FUNDAMENTALS OF ASTROLOGY

Fundamentals of Astrology

M. Ramakrishna Bhat

MOTILAL BANARSIDASS PUBLISHERS
PRIVATE LIMITED • DELHI

6th Reprint: Delhi. **2013**
First Edition: Delhi, 1967
Second Revised Edition: Delhi, 1979
Third Edition: Delhi, 1988

ISBN: 978-81-208-0275-9 (Cloth)
ISBN: 978-81-208-0276-6 (Paper)

MOTILAL BANARSIDASS
41 U.A. Bungalow Road, Jawahar Nagar, Delhi 110 007
8 Mahalaxmi Chamber, 22 Bhulabhai Desai Road, Mumbai 400 026
203 Royapettah High Road, Mylapore, Chennai 600 004
236, 9th Main III Block, Jayanagar, Bengalure 560 011
Sanas Plaza, 1302 Baji Rao Road, Pune 411 002
8 Camac Street, Kolkata 700 017
Ashok Rajpath, Patna 800 004
Chowk, Varanasi 221 001

Printed in India

by RP Jain at NAB Printing Unit,
A-44, Naraina Industrial Area, Phase I, New Delhi–110028
and published by JP Jain for Motilal Banarsidass Publishers (P) Ltd,
41 U.A. Bungalow Road, Jawahar Nagar, Delhi-110007

PREFACE TO THE FIRST EDITION

In the History of Science, which is a branch of the intellectual history of mankind, not infrequently we come across human efforts which symbolized, as it were, man's own imagery into the knowable world of matter and form. Very often some of these efforts, in their earlier phases, revolved round the faith that man is the microcosm, an integral part of the macrocosm. In different periods of history, the concept of macrocosm and microcosm assumed different shapes and meanings in different culture-areas.

That man is the principal figure and that the earth on which he lives is the centre of the universe are wholly in tune with the crystallized concept of microcosm and macrocosm. An offshoot of this human inclination is that the happenings on earth geographically and in the life of man individually are, of necessity, influenced by the components of the universe, of stars and planets. It seems reasonable to suppose that the proto-elements or earlier forms of astrology could be traced to this inclination of man. Perhaps, in all the ancient civilizations — in Egypt, Babylonia, India and China — when man the food gatherer became man the thinker, the nature of the proto-elements of astrology must have been more or less similar. But those elements were prone to take different shapes till they reached a stage of systematization based on recurring experiences over a long stretch of time. In this process each culture-area tried to introduce its own knowledge of experiences and this knowledge was passed on from one generation to another. Possibly, the science of astrology grew from these experiences and around the knowledge of the triad — man, earth and planets.

There are different schools of thought regarding the place of origin of astrology. It would perhaps be wrong to think of a particular place or group of people as originators of astrology. Equally wrong would it be to imagine that astrology in its present form and practice was disseminated at a particular period of history. In this short compass it is rather difficult to go into the historical influences at work from time to time in relation to the science of astrology. Suffice it to say that astrology, as stated before, gradually evolved and absorbed in its evolution the thought-structure of the culture-area in which it grew. From this standpoint it is futile indeed to think of indebtedness of one country to another, particularly in the remote ancient period when astrology was an active participant in the movement of ideas from one place to another, notably among Egypt, Babylonia, India and Greece. A chronological differentiation in this respect seems at best to be an intellectual exercise and, in effect, a conjecture.[1]

In India, the way in which Nakṣatravidyā, the science of stars, has been thought of even in the Vedic literature shows that it was regarded as one of the intellectual attainments. The word Nakṣatra means star in general as well as an asterism in the zodiacal belt. The star groups or Nakṣatras were referred to as *Devagrahas*. Parts of the body of the Primordial Being, Prajāpati, have been extolled in terms of Nakṣatras (His hand — Hasta, mind — Citra, base — Mūla etc.). The Kālapuruṣa also has been imagined in much the same way by the later exponents of Indian astrology.

In the Vedic as well as the Post-Vedic literature including the Pūrāṇas there are innumerable references to the auspicious days in relation to the Nakṣatras, for marriages, ploughing and the like. Some of them were even thought of in terms of *Puṇya* or *Pāpa* Nakṣatras and prognostications were usually made on that basis. In the Mahābhārata as well as the Rāmāyaṇa there are passages which speak of inauspicious or unlucky movements with reference to Nakṣatras as well as planets. It seems to be fairly certain that the Nakṣatravidyā was held in high esteem in India of the Vedic and Post-Vedic period. A knowledge of the Nakṣatras was necessary for a religious rite (sacrifice) called Nakṣatreṣṭi as well as the Śrauta rite concerning the consecration of the sacred fires. In the Chāndogya, it is stated that among the lores which Maharṣi Nārada knew was also the Nakṣatravidyā or the Science of Stars.

The Science of Stars was, however, not all that noble and worthy of adoration as it developed. Gradually, some profane

1. In this connection refer to what Sir William Jones says in his essay on "The Antiquity of the Indian Zodiac" in the Asiatic Researches, Vol. II. pp. 304-305 and p. 302. See also our edition of the Bṛhat Samhitā, Introduction pp. vi-vii.

accretions and unscrupulous practices crept into the hoary Science, which was designated as the "Eye of Knowledge", and probably the baser side of it began to manifest itself. It was for this reason perhaps that Manu thought of one whose existence depended upon the practice of astrology as unfit to participate in religious rites. Kauṭilya also denounced the use of astrology in ordinary life except by the royal personages in the interests of the kingdom and the subjects. A similar view is expressed in the Gautama Dharma Sūtra. The Taittirīya Brāhmaṇa speaks of an astrologer (of course, a bad one) as fit to be consigned to animals. The famous Astronomer-cum-Astrologer Varāhamihira too condemns a bad astrologer as "Nakṣatrasūcaka", a sinner and one who defiles society. However, he plays extraordinary compliments to a worthy astrologer who, in his view, should know practically all branches of knowledge under the Sun, and be a guide, philosopher and teacher to society (See Bṛhat Saṁhitā, Chapter II). He declares in this context, "One wishing for prosperity should not dwell in a place devoid of a good astrologer. For he is the Eye, and no sin will creep in where he stays". Such an astrologer, he declares, is Paṅktipāvana — sanctifier of a religious dinner.

The foregoing citations illustrate that astrology based on the Nakṣatras and planetary movements was well known to the Indians and that its profane aspects were viewed with great indignation. I hope it is not necessary at this stage of scientific development to refute the charge that astrology is no science. There are persons amongst us who aver that planets do not exercise any influence on human life. We can only refer them to the findings of prominent astronomers and medical men in the West. According to Dr. Bachman of Syracuse University there is a direct relationship between the violent eruptions on the Sun's molten surface and human illness, depression, pain and well-being. Dr. Russel Fields of Washington opines that a certain geometrical position of Saturn with reference to Mars and the Moon could predispose a person to the dread disease of cancer. It is held that the incidence of correlation between solar flares and cardio-vascular disease is too glaring to be ignored. Hence there is nothing unscientific if our astrology explains how the planets in outer space influence human life and behaviour on this earth. After all our earth, we are told, was originally fragment of that flaming ball of burning gases viz. the Sun, about two thousand million years ago.

There is yet another aspect of Indian astrology which needs special mention. Horāśāstra or predictive astrology relating to the horoscopes of individuals emphasizes that *Karma* and *Punarjanma* are powerful determinants of the lives of individuals. This is a characteristic concept of Indian astrology as there does not seem to be any corresponding concept either in the Babylonian or in the Greek astrology. The individual has to perform good deeds and lead a pure life so that he can reap the benefits of good planetary influences in his future birth. Astrology is, therefore, a valuable guide to look up to, in order to have an insight into one's own life, here as well as hereafter. In this respect the method followed by astrology stands in good stead. A knowledge of astrology is incomplete without understanding its premise and methods. Astrology being an ancient heritage is naturally founded on a philosophical and spiritual approach to human life as a constituent of the macrocosm. In this contest we can quote what Cheiro (Count Louis Hamon) remarks in defence of palmistry, substituting 'astrology' for 'palmistry': "It becomes a study not contrary to the dictates of reason, but in accordance with those natural laws that we observe in the shaping of even inanimate objects, which, by demonstrating the effect of a heretofore cause, are in themselves the cause of a hereafter effect." Thus astrology is not only a good guide but warns the wary about the "weak and broken bridges" on the way. The aim of this ancient discipline, therefore, is to correct man's angularities, make him lead his life in conformity with the accepted laws of conduct, evolve psychologically and spiritually and ultimately merge in his Source. The Prāyascittaṣ or expiatory rites prescribed in the Dharma Śāstras suggest that man is no automaton in the hands of an inexorable Fate. It is the conviction of great Sages and Saints that by self-effort coupled with sincere devotion to God and faith in oneself man can rise above the influence of his environments. Indian astrology has a rich and hoary tradition in that it was propounded and propagated by great sages like Manu, Garga, Parāśara, Kaṣyapa and a host of others who had not only observed minutely life around them but also developed the intuitional eye by dint of hard penance and selfless and pure conduct. The reported utterances in trance of Edgar Cayce about astrological entities and re-incarnation bear out in a remarkable manner the findings of these ancient Sages of India. "The twelve Signs of the Zodiac represent soul-patterns. The solar system has eight dimensions through which the soul passes exhibiting levels of consciousness. The soul of the entity is part of the universal consciousness and has dwelt in these environs ... the signs of the Zodiac are Karmik Patterns ... the planets are the Looms, the Will is the Weaver."

As a science astrology has discovered "correct methods and reached correct knowledge about the influence of planets on the human mind and on the day-to-day activities of human beings."[1]

In the pages that follow I have in my own humble way attempted to bring to the fore not only the rationality of astrology but also the nature and structure of the correct knowledge that our forefathers possessed regarding the predictable influences of planets on human beings, and to give a spiritual bias to astrology. The reader is taken step by step in this work from the rudiments viz. the distribution of constellations in the Zodiacal belt which is divided into twelve Signs, and the planetary hierarchy, through the method of calculating the ascendant and other houses of a natal chart, assessment of the strength, influences, aspects, afflictions, mutual relations etc. of the planets, to the final stage of reading the brighter and darker sides of the subject's life, his chances of success and failure, their periods, ingress of the Soul into the mortal coil and exit therefrom as well as its departure to other worlds according to its Karma. I am sure the illustrative charts, appended to explain different rules will be of special benefit to students and lovers of astrology.

Much of the contents of this book had appeared in the pages of the "Astrological Magazine" edited by Prof. B.V. Raman, who invited me to contribute articles on several subjects, especially on the principles of astrology entitled "Lessons in Astrology" over a period of about four years. I therefore take this opportunity of acknowledging my indebtedness to him. My thanks are also due to the many readers of the Magazine who had appreciated my Lessons and asked me to make them available in book form. I am beholden to Śrīmān Shiv Saran Vaish of Pilibhit, who being an eminent astrologer himself, gave

1. Vide P. V. Kane's History of Dharmasastra Vol. 5, Pt. I p. 434.

me fraternal encouragement and inspiration constantly during the publication of the Lessons. I must not forget to remember with gratitude the loving help I have received at the hands of Dr. B. V. Subbarayappa, M.Sc., Ph. D., my friend and erstwhile colleague at Bangalore. I am especially thankful to Śrī Sunder Lal Jain, Proprietor, M/s Motilal Banarsidass, for printing and publishing this work promptly and attractively.

Now it remains for me to lay this work of mine as a humble offering at the holy Lotus-feet of the Lord Śrī Siddhi Vināyaka of Madhupura whose unique grace has been guarding me in all situations.

Om Tat Sat

Delhi, **M. Ramakrishna Bhat**
Vijaya Daśamī :
12th October 1967.

PREFACE TO THE SECOND EDITION

It is a happy augury that the claim of astrology as a discipline worthy of serious consideration is being accepted more and more by unprejudiced thinkers all over the world. It is a pity, however, that there are still a few misguided and prejudiced scientists and rationalists in India and elsewhere who have not yet given up their insistence on their pet theory that distant planets and stars do not exert any influence on the earth and its denizens. It is really baffling to modern scientists as to how the ancient Seers were able to observe and correlate celestial phenomena with terristrial occurrences such as earthquakes, epidemics and the like. The great Varāhamihira, one of the pioneers of Indian astronomy, states[1] that the comets named *Tāmasa-kīlakas, Dark Shafts*, which are seen sometimes on the Sun's disc have enormous effects on weather conditions, human behaviour and health. According to the ancient authors, who must have observed minutely these phenomena now termed solar flares, sunspots etc., they cause dust-storms, earthquakes, famines, pestilence, political changes etc. This, we are told by modern scientists, is due to the flows of corpusles that the Sun sends off that are called sometimes 'Solar Wind' having their own magnetic fields which interact with the magnetic field of the earth and influence terrestrial happenings, affecting the electrical potential of individuals. Dr. Russel Fields of Washington is of the opinion that the incidence of correlation between solar flares and cardio-vascular disease is too glaring to be ignored. If all beings are not affected simultaneously by cosmic radiation etc., it is due to the in-built resistance of such individuals.

The above explanation would be sufficient to explode the myth that outer space and planets have no influence on human beings. In fact earthly beings are the products of solar and cosmic radiations. It is these radiations that sustain the discarnate spirit while moving in space as well as during its stay and development in the mother's womb. Accordingly the

1. Vide the Bṛhat Saṁhitā page 24 new edition (Pub. Motilal Banarsidass, Delhi), V 7 & 129.

Vedic Seers have sung in ecstasy "सूर्य आत्मा जगतस्तस्थुषश्च" — The Sun is the Soul of all that is moving and stationary in the universe.

I am happy to acknowledge the appreciation of the scholars who have recognized the value of this work as a worthy introduction to the science of astrology. I am now offering a revised and enlarged edition of the *Fundamentals of Astrology*. In this new edition some new elements have been introduced in order to make the work more useful to the students of Astrology : A more scientific method of calculating the *Candra-Kriyās*, *Candrāvasthās* and *Candravelās*, a chapter describing in detail the decanates, their forms, character, usefulness etc.

Amṛtaghaṭīs (nectareous periods), periods of risk in the case of birth in the *Gaṇḍānta* constellations, effects of conjunction of five and six planets, a detailed account of the significations of the 12 houses or Bhāvas, effects of planets' occupying the twelve Signs (not houses), planetary configurations for the birth of sub-human beings (*Viyoni-janma*) — all these have been duly incorporated. All sanskrit words have been spelt with proper diacritical marks. Minor errors, wherever detected, have also been rectified. I hope, therefore, this edition will serve the interests of both practitioners and students of astrology in a big way.

Lastly I am beholden to Shri Sunder Lal Jain, Proprietor of M/s Motilal Banarsidass, for his abiding interest in the propagation of our ancient culture wherein is enshrined the science of astrology, and for his inducing me to prepare a revised edition of this work. I pray to the Supreme Lord that by His grace all lovers of pure Indian culture including astrology may be benefited by studying this work and adapt their life to the rules of noble living and thinking for attainment of the ultimate Beatitude.

Om Tat Sat

Vittal, **M. Ramakrishna Bhat**

1st January 1978.

PREFACE TO THE THIRD EDITION

By the grace of the Lord Śrī Siddhivināyaka, this work, whose third enlarged edition is now offered to the learned public, has already found favour with both students and practitioners of this ancient science viz. Astrology, both in the East and West. To make the work more useful to readers, an Appendix on the Pañcāṅga or Almanac, which is a necessary ingredient of the daily life of a cultured Indian like prayers, has been added to the text in this edition, which, I hope, will be appreciated as useful by discerning students of astrology.

Vittal
23rd Jan. 1988

M. R. Bhat

CONTENTS

श्रीसिद्धिविनायको विजयते

CHAPTER I

GENERAL PRINCIPLES

Nobody need be ashamed of entertaining a desire to learn the ancient lore of Astrology. After all the thirst for knowledge is a legitimate ambition of worthy human beings. Astrology is not the Forbidden Fruit. It has been practised and revered in all climes and times. To Hindus especially it is one of their Sacred Sciences or Śāstras. For, it is reckoned as one among the ancillaries or limbs of the Vedas. Some might say that it is only Astronomy that is mentioned as a limb of the Vedas and not Astrology i.e. the science of prediction. The predictive part of astrology is as scientific as the mathematical one, as the former is directly based upon the latter. Moreover the ancient Sages had discovered the truth of predictive astrology through their meditation or penance and intuitional perception. All the authors of Dharma Śāstras—Vyāsa, Vālmīki, Kālidāsa and a host of other poets and seers, have cherished and developed this science of astrology which is one of the corner stones of Indian Culture. So if you have any regard for culture as such, you must necessarily pay your homage to this science. Astrology is as old as the Veda which is held as Apauruṣeya or eternal and only revealed at the commencement of each cycle. In ancient India astrologers were held in high esteem, as they combined both a scientific bent of mind and a spiritual outlook on life as well as a pure life of high moral standard. They practised this lore not for amassing wealth, but for giving guidance to the needy and the distressed. Their aim was to remove the cause of suffering among the people and to turn their minds towards Dharma and God. Hence a reverential attitude is expected of the students of astrology. Readers might be aware of what the Lord says towards the end of the Gītā: "This ought not to be imparted to one who has no penance, no devotion, no interest in the subject and to one who hates Me." This remark applies with equal force to astrology too. The Sun being the

Lord of the planetary kingdom, Haṁsa, the Pure One, ideal of Brahmacarya and Yoga as well as the One praised in the Great Gāyatrī Mantra, ought to be invoked at the commencement of this study for blessing us all, the teacher and the taught, with a clear intellect, an understanding heart and pure thoughts. May we bask in the Gracious Light of that Supreme Effulgence !

According to the Indian system there are nine planets i.e. the seven planets whose names are attached to the week days, and Rāhu and Ketu. Their English names are—Sun ☉, Moon ☽, Mars ♂, Mercury ☿, Jupiter ♃, Venus ♀, Saturn ♄, Dragon's Head or Ascending Node ☊, and Dragon's Tail or Descending Node ☋. The zodiac which is a circle has twelve Rāśis or Signs which the planets traverse during their journey. These Rāśis are called (i) Meṣa—Aries ♈, (ii) Vṛṣabha—Taurus ♉, (iii) Mithuna—Gemini ♊, (iv) Karkaṭaka—Cancer ♋, (v) Siṁha—Leo ♌, (vi) Kanyā—Virgo ♍, (vii) Tulā—Libra ♎, (viii) Vṛścika—Scorpio ♏, (ix) Dhanus—Sagittarius ♐, (x) Makara—Capricorn ♑, (xi) Kumbha—Aquarius ♒ and (xii) Mīna—Pisces ♓.

Fig. I

Mīna 12	Meṣa 1	Vṛṣabha 2	Mithuna 3
Kumbha 11			Karka 4
Makara 10			Siṁha 5
Dhanus 9	Vṛścika 8	Tulā 7	Kanyā 6

Fig. II

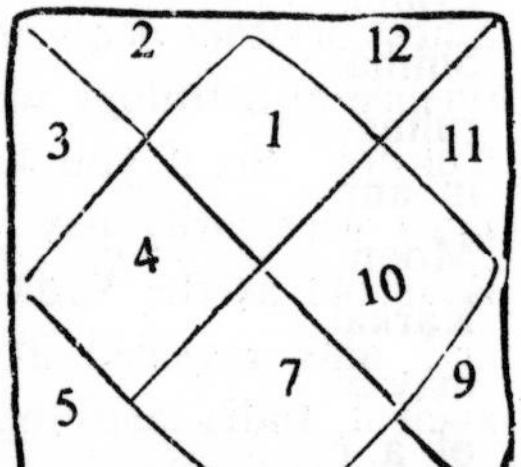

Figure II shows the chart as drawn in North India. The difference between these two is that in the South Indian chart the positions of the several Rāśis never change, whereas in the other the Lagna or Ascendant is put at the top and the counting is done in the opposite direction. You are aware of the fact that the starry firmament contains numberless stars. Now the belt of the zodiac contains 27 constellations or Nakṣatras distributed among the twelve Rāśis beginning from Meṣa. If you divide 27 by 12, you get $2\frac{1}{4}$. So each Rāśi contains two stars and a quarter. In other words each Sign contains nine Pādas or quarters of stars. *Meṣa* has Aśvinī, Bharaṇī and the first Pāda of Kṛttikā, *Vṛṣabha* the remaining three quarters of Kṛttikā, Rohiṇī and the first two Pādas of Mṛgaśiras; *Mithuna*, the latter half of Mṛgaśiras, Ārdrā and the first three quarters of Punarvasu; *Karkaṭaka*, the last Pāda of Punarvasu, Puṣya and the whole of Āśleṣā, *Siṁha*, Maghā, Pūrva Phalgunī and the first Pāda of Uttara Phalgunī; *Kanyā*, the remaining three Pādas of U. Phalgunī, Hasta and the first half of Citrā; *Tulā*, the latter half of Citrā, Svātī and the first three Pādas of Viśākhā; *Vṛścika*, the last quarter of Viśākhā, Anurādhā and the whole of Jyeṣṭhā; *Dhanus*, Mūla, Pūrvāṣāḍhā and the first Pāda of Uttarāṣāḍhā; *Makara*, the remaining three quarters of Uttarāṣāḍhā, Śravaṇa and the first half of Dhaniṣṭhā; *Kumbha*, the latter half of Dhaniṣṭhā, Śatabhiṣak and the first three Pādas of Pūrvābhādra; and *Mīna*, the last quarter of Pūrvābhādra, Uttarābhādra and Revatī.

I have already told you that the Divine Sun is the King and Ruler of the Planetary Kingdom. The Moon is His Consort. So the whole zodiac of 12 Signs belonged to the Divine Royal Couple. The Sun was ruling over the six signs beginning with Siṁha and ending with Makara. His Queen, the Moon, was ruling over the six signs from Karkaṭaka, counting being done in anti-clockwise manner. The idea is that the Sun and the Moon were living in their respective palaces viz. Siṁha and Karkaṭaka, and ruling over their respective dominions. Or it may be said that these two signs are the front and hind portions of a palace, where the husband transacts his business in the front part and the wife in the hind portion. This Couple was noted for their generosity. So each one of the remaining planets, Rāhu and Ketu excepted, went to these luminaries to ask for a house. For, it is natural for a houseless person to wish to have a house to live in. At first Mercury who is closest to the Sun, went to Him and begged Him for a house. Out of pure compassion He gave him a house i.e. Rāśi, next to His own i.e. Kanyā. Mercury was not satisfied with one. So he quietly went by the back door to the Moon and repeated the request without telling Her that he had already got one house from the King. The Moon too gave Mercury a house next to Her own i.e. Mithuna. That is how Budha came to have two houses, Kanyā and

Mithuna. The former is the negative house and the latter the positive one. This news reached the ears of Śukra, Kuja, Guru and Śani also. So they too one after another played the same trick on the generosity of the Royal Couple and each got two houses, leaving only one house to each of the luminaries. Thus Venus became the lord of Tulā and Vṛṣabha (positive and negative respy.), Mars Vṛścika and Meṣa (negative and positive), Guru Dhanus and Mīna (positive and negative), and lastly Saturn Makara and Kumbha (negative and positive).

The odd Signs viz. Aries, Gemini, Leo, Libra, Sagittarius, and Aquarius are called Krūra or Fierce, while the even Rāśis viz. Taurus, Cancer, Virgo, Scorpio, Capricorn and Pisces, Saumya or Gentle. The odd and even signs are also called Male and Female ones respectively. Make the 12 Rāṣis into four groups of three Rāśis each. So the first group would consist of Meṣa, Vṛṣabha and Mithuna. These are called in order Cara or Movable, Sthira or Fixed and Dvisvabhāva or Common Signs. Repeat this process with regard to other groups as well. The same three signs of each group are also called in order Dhātu or Mineral, Mūla or Root and Jīva or Living Being. Now you know that a circle has 360 degrees at its centre. So if a circle were divided into twelve equal parts or sectors, each would get 30 degrees. Thus you see that a Rāśi or Sign consists of 30 degrees.

Horā :—Such a Rāśi is first divided into two equal parts or halves called Horās. So each Horā measures 15 degrees. Who are the owners of these Horās in the several Signs ? They are divided between only two planets viz. the Sun and the Moon. However, there is some difference: In all the odd Signs viz. Meṣa, Mithuna, Siṁha, Tulā, Dhanus and Kumbha, the first Horā is ruled by the Sun and the second by the Moon, while in the even Signs this order is reversed, i.e. the first belongs to the Moon and the next to the Sun. Thus you see that in all there are 24 Horās in the zodiac and out of them 12 are held by the Sun and the remaining 12 by the Moon. Please remember that the word Horā in Greek means an hour. The famous Varāhamihira, however, derives the word from *Aho-rātra* by combining the last and the first syllables of the two words. But let us not worry ourselves at this stage with such subtle matters.

Drekkāṇa :—A Rāśi is further subdivided into three equal

parts of 10 degrees each. Each part is named a Drekkāṇa or Decanate. In each Sign the first Decanate is owned by the lord of the same Sign, the second by the lord of the 5th Rāśi from that and the third by the lord of the 9th Sign from the original one. For example, in Meṣa the first Drekkāṇa is called Meṣa itself and its lord should be Mars, the second Siṁha ruled by the Sun and the third Dhanus owned by Jupiter. In this manner you can easily find out the decanates of all the Rāśis.

Navāṁśa :—A sign is further subdivided into nine equal parts called Navāṁśas. What is the measure of a Navāṁśa in angles ? It is 30° divided by 9. This is equal to $\frac{10}{3}$ degrees or 3 degrees and 20 minutes. Now we must know how these Navāṁśas are counted in the several Rāśis. In respect of this we have to make four groups of three Rāśis each as follows : (1) Meṣa, Siṁha and Dhanus, (2) Vṛṣabha, Kanyā and Makara, (3) Mithuna, Tulā and Kumbha, and (4) Karkaṭaka, Vṛścika and Mīna. In the first group the Navāṁśas begin with Meṣa and end with Dhanus. In other words the first Navāṁśa of Meṣa, Siṁha and Dhanus is Meṣa itself; and the last Dhanus. In the second group the Navāṁśas begin with Makara and end with Kanyā. In other words the first Navāṁśa of Vṛṣabha, Kanyā and Makara is Makara, and the last Kanyā. So you see that the first Navāṁśa of Makara is the same, and the last of Kanyā is Kanyā itself. But the Vṛṣabha-Navāṁśa of Vṛṣabha Rāśi is neither the first nor the last. It is the 5th Navāṁśa. In this manner if you work out you will see that a particular Navāṁśa bears the same name as the Rāśi itself. In the third group the Navāṁśas begin with Tulā and end with Mithuna. So the first Navāṁśa of Tulā is Tulā itself; and the last of Mithuna is Mithuna itself. Lastly the Navāṁśas of the fourth group of Rāśis begin with Karkaṭaka and end in Mīna. Here too you see that the first of Karkaṭaka is Karkaṭaka itself and the last of Mīna is Mīna itself. In this manner you can see that in every Rāśi there is a Navāṁśa which bears the same name. In other words both the Rāśi and Navāṁśa have the same lord. It will be clear to you now that in all the Cara Rāśis the Navāṁśas bearing the same names are the first ones; in all the Sthira Rāśis they are the 5th; and in all the Dvisvabhāva or Common Signs they are the last or 9th.

I have already told you that a Sign consists of $2\frac{1}{4}$ stars or

9 quarter-stars. So you can easily equate a Navāṁśa with a quarter star. Another thing that should be remembered by novices is that since this part has connection with the number nine, in regard to each Rāśi there will be some three Rāśis which do not contribute their names to the Navāṁśas. For an example take Meṣa. In this there are not Navāṁśas having the names of Makara, Kumbha and Mīna. With regard to Vṛṣabha the uninvited Rāśis are different. They are Tulā, Vṛścika and Dhanus. Let me give an illustration for the Navāṁśa Chart :—

Mars	Moon		Ketu Jupiter
Mercury	Rāśi Chart		
Sun			
Rāh	Venus	Saturn	

Venus	Moon	Sun	Saturn Jupiter
	Navāṁśa Chart		Rāhu
Ketu			
Mars	Mercury		

Instead of having two separate charts like this you can have a single chart for both. In the example given above the Moon is in Meṣa in both the charts. What does it mean ? It means that she is in the first Navāṁśa of Meṣa which is identical with the first Pāda of Aśvinī. So if you write the figure I underneath Moon in the Rāśi chart, it would mean the same thing as the above and would save you the trouble of drawing another chart. Similarly write 10 against Ketu, 3 against Jupiter and so on.

Dvādaśāṁśa :—A Rāśi is further subdivided into 12 equal parts termed Dvādaśāṁśa, each subdivision getting an angle of $2\frac{1}{2}$ degrees. Regarding the names of these 12 parts there is absolutely no difficulty, as the Dvādaśāṁśas in each Rāśi begin with the same Rāśi and end with the one that is 12th from it. That is to say, in Meṣa the 12 parts are counted from Meṣa onwards ending in Mīna. In Vṛṣabha the first part is Vṛṣabha itself and the last Meṣa, and so on.

Triṁśāṁśa.:—This is nothing but a one-degree portion of a Rāśi. Hence there should be 30 such parts in each Sign. Do not think that these 30 parts or degree portions belong to thirty planets, which is an impossibility. Their lords are only the five planets viz. Mars, Mercury, Jupiter, Venus and Saturn. The Sun and the Moon have not cared to have any say in this matter. Do not think either that the 30 degrees of a Sign are equally distributed among these five planets. With regard to the distribution of these degrees there is difference in respect of odd and even Rāśis. In the odd Signs i.e. 1, 3, 5, 7, 9 and 11, the distribution is as follows :—The first 5 degrees belong to Mars, the next 5 degrees to Saturn, the next 8 to Jupiter, the next 7 to Mercury and the last 5 to Venus. In an even Sign this order is to be reversed : The first 5 degrees go to Venus, the next 7 to Mercury, the next 8 to Jupiter, the next 5 to Saturn and the last 5 to Mars.

So far I have told you about six Vargas or categories viz. Rāśi, Horā, Drekkāṇa, Navāṁśa, Dvādaśāṁśa and Triṁśāṁśa. These six are called Ṣaḍvargas. Please bear this term in mind and what it signifies, as it is one of the fundamental principles of this science.

Saptāṁśa :—Some authorities speak of a 7th Varga called Saptāṁśa. Here each Sign of 30 degrees is divided into 7 equal parts. The nomenclature of these parts in the several Rāśis is shown below :—In the odd Signs the first part belongs to the particular Rāśi itself and the last to the Sign that is 7th from it, while in the even Rāśis this order is reversed. For example, in Meṣa the first Saptāṁśa belongs to Meṣa and the last to Tulā, while in Vṛṣabha which is an even Sign the first Saptāṁśa belongs to Vṛścika, which is 7th from Vṛṣabha, and the last to Vṛṣabha itself.

Daśāṁśa :—Yet another Varga is spoken of by some scholars. This is called Daśāṁśa or 3-degree portion of a Sign. The word simply means a tenth part. With respect to the lordship of these subdivisions there is some difference : In the odd Rāśis the Aṁśas or parts are counted from the particular Signs themselves and in the even Signs they are counted from the 9th Rāśi from the concerned Sign. For example, in Meṣa the first Daśāṁśa is Meṣa itself and the last is Makara, whereas in Vṛṣabha the first is again Makara and the last Tulā. Here also you see a sort of symmetry. For the last Daśāṁśa of an odd Rāśi happens to be the first Aṁśa of the immediately following even Sign.

Ṣoḍaśāṁśa :—There is yet another subdivision of a Rāśi according to some. That is called Ṣoḍaśāṁśa or a 16th part of a Rāśi. The value of this division is $1\frac{7}{8}$ degrees. The lords of these Aṁśas in an odd Sign are those of the 12 Signs counted regularly from the particular Sign itself and Brahmā, Viṣṇu, Hara and Ravi. In the case of an even Sign this process is to be reversed. There is one more Varga spoken of by some scholars. It is the Ṣaṣṭyaṁśa or $\frac{1}{60}$ of a Rāśi which corresponds to $\frac{1}{2}$ degree.

Ṣaṣṭyaṁśa :—In the case of odd Rāśis the malefic or Krūra $\frac{1}{60}$ parts are the 1st, 2nd, 8th, 9th, 10th, 11th, 12th, 15th, 16th, 30th, 31st, 32nd, 33rd, 34th, 35th, 39th, 40th, 42nd, 43rd, 44th, 48th, 51st, 52nd, and 59th. The rest are Saumya or gentle. In even Signs this order is reversed. That is to say, what are fierce or Krūra in odd Signs become Saumya in even Signs and vice versa. In this manner you have seen ten Vargas or subdivisions of a Rāśi. Of course the most important ones are the first six. This fact being remembered will stand you in good stead when I shall be explaining later the strength of planets.

Characteristics of the Rāśis :—The forms of the twelve signs beginning with Meṣa are in order (1) a Ram, (2) a Bull, (3) a Human Couple of which the man holds a staff and the woman a lute—Vīṇā, (4) a Crab, (5) a Lion, (6) a Maiden seated in a boat holding fire and green plant, (7) a Man holding scales, (8) a Scorpion, (9) a Man holding a bow and having the body of a horse beneath the hips, (10) a Crocodile with the face of a deer, (11) a Man holding a pot, and (12) a Pair of Fish. Signs Karkaṭaka, Vṛścika, Makara and Mīna are termed Watery ones as well as *Aquatic* (moving in water); Vṛṣabha, Kanyā, Tulā and Kumbha are called *Jalāśrayas* or dependent on water and delighting in places abounding in water; and the remaining Rāśis viz. Meṣa, Mithuna, Siṁha and Dhanus, are Land-Signs. Karkaṭaka, Vṛścika and Mīna are also termed Kīṭas or Reptiles. This appellation, however, is mostly applied to Vṛścika. The *haunts* or abodes of these Signs are in order (1) Forest or Plateau, (2) Field or Meadow, (3) Bed chamber or Village, (4) Pond or pit with water, (5) Mountain cave, (6) Land with water and vegetation, (7) Market-place or busy town, (8) Hole, (9) Battle-field or where kings assemble, (10) Forest with plenty of water in it, (11) Place frequented by potters, and (12) Water. Meṣa, Vṛṣabha, Siṁha, the latter half of Dhanus and the first half of Makara are called Quadruped signs. Mithuna, Kanyā, Tulā, the first half of Dhanus, and Kumbha are designated as Human signs. Kīṭas have been already named. Thus you see that $4\frac{1}{2}$ Rāśis come under the Human category, four Rāśis (3 full and two half signs) under the Quadruped, and three under the Reptile category. What about the remaining half Rāśi i.e. the latter half of Makara which is a crocodile ? There is no special name for it except Aquatic or Jalacara.

How do they rise ? Do not be under the impression that all the signs rise in the same manner. Some rise with their heads first and some others with their hind parts foremost. Meṣa, Vṛṣabha, Karkaṭaka, Dhanus and Makara rise with their hind parts first, while Siṁha, Kanyā, Tulā, Vṛścika and Kumbha rise with their heads foremost. Mithuna and Mīna rise both-ways, because their two constituents face each other. The Sanskrit names for these three types of Rāśis are respectively (1) Pṛṣṭhodaya, (2) Śīrṣodaya and (3) Ubhayodaya.

Diurnal etc. :— Those Signs coming under the category of Śīrṣodayas, six in all, are ruled by the Sun and so called Diurnal Signs, while the Pṛṣṭhodayas and Mithuna come under the Moon and so are called Nocturnal ones. Sign Mīna is a Twilight—Sandhyā—Sign.

Quarters represented by the signs :—Meṣa, Vṛṣabha, Mithuna, and Karkaṭaka represent respectively the East, South, West and North. Similarly deal with the remaining two groups of four signs each. If you have to consider eight directions, then take Meṣa and Vṛṣabha for the East, Mithuna for South-East, Karka and Siṁha for South, Kanyā for South-West, Tulā and Vṛścika for West, Dhanus for North-West, Makara and Kumbha for North and lastly Mīna for North-East.

Castes of the Signs :—Karkaṭaka, Vṛścika and Mīna are Brahmins, Meṣa, Siṁha and Dhanus Kṣatriyas, Mithuna, Tulā and Kumbha Vaiśyas, and Vṛṣabha, Kanyā and Makara Śūdras.

The first eight Signs of the Zodiac are termed *Material* Signs and the last four *Philosophical* ones.

Colours of Signs :—The colours of the twelve signs are in order (1) Red, (2) White, (3) Green, (4) Pink, (5) Brown, (6) Grey, (7) Variegated, (8) Black, (9) Golden, (10) Yellow, (11) Variegated, and (12) Deep Brown.

Their Stature :— Aquarius, Pisces, Aries and Taurus are short;

Gemini, Cancer, Sagittarius and Capricorn are of medium length; and Leo, Virgo, Libra and Scorpio, long.

Kālapuruṣa's Limbs :—The whole zodiac consisting of the twelve signs represents the Body of the Supreme termed Kāla or Time. The twelve signs, therefore, stand for the head, face, neck, arms, heart, stomach, abdomen, private parts, thighs, knees, shanks and feet respectively of Kālapuruṣa. Now I must digress a little. When a horoscope is prepared for a child, you will find therein a certain Rāśi being put as Lagna or Ascendant. What does it mean ? You know the zodiac is like a wheel. It appears to revolve as time passes on. So the Rāśis rise, as does the Sun, above the horizon one after another. Thus at the time of birth one of the signs will be rising above the horizon. That is called Lagna. Now the limbs of Kālapuruṣa mentioned above apply to the world as a whole, but when you have to apply this principle to individual cases you have to begin with the Lagna as the starting point. In other words the Lagna will represent the head of the native and the next house his face and so on. I shall tell you later on as to how to calculate the Lagna and other particulars of a horoscope.

Strength of Rāśis :—When any of the Human signs mentioned above happens to be the Lagna, then that sign attains strength; the quadruped ones are strong when they happen to be the 10th house from the Lagna; the Reptile signs are strong when they become the 7th house from Lagna; the Aquatic ones get strength when they come to occupy the position of the 4th house from the Ascendant. For example, let the first half of Dhanus be the Lagna. Then this Rāśi being a Human one becomes strong. As Mīna is the 4th house, it also becomes strong, because it is a Watery or Aquatic Sign. Mithuna and Kanyā, both human Signs, being 7th and 10th houses respectively do not get strength. The names Diurnal, Nocturnal etc. given above are also significant, because they get strength in those periods of time.

Chapter II

PLANETS' CHARACTERISTICS

I have already told you about the Rāśis and their lords. The planets wield different kinds of authority over the Rāśis they are connected with. Meṣa is called the Exaltation—Ucca-house of the Sun, although that house belongs to Mars. The idea is that the Sun is very very strong in that house. Similarly the Ucca Rāśis of the remaining six planets are respectively Vṛṣabha, Makara, Kanyā, Karkaṭaka, Mīna and Tulā. Though these are the Exaltation houses, yet there is a particular degree in them which is termed the Highest Exaltation point. So for the seven planets beginning with the Sun the degrees of highest exaltation are in order the 10th, 3rd, 28th, 15th, 5th, 27th and 20th in their respective exaltation Rāśis. So you can call the Sun really Exalted if he is in the 10th degree of Meṣa. If on the other hand he be in the 20th degree of the same sign, you could only say that he is in his exaltation sign but not in his highest exaltation, as he has fallen from that point. As night follows day, there must be a Rāśi where a planet is debilitated, Nīca, also. Yes. The house 7th from the exaltation Rāśi is called the Debilitation Sign of a planet. So what is the Nīca Rāśi for the Sun ? It must be Tulā as it is the 7th from Meṣa. In the same manner you can easily find out the Nīca houses for the other planets. They are in order Vṛścika, Karkaṭaka, Mīna, Makara, Kanyā and Meṣa. In this matter also there is the lowest degree of debilitation, which is the same as for exaltation. That is, the Sun is in his lowest debilitation if he is in the 10th degree of Tulā. You can now find out which Pāda of the Nakṣatra this highest exaltation or lowest debilitation corresponds to. The former will be in the third quarter of Aśvinī and the latter in the first Pāda of Svātī. Another feature of this subject which you must have noticed is the relationship between the Sun and Saturn, Mars and Jupiter, and Mercury and Venus. For the exaltation of one is the debilitation of the other and vice versa.

Mūlatrikoṇa :—So far you have seen the planets' own houses and exaltation houses. In addition to these there is another house called the *Mūlatrikoṇa* house. You know the Sun's own house in Siṁha. This is his *Mūlatrikoṇa* also. In that case you may find it difficult to distinguish between the two kinds of houses. So there is a way out of this dilemma: The initial 20 degree portion of Siṁha is his *Mūlatrikoṇa*, and the last 10 degree portion his own house or Svakṣetra. Hence if the Sun is anywhere between the commencement of Siṁha and 20 degrees, you should say that he is in his *Mūlatrikoṇa.* Beyond that point you have to say that he is in Svakṣetra or own house. In Vṛṣabha the first 3 degrees constitute the Moon's exaltation portion and the remaining portion of 27 degrees is her *Mūlatrikoṇa.* In Meṣa the initial 12 degree portion is the *Mūlatrikoṇa* of Mars and the remaining 18 degree portion his Svakṣetra. Sign Vṛścika is, therefore, only his Svakṣetra, negative house. For Budha the first half i.e. 15 degree portion, of Kanyā is his Exaltation. Beyond that point a five degree portion i.e. upto 20 degrees, is his Mūlatrikoṇa. And the last 10 degrees are his Svakṣetra. Thus in this one sign you see three types of relationship. Mithuna is his positive Svakṣetra. In Dhanus the first 5 degrees constitute the Mūlatrikoṇa of Guru and the rest his own house. In Tulā the initial 20 degrees are the Mūlatrikoṇa of Venus and the rest own house. Lastly in Kumbha the first 20 degrees constitute Saturn's Mūlatrikoṇa and the rest own house. Now you may ask me about Rāhu and Ketu. Well, I shall tell you their strong houses. Rāhu is considered strong in Karkaṭaka, Vṛṣabha, Meṣa, Kumbha and Vṛścika, while Ketu is strong in Mīna, Kanyā, Vṛṣabha and the latter half of Dhanus. However, there is much difference of opinion about this. Rāhu's Svakṣetra is supposed to be Kanyā, Mūlatrikoṇas are Mithuna and Karkaṭaka, and Exaltation is Vṛṣabha. Ketu's Svakṣetra is Mīna, Mūlatrikoṇa Dhanus, and exaltation Vṛścika. According to another view Rāhu is exalted in Mithuna, has Siṁha as his Mūlatrikoṇa and Kanyā as his Svakṣetra. Ketu is exalted in Dhanus, has Kumbha as his Mūlatrikoṇa and Mīna as his Svakṣetra.

Sex of planets :—The Sun, Mars and Jupiter are males, the Moon, Venus and Rāhu females, and Mercury, Saturn and Ketu eunuchs.

Castes of planets :—Jupiter and Venus are Brahmins, the Sun and Mars Kṣatriyas, the Moon Vaiśya, Mercury of mixed caste, Saturn Śūdra, and Rāhu an outcast. According to another view Mercury is a Śūdra, and Saturn an outcast. There is yet another view according to which Mercury is a Vaiśya.

Their nature :—Mercury, Jupiter and Venus are natural benefics. Similarly the waxing Moon is a benefic. The waning Moon, and Mercury with a malefic are malefics. The Sun, Mars, Saturn, Rāhu and Ketu are natural malefics.

Their qualities :—The Sun, Moon and Jupiter are of Sātvika (pure or good) nature; Mercury and Venus of Rājasa (active, passionate) nature; and the rest viz. Mars, Saturn, Rāhu and Ketu of Tāmasa (dark, ignorant) nature.

Their quarters :—The lords of the 8 directions beginning with the East are in order (1) the Sun, (2) Venus, (3) Mars, (4) Rāhu, (5) Saturn, (6) Moon, (7) Mercury, and (8) Jupiter.

Their colours :—The colours of the nine planets are in order (1) dark red, (2) white, (3) deep red, (4) of the colour of Dūrvā grass or green, (5) of golden hue, (6) white, (7) blue or jet black, (8) of the colour of collyrium, and (9) brown. If you want to know the colour of Māndi, one of the sons of Saturn, it is a mixture of all colours. Now you might have a confusion because of the colours of the Rāśis and planets. Though colours are assigned to the signs, they are influenced by the colours of the planets they are associated with. For example, the colour of Makara is, as you know, yellow. If Saturn is posited in that Rāśi, the latter takes the shade of the planet. Similarly a planet conjoined with another will have its natural colour influenced by that of the other.

Their humours :—The Sun and Mars have Pitta or bile as the chief humour of their body; the Moon and Venus Vāta and Kapha or wind and phlegm; Saturn Vāta or wind; Mercury a mixture of all the three humours; and Jupiter Kapha or phlegm.

Their seasons :—You know that there are six Ṛtus viz. Vasanta, (Spring), Grīṣma (Summer). Varṣā (Rainy), Śarad (Autumn), Hemanta (Dewy), and Śiśira (Winter). These belong to (1) Venus, (2) the Sun and Mars, (3) the Moon, (4) Mercury, (5) Jupiter and (6) Saturn respectively. Mind you there are two lords for summer.

Their gems, metals, tastes etc. :—The Sun's precious stone is Māṇikya or ruby, the Moon's pearl, Mars' coral, Mercury's

Marakata or emerald, Jupiter's Puṣyarāga or topaz, Venus's diamond, Saturn's Nīlam or sapphire, Rāhu's Gomedhika or agate, and Ketu's Vaidūrya or lapis lazuli. In this connection let me tell you the metals owned by the planets : They are in order (1) copper, (2) bell-metal, (3) copper, (4) lead, (5) gold, (6) silver, and (7) iron. The clothes worn by them have the same colours as they themselves possess, but those of Saturn are rags and those of Mars singed by fire. Their *tastes* are in order (1) pungent, (2) salt, (3) bitter, (4) mixed, (5) sweet, (6) sour, and (7) astringent. Lead and tattered clothes are owned by Rāhu, while a mud pot and pieced-together as well as variegated clothes by Ketu.

Their grains :—The grains owned by the nine planets are in order (1) wheat, (2) rice, (3) Āḍhaka or Tuvar, (4) green gram, (5) Bengal gram, (6) Niṣpāva or cow gram, (7) sesamum, (8) black gram and (9) horse gram.

Their birth places :—The countries of birth of the planets in order are (1) Kalinga, (2) Yavana country—the banks of the Jumna (according to another view), (3) Avanti, (4) Magadha, (5) Sindhu, (6) Nikaṭa or Bhojakaṭa, (7) Saurāṣṭra, (8) Ambara or Siṁhala, and (9) Parvata or Antarvedi.

Their ages :—The Sun represents a person aged 50 years; the Moon one of 70 years; Mars one of 16 years; Mercury one of 20 years; Jupiter one of 30 years; Venus one of 7 years (16 according to some); Saturn one of 80 or 100 years; Rāhu one of 100 years. Ketu is similar to Rāhu.

Their Presiding Deities :—The Deities that preside over the nine planets are in order (1) Rudra or Śiva, (2) the Divine Mother, Pārvatī, (3) Kārtikeya, (4) Viṣṇu, (5) Brahman (or Śiva), (6) Lakṣmī, (7) Kāla or Yama (or Rudra), (8) Ādiśeṣa, King of Serpents (or Kārtikeya), and (9) Brahman (or Vighneśvara).

Their natural rays :—Do not think that the rays I am speaking of are the visible ones of the planets. They are the spiritual rays or Kiraṇas of the respective planets. Rāhu and Ketu have no rays. The Sun and others have in order (1) 20, (2) 8, (3) 10, (4) 10, (5) 12, (6) 14, and (7) 16 rays. It will also interest you to know that only the Sun and the Moon are called Luminous planets or Prakāśagrahas, and the next five Tārāgrahas or non-luminous planets. Rāhu and Ketu are Tamograhas or of the nature of darkness.

Their Dhātus or physical constituents :—In Āyurveda seven Dhātus are spoken of as constituting the body. They are (1) Bones, (2) Blood, (3) Marrow, (4) Skin, (5) Fat, (6) Semen and (7) Muscles. These are respectively presided over by the seven planets beginning with the Sun.

Their Elements :—You know there are five elements constituting the entire universe. They are (1) Pṛthivī or Earth, (2) Āpaḥ or Water, (3) Tejas or Fire, (4) Vāyu or Wind, and (5) Ākāśa or Ether. Do not confuse these things with the visible earth etc. These are subtle things of which you see the grosser forms in the world. The Sun and Mars own Fire; the Moon and Venus Water; Mercury Earth; Jupiter Ether, and Saturn Wind.

The Planetary Cabinet :—The Sun and Moon are the Royal Couple, Mars the Commander, Mercury the Crown Prince, Jupiter and Venus Ministers, and Saturn the Servant. These seven planets also represent in order the Soul, Mind, Courage, Speech, Wisdom, and Happiness, Sexual Passion, and Grief of Kālapuruṣa. They also represent the senses and their functions thus :—Mercury governs smell (nose), the Moon and Venus taste (tongue), the Sun and Mars form (eye), Jupiter sound (ear), and Saturn, Rāhu and Ketu touch (skin).

Their Aspects :—The planets have four kinds of aspects. In other words they look at certain houses or planets posited therein in this manner. The mode of looking at the 3rd and 10th houses from the one occupied by a planet is termed a *quarter aspect*; looking at the 5th and 9th is *half-aspect*; at the 4th and 8th houses is $\frac{3}{4}$ *aspect*; and at the 7th house is full aspect. There is a speciality in the case of Jupiter, Mars and Saturn. In the case of Saturn even the quarter aspect is considered to be full. So he aspects *fully* at the 3rd, 7th and 10th houses from the house occupied by him. In the case of Jupiter even a half aspect is considered to be full. So he aspects *fully* at the 5th, 7th and 9th houses from his position. In the case of Mars even a $\frac{3}{4}$ aspect is full. So he aspects *fully* at the 4th, 7th and 8th houses. You remember that Mars and Saturn are among the Malefics. Hence their aspects cannot but have the same nature.

Their Friends :—Even as we have best friends, ordinary friends, neutrals, enemies and inveterate foes, so do the planets in their life. The following Table gives the friends, neutrals and enemies of the several planets. This is their inborn or natural relationship. There is also another kind of friendship called Temporary or Tātkālika. Now look at the Table giving the first type of relations.

Planets	Friends.	Neutrals.	Enemies.
Sun	Moon, Mars & Jupiter.	Mercury.	Venus & Saturn.
Moon	Sun & Mercury.	The rest.	Nil.
Mars	Sun, Moon & Jupiter.	Venus & Saturn	Mercury.
Mercury	Sun & Venus.	Mars. Jup.& Sat.	Moon.
Jupiter	Sun, Moon & Mars.	Saturn.	Mercury & Venus.
Venus	Mercury & Saturn.	Mars & Juptier.	Sun & Moon.
Saturn	Mercury & Venus.	Jupiter.	Sun, Moon & Mars.
Rāhu & Ketu	Mercury, Saturn & Venus.	Mars.	Sun, Moon & Jupiter.

According to others Rāhu is the enemy of the Sun, Moon and Mars; and neutral to Jupiter, while Ketu is neutral to Mercury. In the case of friendship and enmity Rāhu and Ketu are in opposite camps. There is another way of finding this relationship : Find out the lords of the 3rd, 6th, 7th, 10th and 11th houses from the Mūlatrikoṇa house of the planet concerned. Among such planets those that come twice become the natural enemies of the planets concerned and the rest only neutrals to him. For example take the Sun's Mūlatrikoṇa viz. Siṁha. Śukra is reckoned twice as he is the lord of the 3rd and 10th houses from Siṁha. Saturn too gets two houses, 6th and 7th. So these two planets are the natural enemies of the Sun, while Mercury who owns only one house viz. the 11th, becomes a neutral. The remaining ones are his natural friends. Similarly the lords of 2nd, 4th, 5th, 8th, 9th and 12th houses from the Mūlatrikoṇa of a planet, invited twice, become its natural friends and the rest neutral. In this rule there is an important exception to be borne in mind. That is, the lord of a planet's exaltation house is exempted from the operation of this rule. That is why Saturn is only a neutral to Mars and not an enemy, though he owns two houses viz. 10th and 11th from the Mūlatrikoṇa i.e. Meṣa, of Mars. You remember that the exaltation house of Mars viz. Makara, is owned by Saturn. If you work out in this manner you will see that the Moon does not get any enemy at all. As the Sun and the Moon own only one house each, even when they are called once they become enemies. So far I have been telling you about the natural relationships among the planets. Now I shall tell you their temporary friendship etc. You note the position of a planet. The planets that are posited in the three houses in front of and three behind the one occupied by this planet become its temporary friends. That is, those in the 2nd, 3rd and 4th, as well as 12th, 11th & 10th become temporary friends. Let us suppose that the Sun and Saturn are in Vṛścikā, Mars and Jupiter in Tulā, Mercury in Dhanus, Venus in Makara and so on. In this chart for the Sun or Saturn the following four become friends for the time being. They are—Mercury, Venus, Mars and Jupiter. Planets occupying the same house as well as those occupying houses not mentioned in this list are to be considered as enemies. A planet that is friendly to another both naturally and temporarily becomes an Adhimitra or very intimate friend. Similarly one that is inimical to another both-ways becomes an Adhiśatru or bitter enemy. Now a friend by nature but enemy for the present becomes neutral. So too a natural enemy but friendly for the time being becomes neutral. A neutral getting temporary friendship becomes as good as a friend.

Trees of the planets :—The Sun owns or represents trees that are tall and strong inside; the Moon and Venus, creepers; Mars and Saturn, thorny trees; Jupiter, fruit-bearing trees; Mercury fruitless ones; and Rāhu and Ketu, bushes. Venus and the Moon also signify milky and blossoming trees. It should be remembered here that the Moon is called Oṣadhīśa i.e. lord of herbs. Śani owns all sapless and weak trees. Rāhu also rules the Sāla tree.

Their periods :—The seven planets beginning with the Sun preside over (1) a solstice or six months, (2) a moment, (3) a day, (4) a Ṛtu or two months, (5) a month, (6) a fortnight and (7) a year, in order.

Relations signified by them :—The Sun and other planets are called Kārakas or Significators of certain relatives of the native:

Father, mother, younger brother, maternal uncle, children, wife or husband and servant are signified in order by the seven planets. There are many other things for which these planets are Kārakas too. For the present this will suffice. Rāhu and Ketu indicate maternal and paternal grandfathers respectively. There is yet another way of looking at them : In the horoscope of a person born at daytime the Sun represents his father and Venus his mother. Similarly for a night birth Saturn becomes the father and the Moon the mother. In the day-birth Saturn becomes the paternal uncle and the Moon the maternal aunt. The same rule holds good in the case of a night-birth. The Sun similarly stands for the right eye and the Moon for the left one. Jupiter also indicates the eldest brother, and Mercury the adopted son.

Their identification marks :—The Sun, Jupiter, Mercury and Mars have their special marks (like trade marks) on their right side, while the others have them on the left side. The seven planets have the marks in the following limbs in order:—(1) on the right hip, (2) on the left side of the head, (3) on the right side of the back, (4) in the right arm-pit, (5) on the right shoulder, (6) on the left side of the face and (7) on the left thigh or leg.

Their places in a house :—The seven planets rule in order the worship room, bath-room, kitchen, dance-hall, strong room, bed-chamber and a place where garbage is thrown.

Their forms :—Saturn and Mercury look like birds, the Moon like a reptile, Jupiter and Venus like human beings, and the Sun and Mars like quadrupeds. The Moon and Venus are said to be aquatic beings, Mercury and Jupiter are those that move about in a village, and the rest are denizens of the forest.

How they rise :—The Sun, Mars, Saturn and Rāhu rise with their hind part appearing in front, while the Moon, Mercury and Venus with their head foremost. Jupiter rises both ways.

General Characteristics of the Planets

Sun :—He has a square body, pink eyes, sparse hair both on the head and the body. He has no permanent residence, is lazy, weak-kneed, has attractive countenance and speech. He is valiant, wrathful and possessed of massive arms. Other characteristics of the Sun which have been already mentioned should also be remembered.

Moon :—The Moon has a corpulent body, is young as well as old, white in complexion, with lovely eyes, black and thin hair, has tender speech and mild temper. She is proficient in politics and intelligent.

Mars :—He has a slender waist, curly and shining hair, fierce red eyes, cruel nature, fickle mind, but a generous heart. He is expert in striking hard and bears marks of burning and weapons. He is well disciplined and valorous. His voice is queer.

Mercury :—He is green like the Dūrvā grass, full of veins, pleasant in speech and fond of fun and frolic. He has red and long eyes. He governs the skin. He is well-versed in politics and has lots of information on various topics. He has even limbs. Mark his Sanskrit name Budha which means learned.

Jupiter :—He has golden complexion, brown eyes and hair, corpulent and tall body. He is very wise and learned as well as of noble demeanour. He is very eloquent and governs wealth. His voice resembles the sound of conch or the lion's roar. He is also adept in politics.

Venus :—He has black curly hair, huge body and thick limbs, greenish complexion, amiable and attractive personality, broad eyes and plenty of virility. He is hen-pecked and given to fraud.

Saturn :—He is dark, lame, lazy, with sunken eyes, lean and lank body, prominent veins, thick nails and protruding teeth. His hair is coarse and thick. He is dirty, angry, dreadful, full of wrinkles, clad in black clothes, foolish, and a tale-bearer. His hands and feet are very long. He is merciless and melancholic.

The Haunts and other things signified by the Planets

Sun :—A Śiva temple, open area, desert, devotee of Śiva, physician, king, sacrificer, chief minister, tiger, deer and the Cakravāka bird. He represents also the following :—Copper, gold, father, effects of meritorious deeds, soul, happiness, prowess, courage, valour, victory in battle, government service, popularity, mountaineering, enthusiasm and sharpness.

Moon :—Durgā temple, women's apartments, watery place, herbarium, a place where honey is kept (or one of liquor), a worshipper of the deity called Śāstā, woman, washerman, husbandman, aquatic things, hare, antelope, crane, Cakora bird, mother's welfare, mental peace, sea-bath, chowries, umbrella, fan, fruits, tender articles, flowers, corn, agriculture, renown, pearls, bell-metal, silver, milk and other sweet things, clothes, cows, good meals, health and beauty.

Mars :—Places frequented by thieves and Mlecchas, fire-place, battle-field, cook, soldier, goldsmith, ram, cock, jackal, monkey, vulture, strength, produce of lands, nature of brothers, cruelty, battle, daring deed, hatred, gold, kitchen, thieves, enemies, weapons, attachment to other women, uttering lies, prowess, wounds, command of army, sin and mental elation.

Mercury :—Assembly of scholars, temple of lord Viṣṇu, recreation ground, accountant's office or astrological bureau, cowherd, learned man, artisan or artiste, astrologer or accountant, devotee of Viṣṇu, Garuḍa, Cātaka bird, parrot, cat, learning, eloquence, proficiency in arts, cleverness in propitiating Gods, intelligence, sacrifice, truthfulness, oyster-shell, kinsmen, rank of a Yuvarāja, friends and sister's children.

Jupiter :—Treasury, Aśvattha tree, dwellings of Gods and Brahmins, astrologer, minister, preceptor, great Sannyāsin, dove, horse, swan, knowledge, virtues, son, Svadharma, teaching profession, nobility, all-round progress, knowledge of scriptures, final beatitude, faith, devotion to Gods and Brahmins, penance, sacrifice, control over the senses, longevity and happiness of husband, compassion, and royal honour.

Venus :—Street of harlots, harem, dance-hall, bed-chamber, musician, wealthy person, sensualist, merchant, dancer, weaver, courtesan, peacock, buffalo, cow, parrot, wealth, vehicles, clothes, ornaments, buried treasures, dance, vocal and instrumental music, wife, conjugal felicity, scents, flowers, sexual dalliance, bed, house, prosperity, poesy, addiction to many women, sportive movements, passion, ministry, winsome speech, festivity and marriage.

Saturn :—Place where outcasts live, dirty area, temple of Śāstā, oil-monger, servant, vile person, hunter, blacksmith, crow, cuckoo, longevity, death, fear, degradation, misery, illness, humiliation, poverty, servitude, calumny, sins, pollution, censure, misfortune, constancy, taking shelter under ignoble persons, buffalo, lethargy, debt, iron, agricultural implements, prison and imprisonment.

Rāhu and Ketu :—Ant-hill, dark holes tenanted by snakes etc., Buddhist, snake-charmer, donkey, ram, wolf, camel, serpent, mosquito, bug, owl and insect.

Planets' points of strength :—Every planet is strong in his own Rāśi, Navāṁśa, decanate, exaltation sign, weekday etc.

Sun :—The Sun is strong in addition in the Uttarāyaṇa i.e. from the moment of his entering the sign Makara till he steps into Karkaṭaka, and in his own Horā. His strength is middling when he is situated in a friend's house. He is strong in the initial part of a sign, of moderate strength in its middle and weak in its end. He is weak at the twilight and also during his eclipse.

Moon :—She is strong in her southerly course, in her own Horā, at night, in the bright fortnight for the first ten days she has moderate strength, she is very strong for the next ten days i.e. till the 5th day in the dark fortnight, and weak in the last ten days. When she is to the North of planets or goes in a clock-wise manner around them, or when she is aspected by or conjoined with benefics, or when she is aspected by all the other planets, she becomes strong. She is weak at the commencement of a Rāśi, of moderate strength in the middle and strong at the end. She is strong in all houses when full.

Mars :—He is strong when he is Vakra or retrograde, bright, in Kumbha, Mīna, in his southerly course, at night, in any Sign that happens to be the 10th from the Lagna and in the beginning of a Sign. He is weak in the middle of a Rāśi and of medium strength at its end.

Mercury :—He is strong when he rises after his eclipse, in Dhanus, both by day and night, during his retrograde motion, and in the middle of a Rāśi. He is weak at the end of a Sign and of moderate strength at its commencement.

Jupiter :—He is strong also in Vṛścika, in his northerly course, in the fore-noon, and in the middle of a Sign. He is of moderate strength in the initial part of a Sign and weak at its end. He is strong also when retrograde, povided he is not debilitated.

Venus :—He is strong also in the 3rd, 6th and 12th houses from the Ascendant, when retrograde, when in front of the Sun, in the afternoon, when posited to the North of planets and in the middle of Signs. He is strong when conjoined with the Moon. He is weak in the beginning of a Rāśi and of moderate strength at its end.

Saturn :—He is strong in the dark fortnight, at night, when he is retrograde, in his southerly course, while rising in the Ascendant, and while moving slowly. He is weak, middling and strong in the beginning, middle and end respectively of a Rāśi.

Rāhu :—He is strong in Meṣa, Vṛṣabha, Karka, Vṛścika and Kumbha, in conjunction with the Sun or Moon, and at the end of a Sign.

Ketu :—He is strong in the latter half of Dhanus, in Mīna, Kanyā, Vṛṣabha, at night, when a meteor or rainbow is seen.

Thus have I told you something about the strength of the planets. Please remember that every planet is strong in his own house etc. mentioned above. Similarly there are certain Bhāvas in a horoscope wherein the planets are strong. This I shall take up after telling you how to calculate the lagna and other Bhāvas and how to locate the various planets in the different signs of the chart.

CHAPTER III

LAGNA AND OTHER HOUSES

How to cast a horoscope :—Formerly when watches were not available, people used to find out the time of birth from the shadow at daytime, and from the stars in the heavens at night. Now that we have watches giving the Indian Standard Time the difficulty of looking up to the sky or down on the ground is obviated. So what you have to do to start with is to ascertain the correct time of birth as well as the place of birth. Then have before you Lahiri's "Tables of Ascendants" and the Ephemeris for the year. The ascendant (lagna) and other houses (a Rāśi and a house in a horoscope need not be identical) vary according to the latitude of the place. To calculate the ascendant you have to convert the time in I. S. T. to the Local Mean Time which you can read from the last page of Lahiri's Ephemeris. For example you find against Delhi :—Latitude 28-39; Longitude 77-13; Local time by correction to I. S. T. minus 21 m. 8 s. and lastly correction to Indian Sidereal Time+(plus) 3 s. Hence you will deduct 21 minutes 8 seconds from the I. S. T. in order to get the Local Mean Time (L. M. T.) at Delhi. You will also find for each day of the year the Sidereal Time (S. T.) at noon, correction to which is given above as plus 3 seconds. Then you will find the Sidereal Time for the moment of birth. This is worked out thus :—Find the difference between the L. M. T. and the noon i.e. 12 hours. It is minus if the L. M. T. is before noon, and plus if it is after the noon. The Sidereal equivalent of this difference is got by adding to it 10 seconds per hour. If the birth is before noon, deduct this sidereal equivalent from the Sidereal Time (S. T.) at noon; if it is afternoon, add it to the S. T. at noon. The result you get is called the Sidereal Time (S. T.) for the moment of birth. Now you can read from the Tables of Ascendants the particular degree of the Rāśi (Sign) that rises at the place.

Let us take a practical example : A male born on September 8th, 1957 at 9.55 A.M, I .S. T. at Bombay. You will find in the Tables under "Principal Cities ..." the Latitude, Longitude etc. of Bombay. In the 4th column you find minus 38 m. 44 s. for getting the L. M. T. So deduct from 9 h.-55 m.-0 s., 0 h.-38 m.-44 s. You will get 9 h.-16 m.-16 s., which is the L. M. T. Now find out the difference between this and noon i.e. 12 hours. It is 2 h.-43 m.-44 s. Add the correction to this at the rate of 10 seconds per hour. It is 27 seconds. So the sidereal equivalent comes to 2 h.-44 m.-11 s. As the birth (i.e. L. M. T.) is before noon, this figure, viz. 2 h.-44 m.-11 s., should be subtracted from the S. T. at noon. We can get this S. T. at noon either from the Ephemeris for the year or from the "Tables of Ascendants". From Table I in the latter we get 11 h.-7 m.-27 s. against September 8th. From Table II we get+0 m.-46 s. for 1957. So we have to add 46 seconds to 11 h.-7 m.-27 s. That comes to 11 h.-8 m.-13 s. In the Ephemeris it is given as 11 h. -8 m.-14 s. This is not all. We have to make the correction to the Indian S. T. at noon. We find this to be plus 6 seconds for Bombay. So the final S. T. at noon becomes 11 h.-8 m.-20 s. To get the S. T. for the moment of birth you will now deduct the figure 2 h.-44 m.-11 s. (the sidereal equivalent) from the S. T. at noon viz. 11 h.-8 m.-20 s. This will give you the required S. T., 8 h.-24 m.9 s. On page 29 of the Tables you will get the ascendants for Bombay in signs, degrees and minutes for all hours within intervals of every 4 minutes. Under 8 h. and against 24 minutes you will find 6^s-10°-46′. This shows that the ascendant is Libra or Tulā and the degree ascending is the 11th. Now you will have to work out the fraction of minutes of arc corresponding to the 9 seconds you see in the S. T. For 8 h. 28 m. of S. T. the figure for the ascendant is 6^s-11°-41 . This shows that for a difference of four minutes in the S. T. the increase in the ascendant is 55' only. So for 1 minute it would be $\frac{55}{4}$ minutes. If for 1 minute or 60 seconds the increase is $\frac{55}{4}$, then what is it for 9 seconds ? It is equal to $\frac{55}{4} \times \frac{9}{60} = \frac{33}{16}$ minutes or 2 minutes and 4 seconds (for practical purposes). Adding this to the figure for ascendant already obtained we get 6^s-10°-48′-4″. This is not the final figure. At this stage you are called upon to effect a further correction called the Ayanāṁśa-correction or the correction due to the precession of equinox. This you will find on page 6 of the Tables. It is minus 16 minutes for 1957. By deducting 16 minutes from the above figure viz. 6^s-10°-48′-4″

we get 6^s-10°-32′-4″ as the final figure for the ascendant of birth. This is called the *cusp* or centre of the first Bhāva or Lagna. Now what is the Navāṁśa ($\frac{1}{9}$ of a Rāśi) of this ? As one Navāṁśa consists of 3°-20′, it is more than three. That means that it is the 4th Navāṁśa upto 13°-20′. You know that in Libra (Tulā) the Navāṁśas begin from the same sign. Hence the Navāṁśa Rāśi happens to be Capricorn or Makara. So you write the word Lagna in sign Libra and put the number 10 to indicate its Navāṁśa. This does not mean that its Aṁśa is the 10th. For, there cannot be a tenth part where there are only nine. On the other hand it means only that the Navāṁśa Rāśi is identical with the 10th sign of the Zodiac which is Capricorn. This system will obviate the difficulty of drawing another diagram for the Navāṁśas. Note that the strength of planets is mainly based on their Aṁśas.

After getting the figure for the ascendant you will proceed to find out the figure for the cusp of the 10th house or the Meridian Cusp (M. C.), which is essential for calculating all the remaining houses or Bhāvas. The Bhāva-cakra or Diagram of Houses is known as the Calita Cakra in the North. What is the basis for the figure of the 10th house ? It is the same S. T. (sidereal time) you have obtained for the moment of birth. On page 8 of the Table you will find the figures for the 10th house for all places on the earth. There you will find 3^s-10°-41′ against 24 minutes under 8 hours. The figure for 28 minutes is 3^s-11°-39′. So the increase for 4 minutes of S. T. is 58 minutes of arc. Hence the increase for 9 seconds it is 2 minutes 10 seconds. Add this to the figure 3^s-10°-41′. You will then have 3^s-10°-43′-10″. Make the Ayanāṁśa correction as before by subtracting 16 minutes from this figure. Then you get the M. C. which is equal to 3^s-10°-27′-10″. In this example you find both the ascending degree and the M. C. degree to be the same. It need not be the same. If you work out the ascendant and the M. C. for a male birth at Delhi on 10th December 1962 at 9-05 A. M. I. S. T., you will find that the figure for the former is 8^s-21°-36′-9″ and for the latter 6^s-8°-10′-35″. This would show that the houses are not of equal length. Let us now try to get the figures for the remaining ten houses. For this purpose we have to work out first the 11th and 12th houses. This is done as follows :—Subtract the figure of the M. C. from that of the ascendant. Divide the result by 3. Then add the quotient to the figure of the 10th house (M. C.) to get the figure of the 11th house. If you add the quotient again to the figure of the 11th house, you will get that of the 12th house. By adopting this procedure you will get 4^s-10°-28′-48″ for the cusp of the 11th house, and 5^s-10°-30′-26″ for that of the 12th house. Now you have the figures for the cusps of four houses viz. the first, tenth, eleventh and twelfth. Now your task is easy : You will get the cusp of the 7th house by merely adding 6 signs to the figure of the ascendant. So the 7th house will be $=0^s$-10°-32′-4″. Similarly you will get the cusp of the 4th house (which is also known as Nadir) by subtracting 6 signs from that of the M. C. So you get 9^s-10°-27′-10″ for the 4th house. Similary get the 5th house and the 6th house by deducting 6 signs from the cusps of the 11th and 12th houses respectively. They will be 10^s-10°-28′-48″, and 11^s-10°-30′-26″. Now only the second, third, eighth and ninth houses remain to be fixed. By adding 2 signs to the figure for the 12th house you will get the cusp of the 2nd house; and by adding 4 signs to that of the 11th house you get the figure for the 3rd house. By adding 6 signs to the 2nd house and to the 3rd house severally you get the 8th and 9th house-cusps. The following table gives the above results in a clear form :—

Bhā-vas	Longitudes (Cusps)	Sandhis (Junctions)	Bhā-vas	Longitudes (Cusps)	Sandhis (Junctions)
I	6^s-10°-32′-4″	5^s-25°-31′-15″	VII	0^s-10°-32′-24″	11^s-25°-31′-15″
II	7-10-30-26	6-25-31-15	VIII	1-10-30-26	0-25-31-15
III	8-10-28-48	7-25-29-37	IX	2-10-28-48	1-25-29-37
IV	9-10-27-10	8-25-27-59	X	3-10-27-10	2-25-27-59
V	10-10-28-48	9-25-27-59	XI	4-10-28-48	3-25-27-59
VI	11-10-30-26	10-25-29-37	XII	5-10-30-26	4-25-29-37

Now if you add the figures of two contiguous houses and divide the result by two, you get the Sandhi or junction of those two Bhāvas. For example, let us find out the Sandhi between the 12th and Lagna Bhāvas. By adding the two figures, 5^s-10°-30′-26″ and 6^s-10°-32′-4″ and dividing the result, 11-21-2-30, by 2, we get the figure, 5-25-31-15 which is the Sandhi between the 12th and the 1st Bhāvas. What does it mean ? It means that the lagna Bhāva starts from 25-31-15 of Kanyā, and the 12th Bhāva extends upto that point. The Lagna therefore, extends from this point to 6^s-25°-31′-15″.

Thus you will see that the Lagna is always 30 degrees in extent. Now if a planet were posited in Tulā, say in the 28th degree thereof, then that planet, though situated in the Lagna Rāśi, would not be in the first Bhāva, but in the second. If a planet, on the other hand, is posited in the same degree as the Sandhi, it should be put in the Sandhi and it belongs to neither Bhāva. Such a planet is utterly ineffective in conferring good or bad results on the native. Please bear this important principle in mind for future guidance. In this case all the 12 Sandhis occur in the 26th degree of the concerned Signs. For assigning a planet to a Sandhi it is not necessary that the planet's longitude must be identical in every detail with the Sandhi. It is enough if both are in the same degree.

After this you have to find out the longitudes of the planets or the Grahasphuṭas for the time of birth. For this purpose you can utilize Lahiri's Indian Ephemeris for 1957. Therein see pages 22 and 23, where the Nirayaṇa longitudes of the planets are given for 5-30 A.M. for each day. The Sun's longitudes at 5-30 A.M. on the 8th and 9th of September are 4^s-21°-48′-4″ and 4^s-22°-46′-20″ respectively. The difference between these two figures will give you the Sun's motion during a day or 24 hours. It is 0°-58′-16″. Now find out the difference between the time of birth and 5 hr. 30 m. which is our starting point in the Ephemeris. It is 4 h. 25 m. By simple rule of three you can find out now how far the Sun could advance in 4h. 25m. Divide 58′-16″ by 6. You get the Sun's motion for 4 hours. This comes to 0°-9′-43″. From this you can work out the motion for 25 minutes after finding it out for one hour. So for the interval of 4 h. 25 m. the Sun's motion is 10 m. 43 s. By adding this to the Sun's it comes to 4^s-21°-58′-47″. In the same manner you can calculate the longitudes of the other planets as well. In the case of fast-moving planets however there is a small correction noticed on page 61. I shall give you now the consolidated results in the following Table :—

Lagna	$=6^{s}$-10°-32′-4″.	Venus	$=5^{s}$-29°-33′-4″
Sun	=4-21-58-47	Saturn	=7-15-0-22.
Moon	=10-10-51-45.	Rāhu	=6-18-52-5.
Mars	=4-26-26-0.	Ketu	=0-18-52-5.
Ret. Mercury	=4-25-17-0.	Gulika	=9-0-8-31.
Jupiter	=5-13-0-12.	Māndi	=9-23-23-52.

Note :—Here Mercury is retrograde. Hence in his case and in that of Rāhu the motion in degrees etc. is to be deducted from the position given for 5-30 A.M. Ketu's position is Rāhu's increased by 6 Signs.

Now I must tell you how to calculate the position of Gulika. For this you must first find out the length of the day (or night in the case of a night birth) in Ghaṭīs. In this case it is 30 Ghaṭīs 57 Vighaṭīs. Now the day of birth is Sunday. The length of the day is to be split into 8 equal parts which are presided over by the seven planets in order beginning with the lord of the week-day concerned. Here it is the Sun. What about the 8th part ? It has no lord.[1] Now that part which belongs to Saturn is that of Gulika who is a son of the former. Here it is the 7th part where we have to locate Gulika. Find out the initial point of the 7th part which is the end of the 6th one. This will give you the time of rising of Gulika. The end of the 6th or the beginning of the 7th part is 23 Ghaṭīs 13 Vighaṭīs. The sunrise on that day at Bombay is at 6-25 A.M. Then what is the time corresponding to 23-13 Ghaṭīs ? It is 9 h. 17 m. Add this to the time of sunrise. You get 3-42 P.M. which is the time of Gulika's rising. Just as you have calculated the Ascendant for 9-55 A.M. so have you to do for 3-42 P.M. on that day. The sidereal time for that time is 14h 12m 6s, for which the Ascendant is 9^{s}-0°-8′-31″. This is the position of Gulika. In the case of a night birth the lordship of the first part is not that of the lord of the week-day, but the one that is 5th from him. So if there is a birth on the night of Sunday, the first part of the night would be presided over by Jupiter and Gulika's position is in the beginning of the 3rd part.

1. According to one authority it is presided over by the lord of the first part.

At this juncture an explanation becomes necessary : Saturn is said to have two sons viz. Gulika and Māndi. There are some authorities that make no distinction between the two. There are yet some who do not recognize at all these two minor planets. But the rising of Gulika is strictly avoided in Electional astrology or Muhūrta Śāstra. Māndi's presence is needed for verifying the ascendant and longevity according to Mantreśvara, a reputed writer on astrology. The distinction between these two minor planets (Upagrahas) consists in the fact that the methods for calculating their rising periods are quite different. I have already explained the procedure for finding out the presence of Gulika in the horoscopic chart.

Māndi's rising is calculated as follows :—As before find out the duration in Ghaṭīs etc. of the day or night, as the case may be. If the duration of the day is of 30 Ghaṭīs, Māndi would rise at the end of 26 Ghaṭīs on Sunday, of 22 Ghaṭīs on Monday, of 18 on Tuesday, of 14 on Wednesday, of 10 on Thursday, of 6 on Friday, and lastly of 2 Ghaṭīs on Saturday. In the case of night births the 5th from that of the particular week day will have to be considered. If the duration of the day or night is more or less than 30 Ghaṭīs, the above Ghaṭīs given for the rising of Māndi will have to be altered proportionately. In our example it would be $\frac{30—57}{30} \times \frac{26}{1}$ Ghaṭīs. That comes to 26 Ghaṭīs 49 Vighaṭīs or 10 h. 43 m. 36 s. from sunrise. Hence we have to calculate the ascendant for 5h 8m 36s P.M.

Now it would be clear to you as to why these two planets are not identical. Now the sidereal time (S. T.) for the above moment, which you can work out as shown already, comes to

—	Ketu 6	—	—
Moon 10	Rāśi with Aṁśa		—
Māndi 5			Sun 7 R.Merc.8 Mars 8
—	Sat. 8	Lag.10 Rāhu 12	Jup. 1 Ven. 6

—	Ketu	—	—
Moon	Bhāva Chart		—
Māndi			Sun Mercury
	Saturn	Lagna Rāhu Venus	Mars Jupiter

15 h. 38 m. 56 s., for which the ascendant is 9s-23°-23′52″. This is the exact position of Māndi for that day. For the present we shall take into consideration only Māndi and not Gulika.

Now let me draw the charts with the planets in them. (See p. 29)

In the first chart you find the planets in the different Signs as well as their Navāṁśas. Under the Moon you see the figure 10, indicating that the Navāṁśa Rāśi of the Moon is Makara. Now you have the key to find out which planet is in which Bhāva. For, the chart on the left is only that of Rāśis and not of Bhāvas. You remember that in this case all the Sandhis are situated in degree 26. Is there any planet that is in this degree in any Rāśi ? Yes, Mercury is in that degree in Siṁha. You know that is the Sandhi between XI and XII Bhāvas. So Mercury will have to be put in the Bhāva chart between these two Bhāvas. Just see also if there is any planet beyond 26th degree. There are only two, viz. Mars and Venus. Their longitudes are in order 4-26-26-0 and 5-29-33-4. In which Bhāva do these degrees fall ? They are in the 12th and Lagna Bhāva respectively. So Venus though posited in the 12th house in the Rāśi chart. comes to the Lagna or the first Bhāva in the Bhāva chart. Similarly Mars appearing in the 11th Rāśi is actually in the 12th Bhāva.

Now look at the Bhāva chart. When you read the Bhāva chart, you should not mention the names of Rāśis. So, though Venus is in Kanyā, he is in I Bhāva and not in Tulā. Apply the same principle to Mars as well. Note also that if Mercury is in Bhāva-Sandhi (junction of houses), Venus is in Rāśi-Sandhi (junction of Signs). For the latter is in the 30th degree of Virgo. It may interest you to know also that the Moon occupies the very centre or cusp of the 5th house. This is a source of strength to the planet.

You have already learnt that in an individual's horoscope the Lagna stands for the head, the second house for face, and so on. This is not all. For, each of the 12 houses represents a number of things which you should know in detail.

First House : Body, limbs, happiness, misery, old age, knowledge, birth place, fame, dream, strength, dignity, politics, longevity, tranquillity, age, hair, stature, pride, livelihood, gambling, stigma, honour, skin, sleep, proficiency, loss of wealth, insult of others, one's nature, recovery from illness, dispassion, doing one's duty, engagement in cattle-breeding, loss of decorum and blame from one's own classmen.

Second House : Speech, wealth, belief in sacred tradition, supporting others, nails, food, truth and falsehood, tongue, eyes, clothes, diamond, copper, gems, pearl, zeal, artificial preparation (witchcraft ?), family, trade and commerce, liberality, industriousness for earning money, help, friend, lustre, miserliness, oratory, learning, gold, silver, corn, modesty, nose, firmness of mind, personal attendant, going and coming and vivacity.

Third House : Courage, brothers, battle, ears, legs, path, holy place, mental confusion, capacity, paradise, causing sorrow, dream, soldier, valour, kith and kin, friend, movement, throat, tasty food, partition of property, strength, ornaments, virtue, delighting in learning lores, sports, gain, physical growth, noble descent, servant, the part of the palm between the forefinger and the thumb, small boat, a big undertaking, and one's own religious duty.

Fourth House : Education, kingdom, house, vehicles, oil bath, mother, friend, kinsman, caste, garments, well, water, milk, happiness, perfume, popularity, potent medicine, trust, falsehood, platform, victory, perspiration, agriculture, field, installation of wells, gardens etc., maternal relations, reasoning intellect, father, wife, hoarding wealth, mansion, art and architecture, house-warmimg, conclusion, character, brilliance, paternal property, ambrosia, the art of giving clues to the place where stolen goods are concealed, anthill, Vedas, scriptures, buffaloes, cows, horses and elephants, and produces of wet lands.

Fifth House : Progeny, father, religious merit, king's minister, good character, mechanical art, mind, learning, foetus, discrimination, umbrella, stories, auspicious invitation, garments, great project, paternal property, intuition, fortune derived through wife, liaison with courtesans, dignity, greatness, secret, politeness, journalism, well-being, friendship, poetic compositions, stomach, undertaking a work, repetition of Mantras, well-earned affluence, gift of food, wisdom, contemplation, ways of earning money, labour, festivities, scholarship and hereditary ministership.

Sixth House : Disease, obstacle, fighting, maternal uncle, phlegm, glands, cruel deeds, lunacy, boils, enemy, hatred, miserliness, sickness, wounds, venereal disease (gonorrhoea), food, weariness, debt, calumny, enemy's power, consumption, heat, ulcers, mental depression, anguish, enmity with people, incessant eye-trouble, receiving alms, untimely meals, loss of learning, cousins and other blood relations, gain, strain, poison, fetters, colic, guarding one's own reputation, urinary complaints, dysentry, six tastes, reproof, slaves, thieves, calamity, prison, and misunderstandings with brothers etc.

Seventh House : Marriage, unchastity, lustful person, victory, hostility to women, deviation from path, scents, songs, flowers, sumptuous food and drink, betel chewing, journey, curd, forgetfulness, acquisition of clothes etc., semen, husband and wife, genital organ, urine, anus, trade, milk, honeyed drink, eating soup and ghee, gift, loss of valour, overthrow of the enemy, money locked up elsewhere, controversy, sexual union, adopted son, foreign country, sexual secrets, and theft.

Eighth House : Longevity, happiness, defeat, wealth left behind by a deceased person, afflicted face, death, suffering, urinary disease, quarrel for food, calamity, brother's enemy, trouble to wife, tuft of hair, enemy's fortress, laziness, punishment by the king, fright, loss of wealth, creditor, long-standing money, arrival of a wicked person, sin, killing a living being, mutilation of a limb, decapitation, distressing talk, misfortunes or portents, zeal for committing cruel deeds, warfare, and intense mental suffering.

Ninth House : Charity, virtue, pilgrimage, penance, reverence to elders, medicine, conduct, purity of mind, worship of God, endeavour to acquire learning, affluence, travel, conveyance, fortune, diplomacy, prowess, moral story, religious bath, nourishment, company of the virtuous, patrimony, children, prosperity of eight kinds, horses, elephants and buffaloes, coronation hall, establishment of spiritual (Vedic) values, sacrificial rite, and treasure.

Tenth House : Trade and commerce, honour from the king, riding a horse, athletics, kingly duty, servitude, agriculture, physician, fame, treasures, and hoarded wealth, sacrifices preeminence, teacher or elder, machine (talisman), incantation, mother, expansion of merits, medicine, thigh, Gods, accomplishment of Mantra, wealth, adopted son, lord, self-respect, road, honourable living, sovereign, education, seal of authority, subjugation and command.

Eleventh House : Allround gain, receipts, bad desire, dependence, eldest brother, paternal uncle, worshipping the Deities and the virtuous, learning, gold, clever ways of earning money, paternal property, knee, love of gems and ornaments, king's wealth, lost wealth, fine arts, making ornaments for one's sweetheart, intelligence, ministership, brother-in-law, dawn of fortune, realization of one's desire, cooking, desire, mother, longevity, ears, shanks, and painting.

Twelfth House : Disturbance to sleep, mental affliction, feet, fear of the enemy, imprisonment, liberation from pain and debts, horses, elephants, paternal property, enemy, ascent to Heaven, left eye, people's enmity, loss of a limb, becoming a paramour, dissolution of marriage, renouncing the couch, loss of job, mental aberration, wretchedness, fetters, loss of happiness of paternal uncles, disputation, anger, bodily injury, death, going abroad, allround loss and death of wife.

CHAPTER IV

PLANETARY STRENGTH

In the preceding Chapter, I had told you how to calculate the Lagna and other Bhāvas. Now I shall tell you some other points of strength of the planets with reference to the Bhāva chart. Where would the Sun be strong in this chart ? He is strong in the Lagna if it happens to be Meṣa, Siṁha, Dhanus or Mīna. He is also strong in any of these if it is the 10th house from the Lagna. Elsewhere he is weak. In the chart given in the previous Chapter the Sun is in Leo, his own house, but it is neither the Lagna nor the 10th house. So you cannot give him credit on this score. Still it should be borne in mind that he is in his own house which is a source of strength, as you remember. Another point is that all malefics are strong in the 3rd, 6th, and 11th houses from the Ascendant. So do not suddenly make deductions from stray rules. But the Sun here is in his debilitation Navāṁśa. There is a statement in Sanskrit—"Grahāṇām Aṁśakaṁ Balam" which means, the strength of planets depends more on that of their Navāṁśa Rāśis.

The Moon is strong in Gemini, Virgo, Pisces and the first half of Sagittarius, when these happen to be the Lagna or the 7th house. She is strong in the 10th house identical with Taurus or the latter half of Sagittarius. When she occupies Gemini or Cancer identical with the 4th house, she is strong. From this you will understand that the Moon is strong if posited in the 10th for Siṁha-lagna. Vṛṣabha is her exaltation and she is in the 10th which is called the Zenith. So for Siṁha-lagna people she is very powerful in Taurus, though she may be the owner of the 12th house. In the given chart she is in Kumbha. So she gets no special strength.

Mars is strong in Kumbha lagna. So is he in Cancer and Scorpio when they are the 7th house. So too is he in the first half of Capricorn, and Gemini when they happen to be the 10th house. The first half of Dhanus identical with the 4th house makes him strong. Though Cancer is his debilitation, he is considered to be strong, if that Rāśi is the 7th house.

This fact must be noted. In the given chart Mercury being in Sandhi becomes powerless. Mars, lord of 2nd and 7th houses is in the house of loss.

Mercury is strong in the following positions :—In Makara, Siṁha, Karka and Vṛścika as Lagna; in Dhanus as 4th house; in Vṛṣabha as the 7th house; and in Mīna as the 10th house. In our example he is retrograde i.e. Vakra or going backwards. Mercury is at the junction between 11th house and 12th house here. So he must be declared to be weak. Another point is that he is combust i.e. he is very close to the Sun that he is invisible. This fact takes away much of his strength too.

Jupiter is strong in Meṣa , Vṛṣabha, Siṁha, Vṛścika, Dhanus and Mīna as the Lagna, 4th or 10th house. In our example he being in the 12th house must be declared to be weak. However, sign Virgo is good for him.

Venus is strong in Meṣa, Siṁha, Vṛścika and Kumbha as the Lagna; in the latter half of Dhanus, and Vṛścika as the 7th house; in the first half of Ḍhanus, Mīna, Siṁha and Vṛścika as the 10th house; and in the latter half of Makara as the 4th house. In the given example Venus is in the last degree of Kanyā which is his debilitation sign. Though he is in the Lagna Bhāva, he does not get any strength.

Saturn is strong in Tulā and Kumbha as Ascendant or the 4th house; in Siṁha as the 10th house; and in a Rāśi other than the Pṛṣṭhodayas—those that rise with their backs foremost—as the 7th. Rāhu is strong in the 10th house, if it is one of the Rāśis already mentioned as his strong positions. Here Saturn is not strong. So are Rāhu and Ketu.

When examining a chart you are no doubt observing the Navāṁśas of the planets. There is a particular way of looking at these Aṁśas : For example, if the Aṁśa of a planet represents a Sign which happens to be a Dussthāna, bad house i.e. 6th, 8th or 12th, then it is considered to be not so beneficial. Similarly are those Navāṁśa Signs that are occupied by Māndi and other malefics. In our chart Māndi occupies Capricorn which happens to be the Navāṁśa of the Moon. Hence on that score the Moon suffers. So does the Lagna. Māndi's Aṁśa is 5 i.e. Leo, which is occupied by the Sun, R. Mercury and Mars. So these planets suffer from some affliction of a subtle nature. But if a Navāṁśa Sign, though occupied by a malefic, is aspected by a benefic, we should expect pretty good results. Look at the Lagna, whose Aṁśa is Capricorn. Though it is tenanted by Māndi, yet Jupiter's beneficent rays fall on that Sign and Māndi. Of course it is also aspected by the malefic Saturn. However, as Saturn is the lord of that house as well as the Yogakāraka for this Lagna—A planet that owns both a Kendra and a Koṇa house is called Yogakāraka, bestower of benefits—his aspect cannot be harmful despite his malefic nature. Similarly planets that occupy constellations that are 3rd, 5th or 7th counted from that of the ascendant or the Moon yield untoward effects. You may bear in mind that *planets do not exercise their aspects in the Navāṁśa chart as they do in the Rāśi chart.*

Now in the chart the houses have different names : The 1st, 4th, 7th and 10th are termed Kendras or Angles; the 5th and 9th are called Trikoṇas or Trines; the 2nd, 5th, 8th and 11th are called Paṇaphara; and the 3rd, 6th, 9th and 12th are termed Āpoklima. The synonyms of Kendra are (1) Kaṇṭaka and (ii) Catuṣṭaya. Āpoklima is otherwise known as Carama and Paṇaphara as Madhya Kendra. The 12 Bhāvas are respectively called (i) Tanu—body, (ii) Artha—wealth, (iii) Sahaja—brother, (iv) Bāndhava—kinsman, (v) Putra—son, (vi) Ari—enemy, (vii) Kalatra—wife or husband, (viii) Nidhana—death, (ix) Dharma—religious merit, (x) Karma—profession, (xi) Āya—profit, and (xii) Vyaya—loss. The 4th and 8th houses constitute Caturaśra—Square; and the 6th and 11th, Ṣaṭ Koṇa. The 3rd, 6th, 10th and 11th houses are called Upacayas or houses of progress. Another way of looking at this matter is the following :—Mercury and Jupiter are always strong in the Lagna, whatever be the Rāśi : the Sun and Mars in the 10th; the Moon and Venus in the 4th house, and Saturn in the 7th. This is called Digbala or Directional Strength. For, as you know, the Lagna represents the East, the 4th North, 7th West, and 10th South. As in the case of the limbs of Kālapuruṣa you start with the Lagna in a horoscope, so for the quarters too you have to begin with the Lagna instead of Meṣa. The four houses mentioned here happen to be the Kendras or Angular houses. All planets are strong in Kendras, especially benefics are very strong there; they are moderately strong in Paṇaphara houses; and weak in Āpoklimas. It is to be remembered that for malefics ownership of Kendras is very good, while for benefics occupation of Kendras is beneficial.

Planets have a sixfold strength: Kālaja or one born of the time (Temporal), Ceṣṭā (motional), Uccaja or one derived from its exaltation position, Dik (Directional), Ayana or one derived from its declination, and Sthāna (positional). Mars, Venus and the Moon are strong at night. Mercury is strong always. The rest are strong during the day. According to Horāsāra even Saturn is strong at night. The benefics are powerful in the bright fortnight and the malefics in the dark fortnight. The strength of planets is measured in Rūpas. Planets presiding over the year, month, day and hour get $\frac{1}{4}$, $\frac{1}{2}$, $\frac{3}{4}$ and 1 Rūpa respectively as their temporal strength.

The Sun gets the Ceṣṭābala in his Northerly course; the Moon gets it when she is full; and the others get it when they are retrograde. In planetary war—when two planets are posited in the same degree, they are said to be at war, and that planet which is to the North of the other is called the Victorious one (of course there are many varieties of victories)—the victorious planets as well as those that are possessed of plenty of brilliant rays also get this Ceṣṭābala.

Planets get their Uccabala of 1 Rūpa when they are in their highest exaltation.

The Ayanabala is got by Mercury, Saturn and the Moon when they are in their Southerly course, and the rest in their Northerly one. Now the last or sixth is the Sthānabala or positional strength. I have already told you the six Vargas viz. Rāśi, Horā, Drekkaṇa, Navāṁśa, Dvādaśāṁśa and Triṁśāṁśa, occupied by the planets in a horoscope. Consideration of a planet's position in exaltation, own house, friendly house etc. is the basis of this Positional strength. Planets posited in Kendras get one Rūpa as their strength, those in Paṇaphara $\frac{1}{2}$ Rūpa, and those in Āpoklima $\frac{1}{4}$ Rūpa. A planet in his own Navāṁśa is said to be strong in Sthāna. A planet in exaltation gets 1 Rūpa, $\frac{3}{4}$ in Mūlatrikoṇa, $\frac{1}{2}$ in his own house, $\frac{1}{4}$ in a friend's house and nil in inimical house, depression and combustion. There is another kind of this Bala: A hermophrodite (eunuch) planet is strong in the middle of a Rāśi, a male planet in its initial part, and a female planet at its end. Similarly among the planets Mars is naturally twice as strong as Saturn,

Mercury is 4 times as strong as Mars, Jupiter 8 times as Mercury, Venus 8 times as Jupiter, the Moon sixteen times as Venus, the Sun twice as the Moon, and lastly Rāhu is twice as strong as the Sun. So you understand now that the strength of the luminaries is very important for the well-being of a native. A planet though otherwise strong will spoil the Bhāva it occupies and owns, if it is eclipsed. Even if such a planet should form any Yoga, it would not be of much value. If benefic planets are stronger than malefics, the native will become fortunate, attractive, brave and brilliant. If the contrary is the case, sinful, cruel and foolish fellows are born. Planets are said to be badly posited when they are eclipsed, debilitated (Nīca) in Rāśi or Navāṁśa, posited in the Sign of an enemy, in the 6th, 8th or 12th house from the Lagna. In other positions they are said to be well-placed. If a planet is retrograde or brilliant with rays, it is said to be strong in spite of its occupation of its debilitation or inimical Sign or Aṁśa. Generally all planets, therefore, are strong in their exaltation; the Moon is strong when she has the Pakṣabala; and the Sun is strong when he has the Digbala in full i.e. in the 10th house from the Lagna which is also known as the Meridian. The remaining five get it when they are retrograde. Remember this point well viz. retrograde motion confers a good deal of power and strength equal to that of exaltation on a planet. Rāhu is strong in Meṣa. Vṛṣabha, Karka, Vṛṣcika and Kumbha, and Ketu in Vṛṣabha, Kanyā, latter half of Dhanus and Mīna. Still the houses of benefics who are strong and well-placed in the horoscope will prove beneficial to all the malefics.

You must be anxious to know the relative importance and value of the six or seven Vargas already mentioned. The effect is full in a Rāśi, and $\frac{1}{2}$ in the remaining six Vargas. It is $\frac{1}{4}$ in Ṣoḍaśāṁśa ($\frac{1}{16}$), Daśāṁśa ($\frac{1}{10}$), and Ṣaṣṭyaṁśa ($\frac{1}{60}$).

If the Lagna happens to be a Human Rāśi (Gemini, Virgo, Libra, first half of Sagittarius, and Aquarius), its strength is 1 Rūpa; if it is Scorpio, the strength is $\frac{1}{4}$ Rūpa; if any of the rest, the strength is $\frac{1}{2}$ Rūpa. The strength of the Ascendant is equal to the total strength of its lord. If that lord occupies an Upacaya house (3, 6, 10 or 11), the Lagna will attain great strength. The same effect accrues to it when it is occupied or aspected by its lord, Mercury or Jupiter and when conjoined with Venus and without the aspect or conjunction of other planets. For day-births the diurnal Signs are strong and for night-births the nocturnal ones.

I have mentioned above that to be posited in Kendras is a matter of considerable strength for planets. Among the four Kendras the Lagna-Kendra is the strongest, next in importance is the 7th, next to that is the 10th and last is the 4th which is called Pātāla or Netherworld. You might remember the two kinds of friendship etc. existing among the planets, natural and temporary. Of these the former is more powerful and lasting. Although Venus is 8 times as strong as Jupiter, still Jupiter being the Preceptor of the Gods and philosophical in nature, has no parallel in conferring good results on humanity. He is, therefore, very powerful in warding off evil influences and conferring all sorts of benefits. Venus has only half the strength of Jupiter in these matters, while Mercury only ¼ of Jupiter's power. However, the strength of the Moon is the primary cause of that of all the planets. So if the Moon is weak in a horoscope, much of its power is lost.

There is another source of strength : Just as we have several moods such as happy, depressed etc. even so do the planets. There are eleven Avasthās or moods viz. (1) Pradīpta or Blazing, (2) Sukhita or Happy, (3) Svastha or Well, (4) Mudita or Delighted, (5) Śānta or Tranquil, (6) Śakta or Capable, (7) Nipīḍita or Tortured, (8) Khala or Base, (9) Suduḥkhita or exceedingly Distressed, (10) Atibhīta or greatly Frightened, and (11) Vikala or Infirm. A planet in exaltation is the first; one in his Mūlatrikoṇa is the second; one in his own house is the third; one in a friend's house is the fourth; one in the Varga of a benefic planet is the fifth; one with a mass of brilliant rays the sixth; one defeated in a planetary war the 7th; one posited in the Varga (Rāśi, Horā etc.) of a malefic the 8th; one in an inimical house the 9th; one in debilitation the 10th; and lastly an eclipsed one is the 11th. The effects of these Avasthās will be corresponding to their appellations. The good effect of a planet in the Pradīptāvasthā will be full and in the last nil. In the others it is proportionate to the place between the two extremes.

It is very essential for a long and happy life to have the Lagna and the Moon as well as their lords to be strong. What is meant by the Lord of the Moon ? It is the lord of the house occupied by her. So see if the benefics in a horoscope possess considerable strength in their six Vargas (Rāśi, Horā, Drekkāṇa, Navāṁśa, Dvādaśāṁśa and Triṁśāṁśa). See also if the Lagna occupies benefic Ṣaḍvargas. If the lords of these Vargas are also strong, the native will be king or similar to him. If the lord of the rising Navāṁśa of the Lagna is strong, the native will be happy; if that of the rising decanate is strong, he will be equal to a sovereign; and if that of the Lagna-Rāśi is strong, he will be actually a king possessed of immense fortune. If malefics occupy odd Signs and Sun's Horā, the native will be strong, cruel, wealthy, whereas if benefics occupy even Rāśis and the lunar Horā, he will be brilliant in appearance, modest in speech, and of amiable nature. The results will be mixed if these conditions are of a mixed nature.

Decanates

I have to tell you now about the nature and quality of the 36 decanates in the zodiacal circle. The following are called Āyudhadrekkāṇa (Weapon) and are malefic :—The *last* decanates of Meṣa, Mithuna, Siṁha, Tulā and Dhanus, the *first* of Meṣa and Dhanus, the *middle* ones of Mithuna and Kanyā. The *middle* one of Scorpio is termed Pāśa (Noose) which is also malefic. The *first* of Capricorn is *Nigaḷa* (Fetters). This too is bad. Gṛdhrāsya (Vulture-faced) which is malefic is constituted by the following :—The *first* of Leo and Aquarius, and the *middle* of Libra. The *last* decanate of Taurus is called Vihaga or Bird. The *first* of Cancer is Kolāsya or Hog-faced. The Ahi—Serpent, decanates are the *first* of Scorpio, the *last* of Cancer and Pisces. Catuṣpād or Quadrupéd decanates are the *middle* ones of Meṣa and Vṛṣabha, the *first* of Leo and the last of Scorpio. Persons born under these decanates will be poor, vile and cruel. There is another way of looking at the decanates: In a movable Sign the three decanates are in order good, moderate and bad; in a fixed Sign they are bad, good and moderate; and in a dual one they are bad, moderate and good.[1] Now see if the lord of the rising decanate is in his own Varga i.e. own Rāśi, Navāṁśa etc., conjoined with benefics, posited in his exaltation

1. See Chapter XVIII on Decanates.

or friendly house. See also if the lords of the Triṁśāṁśa, Dvādaśāṁśa of the Lagna and its Horā are strong. If these conditions are satisfied, the native will be a paragon of virtues, pure, skilful, long-lived, compassionate and blessed with royal pleasures, sons and renown.

Now I would ask you to apply the knowledge of what you have learnt so far to the chart given in the previous chapter. First of all the Lagna i.e. Tulā, is a Human sign. So it gets strength. The 10th viz. Cancer, is not a Quadrupéd sign. So it cannot get strength on that point. The 7th too fares the same fate as it is not a Reptile sign. The 4th house viz. Capricorn, gets strength as it is an Aquatic sign. Note that the Lagna is also diurnal and strong for the day-birth. If you consider the Digbala conditions none of the planets gets it. Venus gets some strength on account of his presence in the Lagna-kendra although he is at the fag end of the sign Virgo which is termed Rāśi-Sandhi. There are four kinds of Sandhi viz. Rāśi-sandhi, Ṛkṣa-sandhi, Tithi-sandhi and Dina-sandhi, whose effect is not happy. I hope these terms are easy. As Rāhu and Ketu are in Kendras they too get some sort of strength, though malefics are expected to be elsewhere. On account of the Kendra rule Venus and Rāhu and Ketu should get 1 Rūpa each. Saturn, the Moon and the Sun get ½ Rūpa each as they are in Paṇapharas. Jupiter and Mars being in Āpoklima get only ¼ Rūpa each. The Sun being in his own house gets ½ Rūpa and Mercury nil being combust. Venus being in depression shares the same fate. Jupiter being in enemy's house is in the same predicament. Saturn being in inimical position follows suit.

As the birth is in the daytime, Mars, Venus and the Moon do not get Kālabala or temporal strength. The rest are possesed of that strength. As the birth is in the bright fortnight, all the benefics viz. Jupiter, Venus and the Moon get strength.

As the Sun is in Dakṣiṇāyana he does not get the Ceṣṭābala. The Moon being full gets it. Why do you call the Moon full or powerful ? After 10 days in the bright half she is full or powerful for 10 days. The birth is on the 14th lunar day of the light half. Mercury being retrograde gets this strength. The remaining planets do not get it.

The full Uccabala of 1 Rūpa is not won by any planet, but won't they get at lest a portion of that ? Yes, they will. This can be got by calculation. I shall just point out the method of doing that. You know a planet's Uccabala is zero when it is in its lowest debilitation. When it proceeds from that point gradually to its highest exaltation i.e. when it covers an angle of 180 degrees, it gets one full Rūpa as its strength. So by rule of three you can easily find out its strength. Let me now show you the strength of the Sun : You remember his Sphuṭa or longitude, 4^s–21°–58′–47″. Here he is going to his debilitation i.e. he is Avarohin. His lowest debilitation is 6^s–10°–0′–0″. Find out the difference between his actual position and the one where he has no strength at all. By subtracting the former from the latter we get 1^s-18°-1′-13″. For this much he will get some credit. For 180 degrees it is 1 Rūpa, then for 48 degrees (leaving off the small fraction of a degree) what is it ? It is $\frac{48}{180} = \frac{4}{15} = {\cdot}27$ Rūpa. In this manner you have to work out the Uccabala for the others as well.

The Ayanabala or declinational strength is got by the Sun, Moon, Mars and Saturn. For finding out the declination of the planets you refer to pages 22 and 23 of Lahiri's Indian Ephemeris for 1957. The others do not get it.

Now we have to consider the Ṣaḍvarga strength of these planets. The Sun is in his own Rāśi—this is very good—, and is in the Horā of the Moon, in the decanate of Mars (both these are his friends), in the Navāṁśa of Tulā, which is his debilitation and inimical house and so bad, in Dvādaśāṁśa he is in the sign of Mars again, and lastly he is in the Triṁśāṁśa of Mercury, a neutral. Thus he has strength in respect of four Vargas viz. Sign, Horā, Drekkāṇa and Dvādaśāṁśa. While considering this Ṣaḍvarga-strength you have to see if the planet concerned is in his own Rāśi, exaltation or friendly house. In Triṁśāṁśa, of course, you consider whether the planet presiding over that Aṁśa is himself or his friend. You have seen in the case of the Sun that he has three Vargas belonging to his friends. This is a sort of combination of three sources of strength. In the same manner a planet may be in his own Rāśi, Decanate, Navāṁśa etc. If you take the luminaries there is a possibility of their being in their own sign, Horā, Decanate, Navāṁśa and Dvādaśāṁśa. In the case of the others too it is five, leaving off Horā but adding Triṁśāṁśa. In the case of 10 Vargas there is a possibility of 8 such combinations. Such combinations are called by special names. The combinations of 2, 3, 4, 5, 6, 7, 8 and 9 Vargas are called in order *Pārijāta*, *Uttama*, *Gopura*, *Siṁhāsana*, *Pārāvata*, *Devaloka*, *Suraloka* and *Airāvata*. In the case of the Sun, as stated above there is a combination of five friendly Vargas. So it should be called Siṁhāsana. The best combination is of Exaltations in the Vargas, next best is that of own houses and lastly that of friendly houses. However the combination of own and exaltation houses may be allowed. Now I shall enumerate the effects of these special combinations called Vaiśeṣikāṁśas.

Pārijāta :—The native becomes noble, virtuous, wealthy, happy and powerful. *Uttama* :—One becomes noted for his good conduct and character, modest, and efficient. *Gopura* :—He will be endowed with noble ideas, lands, cattle and houses. *Siṁhāsana* :—He becomes a favourite of kings or equal to them. *Pārāvata* :—He will own good horses, elephants, vehicles and such other royal emblems. *Devaloka* :—He gets wide fame, and rulership of a kingdom. *Suraloka* :—He gets good fortune, kingdom, wealth, corn and good family. *Airāvata* :—He becomes equal to Indra, and is respected by kings. In the example given you can independently work out which of the planets have attained Vaiśeṣikāṁśas and to what extent.

Now for your convenience and verification I give the results of these ten Vargas in a tabulated form :—

Planets	Rāśi	Horā	Decanate	Navāṁ.	Dvāda.
Sun.	Own.	Friend.	Friend.	Enemy	Friend.
Moon.	eut.	Do.	Do.	Neut.	Do.
Mars.	Friend.	Do.	Own.	Own.	Enemy.
Mercury.	Do.	Enemy.	Neut.	Neut.	Own.
Jup.	Enemy.	Friend.	Do.	Friend.	Neut.
Ven.	Debil.	Enemy.	Own.	Debil.	Enemy.
Sat.	Enemy.	Do.	Neut.	Enemy.	Friend.
Planets.	Triṁś.	Saptā.	Daśā.	Ṣoḍa.	Ṣaṣtya.
Sun.	Neut.	Enemy.	Friend.	Friend.	Krūra.
Moon.	Do.	Neut.	Exalt.	Own.	Saumya.
Mars.	Do.	Do.	Own.	Hara.	Do.
Mercury	Friend.	Do.	Neut.	Viṣṇu.	Krūra.
Jup.	Own.	Enemy.	Enemy.	Enemy.	Do.
Ven.	Neut.	Friend.	Friend.	Friend.	Do.
Sat.	Do.	Enemy.	Neut.	Do.	Saumya.

There is another point to be remembered here. You know in the example chart Saturn is in Scorpio both in Rāśi and Navāṁśa. This sort of identity in respect of the Sign and Navāṁśa is termed Vargottamāṁśa. Its effects are similar to those of a planet situated in his own house. In this example though Saturn is posited in an inimical house, yet being in Vargottamāṁśa he must yield only good results.

The calculation of the Balapiṇḍa i.e. total strength of planets in Rūpas can be done according to the principles already enunciated. For the present you will just note that the Sun and other planets are considered strong when they are possessed of $6\frac{1}{2}$, 6, 5, 7, $6\frac{1}{2}$, $5\frac{1}{2}$, and 5 Rūpas respectively in total Ṣaḍbala.

Now see how the lord of the rising decanate is. Who is he ? He is Saturn. Save for the Vargottamāṁśa he gets very little Ṣaḍvargabala. Now consider the Lagna itself. Who are the lords of its Triṁśāṁśa, Dvādaśāṁśa and Horā ? Are they strong ? The Horā-lord is the Sun. That of the Triṁśāṁśa is Jupiter, and that of the Dvādaśāṁśa Saturn. All of them can be said to be strong. Remember also that the rising decanate is called Gṛdhrāsya (Vulture-faced). I have already told you that for the Moon her Pakṣabala is of paramount importance, while the Sthānabala is very important for others. So when you begin to examine horoscopes you will pay particular attention to this rule. From the Table given above you can find out which of the planets have strength in the several Vargas. If 9, 8, 7, 6, 5, 4, 3, 2 and 1 out of the 10 Vargas be weak, the effects would be (1) destruction, (2) grief, (3) disaster, (4) unhappiness, (5) fond of kinsmen, (6) leader of relations, (7) favourite of kings, (8) a wealthy king, and (9) foremost of kings.

There is the age of planets depending on their positions in the signs. In odd signs the first six-degree portion represents a planet's infancy, the second part his boyhood, the third his youth, the fourth his old age and the last his death. In an even sign this order is to be reversed. So the Sun becomes old, Mars and Mercury lifeless. The Moon is in boyhood. Venus is in infancy. Jupiter is a youth. So is Saturn.

There is another way of finding out the ages of planets. A planet occupying its *own* or *friendly* house is said to be in *Boyhood*; one in its *Mūlatrikoṇa*, in *youth*; in *Exaltation*, in the position of a Prince or *Yuvarāja*; in *Inimical* house, in *Old Age*; and in *Debilitation*, in *Death*.

CHAPTER V

MOON'S STATES AND CONSTELLATIONS

You might remember my remark to the effect that the Moon's strength is the very basis for that of all the planets. Hence I shall tell you now other methods of finding out her potency: There are three elements called (i) Candrakriyā or Moon's Activity, (ii) Candrāvasthā or Moon's State, and (iii) Candravelā or Moon's Time.

Candrakriyā :— There are 60 Candrakriyās. Generally a star is supposed to have a duration of 60 Ghaṭīs. If that be true, there would be no difficulty in calculating His *kriyā*. For there would be one *Candrakriyā* for every Ghaṭī of the star. But that is not the reality. The duration of stars is sometimes more than 60 Ghaṭīs and at others less than 60. Hence we shall have to find out the total duration of a star in Ghaṭīs and divide it equally among the 60 Candrakriyās. Consequently a Candrakriyā may last for more or less than one Ghaṭī, as the case may be. Now find out the total duration of the star-concerned in Ghaṭīs and also the portion of the star that has already elapsed, in Ghaṭīs. Divide the total duration of the star by 60. The quotient will tell you the duration of one Candrakriyā. Now divide the elapsed portion of the star by this quotient. The result will show the required Candrakriyā. Let us apply this rule to our example. By a reference to page 40 of the Ephemeris you will find that the star Śatabhiṣaj began at 1-26 A.M. that day and continued till 4-24 A.M. the next day. So its total duration was 26 hrs. 58 mts. or 67 Ghaṭīs 25 Vighaṭīs. The elapsed period of the star at birth was 8 hrs. 29 mts. or 21 G. $12\frac{1}{2}$ Vig. Now what is the duration of one Candrakriyā? It is $\frac{\text{Total duration}}{60}$ or $\frac{67^{g}—25^{v}}{60} = \frac{4045}{60}\text{Vig.} = 67\frac{5}{12}$ Vig. Since the divisor is 60, the number for both the total duration and a single Candrakriyā is the same, only the units of time being different. Now divide the elapsed period of the star viz. : 21^{g}-$12\frac{1}{2}^{v}$ or $1272\frac{1}{2}$ Vig. by $67\frac{5}{12}$ Vig. That is $\frac{2545}{2} \times \frac{12}{809} = 18\frac{708}{809}$

It means that it is the 19th Candrakriyā, whose effect is "good character".

Another method of working this out is the following : You know that a constellation contains 13°-20′ or 800 minutes. If this figure is divided by 60, you get the value of one Candrakriyā, which is again 800 seconds. Now taking the longitude of the Moon in the given example on page 28 *supra*, 10^s-10°-51′-45″, we find that it is the second quarter of Śatabhiṣaj, the Moon having traversed 4°-11′-45″ in this Star. Now converting the elapsed part of the star into seconds, we get 15,105 seconds. By dividing this by 800 seconds you get $18\frac{141}{160}$ or the 19th Candrakriyā.

Now note the effects of all the 60 parts in order. (1) One falls from his position, (2) becomes an ascetic, (3) runs after other women, (4) becomes a gambler, (5) mounts a lordly elephant, (6) is seated on the throne, (7) becomes a ruler of men, (8) destroys enemies, (9) commands an army, (10) becomes virtuous, (11) dead or exhausted, (12) one whose head is chopped off, (13) whose hands and feet are wounded, (14) a prisoner, (15) spoilt or missing, (16) becomes a king, (17) Vedic scholar, (18) addicted to sleeping, (19) one of good character, (20) practises meritorious deeds, (21) of noble birth, (22) acquisition of a treasure, (23) belonging to a famous family, (24) engaged in expounding scriptures, (25) destroyer of foes, (26) sickly, (27) conquered by enemy, (28) wanders away from his country, (29) a servant, (30) loses wealth, (31) member of a royal court, (32) a good counsellor, (33) a governor, (34) has a wife, (35) frightened by elephants, (36) cowardly in fight, (37) always timid, (38) lies incognito, (39) giver of food, (40) falls into the fire, (41) oppressed by hunger, (42) eats food, (43) wanders aimlessly, (44) flesh-eater, (45) wounded by weapons, (46) married, (47) holds a ball in his hand, (48) plays at dice, (49) becomes a king, (50) distressed, (51) lies on his bed, (52) one that is served by his enemies, (53) accompanied by friends, (54) a Yogin, (55) in the company of his wife, (56) eats sumptuously, (57) drinks milk, (58) performs meritorious acts, (59) healthy or self-possessed, and (60) lives happily.

Candrāvasthā :— There are 12 Avasthās or conditions of the Moon. As in the case of the *Candrakriyā*, you have to find out the total duration of the star as well as its elapsed part in Ghaṭīs. Divide the total duration by 12. The quotient you get is the value of one *Avasthā.* If the total duration be 60 Ghaṭīs, that of one *Avasthā* would be $\frac{60}{12} = 5$ Ghaṭīs. But it is not always the same, as shown in the previous case. So what you have to do is to divide the total duration viz. 67^g-25^v, by 12. That is $\frac{4045}{12}$ Vig. or $337\frac{1}{12}$ Vighaṭīs. This is the duration of one *Avasthā.* Now divide the elapsed part of the star converted into Vighaṭīs by $\frac{4045}{12}$ Vighaṭīs. That is $\frac{1272.5}{4045} \times 12 = \frac{3054}{809}$ $= 3\frac{627}{809}$ This means the *Candrāvasthā* is the 4th; whose effect is 'Kingship'.

Another method :— Divide the total longitude of the star viz. 800 minutes, by 12. The quotient will give you the value of one *Avasthā* in minutes. This is $\frac{200'}{3}$. If you divide the elapsed part of the star in minutes i.e. 251.75′ by $\frac{200'}{3}$ you get the particular *Candrāvasthā*. So $\frac{251.75}{200} \times 3 = \frac{30.21}{8} = 3.78$ which means that it is the 4th *Avasthā.*

The results are (1) going abroad, (2) becoming an esteemed favourite of a great king, (3) loss of life through service, (4) kingship, (5) interested in the merits befitting one's family, (6) sickness, (7) holding a royal durbar, (8) fear, (9) being tortured by hunger, (10) marriage with a young lady, (11) attachment to a cosy and lovely couch, and (12) eating sumptuous food.

Candravelā :—There are 36 Velās or Periods of the Moon. As explained above, you have to divide the total duration of the star by 36. The quotient you get will give the value of one Velā. So by dividing 67^g-25^v or 4045 Vig. by 36 we get $\frac{4045}{36}$ Vig. as the value of one Velā. Now divide the elapsed part of the star in Vighaṭī by $\frac{4045}{36}$. The result is the required Velā. So

$\frac{2545}{2} \times \frac{36}{4045} = 11\frac{263}{809}$ which means that the *Velā* is the 12th whose effect is 'sexual congress'.

Another method :— Divide the total longitude of the star viz. 800 minutes, by 36. The quotient gives you the value of one *Velā*. This is $\frac{200}{9}'$ Now by dividing 251.75′ i.e. the elapsed part, by $\frac{200'}{9}$ you will get $\frac{251.75 \times 9}{200} = 11.33$ which gives the 12th *Velā*.

Now the results in order are (1) disease of the head, (2) joyousness, (3) performing sacrifice, (4) living in happiness, (5) eye-trouble, (6) happiness, (7) amusement in the company of women, (8) high fever, (9) gold ornaments, (10) shedding tears, (11) drinking poison, (12) sexual congress, (13) stomach-ailment, (14) sport in water, merriment and drawing of pictures, (15) anger, (16) dancing, (17) drinking ghee, (18) sleeping, (19) giving gifts, (20) tooth-ache, (21) quarrel, (22) journey, (23) lunacy, (24) swimming in or crossing water, (25) hostility, (26) an enjoyable bath, (27) hunger, (28) fear, (29) acquisition of śāstraic knowledge, (30) wantonness, (31) assembly, (32) fighting, (33) doing meritorious deeds, (34) committing sins, (35) perpetrating cruel deeds, and (36) great joy. These three kinds of the Moon's strength can be used with advantage.

Now we have to understand the vulnerable degrees in each sign of the zodiac for the planets. The following table gives the Mṛtyubhāgas or fateful degrees of the Moon and other planets as well as the Lagna :—

	Meṣa.	Vṛṣa.	Mith.	Kark.	Siṁ.	Kan.	Tu.	Vṛ.	Dha.	Mak.	Kum.	Mina.
Moon	26	12	13	25	24	11	26	14	13	25	5	12
Do	8	9	22	22	25	14	4	23	18	20	21	10
								(according to others)				
Sun	20	9	12	6	8	24	16	17	22	2	3	23
Mars	19	28	25	23	29	28	14	21	2	15	11	6
Mercury	15	14	13	12	8	18	20	10	21	22	7	5
Jupiter	19	29	12	27	6	4	13	10	17	11	15	28
Venus	28	15	11	17	10	13	4	6	27	12	29	19
Saturn	10	4	7	9	12	16	3	18	28	14	13	15
Rāhu	14	13	12	11	24	23	22	21	10	20	18	8
Ketu	8	18	20	10	21	22	23	24	11	12	13	14
Māndi	23	24	11	12	13	14	8	18	20	10	21	22
Lagna	1	9	22	22	25	2	4	23	18	20	24	10

Now see if any of the planets or Lagna occupies the fateful degree. By a reference to the longitudes of planets etc. you will come to the conclusion that none is in a fateful degree.

Another point to be considered at a birth is the Viṣaghaṭī which is supposed to be harmful to the subject. The duration of this Viṣa is more or less of 4 Ghaṭīs or 1 hour and 36 minutes. If the duration of a Nakṣatra is 60 ghaṭīs, we have to take the Viṣa-period as of 4 ghaṭīs. Otherwise we have to change it by the rule of three process. The following table gives the Viṣaghaṭīs in the Nakṣatras beginning with Kṛttikā :—

Stars	*Viṣa-ghati from to*	*According to others*	*Amṛtaghaṭīs*
Kṛttikā	31-34	23-26	after 54 Ghaṭīs
Rohiṇī	41-44	6-9	,, 52 ,,
Mṛgaśīrṣa	15-18	25-28	,, 38 ,,
Ārdrā	12-15	—	,, 35 ,,
Punarvasu	31-34	—	,, 54 ,,
Puṣya	21-42	25-28	,, 46 ,,
Āśleṣa	33-36	—	,, 56 ,,
Maghā	31-34	—	,, 54 ,,
Pūrvaphalgunī	21-24	—	,, 44 ,,
Uttaraphalgunī	19-22	—	,, 42 ,,
Hasta	22-25	—	,, 45 ,,
Citrā	21-24	—	,, 46 ,,
Svātī	15-18	—	,, 38 ,,
Viśākhā	15-18	—	,, 38 ,,
Anurādhā	11-14	—	,, 34 ,,
Jyeṣṭhā	15-18	—	,, 38 ,,
Mūla	21-24	—	,, 46 ,,
Pūrvāṣāḍhā	25-28	—	,, 48 ,,
Uttarāṣāḍhā	21-24	—	,, 46 ,,
Śravaṇa	11-14	—	,, 34 ,,
Dhaniṣṭha	11-14	—	,, 34 ,,
Śatabhiṣak	19-22	—	,, 42 ,,
Pūrvabhādra	17-20	25-28	,, 40 ,,
Uttarabhādra	25-28	—	,, 48 ,,
Revatī	31-34	—	,, 54 ,,
Aśvinī	51-54	25-28	,, 42 (46?)
Bharaṇī	25-28	23-26	,, 48 ,,

The idea here is that the period of four Ghaṭīs from 31 to 34 (both inclusive) is inauspicious in the star Kṛttikā. So if there is a birth in this period of Viṣa of any Nakṣatra proper propitiatory ceremonies are to be advised by the astrologer. In the given example birth was during the Viṣa-ghaṭī. Similarly Śāntis are necessary if births take place in the following inauspicious days etc. :—

Kṛṣṇa Caturdaśī or the 14th lunar day of the dark fortnight is bad. Find out the total duration of this Tithi. Make six equal parts of this. If the birth takes place in the very first division no śānti is called for, as it is not inauspicious. In the second part it is bad for the father of the child; in the third bad for the mother, in the fourth bad for the maternal uncle, in the fifth for the entire family, and lastly in the sixth there will be loss of money.

Amāvāsyā :—This is very bad for all auspicious rites as well as for birth, but the Jivātman in his anxiety to come into this world with the idea of working out his Prārabdha is blind to the inauspiciousness of the Tithi. The total duration of Amāvāsyā is to be divided into 8 equal parts. Of these the first part is called SINĪVĀLĪ, the next five DARŚA, and the last two KUHŪ. Birth at SINĪVĀLĪ will ruin wealth; at Darśa the parents will be reduced to penury; at Kuhū the evil effects are untold and manifold.

Mūla Nakṣatra :—Birth in the first Pāda of this star is injurious to the father, in the second to the mother, in the third it will cause loss of money, and in the 4th it is good. This process is to be reversed in the case of Āśleṣā. Jyeṣṭhā Nakṣatra also is not quite good, especially when the new-born has elder brothers or sisters. The last Ghaṭī of Jyeṣṭhā and the first two of Mūlā together constitute what is called ABHUKTAMŪLA, which is dire in consequences. The authorities are of opinion that a child born in this period should not be seen by the father for 8 years. Similarly the first half of Citrā, the second and third Pādas of Puṣya, the third quarter of Pūrvāṣāḍhā, and the first of Uttaraphalgunī are considered inauspicious. However, Uttaraphalguni is not bad for female birth.

Gaṇḍānta :—The last 5 Ghaṭīs of Revatī and the first 5 of Aśvinī constitute Nakṣatragaṇḍānta. Similarly in the case of the other two pairs viz. Āśleṣā and Maghā, and Jyeṣṭhā and Mūla. These are also inauspicious. There is a Tithigaṇḍānta : The last two ghaṭīs of the 5th, 10th, 15th and 30th lunar days with two ghaṭīs at the commencement of their immediately next Tithis constitute the Gaṇḍānta. Similarly the last ½ Ghaṭīs of the Ascendants, Cancer, Scorpio and Pisces, and the initial ½ ghaṭīs of Aries, Leo and Sagittarius are Rāśigaṇḍāntas.

The periods of risk caused by *Gaṇḍa* are the following :—

1) 16 years in the case of *first* quarter of *Aśvinī*.
2) 8 years in the case of *first* quarter of *Maghā*.
3) 1 year in the case of *Jyeṣṭhā*.
4) 4 years in the case of *Citrā* and *Mūla*.
5) 2 years in the case of *Āśleṣā*.
6) 1 year in the case of *Revatī*.
7) 2 months in the case of *Uttaraphalgunī*.
8) 3 months in the case of *Puṣya*.
9) 9 months in the case of *Pūrvāṣāḍhā* (Harmful to the father).
10) 12 years in the case of *Hasta* (Do.)
11) Immediate danger to father in the case of *Abhuktamūla*.

Should one born under *Abhuktamūla* live, one makes one's family illustrious, be wealthy and lord of a big army.

Exception to Gaṇḍadoṣa :—This Doṣa would be harmful only if the lunar month of birth be *Jyeṣṭha*, *Āṣāḍha*, *Mārgaśīrṣa*, *Pauṣa* and *Māgha*.

Pañcamāriṣṭa :— This peculiar Doṣa is not met with in Astrological works; but it is mentioned as a major fault in works on Dharma Sāstra. If the 5th house from the Lagna is occupied by any planet it causes this Ariṣṭa or trouble. If the planet in the 5th is the Sun, the subject's father will have trouble; if it is the Moon, his mother; if Mars, his brothers or sisters; if Mercury, his maternal uncle; if Jupiter, maternal grandfather; Venus, mother's sisters; if Saturn, Rāhu or Ketu, the child itself. In our chart the Moon is in the 5th house.

Ekanakṣatra :— It is considered inauspicious, if the child on the one hand and its father, mother, brother or sister on the other have the same star. Then too proper propitiation is advised.

Other inauspicious factors :— I have told you that the planets stand for some relations of the subject. In other words, they are called the Kārakas of relatives. If the Kārakas occupy the Bhāvas denoting the particular relations, they prove harmful to those relations. So if the Sun is in the 9th house, it is bad for the father. The Moon in the 4th is bad for the mother; Mars in the 3rd for brothers; Jupiter in the 5th for children;

Venus in the 7th for the partner in life. In the case of Saturn they say that the 8th house which stands for Āyuṣya or longevity being occupied by him conduces to that. Whatever the authorities may say it is an observed fact that Saturn in the 8th Bhāva creates a good deal of troubles and worries. Besides that you have to see from which planet he is in the 8th house. That Bhāva belonging to that planet and things presided over by him will have plenty of headache.

There are other troublesome elements like DINAMṚTYU and DINAROGA. What are these ? The first is formed by the following :— The first Pāda of Dhaniṣṭhā and Hasta, the second of Viśākhā and Ārdrā, the third of Uttarābhādra and Āśleṣā, and the fourth of Bharaṇī and Mūla. If a birth takes place at *daytime* in any of these Pādas of stars, the Doṣa called Dinamṛtyu is caused. In other words it is fatal to the child. Of course you should not jump into that conclusion only on the basis of this single factor. On the other hand, if the birth in a Dinamṛtyu star-Pāda occurs at night, there is no trouble at all. The same remark applies to what is called Dinaroga too. The following are termed Dinaroga :—The first quarter of the stars Āśleṣā and Uttarābhādra, the second of Bharaṇī and Mūla, the third of Uttaraphalgunī and Śravaṇa, and the last of Svātī and Mṛgaśiras.

Effects of Stars

Aśvinī :—One born under this star becomes learned, resolute, clever, engaged in his own Dharma, prominent in the family, full of self-respect, eats sparingly, highly respectable and of moderate means.

Bharaṇī :—He will be fickle-minded, capable of controlling himself, addicted to women, fond of brothers, proud, courageous, long-lived, helper of friends and having a few children.

Kṛttikā :—Free from confusion, strong, wavering in mind, eater of all kinds of food, very powerful, truthful, owner of many houses and a prattler.

Rohiṇī :—Has plenty of hair on the upper part of the body, leader of groups, has moles on the face or mouth, sides and the back, is fraudulent, unhelpful to his mother, rich and learned.

Mṛgaśiras :—He will have a vacillating mind, a broad body, be sickly in childhood, inadvertant, enthusiastic, has many enemies and troubles.

Ārdrā :—Fickle-minded, crafty in speech, usurper of others' wealth, boastful, proud, with few children, long-lived and receiving money from the Government.

Punarvasu :—Charitable, happy, of very good character, not learned, sickly, thirsty, easily satisfied and weakminded.

Puṣya :—Cruel, irascible, intelligent, stubborn, eloquent, learned in many Śāstras, helper of relatives, has cleptomania and wealth and is independent.

Āṣleśā :—Cruel, fickle, eloquent, leader of groups, wealthy, learned, having much exertion, deceitful and with few children.

Maghā :—Learned, modest, of deep-rooted enmity, cruel, praised by the good, having many servants and riches, enjoying pleasures, industrious and devoted to Gods and elders.

Pūrvaphalgunī :—Of sweet speech, generous, mean, spending much money, with obedient servants, famous, liked by kings, and afraid of fights.

Uttara-Ph. :—Liked by women, handsome, leader of men, learned, getting wealth from the king, having many wives, of generous disposition, talkative, and given to sensual pleasures.

Hasta :—Voluptuous, clever, eloquent, of a thievish mind, rich, fond of foreign countries, eager to fight, and destroyer of enemies.

Citrā :—Wicked, liked by women, (or liked by wicked women), sinful, engaged in various pursuits, fond of disputations, happy, living in another country, and wearing colourful clothes and garlands.

Svātī :—Happy, self-controlled, merciful, of sweet speech, engaged in Dharma, indebted, living abroad, hater of kinsmen, and dressed sparsely, has few children.

Viśākhā :—Odious, prattler, having children and wife, wise, rich, devoted to Gods, elders and Brahmins, not charitable, and afflicted with eye-disease.

Anurādhā :—Oppressed by hunger and thirst, dejected, kind, devoted to Dharma, handsome, fond of wandering, and living abroad.

Jyeṣṭhā :—Content, intent on Dharma, endowed with many children and friends, very irascible, troubled by kinsmen, and leader of his clan.

Mūla :—Learned, happy, rich, sickly, handsome, of thievish leanings, of vacillating mind, eldest of the family, and a king.

P. Āṣāḍhā :—Of firm friendship, humble, with many children, leader of men, wise, eater of sumptuous food, faithful to his wife, and beloved of the king.

U. Āṣāḍhā :—Fond of mirth, modest, having many enemies, distressed, possessed of superior intellect, wanderer, with many wives, and kind.

Śravaṇa :—Learned, living away from birth-place, with an excellent wife, rich, famous, with few children, and many foes, spending lavishly, happy and lordly.

Dhaniṣṭhā :—Rich, heroic, charitable, bereaved of his wife, happy in alien lands, talkative, untruthful and fond of music and dance.

Ṣatabhiṣak :—Voluble, deceitful, in servitude, without sons and brothers, rich, fickle-minded, miserly, engaged in playing tricks and destroyer of enemies.

P. Bhādra :—Exceedingly fond of women, of inconstant residence, hard to be won over, given to enjoyment of pleasures, getting wealth from the king, long-lived, mean, and intent on his work.

U. Bhādra :—Eloquent, happy, blessed with children, having permanent enemies, virtuous, timid, greedy and anxious to improve his strength and wealth.

Revatī :—Living the full span of life, attractive in apprearance, under the control of women, possessed of self-respect and pride, jealous, of valiant heart and rich.

In the case of female birth the following stars are said to be bad :—Ārdrā, Āśleṣā, Śatabhiṣak, Puṣya, Mūla, Citrā, Jyeṣṭhā and Kṛttikā.

Uḍu-Daśā

Before proceeding further I should like you to understand the Uḍudaśā system which also will stand you in good stead in determining the span of life. Ancient Sages have declared that the span of human life is 120 years. This period is distributed among 9 planets thus:—The Sun's Daśā coming first in this scheme lasts for six years, the next of Moon for 10 years, then of Mars for 7 years, then of Rāhu for 18 years, then of Jupiter for 16 years, then of Saturn for 19 years, then of Mercury for 17 years, then of Ketu for 7 years and lastly of Venus for 20 years. Though the Daśā-order is this, do not think that all persons begin with the Sun's Daśā or major period. As this is called Uḍudaśā—Uḍu means star—the major period is found out from the *star* tenanted by the *Moon* at the time of birth. The following Table will show the stars which produce the Daśās of the different planets :—

Sun :—Kṛttikā, Uttaraphalgunī and Uttarāṣāḍhā.
Moon —Rohiṇī, Hasta and Śravaṇa.
Mars :—Mṛgaśiras, Citrā and Dhaniṣṭhā.
Rāhu :—Ārdrā, Svātī and Śatabhiṣak.
Jupiter :—Punarvasu, Viśākhā and Pūrvābhādra.
Saturn :—Puṣya, Anurādhā and Uttarābhādra.
Mercury :—Āśleṣā, Jyeṣṭhā and Revatī.
Ketu :—Maghā, Mūla and Aśvinī.
Venus :—Pūrvaphalgunī, Purvāṣāḍhā and Bharaṇī.

Now we have to find out what portion of a particular Daśā is already over in the state of pregnancy and what portion of it still remains at birth. The most popular method of calculating this is the following:—Find out from a good Pañcāṅga the total duration of the particular star of birth, as well as the part that has already elapsed at the time of birth. Then you can easily find out the remaining part of the star. You know for the full star the number of years allotted. Let X be the total duration of the Nakṣatra in Ghaṭīs, Y be the unexpired portion of the star in Ghaṭīs and Z be the number of years allotted to that star. Then the balance of the Daśā in years will be equal to $Y/X \times Z$. Any fraction of a year is to be multiplied by 12 and divided by the same denominator. This will give you the months. If any fraction of a month remains, it should be multiplied by 30 and divided as before. That will give you the days. If the remaining fraction is further multiplied by 60 and divided as before, it will give you the Ghaṭīs. In the present case Dhaniṣṭhā lasted on the previous day till 47 Ghaṭīs and 45 Vighaṭīs. And on the day of birth Śatabhiṣak lasted for 55-15 Ghaṭīs. So its total duration is 67-30 Ghaṭīs. The time of birth in Ghaṭīs is 8-45. On the previous day already 12-15 Ghaṭīs had been covered, and on the day of birth 8-45. So the total of elapsed part of the Nakṣatra is 12-15 plus 8-45 Ghaṭīs. That is 21 Ghaṭīs. From the above table you know that the Daśā-lord for Śatabhiṣak is Rāhu and its duration is 18 years. Now what is the part of the star still remaining ? It is 46-30 Ghaṭīs. So the balance of Rāhudaśā at birth is 46-30/67-30 × 18 yrs. This is equal to 31/45 × 18 = 12 yrs. 4m. 24d. A better method of calculating this would be from the longitude of the Moon. You know her longitude to be 10ˢ-10°-51′-45″. This also gives the second Pāda of Śatabhiṣak. You remember also that a whole Nakṣatra covers 13°-20′. This is equal to 800 minutes. So for one Pāda of a star the number of minutes required is 200. Now the second Pāda of this star will be complete at 13°-20′-0″. So the balance in the second Pāda is 13°-20′-0″ minus 10°-51′-45″ = 2°-28′-15″. Now what is the Daśā for one Pāda of this star ? It is 4½ yrs. Now convert 2°-28′-15″ into minutes. You get 148.25. You know that it is 9/2 yrs. for 200 minutes, then how many years etc. you get for 148.25 minutes ? That comes to 5.93 × 9/16 = 3 yrs. 4 m. 1 d. This is the balance of Daśā in the second Pāda of that star. There are two full Pādas or one full half yet to be covered. For that the Daśā-period is 9 yrs. Add this to 3y-4m-1d. You get then 12 yrs. 4m. 1.d. as the total balance of Rāhu Daśā at birth. I should like you to follow this latter method for calculating the Uḍudaśā. Now you should learn what are called Bhuktis or sub-periods. What do you mean by this term ? The Daśā which I have just told you about is termed Mahādaśā or major period. Just as a country though having one supreme monarch exercising his authority over it has many Governors, District Officers etc., even so though a particular planet may be the lord of the Mahādaśā, yet there are other planets exercising their authority over certain sub-periods called Bhuktis, Antaras etc. In each Mahādaśā the first sub-period—I shall presently explain how to calculate that—belongs to the lord of the Mahādaśā himself. You know in Delhi certain parts of New Delhi are administered directly by the Central Government. The order of the other sub-periods is the same as that of the Mahādaśās. For example, in the Sun's Mahādaśā the first Bhukti belongs to himself, the next to the Moon and so on in the order of the Daśās. Now let us see the method of calculating these Bhuktis. Multiply the number representing the Mahādaśā period by the number of years allotted to that planet whose Bhukti is to be found out. In this product treat the number beginning with the second place as so many months and the figure in the first place multiplied by 3 as the number of days. For example, in Ravidaśā his own Bhukti is $6 \times 6 = 36$. Here the figure 3 shows the Bhukti period of 3 months, and 6 multiplied by $3 = 18$ is the number of days in addition. So the whole Bhukti of the Sun in his Daśā is 3m. 18d. In this manner the Moon's Bhukti in the Sun's Daśā is $6 \times 10 = 60 = 6$ months only, because $3 \times 0 = 0$. So in Rāhumahādaśā the first Bhukti belongs to Rāhu, which is $18 \times 18 = 324 = 32$ months and 12 days. In Rāhudaśā what portion is already over ? It is 5y-7m-29d. Rāhu's own bhukti is 2y-8m-12d plus Jupiter's of 2-4-24 plus Saturn's of 2y-10m-6d. The total is 7y-11m-12d, but our expired portion is only 5y-7m-29d. So by deducting the latter from the former we get 2y-3m-13d, which is the unexpired part of Saturn's Bhukti in Rāhumahādaśā at birth. Just as the major period—Daśā—has the sub-periods or Bhuktis of the nine planets beginning with that of the major lord himself, even so a Bhukti is further sub-divided into Antarāntaras or *minor periods* in the same order. But its calculation is done thus : Convert the Bhukti into days and multiply that by the number representing the years of the Daśā of that planet whose minor period is required. Divide the product by 120. The quotient will give in days, Ghaṭīs etc. the minor period of the concerned planet. Of course you will have to multiply the remainder by 60 and divide the product by 120 in order to get the number of Ghaṭīs in it. Repeat this process to obtain the Vighaṭīs. Let us take an example for a better understanding of this problem : You know that the sub-period of Jupiter in the major period of Mars is 11 months 6 days. By converting this into days you will get 336. Now if you are asked to find out the minor period of Rāhu in this sub-period of Jupiter in the major period of Mars, what you will do is to multiply 336 by 18 and divide the product by 120. This will give you 252/5 days. This is equal to 50d. and a fraction 2/5. If this is multiplied by 60, you will get 24 Ghaṭīs. So this minor period of Rāhu comes to 1 m. 20 d. 24gh. In the same manner you can further sub-divide a minor period into Sūkṣma-Daśā, which can likewise be sub-divided still further into what is called Prāṇa-Daśā. The sūkṣma-Daśā of Jupiter in the above minor period of Rāhu will be $= 252/2 \times 16/120$ days $=$ 6d.-43g-12v. In this Sūkṣma-daśā of Jupiter the Prāṇa-Daśā of Mars will be $252/5 \times 16/120 \times 7/120 \times 60/1$ ghaṭīs $= 23$ gh. 31 vigh.

Chapter VI

RECTIFICATION OF BIRTH TIME

I shall now tell you some methods by which you can rectify the noted time of birth. However, I have to warn you against depending solely on them. One of the methods is the following :—Convert the time of birth in Ghaṭīs etc. after Sunrise into Vighaṭis. Multiply this by 4 and divide the product by 9. The remainder will indicate the number of the star of birth counted from Aśvinī, Maghā or Mūla. If you apply this rule to our example horoscope, you get 525 Vighaṭis. Then $525 \times 4/9 = 233$ and a remainder of 3. But the 3rd star from Mūla would be Uttarāṣāḍhā. This is not correct. We must get Śatabhiṣak. If you take 8g-30v as the time of birth in Ghaṭis, you get a balance of 6 which gives us the star of birth exactly. So according to this the correct time of birth should be 8 Ghaṭis and 30 Vighaṭis after Sunrise. Another method is to multiply the ghaṭis etc. by 4 and add to it the number of the Rāśi the Lagna represents from Meṣa and again add 5, 10 or 15 according as the Lagna is movable, fixed or dual. Divide this sum by 27. Take the balance into consideration. If the birth is in the bright fortnight count the remainder from Aśvini, and if in the dark fortnight, count from Citrā. That star should be the natal star or one of its trines. In the given example this rule does not hold good. But if you take 8-31.5 ghaṭis, you get a remainder of 6 which gives the required star Śatabhiṣak. Yet another method is this :—Multiply the time of birth in ghaṭīs by 6. Add to this the particular date of the solar month. This total would reveal the number of degrees by which the Lagna is removed from the very commencement of the sign occupied by the Sun. It was the 24th day of Siṁha month. If you add this to 50-70, which is the product you get by multiplying the Iṣṭaghaṭī by 6, you get 75°-10′. According to this rule the cusp of the first house or Lagna must be 75°-10′ farther from the beginning of Leo, because the Sun is situated in that Sign. But actually our Lagna-sphuṭa is 6^{s}-10°-32′-4″ i.e. 2s-10°-32′-4″ removed from the initial point of Leo. However, this will help us in locating the Ascendant broadly. I shall give you yet another method :—Note the Rāśi and Navāṁśa occupied by Māndi as well as by the Moon. Now the Lagna of birth will have some connection with this Rāśi. The Lagna may be the 7th, 5th or 9th from the sign or Navāṁśa of Māndi or the Moon, whichever is stronger of the two. In our example Māndi is in Makara in sign and Leo in Aṁśa. The Moon is in Kumbha Rāśi and Makara Navāṁśa. But the latter is stronger. Here the Lagna is actually in the 9th house from the Moon, the degrees of both being exactly the same i.e. 11th. Accoding to another view, the Lagna may be trine to the lord of the sign or Aṁśa of the Moon or Māndi.

There are some simple rules to find out the sex of the child. In this case too you have to be doubly careful before pronouncing judgment. Convert as before the Iṣṭaghaṭīs etc. into Vighaṭīs. Divide this by 225. Now you may have a remainder upto 225. What you have to do with the remainder is this : have five groups of 15, 30, 45, 60, 75, i.e. from 1 to 15 first group, 16 to 45 second, 46 to 90 third, 91 to 150 fourth, and 151 to 225 fifth. In the odd groups male births are indicated. Take our example. Divide 525 by 225. You will get a remainder of 75. This falls in the third group. So the child must be male. Another method is to multiply the Iṣṭaghaṭī by 4 and to add to it the number of Rāśis alone in the Lagna-sphuṭa. Divide the result by 8. If the remainder is an even number, it is male, and if odd, it is female. In our example, 8-45 × 4 plus 6 41. Leave off the Vighaṭīs. In this case there are no Vighaṭīs. By dividing 41 by 8 you get one as remainder, which being an odd number indicates female birth. Hence the time of birth will have to be suitably modified.

I shall tell you another interesting point in this context. From the Lagna of birth you can find out the direction of the lying-in-chamber in the house. If the Ascendant be Aries, Cancer, Libra, Scorpio or Aquarius, the chamber would be in the eastern portion of the house; if Leo or Capricorn, in the south; if Taurus, in the west; and if Gemini, Virgo, Sagittarius or Pisces, in the north. Before making any pronouncement you will have to see which of the two viz. the Lagna or its Navāṁśa, is stronger. In case the Navāṁśa is stronger, then you will have to give the direction indicated by that sign and not by the Lagna-Rāśi. What do you mean by the Navāṁśa being stronger ?

See if that particular sign whose name the Aṁśa bears is well aspected or occupied and also see if its lord is strong, in benefic house and has the aspect of and association with benefics. You can similarly find out the direction which the lying-in-chamber faces. The planet that occupies a Kendra position in the birth chart gives the direction. You know the quarters presided over by the planets. Suppose there are many planets in Kendras, then you will have to declare the direction from the strongest of them.

The women or obstetricians etc. in attendance on the expectant mother would depend on the number of planets posited between the Ascendant and the Moon. The number of persons standing or waiting outside is equal to the number outside that range. The quantity of oil in the lamp will correspond to the portion of the sign yet to be covered by the Moon in the particular Rāśi occupied by her. The part of the wick remaining is to be guessed from the part of the sign of Lagna that has not yet risen. The nature of the lamp whether movable or fixed is to be deduced from the nature of the Rāśi occupied by the Sun. These details may not be needed now in view of the existence of maternity homes and electric lights. Still I have given them because of their scientific character and interest.

It is said that if in the chart the Moon does not aspect the Ascendant, the child's father must have been away from home at the time of birth. This means that the Moon should be in the 7th house from the Lagna for the father to be at home. I advise you not to take this Yoga too literally. See if the lord of the 9th house is in the visible hemisphere—six signs counted backwards from the Lagna—and in a fixed Rāśi or Aṁśa and has some sort of connection or aspect on the Lagna or its lord and the Moon or the lord of its Rāśi. If these conditions are satisfied, you can say the father was at home. In the above condition i.e. when the Moon does not aspect the Lagna, if the Sun is posited in the 9th or 8th house, which is movable, fixed or dual sign, the father is in another village, in his own village or on his way home respectively.

CHAPTER VII

SPAN OF LIFE

Sages of yore have declared that it is not possible to determine the span of life of a human being until he is 12 years of age. For he may die within four years owing to the previous sins of his mother, or within 8 years on account of the sins of his father, and lastly by his own sins. The cause of his death during this period called that of Bālāriṣṭa is termed Bālagrahas or evil spirits. To ward off this evil influence people are advised to perform propitiatory Homas on the day of the child's Janmanakṣatra and to take proper medical advice also. According to another view, the Bālāriṣṭa period lasts only for 8 years. There is another Ariṣṭa called Yogāriṣṭa, evil planetary configurations, which might cause death before the age of 20. If the span extends beyond 20 but not beyond 32, it is termed short life or Alpāyus; if the life extends upto 70, it is Madhyama or moderate span; and beyond that it is full. Still, the human span of 100 years being divided into 3 equal parts would give us the three types of life.

There are some Yogas or planetary configurations which lead to early death of the native. If the Ascendant at birth is the very end of a Sign which is aspected or occupied by malefics, immediate death is possible. If it is at a Gaṇḍānta mentioned above, the father, mother or the child itself may quit the world. Should the child survive, it would become prominent or a king. If the birth is in any of the four kinds of Sandhi mentioned elsewhere which receives the aspect of malefics or is conjoined with them, early death is to be predicted. Though you may be sure of the coming end, you ought not to utter an inauspicious word to the querent. Your business is to say that there are many evil influences which should be warded off by means of proper worship, prayers etc. of the planets and the deities presiding over them. The end and aim of Astrology is not merely to predict coming events but to strengthen the devotion of people to God and thus lead them on to the path of spirituality culminating in self-realization. In fine, an astrologer should be a practical philosopher. Now coming back to our topic, if the Moon is in the fateful degree of the particular Rāśi, the child may have early death, provided it is a Kendra house or the 8th from the Lagna. The following are some other Yogas leading to early death :—

1. The Kendras and the 8th house are exclusively occupied by malefics.
2. Malefics occupy the first and 8th houses.
3. Malefics are posited in the Lagna and the 7th house.
4. The Moon or the Ascendant is hemmed in between malefics.
5. The weak Moon occupies the 6th, 8th or 12th house.
6. The weak Moon conjoined with malefics is in 1st, 5th, 7th or 9th.
7. Malefics are posited in the 7th and 8th houses.
8. No Kendra or Koṇa is occupied by benefics.

Note that in the above cases, if there is the conjunction or aspect of benefics you cannot predict early death. In such a case you have to state that the native will have trouble through Bālāriṣṭa etc.

If early death is almost certain, you have to find out its approximate time. The following are some of the methods :—If the lord of the Lagna or the Rāśi occupied by the Moon is weak and posited in an evil house i.e. 6, 8 or 12, the child is likely to die within as many years as are indicated by the number of the Sign counted from Aries. If the planet owning the decanate of the Lagna or the Moon is in similar conditions, death is likely to take place in as many months as are denoted by the sign of the decanate. It will die in so many days as are indicated by the Rāśi owning the Navāṁśa of the Lagna or the Moon, if its lord is in similar conditions. Prediction should be made after due consideration of all these Yogas. If there are malefics in the 5th and 8th houses Ariṣṭa or evil influence is to be predicted. There are some more Yogas for early death—

(1) If the lord of the Lagna and the benefics are all placed in Āpoklima houses, i.e. 3, 6, 9 and 12, short life is the result. (2) If the malefics and lord of the 8th house occupy Kendras, the same effect should be pronounced. (3) If the lords of the Lagna and the 8th are inimical to each other, or if the lords of the Candra-iagna and of the 8th therefrom are inimical to each other,

or if the Sun and the Lagna-lord are mutual enemies, the same effect will follow. Please bear in mind that these are the general rules which may be rendered inoperative on account of other powerful factors such as the position of strong Jupiter in the Ascendant. (4) If the lord of the 8th house is by far stronger than the lord of the Lagna, and if he occupies a Kendra, and if at the same time malefics are posited in the 8th and 12th houses, the native is likely to have short life. Even if he should live long, his life would be a burden. (5) If the lord of the Navāṁśa of the Lagna or the lord of the Navāṁśa of the Moon is much weaker than the lord of the 8th from each, short life may be predicted. (6) The same effect will follow, if the lord of the Lagna is combust and in conjunction with malefics or is posited in his depression or inimical house. (7) If four or more planets are posited in the last four houses i.e. 9, 10, 11 and 12, the same is the effect. (8) If the lord of the Lagna, that of the Sign occupied by the lagna-lord and the Lagna itself are not aspected by benefics from Kendras or Koṇas, short life is the result. In addition, the native will be devoid of wife, issue and intelligence. (9) The Lagna or the Candra-lagna should be aspected by the lord of the 8th. Note that an aspect to be effective should be within 12 degrees of the required range i.e. in the case of a seventh-house aspect the distance of the aspecting planet should not be more than 192 degrees, nor less than 168 degrees. (10) The lord of the 8th house from Lagna or the Moon should be aspected by Saturn or Mars, (11) If the luminaries are posited in the 3rd house identical with a malefic Rāśi in conjunction with malefics, the child will be sickly and may not live more than three years. (12) If the Moon be in a Kendra and be conjoined with the lord of the 8th from the Lagna and if the 8th house be also occupied by some planet, immediate death may follow. (13) If the Sun and Mars are jointly posited in the 7th from the Moon, and if Rāhu is in the Lagna, it will quit the world in ten days. (14) Immediate end will follow if there is a malefic in the 7th house from the rising decanate, and the weak Moon in the Lagna. I hope you remember the rising decanate in the given example. It is the second of Libra. That means it is Kumbha Rāśi. There are, of course, malefics in the 7th house from it viz. Leo, but the Moon is neither weak, nor in the Lagna. So this rule cannot be wholly applied to the present horoscope. All the same, the presence of so many malefics in the 7th from the rising decanate is a defect which cannot be ignored. (15) If all the planets are weak and posited in Āpoklima houses, the child will live for two or six months at the most. (16) If at the time of birth a Ketu is rising (there are many kinds of Ketu mentioned by Varāhamihira. You may also take it as the presence of Ketu in the cusp of the Ascendant) being followed by the fall of meteors, by portentous thunder etc., and if the birth is in a cruel Muhūrta (there are altogether 15 muhūrtas at daytime and an equal number at night. Some of them are cruel), immediate death is the result. (17) One born during an eclipse or when there is a misty circle (Pariveṣa) around the Sun or the Moon, when a malefic is in the Lagna or when a malefic aspects it, will live for about three months. (18) If the Moon occupying any one of the houses, 1, 5, 7, 8, 9, 12, and being conjoined with or aspected by malefics is not aspected by benefics, early death will result. (19) Short life is caused when at a day-birth the Moon is in the 6th or 8th house and the Lagna is occupied by its lord, or when the waning Moon is aspected by both benefics and malefics. (20) The waning Moon or Lagna-lord occupying the 8th house is aspected or joined by Rāhu causes death in the 7th year. (21) The Lagna-lord occupying the 7th house along with Rāhu causes death in 21 days, months or years. (22) The weak Moon being aspected by Rāhu in conjunction with other malefics, and the lord of the Janma-Rāśi being eclipsed cause death in the 6th or 8th year. (23) Add up the longitudes of the Sun and the Moon. If this sum represents a Kendra or 9th house occupied by malefics, death is certain by poison or drowning. You may use this principle in the case of our example chart. By adding the two longitudes we get 3-2-50-32 which is the first Navāṁśa of Cancer. This is no doubt a Kendra, but it is vacant. (24) When the Moon occupying the fateful degree in a Sign is conjoined with only malefics without any association of benefics, or is posited in a Kendra or the 8th house, the child will die along with its mother. All these are to be taken as examples of Bālāriṣṭa.

The following are Yogas leading to long and medium lease of life—*Long life*—Benefics and lord of Lagna should be in Kendras. The same being in Paṇaphara houses (2, 5, 8, 11) cause medium life. If malefics and the lord of the 8th house occupy Āpoklima and Paṇaphara houses, long and medium life respectively are caused. If the three pairs of planets mentioned on page 63 *supra* under (3) are friendly, long life is the result; if they are neutral medium life. On the same page under (5) if the first mentioned planet is much stronger than the one mentioned next, long life is the result. If the Lagna-lord being very strong is posited in a Kendra and is aspected by benefics and not at all by malefics, the subject will be blessed with long life, virtues and prosperity. A strong Jupiter in the Lagna can singly ward off a hundred evil Yogas. Similarly the presence of the Sun for a day-birth and the Moon for a night-birth in the 11th Bhāva from the Lagna has the power of warding off a crore of Doṣas according to Sage Garga. If the waxing Moon is posited in a Kendra, Koṇa or the 11th house and in the Navāṁśa of Jupiter, the Sun or herself, the subject will be rid of all troubles and will perform many meritorious deeds. Note that for long life and prosperity the excellence of the Moon, the lord of her Rāśi and the Lagna-lord coupled with the aspect of benefics is essential. So while judging a horoscope you must first see if Jupiter and the Lagna-lord are in Kendras and if the malefics are away from Kendras, Koṇas and the 8th house. If that is the case the native will live a hundred summers enjoying happiness, health and virtues. Similarly a single strong benefic posited in Kendra without any association of the lord of the 8th house removes all Ariṣṭas. The same is the case when the Lagna or the Moon is aspected by all the planets.

Now I shall tell you another method of finding out the three kinds of longevity. Consider the following three pairs of Rāśis : (1) The decanates of the Lagna and Moon, (2) the Navāṁśa Rāśis of the Lagna-lord and of the Rāśi-lord, and (3) the Dvādaśāṁśa Rāśis of the lords of the Lagna and the 8th house. If in these pairs both are movable or one fixed and the other dual sign, long life is to be predicted; if both are dual or one movable and the other fixed, medium life; and if both are fixed or one dual and the other movable, short life. Let us apply this principle to our example : The decanate of the Lagna is Aquarius, a fixed sign, and that of the Moon is Gemini, a dual sign. So you have a pair of fixed and dual signs. What is the effect of this ? It is long life. Now consider the Navāṁśa Rāśis of the lords of Lagna and the Candra Rāśi. The lord of the first is Venus whose Navāṁśa is Virgo, a dual sign; the lord of the second is Saturn whose Aṁśa is Scorpio, a fixed sign. The result again is long life. Now take the last pair, viz. the Dvādaśāṁśas of the lords of the Lagna and the 8th house. The first is Leo, a fixed sign; and the second is also the same, as its lord is the same as that of the Lagna. But this cannot be a good mode of judgment. So in such cases where these two lords are identical what you have to do is to consider the pair of Dvādaśāṁśas of the lords of the Candra-Rāśi and its 8th house. In the present case Saturn's Dvādaśāṁśa Rāśi is Taurus, and that of Mercury, lord of the 8th from the Moon, is Gemini—one fixed and the other dual, the result whereof is long life. In the given chart no doubt the Ascendant is considerably weakened by the presence of the malefic Rāhu and the debilitated Venus who is in Rāśi-sandhi. One redeeming feature of this, however, is that the Dusthānas i.e. 6, 8 and 12, are devoid of malefics. The 12th house is occupied by a benefic viz. Jupiter. Remember this point very well that benefics in bad houses minimize their evil effects. He, therefore, will guard the life of the native. At the same time you have to bear in mind that Jupiter in a bad house indicates lack of Bank-balance in respect of Pūrvapunya, which generally causes great hardship and disappointments in life. The presence of the Sun in the 11th which is his own house is a point in favour of the native. Venus in spite of his weakness is a natural benefic and posited in the Lagna Kendra and the full Moon in a Koṇa. There are of course some Yogas of short life also. The lord of the 8th house from the Moon viz. Mercury, is aspected by the malefic Saturn and conjoined with two other malefics. You may argue that there is the aspect of the strong Moon too. I agree, but look at the degrees occupied by the Moon and Mercury. The distance between the two is 165 and odd degrees. So this aspect is not very effective. Another point in favour of Alpāyus is the debilitation of the Lagnādhipa. Yet another is the presence of four planets in the last 4 Signs. Venus who is the Lagna-lord, and Mercury, lord of the Sign occupied by the Lagna-lord, are not aspected by any benefic. On the contrary the latter is aspected and joined by malefics. This is another point for the same effect. The Sun and Mars are in the 7th from the Moon, and Rāhu in the Lagna. (Refer to (13) on page 64 *supra*). Here also you have to observe minutely how far the Sun and Mars are removed from the Moon. Here the question of the aspect-range does not arise, as it relates to the house. How are we, then, to find out in which houses are the different planets posited with regard to the longitude of the Moon ? We have to proceed exactly in the same manner as we did for the Bhāvas. Now you know the Sphuṭa of the Moon. Take that as the longitude of the Lagna for your current purpose. From page 159 of the Nirayana Tables of Houses you can read the sidereal time viz. 16-32.5 corresponding to this Lagna, and from that the cusps of the houses 10, 11 and 12 also. As I have already shown the method of working out the Bhāva chart, here I shall not repeat it. I am only giving the result which you can verify by your calculations. In this new Bhāva chart of the Candralagna we find that Venus is in the Sandhi between Bhāvas 8 and 9. So is Mars between 7 and 8. Jupiter is exactly in the cusp of the 8th Bhāva. Generally astrologers do not calculate the Bhāvas for the Candralagna. If you want to be quite scientific, then you will have to do this also. So now you see that though the Sun and Mars are in the 7th Rāśi from the Moon, yet for practical purposes only the Sun can be recognized as occupying that position. These are some of the clues for finding out the logevity of a person. There are many more such as the Daśā-systems. This will be taken up later on.

I should like to tell you here that the year 32 in a person's life is critical. It is called Dvātriṁśadyoga. If this coincides with any Daśā-sandhi or other bad period, the native may quit the world, provided there are Yogas for short life. This is the reason for the statement that it is a bad time for a person when Saturn in his transit passes through the position occupied by him at birth. I must tell you now as to how long do the planets stay in a house during their transit. The Sun generally takes one month, the Moon two days and a quarter, Mars two months, Mercury one month, Jupiter one year, Venus one month, Saturn two years and a half and Rāhu-Ketu one year and six months. According to this measure Saturn makes one complete circuit in 30 years. In the case of short life death takes place in the first round of Saturn, of medium life in the second round, and of long life in the third. Now you must be anxious to know when exactly death is likely to take place. The following is the method for finding this : Add up the longitudes of the Sun, Moon,

Jupiter and Saturn at birth. When Saturn passes through the position indicated by this sum in one of his rounds death is likely to overtake the native. If you add up the figures for these planets in the given chart you will get 4-0-50-46.

I am giving below some more Yogas for infant mortality according to Sage Mṛkaṇḍu:—

1. If Venus is weak and is in a house other than a Kendra or Koṇa, if the lord of the Ascendant and Jupiter are afflicted by malefic aspect, if Saturn is in the Aṁśa of the Lagna, and if he has the aspect of Ketu, the child will die within a year.

2. If no benefic is posited in a Kendra, if Saturn being posited in an Aṁśa of Venus is aspected by Ketu and Venus, it will be within two years.

3. If Saturn is in an Aṁśa belonging to Mercury and receives the aspect of Mercury and the Sun, it will be within three years.

4. If Saturn occupying an Aṁśa of Jupiter receives the aspect of the Moon and Jupiter, death will occur in four years.

5. If Saturn occupying the Aṁśa of the Sun is aspected by the Sun and Venus, death will take place in five years.

6. If Saturn is in the Aṁśa of the Moon receiving her aspect, and if the lord of the Lagna is in the 12th house, the maximum lease of life is six years.

7. If Saturn being in the Aṁśa of Pisces receives the aspect of Venus, it will be in 8 years.

8. If the Aṁśa of Saturn is Capricorn and if he is aspected by Mercury, it will die in 10 years.

9. If the Aṁśa is Sagittarius, and if Saturn is aspected by the weak Moon, it will be in 11 years.

10. If the Aṁśa is Aries and the aspecting planet the Sun, death will occur in 12 years.

Now let us consider some examples—Case No. 1—Birth on 10-5-1956, death on 3-1-1957—lived for about 8 months, female.

Explanation :—The figures by the side of the Lagna and planets indicate the Navāṁśa signs. The Sun is in the 11th Bhāva, Jupiter in the 2nd. The Ascendant is the 10th degree of Cancer. The very first thing we have to consider in this chart is the utter weakness of the Moon, owner of the Ascendant, as the birth took place on Amāvāsyā. The malefic Mars aspects the Moon very powerfully. All the malefics are in Kendras and Koṇa.

Note also that Jupiter is not in Kendra, as he has gone to the 2nd Bhāva. There is strong Pañcamāriṣṭa as two malefics are in the 5th house. There is a malefic in the 7th house from the sign indicated by the rising decanate, and the Moon too is weak

—	Sun 8 Moon 7	Merc 2 Ketu 2	Venus 9
—	Case I		Lag 6 Jup 12
Mars 4			—
—	R. Sat 6 Rāhu 8	—	—

though not in the Lagna. Look at the first Yoga given above according to Sage Mṛkaṇḍu. Those conditions are satisfied to the extent of about 60 per cent. See Yoga No. 3. Saturn is in the Aṁśa of Mercury and receives the aspect of both Mercury and the Sun. Hence it should have died within 3 years. Remember also that not a single benefic is in a Kendra. A superficial glance at the chart would make one wax eloquent on the excellent Yogas like Kesari, Rucaka, Haṁsa etc. But what is the use of all that when the Bālāriṣṭa is so powerful ? What is the earthly benefit of the bright Sun to a blind man ?

Case II. Male born on 9-7-1955 and died on 25-2-1956, lived for about 8 months.

Explanation :—The birth was at 6-18 P. M. which was Sandhyākāla. See how the Lagna is afflicted by the presence of Rāhu, Saturn in the 11th and the Sun, Mercury and Ketu in the 7th. And Venus in the 7th is not helpful either. Malefics are in the 1st, 7th and 8th (also in the 11th). Both the Lagna and its lord are powerfully aspected by Saturn. The Lagna-lord, though in exaltation, is in a Dusthāna along with Mars and Māndi and in Vipattārā. The 5th from the Moon is also tenanted by malefics.

Lord of Lagna-decanate i.e. Mars, is debilitated and in a Dusthāna. Death took place in Rāhu's Daśā, Budha's Bhukti and Ketu's Antara therein. Mercury and Ketu who are in the Māraka place from Lagna, are within one degree from each

—	—	—	Ketu 7 Merc 7 Ven 9 Sun 1
Moon 10	II		Mars 5 Jup. 7
—			—
Lag. 5 Rāhu 1	—	R. Sat 1	—

other. The presence of Rāhu in the Lagna which is aspected by Saturn, who presides over burial grounds, suggests that the child must have died of some bad disease caused by an evil spirit haunting the cremation ground. Note also the Navāṁśa of Rāhu, the serpent, denizen of Pātāla. It is Mūla-1 presided over by demon. The child died of epilepsy. The day of birth was a Saturday and of death also was the same. This factor is very significant inasmuch as the disease afflicting the child was one belonging to the nature of Saturn. At the time of death too Saturn and Rāhu were together in Scorpio, the 12th house from the Ascendant at birth. Mars at death was in Sagittarius. The Lagna of death is understood to be Aquarius which was the Moon's position at birth. On the day of death the Moon had gone to the 8th house from Janma-lagna, whose lord again is aspected by Saturn at the exit too. The Ascendant at death is the 3rd from the initial one. That is as good as the 8th.

Case III. Male born on 15-3-1953 died in Sept. the same year, lived for about six months. Birth was on Amāvāsyā though at the time of birth it was just over. Balance of Śani Daśā was 17 yrs. 4 m. 13 d.

Explanation :—Tulā Lagna with Saturn in it (though retrograde) is supposed to give Rājayoga. Two benefics are aspecting the Lagna. With all these the God of death would not spare the child. Why ? The Lagna-lord has gone to the Māraka

R. Mer 6 Moon 5 Sun 4	Mars 2 Venus 3 Jup. 8	—	—
—	III		Ketu 9
Rāhu 3			—
—	—	Lag. 11 R. Sat. 7	—

place along with its lord. The malefic Saturn in the Lagna is aspected by another malefic, Mars, who is also very strong. Thus the lord of Lagna is considerably afflicted. The presence of Jupiter there does not mend matters appreciably, as the distance between the two (Venus & Jupiter) is about 18 degrees. The Moon, owner of the 10th house, is combust and in association with other malefics. The 4th and 10th Kendras too are occupied by malefics, and the latter Kendra is aspected by two powerful malefics, Saturn and Mars. When Karmasthāna, its lord and the Lagna and its lord are rendered powerless, how can the Ātman stay in the body ? Again, the weak Moon in conjunction with malefics is in a Dusthāna viz. 6th. The 5th house from the Moon is occupied by a malefic and afflicted by malefic aspects thereby causing a very strong Ariṣṭa. The Lagna-lord afflicted by malefic conjunction is in the 7th house. Saturn being in the Aṁśa of Venus is aspected by him. This is a part of one of the conditions mentioned by Mṛkaṇḍu for early death. If you take Candra-lagna, there is the powerful malefic in the 8th house. And it was in the Daśā of this planet that both birth and death took place. The child could not survive even the Bhukti of Śani. Now look at the star occupied by Śani. It is Citrā—III which happens to be the Vadhatārā, 7th from the natal one. The lord of Candra-lagna is conjoined with the lord of the 8th (who is aspected by Saturn—which is an Alpāyuryoga) and another malefic.

Case IV. Female born at 9-30 P.M. on 4-8-1952, died at 3 P.M. on 16-9-1952. Balance of Sun's Daśā was 3 yrs. 4 m. 6 d.

Explanation :—According to Sage Garga the presence of the Moon in the 11th for the night-birth should ward off a crore of faults, but here you see death overtaking the child in about a month. Why ? Strong malefics are in the 5th, 7th and 8th houses. Lagna is aspected by Saturn. No Kendra is occupied by a benefic. The lord of the Lagna too is aspected by Mars. The lord of Lagna-Navāṁśa, Mercury, is in a Dusthāna along with the lord of the 8th. There is strong Pañcamāriṣṭa. Death took place in the Bhukti of Jupiter in the Daśā of the Sun who is

Lag. 6	Jup. 8	—	—
—	IV		Sun 9 Ketu 12
Rāhu 6 Moon 10			R. Merc 1 Ven. 1
—	—	Mars 2	Saturn 3

posited in the Vadhatārā, being lord of the 8th house from the Moon and one of the strong malefics causing the Ariṣṭa. The lord of Bhukti too is the owner of the Lagna. On the day of death the Sun had just entered Virgo, the 7th house from the natal Ascendant afflicted by Saturn. In this case too the Lagna of death coincides with the position of natal Moon, who has gone to the 7th house viz. Cancer, from her original position. The star on the latter day was again Āśleṣā, Vadhatārā:

Case V Male born at 1-45 A.M. on 18/19-7-1950—died on 11-10-1950. Balance of Śukra-Daśā was 15 yrs 5m. 11 d.

Explanation :—There is Kesariyoga, Parivartana between the luminaries, and both Jupiter and Moon have Vargottamāṁśa. Still the child could not survive even full three months. Why ? As I have said elsewhere, Yogas will be effective only if the native has a long lease of life, and not otherwise. In this example Rāhu is in the 12th opposed by Mars and Ketu from the 6th. This is a powerful cause for Bālāriṣṭa. The Moon is conjoined with Saturn who has exaltation Aṁśa. In this connection I must tell the readers that malefics in strength have greater power to do mischief than benefics to render help. The Moon is without Pakṣa-bala and so weak. That causes powerful Pañcamāriṣṭa, though Jupiter may aspect it. The Lagna-

Rāhu 6	Lag 8	—	Venus 7
R. Jup. 11	V		Sun 4 Merc. 7
—			Moon 5 Sat. 7
—	—	—	Mars 5 Ketu 12

Navāṁśa is Scorpio, which is the 8th from the Lagna. Venus is in the 2nd Bhāva and the Sun in the junction between the 3rd and 4th Bhāvas. Venus becomes Māraka. There is no benefic in any Kendra. Lord of the Ascendant and its Aṁśa is in a Dusthāna viz. 6th. The 8th house from the Moon is again occupied by Rāhu, and its lord is aspected by another malefic viz Saturn. Death took place in Śukra-daśā, Candra-bhukti. Both these planets have the portfolios of Despatch, one being Māraka and the other producer of Ariṣṭa. Death took place on Amāvāsyā in the month of Kanyā. Five planets excluding Ketu were gathered together in Virgo at that time. Mars had gone to the 8th house from the natal Lagna. The star on that day was Hasta, Vipattārā, presided over by the Moon herself. This shows that the Ariṣṭa was mostly due to the peculiar circumstances of the Moon.

Case VI. Female born at 7-27 A.M. on 27-7-1948, died at 6-30 P.M. on 18-4-1949.

Explanation :—The Lagna is the 30th degree of Cancer and so it partakes of the effects of Gaṇḍānta Lagna. Saturn who is at the very commencement of Leo is likewise in Gaṇḍānta position. His own Daśā for about six months remained at birth. From this itself one could make out that Saturn was out for mischief. The birth took place in fact during the transition between the major periods of Saturn and Mercury. For

Moon 8	Rāhu 6	—	Ven. 8 Merc. 2
—	VI		Sun 7 Lag. 12
—			Sat. 1
—	R. Jup. 11	Ketu 12	Mars 1

transition means a period of one year comprising 6 months on this side and 6 months on the other side of the end of a Daśā. As the child died in the 9th month, it is clear that the child expired during the transition. This accords well with the position of Saturn. Even the Moon can be said to be at the fag end of Uttarabhādrapada. She is in her debilitation Aṁśa and is aspected by powerful Mars. Saturn is in Lagna-bhāva and Mars in the 2nd, Sun in the 12th and Venus in the 11th. The

Lagna is surrounded by malefics. No benefic occupies a Kendra. The 5th and 8th houses from the Moon are tenanted by malefics causing strong Bālāriṣṭa. There is a malefic in the 7th house from Pisces which is the Sign of the Lagna-decanate. The lunar day on both the days of birth and death was the 6th of the dark fortnight. If Saturn is in the Lagna-bhāva in the natal chart, he aspects the Lagna of death, which is the 8th from the natal Moon. If Mars aspects the Moon in the former chart, he takes the position of the natal Moon in the latter, and he is square to her too. In the latter the Lagna is considerably weakened by the presence of Ketu, and by the aspect of Saturn, Mars, Sun, Mercury, Venus and Rāhu. Venus, the lord of Lagna, is completely combust. Death took place when the Sun in his transit passed through the Sign Aries, which is the Aṁśa of the lord of 8th viz. Saturn. The Moon too was then in Sagittarius which is trine to Aries that is the Aṁśa Rāśi of Saturn, lord of 8th.

Case VII. Male born at 6 A.M. on 8-3-1946, died at 6-20 P.M. on 13-12-1950, lived for about five years.

Explanation :—Balance of Śukradaśā was 8 yrs. 6 m. 9 d. Though Jupiter is in the 9th, there was no help from that

Merc. 7 Ven. 4	Moon 7	—	Rāhu 7 Mars 1 Sat. 2
Sun 2 Lag. 10	VII		—
—			—
Ketu 1	—	Jup. 8	—

quarter. No benefic occupies a Kendra. The Ascendant is occupied by the Sun.

Three malefics are posited in the 5th house. The lord of the

8th is aspected by Saturn. Birth was at a Sandhyā. The Moon in the 3rd in the house of a malefic is not happy, when she is not quite strong. There is the malefic Ketu in the 7th from Gemini which is the decanate of the Ascendant. The chart has very powerful Bālāriṣṭa. On the day of death among the malefics causing the Ariṣṭa Saturn had gone to the 8th house from the natal Lagna, Rāhu to the 2nd thus opposite Saturn, and Mars to the 12th along with the Moon. The Sun was trine to the sign occupied by Mercury, lord of 8th house in the natal chart. The Moon had similarly gone to the sign that is trine to the Aṁśa of the natal Sun. Thus the chart of exit becomes interesting when put by the side of the natal one. Note also that both birth and death took place in the major period of Venus who is situated in the Māraka-place along with the lord of the 8th. At birth the sub-period was that of Jupiter and at death it was of Mercury who has the portfolio of Despatch, as he is the lord of the 8th, posited in the Māraka-place, in the 7th star (Vadhatārā) and debilitated to boot. Venus is the lord of Māraka from the Moon. It may rightly be asked as to why death did not occur during the sub-period of Saturn as he is one of the Ariṣṭa-producing planets. Saturn is Lagna-lord and being retrograde attains great power. Moreover Jupiter casts his aspect (though not quite full) on him. Besides that he is in trine to the Lagna. Hence, though he may cause Ariṣṭa, yet he may not cause death, which is the function of the lord of the 8th, and the combination of Venus and Mercury has Saturn and other malefics in square. For these reasons Saturn must have asked Mercury to do the task of carrying away the soul, as it was expected of him on that occasion.

Case VIII. Male born at 7 P.M. on 9-9-1951, died app. at 9 P.M. on 18-1-1953. Balance of Ketu-daśā was 5 yrs. 6 m. 20 d.

Explanation :—The birth was almost during Sandhyākāla. Mūla-I is highly inflammable. Rāhu is in the 12th house receiving the aspect of Mars who has gone to the 6th Bhāva, though occupying the 5th Rāśi. The Sun too has gone to the 7th Bhāva. Thus the Ascendant receives the aspect of two malefics. Jupiter has practically gone to the border of the 1st Bhāva. Note also that the first condition of Sage Mṛkaṇḍu given elsewhere is practically satisfied. Even the 4th one is partially satisfied. Death occurred in Ketu-daśā Maṅgala-bhukti. In Rāśi these two are in Dvidvādaśa positions. Ketu being in a Dusthāna along with the lords of 6, 7, and 8 and in the star presided over by Venus, lord of the 8th, has the port-

R. Jup. 9 Lag. 5	—	—	—
Rāhu 12	VIII		Mars 10
—			R. Mer. 3 R. Ven. 5 Ketu 6 Sun 7
Moon 1	—	—	Sat. 12

folio of undertakers. Even Mars is bad for the reason given above, owing to his malefic nature and being in a Dusthāna in Bhāva chart. The weekday of death also was a Sunday as of birth. At death Ketu was in the 5th from the natal Ascendant and 8th from the natal Moon. Mars was in the 12th from that Lagna. The Moon too was in the 12th. Ketu and Mars were in quincunx positions. The Lagna of death was Leo which is the Navāṁśa of the natal Ascendant. Saturn in transit had come exactly to the Aṁśa of the 8th from the natal Lagna. Jupiter was in Aries which is trine to Leo occupied by Venus, lord of the 8th. At birth the Sun is in Taurus Dvādaśāṁśa, and at death he had gone in transit to Capricorn that is trine to that. The Moon in transit had gone to Aquarius which is trine to Libra that is the Aṁśa of the Sun. Even the Lagna of death is the house occupied by the lord of the 8th.

Yogāriṣṭas :—I shall now give some more planetary configurations which lead to early death. (1) When the lord of the Lagna or of the Janma Rāśi is eclipsed, without any benefic aspect, and when the Kendras are occupied by malefics, the subject is likely to die in his 20th year. (2) When Mars is in the Ascendant, and when the Sun and Saturn possessed of great strength occupy Kendras, death is likely to occur within 20 years. In the absence of that the subject wil break his limbs or be afflicted with some disease. (3) The weak Moon posited in the 8th house and in her debilitation Aṁśa will cause death. If in this Yoga the Moon is aspected by Mars and Saturn, the native cannot live beyond 25 years. (4) Death before 20 years is the result of the Lagna being a movable sign and occupied by Mars and the Sun, and of the 10th house being occupied by Jupiter, and of the 5th or 9th being occupied by the Moon. (5) When malefics are in the 8th house from the Moon, benefics being weak occupy Āpoklima houses from the Lagna, and the Moon herself is in the 6th or 8th house, the maximum span is 25 years. (6) When the lords of the 8th houses from the Lagna and the Moon are both in Kendras, when a planet is in the 8th house from the Lagna and when both Lagna and the Moon are weak, the subject will live for 30 years at the most. (7) the same effect will be there when the 2nd and 12th houses are occupied by malefics in conjunction with Jupiter and Rāhu, and when the Moon is in the 7th or the 8th house. (8) The result is the same when the 7th house from the Sun is tenanted by a malefic, Rāhu and Jupiter, and the Moon is in the 6th or 8th house from the Lagna. (9) Lagna occupied by Jupiter and Venus, the 5th by Mars and Saturn, and the Moon being weak cause short life. (10) Short life i.e. death in 28th year, is caused by the combination of the two luminaries and Rāhu in any sign and by Jupiter in 12th house. (11) Death at 32 years occurs when the Moon and the lord of the 8th from Lagna are in Kendras, when a planet is in the 8th house, provided there is no benefic aspect or conjunction for any Kendra. (12) One lives for 30 years when the weak Moon is in her own house, the lord of 8th in a Kendra, a malefic in the 8th and Lagna-lord also weak. (13) Death at 27 years results under the following conditions. Add up the longitudes of the lords of the Lagna and the 8th. If this result indicates a Kendra or the 8th, and if a malefic should occupy such a house, make this prediction. (14) Lord of the 8th in a Koṇa (5th or 9th), the Lagna-lord in the 8th being aspected or conjoined with malefics—longevity is only 24 years, despite benefic aspects on the two. (15) Lagna has a malefic in it, Jupiter aspected by Saturn or conjoined with Rāhu, some planet is in the 8th—death at 22 years. (16) Lagna is occupied by its lord, the 4th house by the luminaries along with malefics, and the lord of the 8th in a Kendra—3 years. (17) Lord of the 8th in a Kendra and the lord of Lagna powerless—30 or 32 years. (18) Both the Moon and Lagna-lord being weak and aspected by malefics are posited in Āpoklima houses—40 years. (19) Birth at twilight, Jupiter and Venus in Kendras and Lagna-lord conjoined with malefics in Āpoklima—36 years. (20) The Sun hemmed in between malefics occupies the Lagna which is an inimical sign for him—the subject becomes sickly and lives for 36 summers. (21) Birth during Gulika-kāla, the Sun and Moon in Lagna, and benefics in houses other than Kendras and the 8th—36 years. (22) Lord of 8th in the Lagna which is a fixed sign, and a benefic in the 8th—40 years. (23) Navāṁśa of Lagna-lord is the 8th Raśi and that of the 8th-lord the Lagna Rāśi, and these planets are conjoined with malefics—50 years. (24) Kendras are devoid of planets, Lagna-lord unassociated with malefics, malefics occupying the 5th—maximum 60 years. (25) Lagna-lord in the 12th, weak or with malefics, and Jupiter not in Lagna—60 years. (26) 8th-lord in a Kendra, Mars in Lagna, and the Sun and Saturn in the 3rd and 6th—44 years. (27) The Moon occupying the Lagna in Vargottamāṁśa and receiving malefic aspect, and benefics without strength—48 years. (28) Benefics in malefic signs or Aṁśas, malefics in Kendras and the benefics in houses other than Kendras—medium life. (29) Saturn in Lagna which is a dual sign, and the Moon in the 8th or 12th—52 years. (30) Lagna in Cancer or Scorpio being occupied by the Sun along with another malefic, the 2nd house occupied by the Moon, and Kendra not by Jupiter—50 years. (31) Malefics in 4th and 8th houses from Lagna or the Moon and not aspected or joined by benefics—medium life. (32) Malefics in 4th and 10th, 8th also occupied by malefics, the Moon in the 12th, and Jupiter and Venus joined together in some house—ditto. (33) Lagna-lord in Navāṁśa owned by Saturn, and the Moon conjoined with the lord of the 8th occupies 6th, 8th or 12th—maximum 58 years, (34) When all the planets are posited in 6th, 8th and 12th houses, a Rājayoga is formed. One born under this Yoga will live for 58 years. (35) Malefics being posited in 6th, 8th and 12th houses from the Lagna-lord, and benefics not in the 8th—60 years. (36) Malefics being posited in cruel houses, and benefics in Kendras—

80 years. If the above houses are occupied both by benefics and malefics, he lives for 60 years. (37) Jupiter and the Moon in the 4th, the strong lord of Lagna in the 11th, and Mercury in the 10th—80 years. (38) When the Sun, Mars and Saturn, occupying Jupiter's Navāṁśa, are in Kendras, Jupiter in the Lagna, and the rest in houses other than the 8th, the lease of life in 85 years. (39) Malefics in cruel houses, benefics in benefic houses, and Lagna-lord possessed of strength—100 years. (40) Even though Mars may be in the 8th and the Sun in the 1st, one may live for 100 years, provided Jupiter is in a Kendra. (41) The Sun, Mars and Saturn in movable Navāṁśas, Jupiter and Venus in fixed Navāṁśas, and the rest in dual Aṁśas long life or kingship. (42) Benefics in odd Aṁśas and in 4 and 9, malefics in even Aṁśas and in the Lagna, and the Moon too in full strength in the Lagna—100 years and sound health.

Here I have given some Yogas which give general principles for deducing the lease of life of the subject. You will have to apply these principles judiciously taking into consideration many factors like the position and strength of the lord of the Lagna as well as of the benefics, especially of Jupiter. There are some Yogas which give the native numberless years of life. I shall give below a few of them:—(1) Mercury, Jupiter and Venus posited in the same Navāṁśa, Sign or the Ascendant, and Saturn in the 9th—life for a Yuga of a thousand years through Kāyakalpa and such other means. (2) Mercury, Jupiter and Saturn (or Venus) in the same Aṁśa and in the 1st, 4th, 6th, 8th or 9th—two thousand years. (3) All planets in the Navāṁśa of Jupiter and in Kendras, 9th or 2nd house—one renounces worldly life in boyhood, composes many Śāstras and lives a Yuga. (4) The Sun, Mars and Jupiter—all in the Navāṁśa of Saturn—occupying Kendras or the 9th, in strength and the Moon in the Lagna at the end of a Sign—great wealth and life of a Yuga. (5) Lord of 9th in that and the Moon in the Aṁśa of Mars being aspected by Mars—this is a Muniyoga producing a great sage who writes śāstras and lives a Yuga. (6) When the waxing Moon occupies the 1st or 11th house and the sign or Aṁśa of her exaltation or friend, and when Saturn being strong is situated in the 9th, the subject will live for numberless years. (7) If Jupiter and Saturn are in the same degree and occupy together 2nd, 9th or 10th, and the Sun along with Mercury is rising in the Lagna, the native will be a great sage and will live very very long.

CHAPTER VIII

RĀŚI-EFFECTS

I shall now explain to you the effects of birth in the several Rāśis. These are common to the Lagnas and Candralagnas.

Aries:—The native will have round eyes, be popular, very unsteady, will have cattle, be oppressed by heavy expenditure, wandering, talkative, eating sparingly, walking, wise, honoured in an assembly, of bilious nature, honoured by women, having very few children, angry, full of valour, eldest of the children, very stingy and troubled by kinsmen.

Taurus:—He will be round, strong, with plump thighs and a big face, enjoying pleasures of life, happy, learned, seated in mountains and caves, clever, adept in expounding various theories, devoid of elders and children, or having only female children, forgiving, happy in the middle and last parts of life, bright and devoted to wife. He may have marks or moles on his back, face or sides.

Gemini:—He will be handsome like Cupid, with a broad face and clear speech, unsteady, either impotent or very voluptuous, with a few children, fond of gambling and music, hater of relatives, phlegmatic and windy in constitution, fond of wife, charitable, fond of jokes, clever, powerful and fond of eating and drinking. He will have a prominent nose, curly hair and dark eyes. He lives always indoors.

Cancer:—He will be intelligent, virtuous, will command his relatives, be proud, troubled by fire and wind, talkative, of strong body, with a few children, will have connections with many women, be an astrologer, prompt, happy, of low income, learned, having secret sons, knower of many languages, always in company and receiving wealth from a king.

Leo:—He will be dignified, prosperous or respectable, with a broad face, intelligent, virtuous, enjoyer of pleasures, deceitful, of charming face, merciful, fearless, getting angry for trifles for a long time, emaciated by hunger, endowed with innate strength, very rich, obedient to his mother, adhering strictly to his principles, valiant, living alone, not firm and having not many sons. He has reddish eyes.

Virgo:—He is slovenly, with very little wealth and happiness, wise, religious-minded, hater of relatives, of phlegm and wind in constitution, with many daughters and few sons, of lovely face, liked by damsels, fickle, learned, long-lived, of sweet speech, intent on money, of peaceful end and taking delight in others' prosperity.

Libra:—He will be virtuous, religious-minded, with a magnanimous heart, a smiling face, having wife, troubles, clever in trade, fond of mirth, full of knowledge, helping relatives, devoid of sons, lean, wealthy, with a God's name as an additional one, eating liquid food, and be the youngest child of his parents.

Scorpio:—His eyes will be similar to honey in colour; he will be without elders and preceptors, clever in disputations, with a long face, of cruel deeds, favourite of a king, without a happy end, sickly in childhood, of short life, befriended by others, inclined towards poetry, powerful, a religious hypocrite, oppressed by sloth and exhaustion and fond of low-class men. His soles and palms may be marked with lotuses.

Sagittarius:—He will have a long and attractive face, big nose and ears, many enemies, dark eyes, learning in Śāstras, self-control, money spent away, losses, grandchildren, but he will hate his own sons, be honoured by scholars, full of self-respect, valiant, virtuous, of very long life, miserly and devoid of sons and wife.

Capricorn:—He will be of a short stature, clever, full of prowess, without money in the middle part of his ife, of wandering habits, fickle, with wicked intentions, troubled by hardships, courageous, liked by the people, with dissipated knowledge and energy, shameless, attached to an old woman, with a feminine heart, windy and unhappy on account of children.

Aquarius:—He will commit sins secretly, his body will be pot-like, he will be talkative, will have many children and happiness. He will lose his ancestral wealth, be wandering, inimical towards the good and deaf, will have heart-disease, be jealous, lazy, wicked, lustful, greedy, fond of scents and flowers, utilizing others' wealth, with an obsessed mind and troubled by his own actions and words.

Pisces:—He will have a symmetrical and handsome body, fine eyes, strength, dignified speech, residence in a foreign country, conquest over enemies, many wives, great learning, honour in an assembly, fame, royal favour, enjoyment of pleasures, attachment to his wives and good fortune. He will drink plenty of water, and enjoy the wealth of the seas. He will also be grateful.

Effects of planets occupying exaltation, own, friendly etc. houses:

Exaltation:—The subject is likely to become a big land-lord or king, receiving homage from kings and being possessed of immense wealth. He will be endowed with excellent virtues, victorious everywhere, famous, charitable, courageous, clever and diplomatic.

Own house:—The person concerned will have during the Daśā of that planet power and pelf through his king; he will stay in his own house permanently; he will acquire a new house and fertile lands, receive respect from the people, and recover all lost articles.

Friendly house:—He will achieve his objects with the help of friends, make new friends, have the good fortune of the company of wife and sons, will enjoy wealth and corn, will be charitable and friend of all and enemy to none.

Inimical house :—He becomes lowly, eats others' food, stays in others' houses, becomes indigent, is troubled always by rivals and foes, and even a friend turns out an inveterate enemy.

Debilitation:—He will have a fall from his position, poverty, contraction of debts and indulgence in wicked acts. He will make friends with the ignoble, be in servitude, will walk long distances and do unprofitable tasks. He will reside in the country of barbarians or an unhealthy place.

Combustion:—He may quit the world in a short time in the period of the concerned planet, will be deprived of his wealth, wife and children; he will quarrel for nothing; he will be the object of scandal, humiliation and defeat.

A planet posited in a *neutral* house will enable one to maintain his status quo. You might remember what I have told you about retrograde planets. Whether a planet is in an inimical house or in depression, it will produce such effects as if it were posited in its exaltation, provided it is retrograde. The effects of Vargottamāṁśa—a planet occupying the same Rāśi both in the Rāśi and Navāṁśa charts—are equal to those of one in his own house. Here you must be anxious to know what would be the effect if a planet were debilitated both in Rāśi and Aṁśa, e.g. Venus in the last Navāṁśa of Virgo. Though you may technically call it a case of Vargottamāṁśa, yet in fact it is extremely bad.

There are different effects for the different Navāṁśas occupied by the Moon or Ascendant:

Aries:—A person born in the Meṣa Navāṁśa of any Rāśi will be very cruel, mean-minded, leprous, thievish, of defective eyes, or restless mind, bilious in temperament and passionate. The native is likely to suffer from disease at the ages of 12, 25, 50 and 65 years.

Taurus:—This Aṁśa produces intelligence, sumptuous food, big belly, strength, long face, queer gait, rolling eyes and many daughters. The Aṁśāriṣṭa is likely to be felt at the ages of 10, 22, 32 and 72.

Gemini:—The native will be amiable, fickle, eloquent, well-versed in Śāstras, enjoyer of life, humble, not constant in respect of women, very brainy and without wife. The fateful years are 16, 24, 34, 40 and 63.

Cancer:—He will be irritable, of uneven limbs, wealthy, of crooked eyes, intent on living in a foreign country, helping his kinsmen and inflammed by his own men. The fateful years are 8, 18, 22, 31, 72 and 80.

Leo:—He will be living in a lonely place, be very proud, with a thin belly, knower of practically every thing under the Sun or a popular king, of weak teeth, strong and mentally distressed. The Ariṣṭa is in the years, 10, 20, 30, 60 and 82.

Virgo:—He will be happy in childhood, a master of arts, impotent, a gallant, good-looking, having few sons, engaged in others' tasks, munificent and living in a foreign country. His bad periods are the years, 20, 50 and 60. He will live 108 years with his wealth ever increasing.

Libra:—The person will not reside in a single house for a long time, have a lean and lank body, not having many children, miserly, hater of kinsmen, suffering from phlegmatic troubles, and almost penniless. His vulnerable periods are the 3rd, 23rd, 38th, 54th and 76th years.

Scorpio:—He will be without father or elders, murderous, intelligent, cruel, weak-eyed, tall, with a rotund belly, and committing sins secretly. There may be danger to his life in any of the years, 13, 18, 23, 28, 55 and 70.

Sagittarius:—He will be very virtuous, with wealth earned by his own labour, with a long neck, lazy, easily satisfied, with a broad nose, eloquent and lord of wealth. His life may be in danger in the 4th, 9th, 16th, 36th, 44th, or 72nd year of his life.

Capricorn:—He will be short-limbed, fickle-minded, cruel, quick-footed, indulging in sensual pleasures, not attractive in the eyes of women, of windy constitution, and nick-named by his enemies. He will have risk in the 19th, 27th, 34th, 49th, 54th or 68th year of his life.

Aquarius:—He will be a tale-bearer, merciless, deceitful, weak, fickle, long-limbed, wanderer, spendthrift and miserable at heart. His vulnerable years are 7, 14, 20, 28, 32 and 61.

Pisces:—He will run after women, have a slender body, have a profession connected with water or water-products, be learned, with his belly like that of fish, living in another's house, wealthy and having many wives. His dangerous periods are the 10th, 12th, 21st, 26th, 52nd and 61st years of life. I have told you already that the 32nd year is a critical period in a man's life. Similarly the 8th year and 59th are also considered critical by sages of yore. If these vulnerable periods synchronize with an evil Daśā and Bhukti, death of the native is pretty certain. Otherwise he will suffer from illness. The effects given above for Navāṁśas hold good also for Dvādaśāṁśas. You can now apply the knowledge so far acquired to the chart we have taken as an example. The Lagna is Libra and the Moon is in Aquarius. The Navāṁśa of both is Capricorn. The Lagna-Dvādaśāṁśa is Aquarius and of the Moon Gemini.

As the moon occupies a pre-eminent position in the planetary world, her position in a Rāśi, Navāṁśa etc. and the aspect of the planets on her determine the native's character and other details of life and personality. So I should like to explain here the effects of the aspect of the planets on the Moon when she is posited in the different Signs and Aṁśas.

When the Moon is posited in *Aries* and aspected by Mars, the native becomes a king; if by Mercury, learned; if by Jupiter, king; if by Venus, one equal to a king; if by Saturn, a thief; and if by the Sun, poor. If the Moon is in *Taurus* and aspected by these planets in the order just mentioned, the results will be in order (i) poor, (ii) thief, (iii) respected by the world, (iv) a king, (v) wealthy, and (vi) a servant. If she be in *Gemini* and aspected by Mars and others in the same order, the effects will be (i) a blacksmith, (ii) a king, (iii) learned, (iv) obdurate, (v) a weaver, and (vi) poor. The Moon in *Cancer* being aspected by these planets produces (i) a warrior, (ii) learned man, (iii) wise man, (iv) king, (v) one who works on metals, and (vi) one who suffers from eye-disease respectively. If she occupies *Leo* and is aspected by the same planets, the effects are in order (i) a king, (ii) an astrologer, (iii) wealthy, (iv) king, (v) barber, and (vi) a great king. If she is aspected by these planets while staying in *Virgo* the effects will be in order (i) efficient, (ii) king, (iii) commander of an army, (iv) skilful, (v) landlord, and (vi) king. In *Libra* she being aspected by them produces in order (i) a rogue, (ii) king, (iii) goldsmith, (iv) merchant, (v) tale-bearer, and (vi) wicked. In *Scorpio* the effects of their aspects are in order (i) a king, (ii) father of twins, (iii) king, (iv) dealer in clothes or washerman, (v) one of defective limbs, and (vi) poor. In *Sagittarius* the effects are (i) a cheat, (ii) protector of kinsmen, (iii) king, (iv) leader and supporter of many, (v) a rogue, and (vi) ostentatious person. In *Capricorn* the effects are (i) king, (ii) monarch, (iii) ruler of the earth, (iv) learned man, (v) opulent, and (vi) poor. In *Aquarius* the effects are (i) one addicted to other's wives, (ii) king, (iii) king, (iv) master of concubines, (v) a great king, and (vi) respected by the people respectively. In *Pisces* the effects are (i) perpetrater of crimes, (ii) of sharp intellect, (iii) king, (iv) learned, (v) one who picks holes in others, and (vi) one who commits sins. Remember that these effects are also applicable to the different Dvādaśāṁśas occupied by the Moon when she is aspected by the several planets.

Now I shall explain the effects of the position of the Moon in the different Navāṁśas being aspected by the planets:—If the Navāṁśa of the Moon is *Aries* or *Scorpio* and if she is aspected by the Sun, Mars, Mercury, Jupiter, Venus, and Saturn the effects will be in order (i) a Police officer, (ii) one fond of murders, (iii) skilled in warfare, (iv) king, (v) wealthy, and (vi) quarrelsome fellow. If the Aṁśa is *Taurus* or *Libra*, the effects are (i) a fool, (ii) one addicted to immoral behaviour, (iii) a good poet, (iv) author of good literary works, (v) intent on getting happiness, and (vi) a moral wreck. If the Navāṁśa is *Gemini* or *Virgo*, the effects in order are (i) an actor, (ii) thief, (iii) an eminent poet, (iv) minister, (v) musician, and (vi) clever artisan.

If the Navāṁśa is *Cancer*, the effects are (i) one of tiny limbs, (ii) greedy for money, (iii) an ascetic, (iv) an important person, (v) servant of a woman, and (vi) devoted servant.

If the Aṁśa is *Leo*, the effects are (i) hot-tempered, (ii) honoured by the king, (iii) lord of a treasure, (iv) a lord, (v) issueless, and (vi) one committing heinous crimes.

If the Aṁśa is *Sagittarius* or *Pisces*, they are (i) one of renowned strength, (ii) an instructor in military science, (iii) a comedian, (iv) minister, (v) free from lust, and (vi) of good character.

If the Aṁśa is *Capricorn* or *Aquarius*, the effects are in order (i) one with a few children, (ii) miserable in spite of wealth, (iii) interested in honour or proud, (iv) devoted to one's duty, (v) loved by wicked women, and (vi) irascible. Please remember that these effects are applicable to the Navāṁśas occupied by the Sun as well. Among the aspecting planets put the Moon instead of the Sun. You may have a doubt here: What is to be done when the two sets of effects given for the signs and Aṁśas occupied by the Moon are contradictory ? In such a case find out the relative strength of the lords of the concerned sign and Aṁśa. If the lord of the Navāṁśa occupied by the Moon happens to be stronger, do not take into consideration the effects of aspects of the planets on the Moon in a particular sign, but those given for the Aṁśas. In our example the Moon is in Aquarius sign being aspected by the Sun (and Mars and Mercury: the aspect of these two is not effective as they are beyond the 12 degree range). The effect is "respected by the people". Similarly you can read from the results given above the effects in respect of the Aṁśa of the Moon and the Sun.

You have already seen in this chapter what effects the Moon gives rise to when she occupies the different Signs from Aries to Pisces. You must naturally be anxious now to know the effects produced by the other planets when they occupy these Rāśis, as distinguished from Bhāvas.

When the *Sun* occupies the 12 Rāśis beginning with Aries (barring his exaltation point) the following effects will be felt.

Aries : One will be famous, skilful, given to wandering, with very little wealth, and earning one's livelihood by means of weapons.

Taurus : He will be a dealer in clothes and scents, hater of women and proficient in vocal and instrumental music.

Gemini : He will be learned, wealthy and an astrologer.

Cancer : He will be poor, sharp, doing others' work and be tired and constantly going on tiresome journeys.

Leo : He will be living in forests, hills and ranches, intrepid and learned.

Virgo : He will have a feminine body and skilled in calligraphy, drawing, poetry and mathematics.

Libra : He will be a dealer in spirituous liquors, constantly on the move, be a goldsmith and commit despicable deeds.

Scorpio : He will be cruel, adventurous, will earn money through poison and skilled in wielding weapons.

Sagittarius : He will be respected by the wise, wealthy, sharp-witted and a physician or artisan.

Capricorn : He will be vile, ignorant, a mean trader, poor, greedy and interested in others' fortune.

Aquarius : He will be ignoble, indigent and bereft of sons and fortune.

Pisces : He will become affluent by trading in marine products, and be honoured by women.

Mars will produce the following effects in the 12 Rāśis : (1) and (8) Honour from the king, wandering, commanding an army, wealth, trade, wounds in the body, stealing and too many irons in the fire; (2) and (7) become henpecked, untrue to friends, addicted to other women, hypocrite, timid, dressed nicely and harsh; (3) and (6) intolerant, blessed with children, grateful, without friends, adept in music and warfare, miserly, fearless and imploring; (4) wealthy, earning money by over-seas trade, learned, defective of a limb and wicked; (5) poor, enduring hardship, wandering in forests, and having very few children and wives; (9) and (12) will have too many enemies, be a minister, renowned, fearless and having limited issue; and (10) having many sons, plenty of wealth, be a king or his equal, and (11) troubled by grief, poor, wanderer, liar and cruel.

Mercury will cause the following effects : (1) & (8) gambler, indebted, drunkard, atheist, thief, penniless, having a wicked wife, a cheat and liar; (2) and (7) be a teacher, having many children, and wives, intent on amassing wealth, generous, and devoted to teachers; (3) boastful, learned in arts and sciences, affable in speech, and intent on happiness; (4) earning wealth by means of water and hater of relations; (5) hated by women; devoid of wealth, happiness and children, wanderer, ignorant, fond of women and suffering humiliation at the hands of one's own people; (6) charitable, learned, very virtuous, happy, forgiving, inventive and fearless; (9) honoured by kings, learned and wise adviser; (10) and (11) working for others, indigent, sculptor, debtor and doing menial work; and (12) will win over his servants and skilled in the handicrafts of low castes.

Jupiter will cause one, in (1) and (8) to be commander of an army, very wealthy, endowed with wife and sons, charitable, having faithful servants, forgiving, famous and possessed of valour and noble qualities; in (2) and (7), a sound body, popularity, generosity, wealth, friends and sons; in (3) and (6) plenty of fine clothes or following, sons, friends, ministership and happiness; in (4) endowed with gems, issue, wife, opulence, intelligence and happiness; in (5) head of an army and those of (4); in (9) and (12) governor of a province, king's minister or army-commander and rich; in (10) mean, indigent and unhappy; and in (11) as in (4).

Venus makes one, in (1) and (8), addicted to other women, deprived of wealth on account of them and a disgrace to one's family; in (2) and (7), earn wealth by one's own exertion and intelligence (or having innate strength, intelligence and wealth), honoured by kings, leader of one's people, famous and fearless; in (3) one will do king's work, be wealthy and skilled in arts; in (4) will have two wives, a mendicant, timid, and afflicted by deep grief and pride; in (5) will come by wealth through women, have an excellent wife and few children; in (6) will do ignoble deeds; in (9) will be respected for his virtues and rich, in (10) and (11) he will be attractive, curbed by women and addicted to a wicked woman; and in (12) he will be a scholar, very rich, very handsome and receiving homage from kings.

Saturn in (1) makes one foolish, wanderer, a hypocrite and friendless; in (2) loved by a forbidden woman, poor and with many wives; in (3) and (6) shameless, without happiness, wealth and issue, of shaky writing, be a police officer and a chieftain; in (4) be penniless, toothless, ignorant, childless and motherless;

in (5) be mean, without happiness and sons, and a labourer; in (7) famous, rich and head of a clan, city, village or army; in (8) one will suffer imprisonment or a fatal attack, be fickle-minded and merciless; in (9) and (12) be happy at the end or have a peaceful end, trusted in the king's court, will be blessed with worthy sons, wife and wealth, or be the mayor of a city or head of a village or commander of an army; and in (10) and (11) will have liaison with other women, enjoy others' earnings, leader of a village, town or army, will have weak eye-sight, be slovenly, of lasting wealth and power and a good eater.

Chapter IX

ON BHĀVAS

Bhāva-Kārakas:—You are aware of the names of the twelve Bhāvas beginning with the Tanu—Body. Each of these Bhāvas has one or more Kārakas or Significators who are permanent presidents. They are in order (1) the Sun, (2) Jupiter, (3) Mars, (4) the Moon and Mercury, (5) Jupiter, (6) Saturn and Mars, (7) Venus, (8) Saturn, (9) the Sun and Jupiter, (10) the Sun, Mercury, Jupiter and Saturn, (11) Jupiter, and (12) Saturn. From this you can see that the Sun has three portfolios, of the 1st, 9th and 10th. The Moon and Venus have only one each viz. 4th and 7th respectively. Mars has two, the 3rd and 6th. Mercury too has two viz. 4th and 10th. Jupiter has five and Saturn four. From this it would be clear to you that Jupiter and Saturn hold extra-ordinary positions in the life of beings.

Please remember that benefics in auspicious Bhāvas—those except the Dusthanas, 6, 8, 12,—enhance their good effects, while in evil houses they tone down their bad effects. Similarly malefics in good houses, spoil their good effects, except when they own such houses, and enhance the bad effects of the evil houses they are in. I have already mentioned to you the principle that Kārakas should not occupy the particular Bhāvas. I shall content myself here by drawing your attention to Jupiter's Kārakatva. Though he is the Kāraka for five Bhāvas, 2,5,9,10 and 11, yet he is bad only for the 5th Bhāva viz. issue, if he is posited in that Bhāva. For intellectual acumen etc. he must be good even there. When you want to know all about a Bhāva, consider that as the starting point i.e. Lagna, and take the next house therefrom as its house of wealth or family. For example, if you want to know all the details about a subject's father, take the 9th house as the Lagna and proceed further. The 9th house from this new Lagna would give you an idea about the subject's paternal grandfather. Similarly take the 4th house in the case of the mother. This is not all. You know that the significator for father is the Sun. So to supplement your knowledge got through the Bhāva you have to take the Sun as the Lagna and proceed as before. Even this will not give a correct and the whole picture. You have to start again with the lord of the particular Bhāva as the Lagna and repeat the above process. If you put together the knowledge of all these you will have a fairly accurate knowledge of the Bhāva and its relations. The strength of the Bhāva, its Kāraka and lord, as well as aspects etc. should be borne in mind while assessing the worth of a Bhāva. In this connection I am reminded of the relationship or *Sambandha* among the planets in a chart. There are *five* kinds of relationship viz. (1) Exchange of positions between two planets or what is known as planets in mutual reception, (2) conjunction of the two, (3) mutual aspect, (4) to be in mutual Kendras or quadrants, and (5) to be in mutual Koṇas or trines. This knowledge will help you to ascertain if the lord and Kāraka of a Bhāva are in good or bad relationship between themselves. For example, it is bad for the lord of a Bhāva to be posited in a Dusthāna, 6, 8, 12, from that Bhāva. I hold the same view in respect of the relative positions of Kārakas and Bhāvas though some books give a different view.

I shall give below some more ideas about the Bhāva, their lords etc.:—A Bhāva will be capable of yielding its full effects if it is aspected by or conjoined with benefics or its own lord, provided there is neither the aspect of, nor conjunction with malefics. In this connection it is also necessary for all the concerned planets to be free from combustion, debilitation and position in an inimical house. Secondly, a Bhāva is considered to be strong and beneficent when the trines (5th and 9th), 2nd, 4th, 7th and 10th houses counted from that Bhāva are occupied by benefics or by the lord of the Bhāva, and are unoccupied and unaspected by malefics. If malefics are in these positions, or if they aspect them, the Bhāva will be spoiled. Similarly if the lord of any Bhāva is posited in the 8th house counted from the Lagna, then too the effects of that Bhāva will be bad. Likewise if the lord of an evil house should occupy a Bhāva, the latter would suffer unless aspected by a benefic. A Bhāva is also destroyed if the Bhāva, its lord and its Kāraka are all weak, are hemmed in betwixt malefics, are aspected by or conjoined with malefics or enemies only and if malefics occupy the 4th, 8th and 12th houses or Koṇas counted from that Bhāva. The possible time of destruction of any Bhāva can be found out thus:—Note the lord of the 8th house counted from the Bhāva, the lord of the 22nd decanate from that Bhāva, and planets posited in the 6th, 7th and 8th places counted also from the Bhāva. If these planets are weak, they may bring about the destruction of the Bhāva during their Daśā periods. On the other hand the following planets will bring success and prosperity in their daśās to the Bhāva : Malefics in the 3rd, 6th and 11th houses from it and benefics in its Kendras and Koṇas, if these are strong, as well as those planets that are friendly to the lord of that Bhāva. Similarly that Bhāva wherein the lord of the Lagna is posited will generally prosper. If the Lagna-lord is conjoined with the lord of any Bhāva, the fomer will promote the effects of the latter house. *If the lord of a house is weak and posited in an evil house, the harm done to that house will be indescribable. On the other hand if the said lord is strong, the harm will be meagre.* Now you may ask me what would be the effect of the presence of the Lagna-lord in a Bhāva, if the lord were a malefic planet. The answer is that he would promote the effects of that Bhāva. There is a difficulty again here. A planet may own the Lagna and an evil house, 6th, 8th or 12th. For example, Mars is the lord of Aries Lagna as well as of the 8th; or lord of Scorpio-Lagna and of the 6th. In such cases you have to consider him as the lord of the Lagna alone, and not of the other too. The idea is that not much importance could be attached to his ownership of the evil house. So the presence of Mars in the 5th house viz. Leo or Pisces, will not be harmful to issue. If there is also benefic aspect on Mars, the birth of a son will be much quicker. Suppose a planet owns two houses, say 9th and 12th, in the case of Aries-lagna and Jupiter, then the effects of the planet's Mūlatrikoṇa i.e. Sagittarius, will be felt in full, whereas those of the 12th viz. Pisces, which is only his Svakṣetra (own house) will be only half. In the Daśā of such a planet the effects of both the Bhāvas will be felt in their order. In this case Jupiter's Daśā will give in the first half the effects of the 9th and in the latter half those of the 12th house. There is a difference of opinion among the authorities about this. They say that if the concerned planet is posited in an odd house, then it will first produce the effects of the odd house and then of the even house, and *vice versa.* Similarly find out the kind of relationship, whether friend, intimate friend, enemy etc. that subsists between the lord of a particular Bhāva and the lord of the current Daśā. If the latter were the bitter foe of that Bhāva, you may expect great harm coming to that Bhāva during that Daśā.

Next I should like to give the effects of the presence of the planets in the different Bhāvas. Generally speaking, a person born at Sunrise will not be quiet, nor have many children. He will be merciless, will win encomia in battles, be of defective sight and of few words; he will be happy and given to going away from home constantly. If the Sun should occupy the Ascendant at birth, the native would have sparse hair, be lazy in doing work, hot-tempered, tall in stature, self-conscious, impatient, and lean. If the Lagna be Aries, he would be very famous, wealthy, learned and suffering from cataract in the eye. If he is in Libra Ascendant, the native will be devoid of valour and wealth, and will commit very mean acts. He will also lose his children. When the Sun is in the *Siṁha-lagna*, the native will be the leader of his family and night-blind. If the Sign be *Cancer* with the *Sun*, the native would be wise and of a wavering mind. He will also suffer from a tumour in the eye. When the Lagna is *Virgo* with the *Sun* in it, the person will be possessed of wife, but ungrateful. In *Pisces* the effect is that the native will be in the service of women.

The Sun in the 2nd house makes one suffer from some facial disease and stammering; he will be deprived of his wealth by the king or thieves; he will have neither learning nor modesty. The *Sun* in the 3rd makes one strong, brave, prosperous, generous, famous, and angry but inimical to his relatives. The Sun in the 4th deprives one of happiness, relations, lands, friends and house. He will serve the State, and spend away his patrimony, though he may have intelligence and bravery. The Sun in the 5th causes loss of happiness, wealth, logevity and children. He will be very intelligent and speak rapidly and wander in forests. In the 6th he produces a famous king, minister or commander, a virtuous man, wealthy and victorious one, or one very learned and renowned. In the 7th he makes one hostile to the king, deformed, wanderer, humiliated and wifeless or hater of wife. His mind will not be at peace, and he will be of a playful disposition. In the 8th he makes one lose his wealth and friends as well as sight. His life also will be curtailed. He will have few children, poor health and great fame. In the 9th he makes one lose or hate his father, have children and relatives and devoted to Gods and Brahmins. In the 10th he blesses one with sons, vehicles, praises, intelligence, opulènce, strength and fame as well as the status of a king or a high official. He will be brave and fond of war. In the 11th he makes one wealthy and long-lived, free from grief, and a king or leader of men. He may become a favourite of the sovereign and will have trustworthy servants. In the 12th he makes one hate his father, have defective sight, and devoid of children and wealth. He will have a defective limb, some vices and will live away from home. In the above cases see if the Sun is in a Rāśi or Aṁśa that is his debilitation or inimical. If it is so, then he will only aggravate the evil effects of the concerned Bhāvas. In our example chart though the Sun is posited in the 11th house which happens to be Leo, still as his Aṁśa, is Nīca, debilitation, the result cannot but be mixed.

The Moon in the Lagna identical with Aries, Taurus or Cancer makes one rich, happy and equal to a king, provided she is waxing. If she is weak and posited in other Lagnas, the native will be devoid of speech, intelligence and wealth. But generally, when the waxing Moon is in the Ascendant, the subject becomes strong physically, long-lived, fearless, powerful and opulent. If she is weak, the above results will be reversed. If she is in the 2nd house, he becomes very rich, enjoys sensual pleasures, is defective in some limb, and of soft speech. He is also powerful, honoured by women and satisfied with a little. In the 3rd she makes one very miserly, possessed of brothers, passion, strength and valour, a tale-bearer, merciless and cunning. When she is in he 4th, he becomes happy, enjoying pleasues, charitable and endowed with friends vehicles and fame. He will also eat sumptuous meals, be polite, and fond of women. When she is in the 5th house, he will have good sons, wisdom, gentle gait, wife, valour, ministership and wealth through great exertion. In the 6th she makes one short-lived, not intelligent, suffer from stomach complaint, lazy, poor, have many enemies and humiliation. He will also curb his brothers and other kinsmen. In the 7th she makes one of amiable looks, gentle, loved by a young damsel, commander under a king, and charitable. In the 8th she makes one sickly, short-lived, learned, wealthy, enjoyer of pleasures, and valiant. In the 9th she makes one fond of religious acts, eloquent, lord of wealth, successful in undertakings, victorious, and have special predilection for women. He will also be blessed with children. In the 10h she makes one interested in meritorious activities, helper of the virtuous, wealthy by various means, and husband of a learned young lady. In the 11th she makes one high-minded, long-lived, wealthy, and possessed of sons and servants. He will be learned, honoured by the king, humble and owner of cattle. In the 12th she makes one hateful, miserable, lazy and humiliated. He will also have eye-disease, be short of a limb, fickle-minded and be suffering on account of women. Suppose the Moon in the 12th house is posited in her own house or exaltation, in Rāśi and Aṁśa, in that case she will lead to happiness and wealth.

If *Mars* is in the 1st house, the native will have wounds, be brave, strong, very cruel, short-lived, adventurous, rich, self-respecting, fickle, angry, lazy and troubled by bilious disease. In the 2nd he makes one devoid of learning and money, have ugly face, harsh speech, associated with wicked persons, and troubled by heavy expenditure. In the 3rd he causes heroism, virtues, wealth, happiness, unassailability, amiability, hostility towards brothers or lack of brothers, and wealth got by hard labour. In the 4th causes loss of friends, mother, lands, happiness, house and vehicles. He will also be sickly and dwelling in others' houses. In the 5th he causes loss of happiness and sons, many disasters, a back-biting nature and a mean mind. He may act very cruelly and be of bad character. In the 6th he causes excessive lust, wealth, fame, victory, kingship, laziness and mean-mindedness. In the 7th he makes one do improper acts, afflicted by diseases, wander away, lose his wife and defeated by women. In the 8th he makes one have a deformed body, poor, short-lived condemend by men, and devoid of wife and children. In the 9th Mars makes one a murderer or bandit, hateful though being a friend of the king, and without father. In the 10th he makes one a king, cruel, charitable, very intelligent, popular and respected by the elite. In the 11th he makes one wealthy, happy, free from grief, heroic, and virtuous. In the 12th he makes one have deformed eyes, cruel, wifeless, mean, a tale-bearer, and without some limb or one who suffers a fall.

Mercury in the *first* house leads to long life, sweet and clever speech, knowledge of all Śāstras, wealth, and kindness. In the 2nd he makes one earn his wealth by means of his intellectual powers, a poet, of correct and spotless speech, eater of sumptuous food and amiable. In the 3rd he makes one heroic, tolerably long-lived, having good brothers, fatigued and poor. In the 4th he causes scholarship, witty speech, and enjoyment of happiness, friendship, lands, grains and wealth. In the 5th he produces learning, happiness, valour, many sons, and proficiency in Mantras, as well as intelligence, sweet speech and honour from the learned. In the 6th he makes one engaged in hot disputations, idle, of harsh speech, vanquisher of rivals, hater of men, and living in foreign countries. In the 7th he makes one learned, of attractive dress, of all-round greatness, married to a rich lady, well-versed in scriptures, of a generous disposition, and world-famous. In the 8th he makes one widely renowned, long-lived, supporter of a family, a lord, commander of an army, wealthy and intelligent. In the 9th he causes learning, wealth, good conduct, religious life, oratorical powers, proficiency, courage, great enthusiasm and much corn. In the 10th he makes one successful in his undertakings and possessed of good learning, strength, intelligence, happiness, good and meritorious deeds and truthfulness. He will also be very rich, charitable and famous. In the 11th he causes long life, truthfulness, happiness, wealth got from many sources, good character, and honour from women, as well as devoted servants. In the 12th he makes the native wretched, devoid of learning, lazy, cruel, wrathful, a spendthrift, and suffering humiliation.

Jupiter occupying the *Lagna* other than his debilitation makes the subject handsome, meritorious, long-lived, fearless, learned, happy and blessed with children. In the 2nd he causes eloquence, eating of sumptuous food, a lovely face, prosperity, learning, kindness and interest in worshipping Gods. In the 3rd he makes the subject contemptuous, stingy, famous brothers, sinner, of a wicked disposition, poor, and one who does harm to his brothers. In the 4th he blesses one with mother, friends, attendants, sons, wife, happiness, corn, food, dwelling, vehicles etc. In the 5th he causes trouble on account of children, ministership under a king, intelligence, personal charm, and eloquent speech. If he is in the 6th, the person concerned becomes lazy, destroyer of enemies, clever in incantations, diplomatic, humiliated and a king's minister. If he is in the 7th the person will have a good wife and good sons; he will be very charming, learned, and more munificent than his father. If he be in the 8th house, the native would live long, be a servant, poor, sinful (and, according to Pṛthuyaśas, learned, king and free from enemies). If he be in the 9th, he becomes fortunate, famous, a minister prosperous, having children, intelligent, powerful and anxious for meritorious deeds. In the 10th he causes ideal conduct, fame, great wealth and king's patronage. In the 11th he causes wealth, fearlessness, a few children, long life, vehicles, learning, prominence in the family, and lordship of a treasure-house. In the 12th he makes one hateful, of contemptible speech, bereft of children, sinful, lazy and a servant. He may have a defective limb and spend away his wealth through religious acts or on the art of dancing.

Venus in the *Lagna* makes one have a lovely body and attract ive personality, happiness, longevity, virtuous disposition, learning, wealth, and submission to women. In the 2nd he makes one a poet, have wealth of various kinds, diplomatic, modest, kind, and of a beautiful face. In the 3rd he makes the subject bereft of wife, wealth and happiness, miserly, unpopular, addicted to low-born women. In the 4th he causes ornaments, garments and scents. The native will also be happy, merciful, forbearing and blessed with wife and children. In the 5th he leads to unbroken prosperity, kingship, intelligence and acquisition of children, mostly daughters, as well as learning, ministership or command of an army. In the 6th he makes one free from enemies, poor, grief-stricken, corrupted by young women, deceitful, sickly and issueless. In the 7th Venus makes one have a good wife, and attached to prominent persons. In the 8th he makes the native long-lived, lord of the earth, wealthy, sickly, content, having wife and children, and of a vacillating disposition. In the 9th he makes one have a wife, friends, sons and fortune got from the sovereign, as well as endowed with intelligence, Dhārmic nature and enjoyments. In the 10th he causes great fame, good friends, compassion, lordship, love of women, ministership and construction of tank etc. for the use of the people. In the 11th he makes one very rich, addicted to other women, enjoyer of all kinds of pleasures, intelligent, kind, and satisfied with large gains. In the 12th he makes one have the pleasures of the couch, wealth, addicted to women, intent on charity and one who does not perform his religious duties. If this house happens to be his exaltation or own house, the person will be very rich and married to a famous young lady.

Saturn occupying the *Lagna* at birth identical with his exaltation or own house or a house owned by Jupiter, makes the native equal to a king or ruler of a country or city, wealthy, learned and an illustrious scion of his family. If it is any other Rāśi, the subject will be afflicted with miseries from childhood itself, be dirty, lazy, indigent, cruel, wanderer, windy, cheating women or devoid of a limb. *Saturn* in the 2nd makes one have an ugly face, poor, disposed to evil acts, living in a foreign place at a later stage, enjoying vehicles, wealth and pleasures. He will not have paternal property, but be learned and possessed of self-respect and heroism. If he is in the 3*rd*, the native will be very intelligent, generous, happy with his wife, heroic, but lazy and dejected, mirthful and sometimes unkind also. If he is in the 4th, the person will be unhappy, devoid of house, vehicle and mother, sickly in childhood, troubled by relatives, and not having many children. In the 5th he causes wandering, loss of wisdom, wealth, joy, and children, wickedness, roguery, and eye-disease. In the 6th he makes one a voracious eater, wealthy, subdued by enemies, stubborn, and proud; and helpful, very famous and free from enemies and illness (according to some). In the 7th he makes one have a bad wife, poor, wanderer, distressed, mean, and fickle. In the 8th he makes one dirty, poor, suffering from piles, cruel, hungry, despised by friends, weak-eyed, fickle and having a few children. In the 9th he makes a person devoid of fortune, wealth, children, father and religious disposition, and wicked. He will also be diplomatic. In the 10*th* he makes one a king or his minister, rich, devoted to agriculture, heroic, famous, happy, intelligent and leader of his family. In the 11th he makes one long-lived, of permanent wealth and income, healthy, heroic, famous, lordly and clever in sciences and Śāstras. In the 12th he makes one devoid of shame, money and sons, short of a limb, foolish, driven by enemies, unhappy and troubled by inordinate expenditure. The effects prescribed above for the presence of Saturn in the several Bhāvas, whether good or bad, will be heightened when he is conjoined with the lords of such Bhāvas. Please remember that if the planet is in his debilitation or inimical house, the effects mentioned for the several Bhāvas will not come to pass. Also you have to see the various Bhāvas and the planets posited therein with reference to the Candra-Lagna, the calculation of the cusps of houses being done exactly in the same way as from the Lagna. When more planets than one are joined together in a house, you have to be doubly careful in making predictions.

I shall now give the effects of the presence of Rāhu and the rest in the several Bhāvas : *Rāhu* in the 1st causes short life, but strength and wealth also. The person concerned will also suffer from diseases of the upper limbs of the body. In the 2nd he makes one suffer from stammering, and from some disease of the face or mouth, tender-hearted, get wealth from the king, angry and happy. In the 3rd, he makes one proud, hater of brothers, of a stubborn disposition, long-lived and wealthy. In the 4th he makes the subject a fool, giver of sorrow to others, have friends, short-lived and happy off and on. In the 5th house he makes one talk through the nose, bereft of issue, hard-hearted and suffer from stomach-trouble. In the 6th he causes trouble from enemies and evil spirits, diseases of the anus, long life and wealth. In the 7th he makes one reduced to penury owing to his intrigues with women, lose his wife and virility, self-willed and silly. In the 8th he makes the person short-lived, commit impure or sinful acts, have a defective limb, suffer from wind-disease and have very few children. In the 9th he makes one contradict everybody, without religious merits, and leader of a community, village or town. In the 10th he makes the native famous, have few children, engaged in others' activities, fearless and devoid of meritorious acts. In the 11th he makes one prosperous, have few children, long-lived and suffer from ear-disease. In the 12th he makes one commit sins secretly, a spendthrift, and suffer from water-disease (or have trouble from water and diseases).

Ketu occupying the 1st house at birth makes one ungrateful, unhappy, a tale-bearer, shameless, fallen from his position, have a deformed body, and have the association of the wicked. In the 2nd he makes one devoid of learning and wealth, of mean utterances and sinister looks, eat always others' bread. In the 3rd, he causes long life, strength, wealth, fame, food and happy married life as well as loss of brothers. In the 4th he leads to destruction of lands, fields, vehicles, mother, happiness and birth-place as well as to residence in another's house. In the 5th he makes one lose children, suffer from stomach-disease and troubles from evil spirits, have a wicked heart, and bad nature. In the 6th he causes generosity, excellent virtues, firmness, popularity, lordship, destruction of enemies, and achievement of one's ambitions. In the 7th he brings about humiliation, attachment to bad women, disease of the bowels, loss of wife and seminal fluid. In the 8th he produces short life, separation from near and dear ones, quarrels, wounds caused by weapons, and obstacles to all undertakings. In the 9th he causes predilection for sinful activities, unholy or inauspicious things, loss of father and fortune, poverty, and vilification of noble persons. In the 10th he brings about obstruction to meritorious acts, uncleanliness, censurable activities, brilliance, prowess and great popularity. In the 11th he causes hoarding of money, many virtues, excellent enjoyments, availability of all good materials, and achievement of all desires. In the 12th he leads to the commission of sins clandestinely, spending money on questionable pursuits, loss of wealth, eye-disease, and blasphemous conduct or limping gait.

There is a general rule to the effect that Rāhu produces effects similar to those of Saturn, and Ketu similar to those of Mars. In predicting the effects of Rāhu and Ketu it is also necessary to note the planets in whose houses they are posited as well as those whom they are conjoined. Generally these two planets become beneficial if they are posited in Kendras or Koṇas and are connected (this connection is of five kinds viz. being in mutual reception or Parivartana, conjunction, aspect, mutual Kendra positions and mutual Koṇa positions) with the lords of either. Their presence in the house of benefics too is good.

I have already explained to you how to calculate the position of Māndi. If he is in the 1st house, the subject will become a thief, cruel, immodest, devoid of the knowledge of scriptures etc., not very stout, of deformed eyes, with little intelligence and few children, will eat much have no happiness, be licentious, not long-lived, nor brave, dull-witted and irascible. If he is in the 2nd house, the person concerned will not speak pleasantly, will quarrel with others, will be devoid of wealth and corn, will live away from home, will not be able to argue out his case or may be dumb. If he is in the 3rd house, the subject will live separately from his people, have pride and arrogance, be very hot-tempered, will busy himself with the activities for acquiring wealth, be free from grief and fear and brotherless. In the 4th house Māndi deprives one of relatives, vehicles and wealth, makes him unsteady in mind, of base intelligence and short-lived. In the 5th he makes one lose children, intelligence and wisdom, and causes diseases of the stomach as well as hallucinations. In the 6th he enables one to destroy many hordes of foes, makes him have the hobby of demonology, brave and possessed of excellent sons. If he is in the 7th. the person becomes quarrelsome, will have many wives, hate the world, be ungrateful, of little knowledge and very timid. If he is in the 8th, the person will have deformed eyes and face and a short stature. If he is in the 9th, the native will be without father and children. In the 10th he makes one abandon all meritorious deeds and highly miserly. In the 11th he makes one possessed of happiness, children, intelligence, brilliance and good complexion. In the 12th house he makes one devoid of sensual pleasures, wretched, poor, and a spendthrift.

When Māndi is associated with one or the other of the planets, different effects are produced. If *Māndi* is conjoined with the *Sun*, the native will murder his own father; with the *Moon*, he will give trouble to his mother; with Mars, he will lose his brother; with Mercury, he will be a lunatic; with Jupiter he will be a heretic; with Venus he will have liaison with base women; with Saturn he will be leprous and shortlived; with Rāhu he will be afflicted with some poisonous disease; and lastly with Ketu he will have a fire-accident. If the period of rising of Māndi coincides with the Tyajyakāla or Viṣaghaṭī on the day in question, and if one is born at that time, the person born though a king will be reduced to beggary. In the matter of effects Māndi is similar to Saturn. Māndi is the planet that has special capacity to bring about death. But Māndi cannot be rejected outright as a perpetrator of bad things. At times he does good things also. If the lord of the house occupied by Māndi is strong and posited in his exaltation, own or friendly house identical with a Kendra or Koṇa, the subject will be very handsome, owner of chariots, horses and elephants, very famous and ruler of a vast kingdom. There are 8 more Upagrahas viz. Yamakaṇṭaka, Ardhaprahara,

Kāla, Dhūma, Pāta, Paridhi, Indra-Dhanus or Kodaṇḍa and Upaketu. Their position, nature and effects are explained below:

The upagrahas of the nine planets beginning with the Sun are in order (1) Kāla, (2) Paridhi, (3) Dhūma, (4) Ardhaprahara, (5) Yamakaṇṭaka, (6) Kodaṇḍa, (7) Māndi or Gulika, (8) Pāta or Vyatīpāta, and (9) Upaketu. The rising times of *Kāla* during daytime on weekdays are in order at the end of ghaṭīs 2, 26, 22, 18, 14, 10 and 6. Those of *Yamakaṇṭaka* are at the end of ghaṭīs 18, 14, 10, 6, 2, 26, and 22; those of *Ardhaprahara*, at the end of ghaṭīs 14, 10, 6, 2, 26, 22 and 18. *Dhūma* is got by adding 4^{s}-13°-20′ to the Sun's longitude. *Vyatīpāta* is got by subtracting the figures for Dhūma from 12 signs. *Paridhi* is obtained by adding 6 signs to the figures for Vyatīpāta. *Kodaṇḍa* is obtained by subtracting Paridhi from 12 signs. Lastly *Upaketu* is got by adding 16°-40′ to Kodaṇḍa. We have already seen the methods for calculating the positions of Gulika and Māndi. Among these *Yamakaṇṭaka* is powerful in conferring benefits. However, the power wielded by the other upagrahas to do harm is only half that of Māndi. The effects of *Māndi* or *Gulika*, *Yamakaṇṭaka*, *Ardhaprahara* and *Kāla* are similar to those of Saturn, Jupiter, Mercury and Rāhu respectively. Whichever Bhāva or its lord, is conjoined with Dhūma or some other upagraha, will be practically ruined in the following ways: Dhūma will always produce excessive heat, danger from fire, and mental anguish; Vyatīpāta will create danger from horned animals or death through quadrupeds. Paridhi causes fright of water, watery diseases as well as imprisonment. Kodaṇḍa leads to the danger of being hit by stones, wounded by weapons, or falling from a height. Upaketu will be responsible for troubles like a fall, and hitting, destruction of undertakings and peril from thunderbolt. These effects will be experienced by men during the Daśā-period of the planet owning the house occupied by the upagraha. The special effects of Upaketu being in the 12 houses beginning with the ascendant are in order (1) short life, (2) ugly face, (3) courage, (4) sorrow, (5) loss of children, (6) trouble from enemies, (7) loss of virility, (8) death resulting from vices, (9) hostility to father and religion, (10) love of wanderings, (11) gain, and (12) committing faults.

A Bird's-eye View of the Bhāvas:—I have already explained

to you the characteristic features of persons born under different Ascendants. That should give you some idea about the physical and mental make-up of the subject. There are yet other angles from which you can size up the same situation. The ancients say that the physical characteristics of a person would correspond to those of the planet owning the rising Navāṁśa or of the planet that is the strongest of all in the birth-chart. While applying these rules to charts you will do well to consider not one rule alone but all the relevant ones such as the planets posited in and aspecting the Lagna. Similarly the complexion will correspond to that of the lord of the Moon's Navāṁśa. Here too you must consider the Lagna and planets related to it. For, many a time it is observed that despite other factors the native is found to be of dark complexion when the Lagna is occupied or aspected by Saturn, without the aspect of other planets. The development of the various limbs beginning with the head must be measured by the strength of the Lagna and other Bhāvas. If a particular Bhāva is occupied by a debilitated or eclipsed planet, then the limb signified by that Bhāva is likely to be defective or weak.

Lagna or the first Bhāva:—If the Lord of the Ascendant is bright, posited in a Kendra or Koṇa, in exaltation or own house, when the Lagna is occupied by a benefic and when the lord of the 8th house is posited in a house other than a Kendra, the person concerned will be blessed with long life, prosperity, virtues, honour from kings, splendour, a charming personality, strong physique and a good family. He will also be free from fear and of a meritorious nature. Again if the lord of the Lagna is associated with benefics, the subject will live in a good village or in good company; if he is conjoined with a strong planet, the person will be the protégé of a famous king; if the planet is in his exaltation, he will become a king himself; if he is in his own house, the subject also will live in his own native country; if the Sign is movable, he will be wandering; if it is fixed on, he will be in one place; and lastly if it is a common sign, he will remain in one place for some time and then be changing his place. For attaining fame and happiness it is necessary that the lord of the Lagna must be brilliant and well situated. If the said lord is in a Dusthāna, a malefic house, inimical or debilitation sign, the person will be miserable and will live in a slum or wretched place. The native's happiness, power and progress depend largely on the strength of the Ascendant. Sickness, sorrow and calamities are the effects of a weak Lagna.

The Second Bhāva:—If the lord of the 2nd house is posited in the 1st Bhāva and benefics in the 2nd, the subject will be blessed with a happy family, prosperity, excellent virtues, attractive face and far-sightedness. If the Sun is connected (Note connection is of five kinds) with the lord of the 2nd house, the person will utilize his wealth and learning for the benefit of mankind. If saturn is connected with that planet likewise, his learning will be insignificant and of a low order. If the planet so connected is Jupiter, he will be proficient in the Vedas and Dharma Śāstras; if it is Mercury, he will be expert in economics; if it is Venus, he will be clever in lyrical utterances; if the Moon, he will be a moderate scholar of arts; if Mars, he will be proficient in the arts of war and other cruel deeds and be a tale-bearer; if Rāhu, a stammerer; and if Ketu, he will have stammering and utter falsehood. If malefics occupy the 2nd house, the native will be indigent and stupid.

The Third Bhāva:—If the lords of the Lagna and the 3rd house are in mutual reception and strong, the person will have courage, valour, help from brothers and capacity to do daring acts. If the lord of the 3rd house be strong and conjoined with benefics, and if the Kāraka of this Bhāva viz. Mars, is situated in an auspicious Bhāva, the prosperity of his brothers is assured. If, on the other hand, he be weak or ill-placed, his brothers would die. If both the lord of this Bhāva and Kāraka be posited in odd Signs and be aspected by the Sun, Mars and Jupiter, and if the 3rd house also happens to be an odd Sign, the person would have only brothers whose number would correspond to the Navāṁśas of the 3rd Bhāva. The idea is that for the birth of brothers the house or houses given above should be masculine or odd, and the Bhāva-lord and Kāraka should be aspected by male planets. Here the Kāraka happens to be a male planet. So in this case there is no question of the Kāraka being aspected by Mars.

The Fourth Bhāva:—If the lord of the 4th house and the Moon are strong and conjoined with or aspected by benefics, and if benefics, are posited in the 4th, the mother of the subject will live happily. Her happiness will be certain if benefics occupy the auspicious houses counted from the Moon. On the other hand, if the lord of the 4th and Moon are in Dusthānas, without the association and aspect of benefics, or are surrounded by malefics, or are conjoined with or aspected by malefics, the mother will die. If the lord of the Ascendant be in the 4th or the lord of the 4th be in the 1st, if the Moon has the aspect or association of the two planets (lords of 1st and 4th), the native would be able to perform his mother's obsequial rites. In the above conditions it must also be remembered that the conjunction and mutual aspect of the lords of the 1st and 4th also help in the same affair. Instead of the Lagna you can take the Moon and proceed as before. But if these lords of 1st and 4th are posited in each other's inimical or depression Sign or in the 6th and 8th house from each other, the person will not be performing his mother's last rites or helping her in her last moments, provided there is none of the relationships (five kinds) mentioned before between the two planets. This rule can be applied in a similar manner to the cases of father, brother, son etc, as it is based on an appraisal of the strength, position etc. of the particular Bhāva, its Kāraka, the lord of the Bhāva, the Ascendant and its lord.

If the lord of the 4th house and Venus are strong and associated with the 1st or 4th house, the person concerned will have a palanquin for his vehicle, lordship as well as the acquisition of gold, silver etc., costly gems, ornaments, silken robes, couches of comfort, means to the enjoyment of sensual pleasures, cattle, horses and elephants. On the other hand, if the lord of the 4th house be in a Dusthāna, or conjoined with the Sun and Mars, or if the 4th house itself be occupied by the Sun and Mars, the subject's house of birth would be burnt. If this house be occupied by Rāhu and Saturn, the house would be old and dilapidated. If the 4th or its lord be with an inimical planet, his belongings like lands, cattle and vehicles would be usurped by his enemies.

The Fifth Bhāva:—If the 5th Bhāva and its Aṁśa are owned by benefics, or if its lord is posited in the Aṁśa and house of a benefic, or if the lord of this Bhāva is posited in the same Bhāva, or if the lord of the Bhāva has attained a Vaiśeṣikāṁśa (This has been already explained. They are called Pārijāta, Uttama, Gopura etc.) and is posited in an auspicious Bhāva, the subject will be intelligent and honest. Of course, the aspect of benefics too will have good effects on the Bhāva. These fundamental principles will enable you to understand the happiness, longevity, number etc. of children the subject is going to beget. Please read the general principles enunciated in connection with the 5th Bhāva.

The Sixth Bhāva:—If malefics are in the 6th house, or if the lord of the Lagna is posited in the 6th or conjoined with or aspected by the lord of the 6th, possessed of strength, or if the lord of this Bhāva is in a Kendra or is aspected by or conjoined with malefics, the subject will have untold troubles from enemies which cannot be warded off. You will have to apply this rule to other things also signified by this Bhāva.

If the lord of the Lagna is stronger than that of the 6th and is posited in the Rāśi or Aṁśa of a benefic and receives the aspect of benefics, and if the lord of the 4th house too being strong is posited in a Kendra or Koṇa, he will be endowed with a strong body as well as with health and happiness.

If the lord of the 6th is in a Dusthāna or is eclipsed, debilitated or conjoined with enemies, and if the lord of the Lagna is stronger than the lord of the 6th, and if a benefic occupies the 6th, the subject's enemies will be destroyed. Note also the Bhāva with whose lord the lord of the 6th is conjoined, the Bhāva wherein the 6th-lord is posited and the Bhāva whose lord is posited in the 6th. These three Bhāvas will be inimical to the subject. Let us suppose for illustration that in a chart the lord of the 9th is combined with the lord of the 6th house. In that case a *prima facie* case is made out for the native and his father to be at loggerheads with each other. You may similarly apply the other rules and find out if that is the proper prediction.

The Seventh Bhāva:—If the 7th Bhāva is connected in some way with a benefic and its lord is strong, the subject's wife will be devout, endowed with children and all virtues. Apply other conditions given before to find out the health of the partner, her love for the native etc. Greater details of this Bhāva will be given later on.

The Eighth Bhāva:—If the lord of the 8th house is in any Bhāva other than the Kendras and if he is weaker than the lord of the Ascendant, the person will live long bereft of all worries, obstacles and troubles.

The Ninth Bhāva:—If the 9th house be occupied by the Sun or Mars, and its lord occupy a Dusthāna or hemmed in betwixt malefics, the subject's father would die soon. If the death does not take place immediately, it is likely to take place in the major period of the Sun or Mars, or of the lord of the 9th house who is ill placed, or of one of the malefics surrounding the said lord. A strong malefic posited in the 8th house from the 9th too has the power of killing the father of the native. So is the planet situated in the 12th from that Bhāva or its lord.

If the Sun in the case of a day-birth and Saturn of nightbirth, be posited in an auspicious house and aspected by benefics, and if the lord of the 9th be strong, the native's father would live long.

If the Sun and the Moon are posited in trine to Saturn and Mars, the child is likely to be abandoned by its parents. But if the luminaries are aspected by Jupiter, it will live long and be happy. If Saturn owning the 9th house occupies a movable Sign not aspected by any benefic, and if the Sun is in a Dusthāna, the child will live with a foster father.

If the 9th house or its lord is conjoined with or aspected by Saturn and is in a movable Sign, and if the lord of the 12th house is strong, the child will be taken in adoption by somebody.

The Tenth Bhāva:—If the 10th house be occupied by a benefic, or its lord being strong be in a Kendra, Koṇa, own house, or exaltation, or if the lord of the Lagna be in the 10th, the subject would be honoured, very famous, engaged in meritorious activities, long-lived and fortunate like the sovereign.

If the Sun or Mars be in the 10th, the person concerned would be very powerful and popular; if the lord of the 10th is well placed, he will achieve an illustrious task requiring great prowess; if there are benefics in the 10th, he will do things that are beneficial to mankind and praised by the virtuous; and if Saturn, Rāhu or Ketu should occupy the 10th, he would commit forbidden and wicked deeds.

The Eleventh Bhāva :—Note the Bhāva with whose lord the lord of the 11th house is conjoined as well as that house in which the lord of the 11th is posited. You may predict the gain of the things signified by those two Bhāvas. You may do it through the planets occupying the house of gain as well.

The Twelfth Bhāva :—Note the Bhāva whose lord is posited in the 12th as well as that in which the lord of the 12th is situated. You may predict loss of those articles that are signified by these two Bhāvas.

The Time of Fruition of Bhāvas :—You may be interested in knowing as to how the exact time of events like marriage and brith of a child could be arrived at. This can be done in two ways : One is to find out the particular Daśā-period in which the particular event is likely to happen, and the other is by means of the transit of the planets concerned. I shall first take up the latter and explain the former subsequently. The success or aquisition of a particular Bhāva may be predicted to occur at a time when (1) the lord of the Lagna in his transit comes to the concerned Bhāva itself, (2) when he comes to a Sign which is trine to the Rāśi or Aṁśa occupied by the lord of the Bhāva, (3) when the lord of the Bhāva in his transit comes to a Sign that is trine to the Rāśi or Aṁśa occupied by the lord of the Lagna, (4) when he comes to the Lagna itself, or (5) when the two planets (i.e. lords of Lagna & Bhāva) during their transit conjoin or aspect each other. The same event may be predicted through the Kāraka of the Bhāva and Lagna-lord. The idea is that wherever you find the lord of the Bhāva, replace it by the Kāraka and proceed as before. Instead of the Lagna you may take the Moon and consider the question anew. This you may say is rather confusing. To avoid this confusion further directions are given enabling you to locate the period more definitely. That is done through the transit of Jupiter. Find out the Rāśi and Aṁśa occupied by the lord of the Bhāva under consideration. When Jupiter in his transit comes to that Rāśi or Aṁśa-Rāśi or one in trine to that, you may predict that the particular Bhāva can be realized. Similarly the same event may be said to take place when the lords of the Lagna and the Bhāva meet during their transit. It must be remembered in this connection that the lord of the Bhāva should be sufficiently strong at the time of such a conjunction. Suppose somebody asks you to tell him as to when he is likely to be blest with a child. Then you have to find the Rāśi and the Navāṁśa-Rāśi occupied by the lord of the 5th house counted from the Lagna or the Moon. See when jupiter will be arriving at the Sign of either. If there is no possibility of his arriving there in the near future, you may consider a triangular Rāśi to either of the two where he is due to arrive. This method should be adopted only after satisfying yourself that the major Daśā-period is favourable for the success of the Bhāva.

When the lords of the Lagna and the 6th house join together during transit, the native's enemy will be subdued by him, provided the Lagna-lord happens to be stronger than the other. If it is otherwise, the native will be controlled by his enemy. If there is enmity — temporary and natural — between the lords of the Lagna and a particular Bhāva during their transit or if they are posited in the 6th and 8th places from each other in transit, the subject will have at that time rivalries etc. with the person denoted by the Bhāva. On the other hand if these two planets are friendly both ways and join together in a house during their transit, friendship will be formed during that period between the native and the person signified by the Bhāva.

Conjunctions of Planets :—According to Varāhamihira and his son conjunctions of planets are not very happy. It appears that such combinations poison the houses occupied by the combining planets like a mixture of equal quantities of honey and ghee. Still they conduce sometimes to special Yogas, good and bad. So their effects should be understood. Here combination means presence in the same Rāśi. The effects of the combinations will accrue to a native not only in the case of the birth chart but even afterwards when planets combine in their transits. This is the opinion of Pṛthuyaśas. If the Sun is in conjunction with the Moon, the subject will become a mechanic or mason; if with Mars, intent on committing sins; if with Mercury, clever and possessed of intelligence, fame and happiness; if with Jupiter, cruel and ready to help others; if with Venus, he earns wealth by means of weapons or acting; and if with Saturn, becomes clever in metallurgy or pottery.

Moon :—If the Moon is with Mars, the subject deals in hammers, ploughs, women, liquor and pots, and will be bad for his mother; if with Mercury, he speaks sweetly and modestly, becomes clever in economics, and possessed of happiness and fame; with Jupiter, becomes heroic, leader of family, of unsteady mind and very rich; if with Venus, becomes clever in selling and buying cloths; and if with Saturn, he becomes the son of a woman remarried. Though the combination of the Moon and Mars is extolled by Parāśara as an excellent Yoga (Candramaṅgala Yoga), in the opinion of Varāhamihira and others it is not quite good.

Mars :—If Mars is conjoined with Mercury, he will be a

merchant dealing in herbs, roots, oils etc. and be good at boxing; if with Jupiter, becomes Mayor of a City, a king or a rich Brahmin; if with Venus, a shepherd, wrestler, skilful, addicted to other women or a gambler; and if with Saturn, miserable, given to lying and despised. You see from this that Mars is not at all good in combination with Venus or Saturn.

Mercury :—In combination with Jupiter he makes one an actor, fond of music and expert in dancing; with Venus, eloquent, lord of lands; and leader of an assembly; and with Saturn, adept in cheating others, and addicted to sensual pleasures.

Jupiter :—Combined with Venus he makes one very learned, possessed of wealth and wife as well as numerous virtues; with Saturn, a barber, cook or potter.

Venus :—With Saturn Venus makes one have defective eye-sight or small eyes, improve his financial position tremendously on account of his marriage with a young lady. Such a person also becomes good at writing and painting. If more planets combine, the effects should be declared after making a proper adjustment of the above effects.

Next I shall give the effects of the planetary combinations in certain houses reckoned from the Ascendant :—

The Sun and Mercury joining in the 4th or 8th house from Lagna make one have royal qualities, wealthy and virtuous. The *Sun and Moon* being together in the 9th make one rich, in the 10th famous, in the 12th blind and degraded, and in other houses indigent. The *Moon and Saturn* in 5, 6, 10 or 11 make one born in a royal family a king without doubt. The *Sun and Mars* in 1, 8, 10 and 11 denote birth in a very noble family and great strength; in the rest penury is the result. The *Sun and Jupiter* in 1, 9, 10 or 11 conduce to great military power and renown as well as a strong fortress. The *Sun with Venus* in 5, 8 and 10 makes one equal to a king, famous and strong; and in other houses causes poverty and unhappiness. The *Sun with Saturn* in the 2nd or 6th causes unique fame and happiness; and in others loss of wealth. The *Moon and Mars* in the 1st, 5th, 9th, 10th or 11th make one equal to a king and wealthy; and in others, without happiness and relations or friends. You will note the distinction between the two kinds of effects given here. There is no contradiction between the two. In the first I have given the effects of conjunctions without any reference to the houses, while in the second that is made. The *Moon and Mercury* in the 3rd, 6th, 8th or 12th make one expert in poetry and fine arts, and wealthy; and elsewhere fearless but indigent. The conjunction of the *Moon and Jupiter* in any house except the 3rd, 6th and their depressions lead to wealth, good character and possession of wife and children. Note here the special conditions mentioned. The union of Jupiter and the Moon is called Gajakesariyoga (this yoga is also caused by these two occupying mutual Kendra positions). This is a good Yoga (its effects will be given later on) but its effects will not be good if they combine in the forbidden houses or are in mutual Kendras while occupying such positions. The *Moon and Venus* in the 10th house make one clever in trade and commerce, have the enjoyment of fineries and such other luxuries, and lord of wealth; and in the 12th house, get wealth from foreign countries. The *Moon and Saturn* in an Upacaya house (3, 6, 10 and 11) make one rich and happy, but in others one with a weak body, sinful activities, foolishness and hatred for his mother. *Mars and Mercury* in a Kendra confer acquisition of wealth and happiness, and elsewhere fickleness, leadership of wicked women, slovenliness, easy satisfaction and desire to eat others' food. *Mars and Jupiter* in houses other than the Dusthānas viz. 6, 8 and 12, give power, long life, children and good character; while in the forbidden places, vicious habits, sickness and poverty. *Mars and Venus* in the 1st, 4th or 10th make one prominent in the family or leader of the village community; elsewhere one becomes unsteady, under the control of women and doer of vile deeds. *Mars and Saturn* in 2nd, 4th, 5th, 9th or 10th confer children, friends, virtues, wealth, and elsewhere slovenliness and illuck. Similarly their combination in Upacaya houses makes one famous, beloved of the people and equal to a king; while elsewhere one will be always sickly with windy and bilious complaints. *Mercury and Jupiter* joined together cause deafness, eye-trouble and erudition, but in the Dusthānas they make one handsome, famous and virtuous. *Mercury and Venus* make one defective in some limb, clever in hitting and have no wife and children, while in the 1st or 9th he becomes lord of wealth and very prominent. *Mercury and Saturn* together in the 1st, 9th or 10th make one blessed with wealth, wife, children and friends, elsewhere the effects will be bad. *Jupiter and Venus* together in the

1st, 5th, 3rd or 9th confer intelligence, wife, wealth and sons, and elsewhere they cause great misery and trouble caused by diseases. *Jupiter and Saturn* in an Upacaya house make one famous and honoured by the king, and elsewhere he will be devoid of honour and wealth. *Venus and Saturn* joining in the Lagna, a Koṇa (5 or 9) or a Kendra except the 7th make one come under the influence of women, rich, a commander under a king; and elsewhere he will be bereft of courage and wealth.

I think it would be better for you if I gave the effects of the combination of three planets. The following table shows the effects:—

Sun, Moon & Mars:—Sinner, short-lived, without friends, wife and children, infirm, miserly and despised by the people.

Sun, Mars & Mercury:—Hater of his religion, living in a foreign country, stingy, merciless and miserable owing to the loss of his hard-earned money.

Sun, Mercury & Jupiter:—Intelligent, favourite of the sovereign, without money in old age, and fed by others and troubling others.

Sun, Jupiter & Venus:—Charitable, renowned a king, robbed of his wealth by women and gamblers, troubled by enemies and very miserable.

Sun, Venus & Saturn:—Abandons his religious observances, very cunning, grief-stricken, without income, sickly, and have some money in old age.

Moon, Mars & Mercury:—Famous, wise, popular, eloquent and kind-hearted, but poor in middle age.

Moon, Mercury & Jupiter:—Exalted, learned, prosperous, full of prowess and a king.

Moon, Jupiter & Venus:—A king undoubtedly endowed with elephants, horses, chariots etc. as well as with retinue, treasures and other royal appurtenances.

Moon, Venus & Saturn:—Proud, wealthy, kind, enjoyer of pleasures, belongs to middle class, and endowed with sons, friends and cattle.

Moon, Saturn & Sun:—Poor, sickly, miserable, given to begging, without some limb, and living by service and dancing.

Mars, Mercury & Venus:—Sickly in childhood, courteous, learned in fine arts, a prince and very famous in the world.

Mars, Jupiter & Venus:—Enjoying vehicles and retinue, renowned, very prosperous, enjoyer of all pleasures, and endowed with sons and lands.

Mars, Venus & Saturn:—Hostile to his mother, wandering in foreign countries, addicted to other women, ignoble, and will be humiliated by a royal family.

Mars, Saturn & Sun:—Sinner, deceiver of others' wives, short-lived, and dies in a foreign place through poison, fire, weapon or imprisonment.

Mars, Sun & Mercury:—Always wandering, and gets some corn or food at times with difficulty.

Mercury, Jupiter & Venus:—A king, very opulent, courteous, famous and a Governor.

Mercury, Venus & Saturn:—A king, very rich, of steady resolve, long-lived, famous, learned and honoured by the world.

Mercury, Saturn & Sun:—Will have excessive blood, biliousness, hating his own kith and kin, mean, living in a foreign country, and having a lean body full of veins.

Mercury, Sun & Venus:—Endowed with luxuries, wealth and authority, living with parents and relations, and having honour and valour.

Mercury, Saturn & Mars:—Marries a dancing girl, lives in a far-off place, hates his kinsmen, poor, short-lived and loses wife and cattle.

Jupiter, Venus & Saturn:—Leader of the family, having family happiness, of limited means, enjoys pleasures sparingly, famous, and approved or honoured by the public.

Jupiter, Mars & Sun:—Very rich, honoured by the people, learned, free from the fear of enemies and ailments, and having all kinds of happiness.

Jupiter, Mars & Saturn:—Mayor of a city, powerful, capable of enduring hardships, wealthy, jealous and full of self-respect and valour.

Jupiter, Saturn & Moon:—Fond of women, blessed with children, happy, friend of sweet-tongued persons, and devoted to parents, teachers and gods.

Three or more planets joined together in the Lagna, 9th or 10th house, make a person have too many irons in the fire, very virtuous, very intelligent and enjoy pleasures like Kubera.

If the *Moon, Mars & Jupiter* occupy together the same Rāśi

except their debilitations and the 6th, 7th, 8th and 12th, one becomes strong, powerful and wealthy.

Saturn, Moon, Mars & Venus:—If these join in the 1st, 9th or 10th, one will be bereft of family and friends, and gets happiness only after going abroad.

The Sun, Moon, Mars, Mercury & Jupiter:—If these are joined together anywhere, the subject will be an excellent warrior and a clever spy.

The Sun, Moon, Mars, Mercury, Jupiter & Saturn:—The subject will be a robber, addicted to other women, leprous, reviled by kinsmen, issueless, foolish and in exile.

If benefics are together in a house, only excellent results will happen; on the other hand malefics in such a position cause untold miseries, and mixed effects will have to be predicted for the conjunction of both benefics and malefics. If more than four planets combine in a single Sign, you cannot expect very good results; they will be mixed. When you examine a horoscope you have to take into consideration all the above-mentioned points relating to the conjunction of planets and the houses where such conjunctions take place. Besides that you have to bear in mind their (of the planets) relative strength. For even benefics cannot give the good results mentioned above if they are not strong and well placed.

Chapter X

CONCEPTION AND BIRTH

Now we must know something about the astrological causes for the appearance of menses which lead to conception. The biological phenomenon of the monthly course in women occurs in a cycle by the interaction of the Moon and Mars in transit over their radical charts. You may take in this connection that the Moon stands for blood which is a liquid, and Mars for fire. It is this fire that makes the blood overflow on certain days in the month. In Sanskrit the *Cycle* mentioned above is termed *Ṛtu,* meaning Season. When the Moon in her transit comes to a non-Upacaya house counted from the Lagna (Upacaya houses are 3, 6, 10 & 11) in a woman's natal chart and is aspected by or conjoined with Mars, menses set in. These menses are the cause of pregnancy. The Ṛtukāla or the period of fertility of the ovum is said to be 13 nights after bath on the 4th day. In this matter you have to exclude young children, old, sickly and barren women. The impregnation or Niṣeka should take place on a night when the Moon has gone to an Upacaya house with respect to the woman's natal Lagna, and the Moon should be aspected by Jupiter. The Ascendant for the sexual union should also be a benefic Sign or one with a benefic in it. If the male too has his Sun and Venus, strong and in their own Rāśis or Aṁśas in transit and if the night of union is even in that *Season,* the event may lead to the birth of a male child. The following Yogas lead to the effectiveness of the Union : (1) The Sun, Moon, Jupiter and Venus being posited in their own houses, (2) in their own Aṁśas, (3) in the Lagna and being aspected by or conjoined with Mars, (4) the strong Jupiter being in Lagna, the 5th or 9th house on a good weakday ruled by a good Nakṣatra.

The following are some of the Yogas leading to the birth of a son :—(1) The Sun and Jupiter in odd Signs, (2) the lords of the 1st and 5th in conjunction, (3) their mutual aspect, (4) their being in mutual reception, (5) Saturn being strong, posited in an odd house except the Lagna, and not aspected by or conjoined with any planet, (6) all the male planets occupying the 6th and (or) the 11th, (7) the lord of 5th house being very strong, and (8) all the major planets, viz; the Sun, Moon, Jupiter as well as the Lagna occupying odd houses and Aṁśas. Note that all these Yogas refer to Ādhāna or impregnation. No doubt they can be applied while examining the 5th Bhāva too.

The following are the Yogas leading to the birth of a female child :—(1) The Moon, Venus and Mars in even Signs, (2) conjunction of the Moon and Venus in the 5th or 10th house, (3) their being in their own houses, (4) in their own Aṁśas, (5) Rāhu being in the Lagna and being aspected by the Moon, (6) the Moon being in the Lagna and aspected by Rāhu, (7) Venus being in the Horā of the Moon, and (8) Venus being in a Kendra, (9) The Lagna, Sun, Moon and Jupiter in even Signs and Aṁśas.

Birth of Twins:—When Mercury occupies the Ascendant which is a dual Sign, or aspects such a Lagna, or when he is in the 10th, twins will be born. The sex of the twins should be determined from the nature of the Rāśi and Aṁśa occupied by Mercury. The idea is that if both the Sign and Aṁśa are odd Rāśis, both will be males; if one is odd and the other even, one of the twins will be male and the other female; and if both are even, both will be females. I am giving here some more Yogas for the birth of twins:—(1) The Sun should be in a quadruped sign and the rest being strong in dual signs, (2) the lord of the Lagna conjoined with Rāhu in a sign belonging to Saturn should be aspected by Saturn and Mars, (3) the Moon and Venus should be in even signs, or in dual Aṁśas, Mercury in the Lagna, and Mars and Jupiter in odd signs, (4) the lords of the 1st and 2nd houses are together in a sign and are aspected by Rāhu, (5) the Lagna and Moon in even Signs being aspected by a male planet, (6) Lagna is occupied by Rāhu, its lord in the 10th along with a malefic, and four planets in their own or exaltation signs, (7) the Sun and Jupiter in Gemini and Sagittarius aspected by Mercury, and (8) Venus, Moon and Mars in Pisces or Virgo aspected by Mercury.

The following are the six Yogas for the birth of eunuchs—: (1) The Moon and Sun should aspect each other for a day-birth; (2) Mercury and Saturn should aspect each other for a night-birth; (3) Mars aspecting the Sun in an even Sign; (4) Lagna and Moon being in odd Signs aspected by Mars; (5) the

Moon in an even Sign and Mercury in an odd Sign aspected by Mars; and (6) Venus, Lagna and Moon being in odd Aṁśas.

Growth of Foetus :—The Theory of Evolution is well illustrated in the life of the foetus. It is said that the foetus takes ten months for full growth and delivery. You should not think that this is an unscientific statement. It is not. For, it is based on Nākṣatra-month. So the measure of nine full months according to modern science and that of ten months according to our Śāstras are in agreement. In the *First* month of pregnancy the foetus will be in the form of coagulated blood and is presided over by *Venus* ; in the *Second* month it will resemble the Rudrākṣa seed which is round, and is presided over by *Mars*; in the *Third* it looks like a sprout, and is presided over by *Jupiter*. In the *Fourth* it begins to develop marrow and bones, and is presided over by the *Sun*; in the *Fifth* there is the formation of skin, fat and blood, and is presided over by the Moon; in the *Sixth* it develops all the limbs, and is ruled by *Saturn*; in the *Seventh* the senses appear in it, and it is ruled by *Mercury*; in the *Eighth* it will have some activity caused by hunger and thirst; and is ruled by the lord of the Lagna at *Ādhāna*; in the *Ninth* it feels pain etc. and is ruled by the *Moon*; and lastly the child is delivered in the *Tenth* month that is ruled by the *Sun*. The foetus will grow without trouble if the lord of the particular month is strong and unafflicted by malefics or inimical planets. Suppose the planet presiding over a particular month is afflicted, defeated in war or eclipsed. In that month the child in the womb will suffer most and may even perish. If the Ascendant at Ādhāna or impregnation is a movable sign (or the Moon be in such a sign), the birth is said to take place in the 10th month; if it is a fixed one, in the 11th month; and if a dual one, in the 12th month. The rule relating to Ādhāna can safely be applied to queries regarding the health and sex of the child in the womb. If there is a query as to when a particular woman who is pregnant will be delivered of the child, find out the stronger of the two viz. the Ascendant and the Moon. Note the Dvādaśāṁśa of the stronger one. Count as many Rāśis from this Dvādaśāṁśa-Rāśi as there are Dvādaśāṁśas. When the Moon passes through that sign the delivery will take place. For example, let us take Aries as the Ascendant which is stronger than the Moon. Let the 1/12 Aṁśa of the Lagna be Capricorn which is the 10th

Aṁśa. So count ten signs from Capricorn and you come to Libra. So the birth is likely to take place when the Moon passes through Libra. There is another method of finding out the same event. Find out the Navāṁśa of the Moon at the time of query. When the Moon goes in transit to the 7th Rāśi from the Navāṁśa-Rāśi it may take place. If the Moon at the time of query is in Gemini, 7th Navāṁśa, which is Aries, birth may take place when the Moon passes through the 7th from Aries i.e. Libra. Or it may happen when the Moon goes through the Sign owned by the lord of the rising Navāṁśa. If there is a query as to when, whether at day or night time, the delivery would take place, you have to find out whether the Ascendant is a Diurnal or Nocturnal sign, and what part of the sign has already risen above the horizon. If it is a Nocturnal sign, you will predict that birth will take place at daytime when the same proportion of the day as the part of the Lagna above the horizon is has elapsed, and *vice versa.*

Difficult Delivery:—If there are malefics in the 4th and 7th houses from the Moon at Ādhāna or query, if malefics aspect them, the mother will have severe labour pains.

The child to be coiled round with a cord :—Some times the child after delivery is found to have something like a cord coiling round some part of its body. This is found out thus—(1) If the Lagna at birth is Aries, Leo or Taurus that is occupied by Saturn or Mars, the child will be born with a cord wound round the particular limb signified by the Navāṁśa of the Lagna. The same result should be predicted, if the lord of the Lagna is aspected by many malefics or conjoined with Rāhu or Ketu, or if the Ascendant is occupied by malefics. Another Yoga for the same effect is—Rāhu should be in the Lagna which is surrounded by malefics; or the Lagna occupied by Mars should be aspected by the Sun; or the Lagna occupied by Saturn should be aspected by Mars. Yet another Yoga is : If the Moon or the Lagna belonging to a malefic or one with a malefic in it is in the decanate of Mars, and benefics in the 2nd and 11th houses, the issue is likely to be a reptile or a child with a cord wound round its body.

Yogas for illness or death of Couple :—Certain planetary combinations at the time of copulation bring about disastrous consequences to the man or woman or both. This was the reason why our ancients prescribed only certain days and prohibited the rest for sexual congress. When modern sciences are taking long strides, these rules are considered by many as a bundle of superstitions worthy of being discarded. If Mars and Saturn should be opposite, i.e. in the 7th house, from the Sun at the time of copulation, the husband would fall ill. Similarly if these planets should be in the 7th house from the Moon, the wife would suffer. Death would be the result if the Sun or the Moon, as the case may be, should have Mars and Saturn in the 12th and 2nd places, or either of the luminaries is aspected by one of these malefics and conjoined with the other. It has been already pointed out to you that for a day-birth the Sun and Venus represent the father and mother respectively and Saturn and the Moon the paternal uncle and maternal aunt respectively. At night this order is to be reversed. If at copulation these planets occupy odd and even houses (the one representing father odd, and mother even) the couple will be happy. These planets representing the parents yield full effects, good or bad, in the first part of the day or night, as the case may be; and the least in the last part. The following are some of the Yogas leading to the death of the pregnant woman :—

(1) If there are malefics in the Lagna that have not yet risen, the Lagna being unaspected by benefics; (2) if Saturn is in the Lagna receiving the aspect of the weak Moon and of Mars (or the weak Moon is aspected by Mars); (3) if the Lagna and the Moon together or separately are surrounded by two malefics and are not aspected by benefics; (4) if there are malefics in the 4th house counted from the Moon or the Ascendant; (5) if Mars is in the 7th or 8th house from Lagna; (6) if the Sun is in the 12th, Mars in the 4th and Moon weak; (7) if Mars and the Sun are in the 1st and 7th house respectively, death takes place as a result of a surgical operation. There will be abortion if at a Niṣeka Mars and Saturn occupy the Lagna or if the Moon is situated in the house of either or aspected by either. If on the other hand benefics occupy the Lagna or are in conjunction with the Moon or are posited in 2, 4, 5, 7, 9, and 10 and if the Lagna or the Moon is aspected by Jupiter, the foetus will grow unhindered and will be delivered safely in time.

Yoga for freaks :—People might say that there are some strange children born with two heads etc. They might wish to know if there are any astrological reasons for such things. Yes. I shall give here only one Yoga : If Mercury is in the 5th or 9th house, and the other planets weak, the child will have two heads, four hands and four feet.

Yoga for dumbness :—If the Moon be in Taurus and the malefics viz. the Sun, Mars and Saturn, posited severally or jointly in the last portion of Cancer, Scorpio or Pisces, the child born would be dumb. In case the Moon in the above Yoga is aspected by benefics, it may get speech after a long time.

Yoga to have Teeth at Birth :—If Mars and Saturn are in the Signs or Aṁśas owned by Mercury, the child will have teeth at birth itself.

Yoga for the Birth of a Hunch-backed :—If the Moon be in the Lagna identical with Cancer and be aspected by Saturn and Mars, the child will be hunch-backed or dwarfish in appearance.

Yoga for Lameness :—If the Lagna (at Ādhāna) be Pisces and aspected by the Moon, Mars and Saturn, the child will be lame or will have deformed feet.

Yoga for Imbecility or Idiocy :—If a malefic along with the Moon be situated in any of the Ṛkṣasandhis (i.e. the last portion of Rāśis 4, 8 and 12), the child will grow to be an idiot.

Yoga for Dwarfness etc. :—If the Sun, Moon and Saturn should aspect the rising sign which is the last Aṁśa of Capricorn, the child would be a dwarf. When the Lagna is the same having the above aspect and when the rising decanate is occupied by Mars, the child will be born headless; if the decanate is the second, it will be armless; and if the third, it will be devoid of feet.

Yoga for Congenital Blindness :—If the Lagna happens to be Leo and is occupied by the Sun and Moon, and aspected by Mars and Saturn, the child will be born blind. If the same Lagna be aspected by both benefics and malefics, the child would be blear-eyed. If the Sun or the Moon is posited in the 12th house receiving the aspect of malefics, the right or the left eye, as the case may be, will suffer. Of course benefic aspects have always a tempering effect. Remember that these Yogas are mainly meant for Ādhāna, but may be applied with advantage to the natal chart as well.

Another Yoga for Muteness or Imbecility :—If Jupiter be debilitated, and the Moon be in the Sandhi between two Signs or Aṁśas, the child born would be either dumb or imbecile.

Now I should like you to examine an example of twin-birth. This is the chart of the first of the twins, both female, born on 8th July 1951 at 12-45 P.M. The second was born at 2-45

Jup. 9	—	—	Sun 1 Mars 9
Rāhu 12			Merc. 9
—			Ven. 3 Ketu 6 Moon 2
—	—	—	Sat. 11 Lag. 6

P.M. on the same day. The Lagna for the second is the 27th degree of Libra, while that of the first is the 29th degree of Virgo. The second one died exactly after a month. The Moon in the second is in the 8th degree of Leo, while in the first she is in the 7th degree. Now look at the details of the chart in the light of the rules enunciated above. It will also show you how the planetary dispositions do not exactly follow the rules. In this chart none of the rules is perfectly applicable. Mercury is in the 10th Bhāva; the Moon and Venus are in even and dual Aṁśas respectively; Mars is in an odd Sign; the lord of the 2nd house alone (not along with the lord of the 1st) is aspected by Rāhu; the Lagna alone (and not the Moon too) is in an even Sign that is aspected by a male planet viz. Jupiter (the aspect of Mars is not full); the Lagna-lord is in the 10th along with a malefic viz. the Sun, in the Bhāva chart; and the Sun and Jupiter are in common signs (but are not aspected by Mercury). You will see that out of seven planets four are in dual signs, and the fifth, Venus, in a dual Aṁśa. Of the remaining two viz. the Moon and Mercury, one is in even Aṁśa and the other in even Rāśi. Even Rāhu and Ketu have dual Aṁśas.

If in a natal chart the Sun is conjoined with, aspected or surrounded by malefics, the native's father is sure to get into trouble ere long. The effect will be the same if malefics unassociated with benefics occupy the 6th and 8th places from the Sun or the 4th and 8th from him. If the Sun be in the Aṁśa of Mars and be aspected by Saturn, the father would quit the world before the birth of the child. Similarly, if Mars occupying the Aṁśa of the Sun should be posited in the 4th or the 9th house without receiving the aspect of Jupiter and Venus, the child would not see the father.

The mother's welfare should be similarly predicted from the position of the Moon in the chart. If there are only malefics in the 5th and 9th places from the weak Moon, the mother will come to grief. If both Mars and Saturn are posited in the same Aṁśa but in any Signs, or in Kendras with respect to the Moon, the child will be bereaved of its mother and will be brought up by another.

How are we to find out if the father was at home or abroad at the time of the child's birth ? The popular Yoga mentioned for the presence of the father in a distant place or country is the following:—If the Ascendant at birth is not aspected by the Moon, and the Sun be in the 8th or 9th house, the father would not be at home at the time of birth. The idea is that he may be in the same place but not in the house of birth if the Sun is in a fixed Sign. In the above case if the Sun be also in a movable Rāśi, it must be declared that the father was in a distant country. If the Sun be in a dual Rāśi, the father should be on his way home. This picture of the heavens is given for day-births. If the birth is at night, what should be the Yoga for similar effects ? If the Sun aspects Saturn who is in a movable Sign, the father should be in a foreign place. The same effect should be said to follow if the Lagna be occupied by Saturn or the 7th by Mars, or if the Moon be between the Sun and Mars (or between Mercury and Venus, according to others). If the Sun (for a day-birth) and Saturn (for a night-birth) be aspected by Mars, the same effect will follow. On the other hand if both the aspecting and aspected planets are in movable Signs, the father would be dead in the distant place. If the lord of the Lagna be weak, and aspected by or conjoined with Mars, and if malefics be in the 4th and 9th houses, the father would be bed-ridden at the time of birth. If Saturn occupying Leo Navāṁśa be aspected by the Sun, or be posited in the 8th or 12th house, the father would be in a miserable condition. In the illustrative horoscope given in the beginning, the Sun is in a fixed Sign. Hence it should be declared that the birth took place when the father was away but in the same town.

Yoga for Illegitimate Birth:—One should be extremely cautious in making prediction about the legitimacy or otherwise of a child. Still the ancients have given certain planetary dispositions as indicative of illegitimate birth. When Jupiter aspects neither the Lagna nor the Moon, or when he does not aspect the Moon in conjunction with the Sun, or when the Moon with the Sun is further associated with another malefic, the child is said to be born of another person. The same effect is to be pronounced if Jupiter, Moon and Sun are debilitated, Saturn or Mars in the Lagna, or the Lagna, Moon and Venus are not aspected by benefics. However, if the Moon or Ascendant be in a Sign or Aṁśa owned by Jupiter or aspected by him, the child should be *legitimate*. The same effect will follow if Jupiter is in Rāśi or Aṁśa of the Moon, or if the Sun and Moon are posited in each other's Rāśi or Aṁśa.

Yoga for Father's Incarceration:—If Mars and Saturn are in Aries, Leo or Aquarius identical with the 7th, 9th or 5th place from the Sun, the father of the child will be at the time imprisoned in a foreign place, in his own place or while on his way back home, according as the Sign occupied by the Sun is movable, fixed or dual. In this case it is profitable to see if the Sun occupies in addition a Serpent (Bhujaga) decanate or Fetters (Nigala) Drekkaṇa.

Yoga for Birth in Ship or on Water:—When the Moon is full and in her own house, Mercury in the Lagna and benefics in the 4th, birth takes place in a boat. The same will be the result when the Lagna happens to be a watery Sign and the Moon is posited in the 7th house. Or it may happen if the Ascendant at birth is Gemini or Virgo occupied by Mercury, and if the full Moon is in the second Bhāva. Or it may occur on or near water when the full Moon occupying a watery Rāśi is in the second, aspects it or is in the 4th or 10th house from the Lagna.

Yoga for Clandestine Delivery:—This happens when Saturn

occupies the 12th place from the Lagna or the Moon and is further aspected by malefics.

Nature of Place of Birth:—If the Lagna is a *human* Rāśi occupied by Saturn and aspected by Mars, delivery takes place in a burial ground; if the aspecting planets are Venus and the Moon, it is a fine place where some sort of recreation or decoration is done; if it is Jupiter, it is a sacred place; if it is the Sun, the place is a palace, temple or where cows are in plenty; and if it is Mercury, it is in a house of fine arts. Generally the nature of the place of birth corresponds to that of the Rāśi or Aṁśa of the rising Sign. If it is Movable, the birth will be far away, if fixed in one's own house. The idea is that in the first case birth takes place not in the house of the child's father. If it is a dual Sign or Aṁśa, it will be in an out-house. You can also say in which relative's house the delivery took place. I have already told you about the planets that represent the parents and other kinsmen for day and night births. According to the strength of these planets you will have to adjudge whether the birth of the child took place in the house of the father, mother, paternal uncle or maternal aunt.

Abandonment of Child by Mother:—If the Moon occupies the 7th house (or is combust in a house) which is in trine to Mars and Saturn, the child is abandoned by the mother. But if the Moon is aspected by Jupiter, no such prediction would be right. The child will perish being abandoned by the mother, if the Moon in the Lagna is aspected by malefics, and Mars occupies the 7th house; or if Mars and Saturn are in the 11th or the 2nd house. If the Moon in the above cases is aspected by a benefic, the child will pass into the hands of a person belonging to the class represented by the aspecting planets. If the aspecting planets are malefic, it will be rescued by wicked fellows, but it will die soon.

The limbs corresponding to the Bhāvas that are occupied by benefics or malefics will have moles (or similar marks) or scars caused by wounds or ulcers, as the case may be.

Sub-human birth:—You have learnt that some Signs stand for human beings, while some others for minerals and yet others for vegetables. Now I should like to tell you the circumstances under which sub-humans viz. birds, beasts and plants, take birth:

(1) If the lords of the ascendant and IV house be in mutual reception and if the lord of the former be aspected by or joined with other planets, a quadruped will be born. If the aspecting or conjoining planet be Rāhu or Ketu, it will be a goat; if Jupiter, Venus or Moon, a cow; and if Saturn, a buffalo. The creature will come out of its mother's womb with its legs foremost, if the ascendant-lord be in the 10th and Rāhu in the Lagna.

(2) If the lords of V and IV be posited in II and VII and be aspected or joined by malefics, and if a male planet be in a male decanate, the creatures born would be monkeys, pigs, cats and the like.

(3) If all the malefics be very strong and benefics weak, and if a neutral planet (Mercury or Saturn) be posited in or aspecting a quadrant, there would be birth of a being similar in form to the one shown by the Moon's Dvādaśāṁśa, provided that Aṁśa belongs to a *Viyoni* (Sub-human) Sign.

(4) If malefics be strong and posited in their own Dvādaśāṁśas, and benefics being weak be in the 1/12 Aṁśas belonging to others, similar deductions should be arrived at, provided the ascendant is a *Viyoni* sign.

CHAPTER XI

UḌUDAŚĀS

It is necessary here to remember the basic principle that the science of Astrology presupposes a belief in the theory of Karma and of re-incarnation of the individual soul. It is also understood that there is a Supreme Power called God who is the sole dispenser of the effects of actions, good, bad and indifferent, done by human beings in their earthly existence. Astrology helps us in probing the mysterious working of the Law of Karma, provided we approach the subject with reverence and humility. As I have stated elsewhere Astrology is not an ordinary science, but the Science of all sciences. For understanding this super-science, therefore, the ordinary scientific apparatus will not be sufficient. That is why the ancients have laid down that the life of an astrologer should be an exemplar in every respect to the populace. So the predictions of an astrologer would be correct to that extent to which he is able to attune himself to the Sacred Law. This gives the reason why some predictions are fulfilled while others are falsified or partially fulfilled.

When we look at a horoscope and study the various kinds of strength of the planets and the ascendant, we would be able to assess the nature and strength of the merits and demerits of the subject whose effects he or she has to reap in this life. Now comes the question as to when the person is likely to experience the effects of his good Karmas or deeds as well as those of his bad ones. This is called the method of timing certain events in the life of an individual. But the difficulty is that there are several methods prevalent in different parts of India and the world for arriving at the time of fruition of one's Karma. The periods at which they are expected to bear fruit are technically called DAŚĀS. In common parlance the word DAŚĀ means only *condition* or state. We say that a person is passing through the Daśā of a particular planet. So we have to understand from this that it is the period in which that planet exercises its influence solely on account of its *condition* i.e. strength and other special features. In other words it shows, the Daśā or condition, good, bad or indifferent, through which the subject is passing as a result of his past Karma that is suggested by the planetary condition. I have already explained to you the character, features, habitat, activities, humours etc. of the planets. An understanding of that should help you in ascertaining the *condition* or Daśā of the individual concerned. I have also explained in chapter V-51 that under the Uḍudaśā system the span of human life is 120 years and that this is distributed among the nine planets. However the order of the Daśās or Major and Sub-periods of the nine planets is not the same as that of the week days with Rāhu and Ketu added at the end. The Daśās operate as follows:—(i) The Sun's major period of 6 years for the natal stars already mentioned in the above chapter. (ii) After this the period of the Moon for 10 years. (iii) Then that of Mars or Maṅgala for 7 years. (iv) Then that of Rāhu for 18 years. (v) Then that of Jupiter for 16 years. (vi) Then that of Saturn for 19 years. (vii) Then that of Mercury for 17 years. (viii) Then that of Ketu for 7 years. (ix) Lastly that of Śukra or Venus for 20 years. In the case of sub-periods, minor periods, etc. too the same order is followed. The following table gives the major and minor periods of the planets :—(See page 130).

The mutual relationship between a Daśānātha and the lord of a sub-Daśā must also be harmonious for good effects to be reaped. The idea is that lord of an Antardaśā, sub-period, should not be in the 6th, 8th or 12th house from the Daśānātha. During the Daśā of a planet the native will experience or enjoy those substances that are ascribed to that planet, profession appropriate to it, the special effects of the Bhāva, and Rāśi occupied or aspected by it and the effects of the special Yogas produced by it. The measure of these things depends on the strength of the planet concerned. You know that people sometimes change their taste. For example, a man who is fond of sweets at one time prefers pungent things at another period. What is the reason for this ? It is the Daśā that is responsible for it. Similarly a person who was lean in the beginning becomes stout at a later stage. Some persons prefer certain Deities at one time and certain others at another.

Let us suppose that the Daśā of a malefic planet is in progress. Then sets in the sub-period of another malefic. What would be the effects of this period ? They would be pretty dangerous,

Lords of Sub-period	Sun 6 yrs.	Moon 10 yrs.	Mars 7 yrs.	Rāhu 18 yrs.	Jupiter 16 yrs.	Saturn 19 yrs.	Mercury 17 yrs.	Ketu 7 yrs.	Venus 10 yrs.
	m. d.	m. d.	m. d.	m. d.	m. d.	m. d.	m. d.	m. d.	m.d.
	Sun : 3 18	Moon :10 0	Mars : 4 27	Rāhu 32 12	Jup. : 25 18	Sat. : 36 3	Merc. : 28 27	Ketu : 4 27	Venus : 40 0
	Moon : 6 0	Mars : 7 0	Rāhu 12 18	Jup. : 28 24	Sat. : 30 12	Merc. : 32 9	Ketu : 11 27	Venus: 14 0	Sun : 12 0
	Mars : 4 6	Rāhu : 18 0	Jup. : 11 6	Sat. : 34 6	Merc.: 27 6	Ketu : 13 9	Venus: 34 0	Sun : 4 6	Moon : 20 0
	Rāhu : 10 24	Jup. : 16 0	Sat. : 13 9	Merc. : 30 18	Ketu : 11 6	Venus: 38 0	Sun : 10 6	Moon: 7 0	Mars : 14 0
	Jup. : 9 18	Sat. : 19 0	Merc. : 11 27	Ketu : 12 18	Venus: 32 0	Sun : 11 12	Moon: 17 0	Mars : 4 27	Rāhu : 36 0
	Sat. : 11 12	Merc. : 17 0	Ketu : 4 27	Venus: 36 0	Sun : 9 18	Moon: 19 0	Mars : 11 27	Rāhu : 12 18	Jupiter : 32 0
	Merc.: 10 6	Ketu : 7 0	Venus: 14 0	Sun : 10 24	Moon: 16 0	Mars : 13 9	Rāhu : 30 18	Jup. : 11 6	Sat. : 38 0
	Ketu : 4 6	Venus: 20 0	Sun : 4 6	Moon: 18 0	Mars : 11 6	Rāhu : 34 6	Jup. : 27 6	Sat. : 13 9	Merc. : 34 0
	Venus: 12 0	Sun : 6 0	Moon: 7 0	Mars : 12 18	Rāhu : 28 24	Jup. : 30 12	Sat. : 32 9	Merc.: 11 27	Ketu : 14 0

and calamitous if their positions are mutually hostile. In the sub-period of Saturn in the main Daśā of Mars there is some sort of danger to life, provided there is no benefic aspect. You cannot expect much from a weak Daśānātha, though the Antardaśā-lord may be strong. For, the strength of the lord of the main Daśā is the very foundation on which is built the edifice of life with its ups and downs. A malefic planet posited in a malefic's house identical with the 6th or 8th Bhāva and aspected by a bi-ped planet posited in a malefic house, is likely to prove dangerous to the native's life in his Daśā. Similarly the Daśā of a planet that is conjoined with Rāhu, though apparently very good, will be very bad. At the end of the Daśā there will be miseries, losses and wanderings in foreign lands. During the Daśā of a planet that is posited in the 8th Bhāva from *the lord of the Lagna* there is likely to be much affliction to the person concerned; and at the end of that Daśā one may even expect his exit from the world. During the progress of the Daśā of one who is debilitated or who occupies the house of an enemy or is retrograde, the native will be addicted to forbidden acts; he will be forsaken by his kith and kin, will become extremely greedy and will live in a foreign country. Similarly during the Daśā of a planet that is inimical to the lord of the Lagna or the Candra-Lagna, both natal, the native will have mental derangement, troubles from enemies, loss of lands or kingdom, quarrels with wicked fellows and general physical debility. Even though a planet may be expected to take away the native's life during his Daśā, still if the planet at the commencement of his Daśā is strong, aspected by benefics or situated in benefic or Adhimitra Vargas, the impending danger will be averted. So too a victorious planet or one who is conjoined with benefics or one who occupies own house, exaltation or the like will ward off the Ariṣṭas in his Daśā.

If the major period of a yogakāraka planet is in progress, effects of Rājayoga will be experienced in the sub-periods of the concerned significators or Kārakas. Then the succeeding sub-periods of even malefics will maintain and further the Rājayoga. The Daśās and Apahāras or Bhuktis of the following planets, especially when they are weak, will bring about great sufferings : (i) One posited in the 8th house, (ii) one that aspects the 8th house, (iii) lord of that house, (iv) lord of the decanate of the same house, and (v) the lord of the sign occupied by Māndi.

The period or Daśā of a planet that has fallen from its highest exaltation is termed *Avarohiṇī* or *Descending*, while that of one proceeding from its depression is called *Ārohiṇī* or *Ascending*, that of a planet which occupies a friendly house or exaltation (in Sign or Aṁśa) becomes *Madhyā* or *Middling*, and lastly that of one posited in the sign or Aṁśa belonging to its enemy or debilitation is called *Adhamā* or *Worst*. Even though a planet may be combust, depressed or posited in an inimical sign, yet its *Period* (Daśā) will yield mixed effects generally and produce good effects especially in the latter half, provided it occupies an auspicious house (Bhāva) and Aṁśa (i.e. other than 6th, 8th and 12th. ones).

We can also find out as to when a particular relation is likely to come to harm, by means of this Daśā system. You know the relatives signified by the various Bhāvas. Take the Bhāva of that relation and note the planet that occupies the 12th house from that Bhāva, as well as its owner. If the concerned planet is weak, its major period may prove fatal to that relative. There is another way of timing the fruition of a period on the basis of the planet's transit : When the lord of the Daśā in transit comes to the ascendant, or the 3rd, 6th, 10th or 11th house from the Lagna, or when the same planet comes to the Saptavarga Signs (Rāśi, Horā etc.) of the Lagna, or when a benefic or a planet friendly to the lord of the Lagna comes to the latter, the period will prove beneficial. Note that this is not an absolute rule. For, if a planet is utterly spoilt at birth, its Daśā cannot yield splendid results. Similarly you must note which particular house counted from the natal Moon the lord of Daśā in transit comes to occupy. During that period the effects will be similar to those of ordinary transits. So too you can know as to which particular day or days will be good or bad during a Daśā : When the Moon in transit passes through a Sign owned by a friend of the Daśā-lord, the exaltation of the latter or the 7th house, a trine (trikoṇa) or an Upacaya house counted from the lord of the Daśā, good results will be experienced. These favourable effects would also accrue to the relations represented by the houses counted from the ascendant. You can conclude from this that results will not be favourable when the Moon passes through the rest.

The period of a planet that has recommenced direct motion will prove beneficial in respect of honour, valour and wealth as well as recovery of lost property, provided the concerned planet is in an auspicious house and Aṁśa and not in the 8th or 12th house or Aṁśa. On the other hand, the period of a retrograde planet that is depressed or posited in an inimical house will be marked by ignoble activities, censure from kinsmen, absence from home and servitude. Similarly Jupiter and Venus owning kendras or angles are not considered auspicious. So their periods are likely to produce evil effects at least at the end. If they are also posited in a Māraka place, 2nd or 7th, they become powerful causes of death. The Daśā of a planet whose Navāṁśa belongs to a malefic will create obstacles to education in boyhood. So too is the period of one that occupies an Aṁśa belonging to an eclipsed planet. Venus occupying his own house identical with the 8th from the Lagna will cause diseases in his period; but if he be conjoined with malefics, he would bring about the subject's death at the end of the Daśā in spite of his being the lord of the ascendant.

Effects of Daśās

The general effects of the *Sun's* major period are the following :— One will acquire wealth by means of cruel deeds, from kings and through fighting; he will have trouble from fire and beasts, inflammation in the eyes, diseases of the stomach and teeth, severe sufferings of wife and children, separation from elders or parents, and loss of servants and wealth. If the Sun is not well placed in the natal chart, then one is likely to have greater troubles such as quarrels, sudden royal displeasure (i.e. trouble from the rulers), sickness among one's kinsmen, wanderings, boiling temper, and threat to the corn and wealth as well as trouble to one's wife and children. If the Sun is well placed, his Daśā will generally conduce to prosperity, victories, great activity and happiness. He is good in Aries, Gemini, Virgo and Sagittarius; and in Cancer and Pisces somewhat good.

The *Moon's* period generally confers prosperity through Mantras (Sacred hymns), gods, Brahmins and royal favour, acquisition of wealth, woman, wet lands, flowers, clothes, ornaments, scents and tasty dishes. One will also have quarrels with the wicked, loss of wealth and affliction from wind diseases. If the Moon is strong both in position and phase, her Daśā will bestow excellent benefits such as mental peace and all round success. If she is weak, there will be mental troubles, wanderings, trouble to ones mother and lands. Even heart-trouble may be expected in her period, if she is both weak and afflicted. She is good in Signs 2, 3, 4, 5, 6, and 12. The Moon's Daśā will be good in the middle.

Mars causes the following effects :—Acquisition of cattle and wealth through fire, lands, king, fighting or litigation, medicines, falsehood, deceits and various cruel deeds. There will be ailments caused by vitiation of bile and blood, as well as fever, association with low women, quarrel with one's own sons, wife, kinsmen and elders, and dependence on others' wealth. Mars in Aries, Cancer, and Leo produces mixed results, while in Scorpio and Sagittarius good results. His Daśā will be excellent if Mars is posited in his exaltation, facing upwards and in the 10th or 11th house. A planet is said to be Ūrdhvāsya or with upward looks when he is posited in any one of the six signs following the one occupied by the Sun. Similarly if he is in Vargottamāṁśa, the results will be very good. When he is eclipsed or posited in debilitation Aṁśa or in the 8th house, the outcome is likely to be very unfavourable.

Mercury :— Generally Budha causes in his period the arrival of friends, happiness, fame, eulogy of sholars, wealth, lands, horses, favour of elders or teachers, eloquent speeches, helping others, high status and happiness of one's wife, children and friends. Ailments resulting from the vitiation of all the three humours are also indicated, especially if the planet is afflicted or ill placed. During this Daśā the native is likely to take special interest in music and other fine arts as well as in pleasant and humorous talks. Mercury in Meṣa leads to scientific pursuits, heroism, roguery and falsehood. In Taurus he is bad for the mother, causes throat complaints and debts. In Gemini he gives many wives and children, wisdom and two mothers. In Cancer he enables one to earn money by writing poetry and through fine arts, but will wander in other countries and have little wealth and happiness. In Leo one becomes mayor of a city, popular, and rich, receives honour from great kings and tours over fortresses and forests. In Virgo he makes one a politician, writer, poet and victorious over enemies. Libra is pretty good. Scorpio makes one poor, addicted to a maid servant and toil hard at home. In Dhanus one becomes a leader of a party or minister, endowed with wealth, corn, cattle and two names. In Capricorn one gets into debts, lives in a bad place, serves others, wanders, comes to have mean associates and suffers from hallucinations. In Aquarius one becomes indigent and addicted to a wicked woman. In Pisces one becomes well-versed in Vedas and Śāstras and engaged in philosophical speculations as well as a favourite of the great. Here the reader would do well to remember that Pisces is Mercury's Sign of debilitation, and still good results are given here. What does it mean ? Though he may be in Pisces, yet he must not be in lowest debilitation i.e. 15th degree. If the planet has crossed that point, he can be said to be Ārohi — ascending. In the lowest depression, of course, every planet will produce only untoward results. The Daśā of Mercury who is eclipsed will cause loss of position or lands, perpetual mental affliction, loss of money, jaundice, bronchial catarrh etc. The ancients are of opinion that by nature Mercury can produce only mixed effects.

Jupiter causes in his Daśā performance of meritorious works, birth of sons or daughters, honour from the king and great personages, acquisition of good vehicles, wisdom and knowledge of philosophy, meeting with one's wife, children and friends and success in one's undertakings. He may also lead to the bereavement of elders or parents, ear disease and phlegmatic troubles, as well as enlargement of spleen, abscess and the like. The following are the effects of Jupiter's presence in the twelve signs : (1) Leadership of a group, wisdom, wealth from kings, freedom from grief, and company of kith and kin. (2) Trouble from enemies, unhappiness, going abroad, and earning money with little effort. (3) Hatred for women, opulence, agricultural occupation, aversion to family traditions and opposition to the mother or loss of a limb. (4) In the highest exaltation he enables the native to follow his family profession, to become learned, wealthy, illustrious, and enjoy royal pleasures. Elsewhere the effects are not so good. (5) He becomes a judge, gets wealth from the king, and honour, cattle etc. through his virtues. (6) He gets wealth from the queen, quarrels with Śūdras and mean fellows, wanders from place to place, gets cattle wealth, vehicles, clothes and learning. (7) Energy gets impaired, kills wife and children, suffers from ulcers and loss of appetite. (8) Devotion to gods, wandering, great energy, debts of various kinds, disciplined life and popularity. (9) In the Mūlatrikoṇa part Jupiter makes one prominent, wise, a minister or governor, one under the influence of a young woman, wealthy and happy. Elsewhere he gives wealth and happiness from going abroad, causes sacrifices, cattle breeding and farming. (10) Sorrow on account of relative's demise, service of others, penury, and diseases of stomach, ears and private parts, living in a forest, living by agriculture, and trouble on account of trees, water and treachery. (11) Earning money by heroism, tale-bearing, doing vile deeds, hating one's own people and loss of wealth. (12) Wisdom, pre-eminence in the group, preaching religious stories, humility and love of young women. If Jupiter is combust, his Daśā will produce both misery and happiness in equal measure, while in depression and in an inimical house he will cause many diseases and loss of wife, children and wealth.

Venus bestows during his period materials for sports and pleasure, good vehicles, cattle, gems, clothes, ornaments, treasures, pleasures of the couch, intellectual pursuits, proficiency in dancing etc., feeding, voyage, auspicious religious performances, honour from the sovereign, hereditary wealth, physical charm, gain through trade, and agriculture. Trouble to kinsmen, mental anguish and death of elders are also likely. The bad effects are diseases of wind, phlegm and bile, great trouble on account of standing by one's brother's son, enmity with the ignoble, and friendship with atheists. (1) While in Aries he brings about loss of money, honour and happiness through women, wandering, threat to life, lack of endurance, lordly bearing, and favour of a queen. (2) Intelligent, possessed of agricultural lands, cattle and wife, self-contolled, learned in many Śāstras, father of many girls and king's favourite. (3) Wealthy, fond of wonderful talk or stories, living abroad, very energetic and engaged in many activities. (4) Devoted to one's duty, of good character, having two wives, and following many professions. (5) Earns wealth with the help of a distinguished woman, enjoys others' wealth, loses cattle, possesses a few children and is wise. (6) Loses happiness and character, becomes dispirited, fickle-minded, living abroad and forsaken by his wife. If the Aṁśa also is Virgo, the period will be extremely miserable.

(7) Becomes famous; rich in agricultural produce, cattle and money and gets wealth from the wise. (8) Wandering, talkative, doing others' work, quarrelling without cause and havily indebted. (9) High-minded, chief of the tribe, vanquishing foes, adept in poetry and fine arts, king's favourite and happy with wife and children. (10) Enduring hardships, happy, destroyer of enemies, possessing wind and phlegm in the constitution, wedded to a bad wife and having a despicable family. (11) Gets agitated, knows politics, suffers from diseases, runs after women, spoils his own vows, behaves meanly and does little work. (12) Learned, supporter of family, getting wealth from the king and agriculture, prominent and charming in appearance. He may establish a water-shed or sink wells for the benefit of the public. Best results can be expected in the Daśā of Venus when he occupies his exaltation identical with the 10th, 11th or 12th house without the aspect of or conjunction with malefics.

Saturn brings about the following effects during his period : Severe afflictions to one's wife and children through rheumatism and such other wind diseases, loss of crops, improper talk, drowsiness, cohabitation with a wicked woman, emaciation, desertion of servants, going away from home, sudden loss of one's kith and kin, lands wealth and happiness, acquisition of wealth as a result of some turmoil and fighting in the country, of old women and servants, cows and buffaloes, phlegmatic complaints, piles and burning sensation in the feet, hands and all over the body. The person sometimes becomes a big leader of men, wise, popular, mayor of a city or minister, knower of rules and more famous than his father. (1) In Aries the effects are : wandering, working under others, fall, suffering from skin-disease in the feet and other limbs, deceitful and bereft of brothers and kinsmen. (2) In Taurus, one becomes very famous, intelligent, king or king's equal, devoted to Dharma and participates in battles. (3) One is without forbearance, enjoys pleasures and wealth as well as the company of children, loses wealth through theft or women, works for others and is troubled in battles. (4) He is worried, a dependent, without mother, friends and issue, intelligent and suffering from weakness of eye-sight and hearing. (5) He is afflicted with many diseases, has quarrels with wife, children and relations, and possessed of cattle, horses and wealth. (6) He is learned, earning by hard labour, spoiling trees and water, and liked by elders, Brahmins and Yogins. (7) The major, period of exalted Saturn makes one rich in wisdom, wealth and power, learned, getting wealth easily, and happy. (8) One is engaged in murders and imprisonment, in useless wanderings, uttering falsehood, miserliness, mercilessness, and eking out his livelihood by the favour of low-class persons. (9) One becomes happy, healthy, honoured by kings or a king himself, comes by live-stock, wealth etc., lives in the company of his near and dear ones, and takes active part in wars. (10) He earns money by dint of hard work, looks attractive, becomes the favourite of barren and old women, and loses money through confidence-trick. (11) He enjoys pleasures, becomes leader of his tribe, intelligent and blessed with sons, agricultural produce, cattle and wealth. (12) He earns money with little effort, becomes mayor of a city, head of a villge or community, respected by women and yet eager for liberation. When Saturn is eclipsed (There is one view according to which the combustion of Saturn and Venus does not impair their strength), his Daśā will enable the subject just to balance his budget, make him discontented; his reputation will rise very high and suddenly collapse, and he will be tormented by manifold sufferings.

Rāhu's Daśā generally creates trouble from the king, thieves, poison, fire and weapons, illness of children and wife, mental aberration, death of relatives, humiliation at the hands of mean fellows, scandal as a result of breach of etiquette, loss of position, wound in the feet (or kicks) and failure of undertakings. It may also generate wickedness, a terrible disease which cannot be diagnosed, trouble from enemies, diseases of the eyes and head, loss of crops and misunderstandings with friends.

Should Rāhu be conjoined with a benefic, and posited in an auspicious house (i.e. other than the 6th, 8th or 12th), his major period would be beneficial, in that it would bring prosperity equal to that of a monarch, great reputation, success in works and happy life with family. Rāhu's period will be good, if at birth he occupies Virgo, Scorpio or Pisces. The subject is likely to enjoy honour, happiness, lordship of a country (such as governorship), servants and vehicles. All these, however, are liable to be lost at the end of the period. Note that the period of the benefic in conjunction with Rāhu will yield unfavourable results, especially at its end.

Ketu creates in his period troubles from enemies, thieves, rulers, weapons, diseases caused by excessive heat, false charges, stigma to the family, danger from fire, absence from one's native land, sorrow and confusion on account of women, loss of money, commission of offences, diseases of the teeth and feet as well as phlegmatic ailments.

Rāhu and Ketu confer prosperity on a person in their periods, if they are posited in an angle or trine and are connected (in one of five ways) with the lord of either of the two.

Sub-periods

As I have already told you each Daśā has nine sub-divisions or Bhuktis. While reading the following effects of these sub-periods you will do well to remember the general principles enunciated at the beginning of this chapter.

Major Lord — Sun

(*i*) *Bhukti-lord, Sun* :— See the effects of the Sun's Daśā.

(*ii*) *Bhukti-lord Moon* :— Destruction of enemies, end of sorrow, accession of wealth, agriculture, building of houses, meeting of friends, water-disease, consumption and fire-accidents.

(*iii*) *Mars* :— Sickness, ulcers, trouble from enemies, loss of position and money, enmity with relatives, trouble from the government.

(*iv*) *Rāhu* :— New enemies, theft of money, danger from poison, loss of sensation, and diseases of eyes and head.

(*v*) *Jupiter* :— Eradication of enemies, acquisition of all kinds of wealth, worship of Gods and revered persons, earache, and pulmonary ailment.

(*vi*) *Saturn* :— Loss of wealth, separation from children, illness of wife, heavy expenditure, death of elders, loss of servants, clothes etc., slovenliness and phlegmatic trouble.

(*vii*) *Mercury* :— Scabies, boils, jaundice, leprosy, foul gas, pain in the stomach and hips, loss of land, ailments caused by the three humours.

(*viii*) *Ketu* :—Loss of friends, quarrels with kinsmen and family, danger from enemies, theft of money, loss of position, illness of father and severe pain in the head and feet.

(*ix*) *Venus* :— Headache, stomach-ache, piles, agriculture, loss of house, wealth and corn and sickness of wife and children.

Major lord, — Moon

(*i*) *Moon* :— Birth of a daughter, accession of white silk, meeting of great Brahmins, mother's happiness, conjugal happiness.

(*ii*) *Mars* :— Ailments caused by the vitiation of bile, blood and fire, hardships, sufferings, trouble from enemies and thieves and loss of wealth and honour.

(*iii*) *Rāhu* :— Rise of faults and enemies, illness of a relation, danger from wind and lightning and fever due to bad food and drinks.

(*iv*) *Jupiter* :— Doing charity and religious acts, happiness, accession of clothes and ornaments, company of friends and royal favour.

(*v*) *Saturn* :— Many ailments, great sorrow by the illness of wife, children and friends, or death itself.

(*vi*) *Mercury* :— Acquisition of wealth, cattle, elephants, horses, ornaments, happiness, and enlightenment.

(*vii*) *Ketu* :— Mental disease, loss of wealth and relatives, danger from water, and trouble to servants.

(*viii*) *Venus* :— Voyages, acquisition of wealth, woman and ornaments, agriculture, business transactions, birth of a child (or meeting children), meeting friends and gain of cattle and corn.

(*ix*) *Sun* :— Heroism, honour from the king, recovery from illness, destruction of enemies, and diseases of the nature of bile and wind.

Major lord — Mars

(*i*) *Mars* :— See the general effects of the period.

(*ii*) *Rāhu* :— Danger from weapons, fire, enemies, poison and thieves, diseases of the belly, eyes and head, death of elders and relatives, or one's own death.

(*iii*) *Jupiter* :— Religious activities, pilgrimage, entertainment of guests, increase of sons, friends etc., ear-ache or phlegmatic trouble.

(*iv*) *Saturn* :— Untold sufferings to self, elders, wife and children, loss of money, intense grief, trouble from enemies, excessive heat, wind and fire.

(*v*) *Mercury* :— Trouble from enemies and thieves, loss of wealth, cattle and elephants, confrontation with enemies, harrassment from rulers and quarrel with Śūdras or labourers.

(*vi*) *Ketu* :— Danger from lightning, unexpected trouble from fire and weapons, loss of money, absence from house, death of wife or of oneself.

(*vii*) *Venus* :— Defeat in battle or litigation, going away from one's country, theft of wealth, pain in the left eye and desertion of servants.

(*viii*) *Sun* :— Honour from the king, fame in battle, acquisition of wealth, corn, retinue, beautiful harem, happy life and prosperity through valour.

(*ix*) *Moon* :— Gain of wealth, birth of a child, riddance of enemies, acquisition of clothes, gems, bed and ornaments, illness of elders, enlargement of spleen or excess of bile.

Major lord — Rāhu

(*i*) *Rāhu* :— Sight of snakes, illness caused by poison and water, association with another woman, loss of friends, foul words and trouble from the wicked.

(*ii*) *Jupiter* :— Happiness, religious functions, sound health, association of charming ladies and philosophical or Śastraic discussions.

(*iii*) *Saturn* :— Wounds, illness of the nature of wind and bile, quarrels with near and dear ones and loss of servants and position.

(*iv*) *Mercury* :— Birth of a child, accession of wealth, association with friends, impure thoughts, clever activities, ornaments etc.

(*v*) *Ketu* :— Danger from fever, fire, enemies and weapons, headache, convulsion, trouble to elders and friends, suffering caused by poison and ulcers, and quarrels with friends.

(*vi*) *Venus* :— Marriage, comforts of the couch, accession of vehicles and lands, affliction through phlegm and wind and enmity with relatives.

(*vii*) *Sun* :— Trouble from king and enemies, eye-disease, suffering through poison, fire and weapons, and sickness of near and dear ones.

(*viii*) *Moon* :— Death of wife, quarrels, mental agony, agricultural operations, loss of money, cattle children, and friends, and danger from water.

(*ix*) *Mars* :— Loss of position, heart-trouble, eye-disease, danger from rulers, fire, thieves and weapons or death itself.

Major lord — Jupiter

(*i*) *Jupiter* :— All the good effects mentioned against his major period.

(*ii*) *Saturn* :— Company of harlots, intoxicating drinks, rising to eminence, happiness, trouble to wife, children and cattle, heavy expenditure, great fear and eye-disease.

(*iii*) *Mercury* :— Addiction to women, wine and gambling and illness born of the three humours — This is according to some, but according to others only good things such as worship of gods, and Brahmins, association with sons, happiness and prosperity will be enjoyed.

(*iv*) *Ketu* :— Wounds caused by weapons, enmity with servants, mental agony, trouble to children and wife, separation from elders and friends and danger to one's own life.

(*v*) *Venus* :— Acquisition of various articles, cattle, corn, clothes, servants, wife, children, food and drinks, couch and ornaments, religious activities and observances.

(*vi*) *Sun* :— Subdual of enemies, fame, honour from kings, hot temper, acquisition of servants and vehicles, and custodianship of the wealth of a guild, village, city or state.

(*vii*) *Moon* :— Many damsels, destruction of enemies, gain of wealth, grains and exceptional reputation, and interest in religious observances.

(*viii*) *Mars* :— Pleasing relatives, gain of wealth from enemies, good lands, honour and power, trouble to elders, or injury to eyes.

(*ix*) *Rāhu* :— Suffering among relations, intense mental anguish, sickness, fear of thieves, father's illness or stomach disease, trouble from the government and enemies, and one's own death (or loss of money).

Major lord — Saturn

(*i*) *Saturn* :— Increase in agriculture, servants and buffaloes, wind-disease, wealth through a Śūdra or one of low caste, friendship of an old woman, laziness and sinful activities.

(*ii*) *Mercury* :— Happiness, personal charm, woman, royal favour, victory, company of friends, ailments born of the three humours and sickness of brothers and children.

(*iii*) *Ketu* :— Suffering on account of wind, fire and enemies, quarrels with wife and sons, sight of inauspicious things and danger from snakes.

(*iv*) *Venus* :— Happiness, company of friends, wife and children, wealth through agriculture or voyage and spotless fame. (According to Kālidāsa the above effects are applicable only when one of the two viz. Saturn and Venus, is strong or both weak, whereas if both are strong, even a monarch or Kubera will be reduced to beggary).

(*v*) *Sun* :— Death or danger from enemies, sickness among elders, stomach and eye troubles and loss of money and corn.

(*vi*) *Moon* :— Wife's or one's own death, suffering among friends, diseases and danger from wind and water.

(*vii*) *Mars* :— Loss of position, quarrel with one's own people, sickness or fever, danger from fire, poison or weapon, increase of enemies, hernia and eye-disease.

(*viii*) *Rāhu* :— Going astray, death or danger from diabetes and enlargement of spleen, continuous fever and wounds.

(*ix*) *Jupiter* :— Interest in worship of Gods and company of the learned, happy life at home in the company of wife and children and great increase of wealth and corn.

Major lord — Mercury

(*i*) *Mercury* :— All the good effects mentioned against the Daśā.

(*ii*) *Ketu* :— Grief, quarrel, perplexity, convulsion of the body, association with enemies and loss of lands and vehicles.

(*iii*) *Venus* :— Worship of Gods, Brahmins and teachers, doing charity and meritorious deeds and acquisition of friends, clothes and ornaments.

(*iv*) *Sun* :— Honour from the sovereign and a house along with gold, corals, elephants, horses, excellant food and drinks.

(*v*) *Moon* :— Headache, inflammation in the eyes, leprosy, itches, severe pain in the neck and danger to life.

(*vi*) *Mars* :— Danger from fire, eye-diseases, fear of thieves, misery, loss of position and rheumatic ailment.

(*vii*) *Rāhu* :— Humiliation, loss of patron, loss of wealth, risk from fire, poison and water and pain in the head, eyes and stomach.

(*viii*) *Jupiter* :— Freedom from ailments and fear of enemies, realization of the Supreme (or sound learning in the Vedas), honour from the king and success in penance and religious performances.

(*ix*) *Saturn* :— Destruction of religious merit and wealth, frustration of all undertakings and diseases caused by the vitiation of wind and phlegm.

Major lord — Ketu

(*i*) *Ketu* :— Quarrels with enemies and friends, hearing inauspicious tidings, fever, burning sensation all over the body, going abroad and loss of wealth.

(*ii*) *Venus* :— Quarrel with a noble Brahmin, misunderstanding with one's own wife and kinsmen, birth of a daugher, humiliation and annoyance from others.

(*iii*) *Sun* :— Death of father (teacher or elder), fever, hostility of relatives, going abroad, fight against the king, and trouble through vitiation of phlegm and wind.

(*iv*) *Moon* :— Windfalls and sudden loss of wealth, separation from one's son, child-birth accompanied by severe labour pains, birth of a daughter, and acquisition of servants.

(*v*) *Mars* :— Quarrels with one's family-members, destruction of a relative and danger from snakes, thieves, fire and enemies.

(*vi*) *Rāhu* :— Quarrels with enemies, trouble from the king, fire and thieves, fear of snakes, hearing the words of the wicked, and undesirable activities like black magic.

(*vii*) *Jupiter* :— Birth of a son, worship of gods, acquisition of lands, wealth (or treasure), presents and honour from the king.

(*viii*) *Saturn* :— Destruction of servants, trouble from enemies and fight with them, breaking of limbs and loss of wealth and status.

(*ix*) *Mercury* :— Birth of a son, appreciation from a big lord, acquisition of wealth and lands, trouble from the leader of enemies and loss of crops and cattle (or animals).

Major lord — Venus

(*i*) *Venus* :— Enjoyment of clothes, ornaments, vehicles, scents, pleasures of the couch, bodily splendour, and wealth from kings.

(*ii*) *Sun* :— Diseases of the eyes, stomach and cheeks, danger from the ruler and trouble to elders and relatives.

(*iii*) *Moon* :— Intense pain in the head, teeth and nails, diseases born of wind and phlegm, loss of wealth, and sickness through diarrhoea, enlargement of the spleen and consumption.

(*iv*) *Mars* :— Ailments caused by vitiation of blood and bile, acquisition of gold, copper and lands, seduction of a young woman and loss of job.

(*v*) *Rāhu* :— Acquisition of a treasure, birth of a son, pleasant speech, respect of one's own kinsmen, captivity under an enemy and trouble from fire, thieves and poison.

(*vi*) *Jupiter* :— Meritorious deeds, worship of Gods, union with children and wife and various royal pleasures.

(*vii*) *Saturn* :— Honour from citizens, military and king, acquisition of an excellent damsel, wealth and various materials of luxury. (See also the special remarks under Saturn-Venus period).

(*viii*) *Mercury* :— Children's happiness, influx of much wealth, great authority, fame, destruction of enemies and sickness of the nature of the three humours.

(*ix*) *Ketu* :— Loss of happiness and children, danger from fire, great losses, pain all over the body and association with courtezans.

All the remarks made above should be judiciously adopted according to the positions, strength, aspect etc. of planets as well as the status, caste etc. of the person concerned.

Note :— While examining the nature of Daśās and Bhuktis you should bear in mind the principle that these periods of planets will not be favourable if they own or are posited in the 3rd, 5th or 7th star from the natal one. So is the period of the planet that owns the Sign that is the 8th from the natal Moon. Similarly Saturn's Daśā will be bad, if it is the 4th in order; Jupiter's, if it is the 6th and those of Mars and Rāhu, if the 5th.

Chapter XII

YOGAS

Nābhasa Yogas :— These Heavenly Yogas are of four kinds viz. Ākṛti or diagrammatical, Saṅkhyā or numerical, Āśraya or positional and Dala or bilateral. ĀKṚTI yogas have 20 varieties in all. I shall now define these Ākṛti yogas and explain their effects succinctly. *Gadā* : This means a Mace. Here all the planets should occupy adjacent Kendras i.e. they may be (i) in the 1st and 4th houses, (ii) in the 4th and 7th houses, (iii) in 7th and 10th houses, and (iv) in 10th and 1st houses. *Effects* : One who is born with the Gadā yoga will be wealthy, will perform sacrifices and be intent on amassing wealth. *Śakaṭa* : All planets should be in the 1st and the 7th houses. *Effects* : The person concerned will be a coach-driver, sickly and having a bad wife. *Vihaga* or *Pakṣin*. It means a bird. All planets in this yoga should be in the 4th and 10th houses : *Effects* : The person will earn his living as a messenger, will be of wandering habits and quarrelsome. *Śriṅgāṭaka* : All planets should be in the 1st, 5th and 9th houses. *Effects* : The subject will be sweet-tongued and be happy in his old age. *Hala* or *Plough* : All planets should be in (i) 2nd, 6th and 10th houses, (ii) 3rd, 7th and 11th houses, or (iii) 4th, 8th and 12th houses. This means that the planets should be in mutual trines beginning with any house other than the Lagna. He will be an agriculturist, poor, gluttonous, messenger, grief-stricken and deserted by his kinsmen. *Vajrayoga* : All benefics should be in the 1st and 7th houses, and all malefics in the 4th and 10th houses. In this Yoga benefics will be in opposition to benefics and malefics to malefics. *Effects* : He will be brave, handsome, healthy, but luckless, hated by kinsmen and happy in the initial and final portions of life. *Yava* : This is the reverse of Vajrayoga i.e. all malefics should be in the 1st and 7th houses and benefics in 4th and 10th. *Effects* : He will be engaged in observing vows and performing religious rites, charitable, wealthy, but happy and moneyed only in the middle portion of his life. *Kamala* : All the planets should be posited in the four Kendras in any manner. *Effects* : The person will be very famous, virtuous, long-lived, handsome and wielding power. *Vāpī* : All the planets should occupy the four Paṇaphara (succedent) or the four Āpoklima (cadent) houses. *Effects* : He will hoard his money, be miserly, and have some unenduring happiness. *Yūpa* : All the planets should occupy the 1st, 2nd, 3rd and 4th houses. *Effects* : He will be charitable, wealthy, happy, illustrious, truthful and observing vows. *Iṣu* or *Śara* : All the planets should be posited in the 4th, 5th, 6th and 7th houses. *Effects* : He will be engaged in manufacturing arrows, imprisoning thieves, hunting and wandering in forests. He will also be cruel and a bad artisan. *Śakti* : All the planets should be in the 7th, 8th, 9th and 10th houses. *Effects* : He will be mean, indolent, indigent, grief-stricken. and short-lived. *Daṇḍa* : All the planets should be in the 10th, 11th, 12th and 1st. houses. *Effects* : He will be without wife, children and wealth; will be condemned by all and deserted by his kith and kin, will be mean, miserable and in servitude. *Nau* : All planets should be in the seven houses beginning with the Lagna and ending with the 7th house. *Effects* : The person concerned will amass wealth through a profession relating to water, will be famous, strong, greedy and unsteady. *Kūṭa* : All planets should be in the seven contiguous houses beginning with the 4th. *Effects* : The person will be cruel, poor, roguish, a gambler, liar, jailor and dwelling in a mountain fortress. *Chatra* : All planets should be placed in the seven houses beginning with the 7th house. *Effects* : He will be kind-hearted, charitable, of noble disposition, favourite of kings, helping his kinsmen, and be happy and fortunate in the initial and final portions of life. *Cāpa* : All the planets are to be in the 7 houses from the 10. *Effects* : The person will be a liar, thief, jailor, gambler, dwelling in forests, and unlucky in the middle portion of life. *Ardhacandra* : All the planets are to be in the 7 houses beginning from the 4 Paṇaphara or the 4 Āpoklima houses. *Effects* : He will be handsome, commander of an army, of prepossessing manners, favourite of kings, strong and possessed of gems and gold ornaments. *Samudra* : All the planets should be in the 6 even houses viz. 2, 4, 6, 8, 10 and 12. *Effects* : He will be endowed with wealth, sons and enjoyment of pleasures, popular, powerful and equal to a king. *Cakra* : All the planets should be posited in the 6 odd Bhāvas i.e. 1, 3, 5, 7, 9 and 11. *Effects* : He will receive the homage of kings and become a mighty monarch. Thus we have seen the 20 Ākṛti yogas. From the definition of these yogas you must have come to understand that in all these the planets are to be posited in definite geometric patterns.

Saṅkhyāyogas :— These are Numerical yogas based on the number of Rāśis (not Bhāvas) occupied by the 7 planets. You may in this connection remember that some of these Numerical Yogas coincide with some of the Ākṛtiyogas. In such cases you have to designate the yogas by their Ākṛtiyoga names only. The Saṅkhyāyogas are seven in number. They ae (1) *Vallakī* or *Vīṇā* when all the 7 planets are separately situated in 7 Signs (not Bhāvaṣ), (2) *Dāminī* when they are posited in 6 Rāśis, (3) *Pāśa* when they are in 5 Rāśis, (4) *Kedāra* when they are in 4 Rāśis, (5) *Śūla* when they are in 3 Rāśis, (6) *Yuga* when they are only in two Signs, and (7) *Golaka* when all the planets are crowded in a single Sign. Now I shall give the effects of these in order. *Effects of Vallakī* or *Vīṇā* : The person concerned will have many friends, will speak sweetly, be well versed in the scriptures and instrumental music, happy, and will have many servants. *Dāminī* : He will help others, will be wealthy, full of cattle, brave, learned and blessed with children and gems. *Pāśa* : He will be active, talkative, characterless, having many servants and ultimately be imprisoned. *Kedāra* : He will be helpful to many, an agriculturist, truthful, happy, wealthy but of changing moodṣ. *Śūla* : He will be cruel, terrible, lazy, poor, murderous, brave, and a noted warrior. *Yuga* : The person will be a heretic, poor, ostracized by society, and bereft of children, honour, and virtue. *Golaka* : He will be poor, indolent, without education and honour, unclean, and always sad and wretched. From the above description you would be able to say that the Yogas Gadā, Pakṣin (Vihaga) and Śakaṭa of the Ākṛti group are nothing but different types of Yugayoga. Similarly Śṛṅgāṭaka and Hala are only varieties of Śūlayoga. The Yogas Vajra, Yava, Kamala, Vāpī, Yūpa, Iṣu, Śakti and Daṇḍa are varieties of Kedāra. Yogas Nau, Kūṭa, Chatra, Cāpa and Ardhacandra are particular instances of Vīṇāyoga. Samudra and Cakra are special forms of Dāmayoga.

Āśrayayogas which are three in number viz. Rajju, Musala, and Nala, are based on the nature of the Signs occupied by the planets. When Āśrayayogas coincide with Ākṛtiyogas the former are not taken into consideration. But if there is coincidence between the Āśraya and Saṅkhyāyogas, the former should prevail except in the case of Golakayoga. *Rajjuyoga* is formed when the planets are exclusively posited in the movable Rāśis. In these yogas there is no consideration of the Bhāvas. *Effects* : The person concerned will be fond of wandering, will earn wealth in foreign countries, be handsome, cruel and roguish in character. *Musalayoga* : In this all the planets are to be in fixed Signs. *Effects* : He will be active, famous, favourite of kings, heroic, of firm mind and endowed with honour, wealth and knowledge. *Nalayoga* : All the planets are to be in dual Rāśis. *Effects* : He will have either one limb in excess or one less, will have plenty of hoarded wealth, be clever, helpful to kinsmen, and handsome in appearance.

The *Dalayogas* which are only two are based on the nature of the Bhāvas (not Rāśis) and of the planets occupying them. *Srak* or *Mālā* yoga is formed when all the three benefics viz. Mercury, Jupiter and Venus, are posited only in Kendras. In regard to this Dalayoga the Moon is not taken into consideration. So we have three benefics and three malefics. *Effects of Mālā* : He will command all kinds of pleasures, vehicles, garments, riches and happiness, be handsome, and have many loving wives. *Sarpa* : This is formed by the three malefics occupying only Kendras. *Effects* : One will be cross, cruel, poor, wretched, despondent, a drunkard and eater in other's houses. There is yet another point which you should remember in connection with these Nābhasayogas : They take effect throughout the life-time of the subject irrespective of the ruling major Daśā period and sub-period. In our example chart there is one Nābhasayoga only viz. Dāminī, of the Numeral yogas.

Cāndrayogas

In this section I am going to deal with the Yogas that arise from the position of planets with respect to the Moon or vice versa. *Adhamayoga* (Worst) :— If the Moon is posited in a Kendra with respect to the Sun in a natal chart, the resulting yoga is termed Adhama. This may happen in one of four ways : The Moon may be conjoined with the Sun, she may be in the 4th, 7th or the 10th from the Sun. As the name indicates the effects are very bad : The subject's moral calibre will be very low, his financial position deplorable, wisdom practically absent and intellectual powers very meagre. *Sama* or *Madhya* yoga is caused when the Moon is situated in a Paṇaphara house from the Sun. The effect is that the moral calibre etc. mentioned above will be moderate. *Variṣṭha* or Best yoga is formed when the Moon is posited in an Āpoklima house from the Sun. The result is the best position of morals etc. If the Moon posited in her own Aṁśa or in that of a great friend, is aspected by Jupiter, if the birth be in daytime, or by Venus, if the birth be at night, the subject will be very happy and opulent.

Candra Adhiyoga : This yoga is formed when the benefics, Mercury, Jupiter and Venus, are posited in the 6th, 7th and 8th houses from the Moon. It may happen that the benefics may be distributed among these three houses, or they may be in two of the houses or in one of them. The effects of this yoga will be fully realized if in this configuration the benefics are quite strong and are not afflicted by malefics through association or aspect. *Effects* : The subject will become commander of an army, minister or a king. He will live long without diseases and risks, enjoying great prosperity, power and victory over his enemies. In the same manner there is also the *Lagnādhiyoga* formed when the benefics are posited in the above-mentioned houses with respect to the Lagna. The effects of this too are similar to those of the Candrādhiyoga.

Sunaphā : This is formed when there is any planet excluding the Sun in the 2nd house from the Moon. *Anaphā* : This is formed when there is any planet, excluding the Sun, in the 12th house from her. *Durudharā* is formed when there are planets both in the 2nd and 12th houses. According to another view these three yogas are formed in order when threre are planets in the 4th, 10th and both the houses from the Moon. There is yet another view according to which these three yogas are caused by the presence of planets in the 2nd, 12th and both the Rāśis from the one which is the Navāṁśa Rāśi of the Moon. In the absence of these three yogas an unlucky yoga called *Kemadruma* is brought into existence. Now let me give the *Effects of Sunaphā* : The person born with this Yoga will be prosperous, mighty, of virtuous disposition, very famous, well versed in Śāstras, attractive on account of his superior qualities, serene, happy, king or minister and very wise. *Effects of Anaphā* : He will be an eloquent speaker, rich, lordly, free from diseases, of good character, famous, of happy and contented mind, well-dressed and enjoyer of good dishes, drinks, garlands and damsels. *Effects of Durudharā* : He will become famous for the qualities of his speech, wisdom and valour throughout the world, will enjoy independence, happiness, wealth, vehicles and pleasures, will be generous, will take pains to look after his kith and kin as well as his property, be of good character and a leader of men. *Effects of Kemadruma* : The person concerned though born in a royal family would lose his wife, friends, houses, clothes and food, be oppressed by poverty, misery, diseases and wretchedness. He will also be unclean, in servitude, roguish and one whose conduct is hated by one and all. At this juncture it is appropriate for you to know that there are some important exceptions to the Kemadruma Yoga. If there is any planet except the Sun in any one of the Kendras from the ascendant or the Moon or if the Moon is conjoined with any of the five planets beginning with Mars, there is no Kemadruma. Similarly if all the planets aspect the moon, then too the Kemadruma is nullified. In addition to the effects given for these yogas there are certain other features which accrue to the native according to the planet that occupies the 12th or 2nd house from the Moon. If Mars is one of the planets situated in the 12th or 2nd house from the Moon, the person will be energetic, heroic, wealthy and adventurous; if it is Mercury in such a position, he will be clever, of sweet words and proficient in arts; if it is Jupiter, he will be wealthy, religiously inclined, happy and honoured by kings; if it is Venus, he will be very rich enjoying all the pleasures of senses; and if it is Saturn, he will enjoy himself with others' wealth, clothes etc., will have many activities and be a leader of men.

Another Yoga is based on the Moon's position in one of the two halves of the zodiac according to the time of birth. If the birth is at night and if the Moon is in the visible half of the zodiac i.e. in one of the houses from the 7th to the 1st, the result is very auspicious. Suppose the Moon is in the invisible half for the same birth, it is very bad for the native. For a day birth if the Moon is in the invisible half, she will bestow good fortune. There is another yoga based on the position of benefics in the Upacaya houses. If all the four benefics, Moon, Mercury,

Jupiter and Venus, are posited in Upacaya houses, 3, 6, 10 and 11, counted from the Lagna, the person will be *immensely* rich; if three benefics are in such houses counted from the Moon, he will be wealthy; if there are only two benefics, he will be moderately rich; if it is a single benefic, his wealth will be meagre. Ancient authorities consider this *Upacaya* yoga to be very important and unerring in its effect. According to another authority *Vasumat* yoga is caused when all the benefics are posited in Upacaya houses counted from the Lagna or the Moon. The effect of this yoga in addition to what has been given already is that the person will live always in his own house. *Amalā* yoga is caused by the presence of benefics in the 10th house counted from the Lagna or the Moon. Its effects are kingship, wealth, sons, fame and good morals or policy. *Puṣkalayoga* is brought about by the lord of the Sign occupied by the Moon occupying a Kendra (with respect to the Lagna) which must belong to a very friendly planet, along with the lord of the Lagna, when a benefic aspects the Lagna. *Effects* : The person will be wealthy, famous, honoured by great kings, having beautiful ornaments and garments, sweet-tongued, ideal and a lord.

There are some Yogas that are similar to Sunaphā etc. where the reference-planet is the Moon, whereas here it is the Sun. In those three yogas you were asked to ignore the Sun. Here you are asked to ignore the Moon. If benefic planets (except the Moon) occupy the 2nd, 12th and both the houses with respect to the Sun, the resulting three yogas are respectively called *Śubhavesi*, *Śubhavāsi* and *Śubha-Ubhayacarī*. But if these planets are malefic, the three Yogas will be called *Pāpavesi*, *Pāpavāsi* and *Pāpa-Ubhayacarī* respectively. When there are benefics on either side of the Lagna i.e. in the 12th and the 2nd houses, the resulting yoga is termed *Śubhakartarī*. If malefics occupy these houses, the yoga is called *Pāpakartarī*. If there are benefics in the 2nd house from the Lagna unaspected by malefics, the Yoga is called *Suṣubha*. Now I shall give the effects of these yogas in order. *Effects of Śubhavesi* : The person will be very handsome, happy, a paragon of virtues, brave and a king. *Śubhavāsi* : He will be famous, liked by all, very attractive, munificent and king's favourite. *Śubhobhayacarī* : He will have beautiful limbs, will speak sweetly, be an appreciator of beauty, eloquent, famous and wealthy. *Pāpavesi* : He will scandalize others, lose his splendour or appetite, love the mean and be wicked. *Pāpavāsi* : He will be deceitful, will abuse others, be in the company of rogues, wicked and yet quoting the scriptures. *Pāpobhayacarī* : He will be sad at heart owing to bad name in public and be bereft of education, wealth and fortune. *Śubhakartarī* : He will live long, be free from dangers, diseases and enemies, happy and rich. *Pāpakartarī* : He will be shortlived, indigent, unclean, without happiness, wife and children. He will also be short of a limb.

I have mentioned above that the Moon produces good or bad yoga according to her position in the visible or invisible half of the zodiac. Now another yoga similar to that but more broad-based than that is given. That is called the ***Mahābhāgya*** yoga. If the native is *Male* and time of birth *Day* all the three viz. the Sun, Moon and the Lagna should be in *odd* Rāśis. In the case of a *Female* the time must be *night* and the three significators must be posited in *even* Rāśis. What are the effects of this grand yoga ? They are : If it is a male, he will give delight to all by his mere appearance, be munificent, renowed, a king and pure, living for 80 years. A woman having this yoga will enjoy plenty of wealth and long auspiciousness i.e. will live long and predecease her husband, be of ideal character, will be blessed with sons and grandsons and be very fortunate. *Kesari* or *Gajakesari* yoga : When the Moon is posited in a Kendra from Jupiter, this Yoga is brought about. *Effects* : The person will destroy his enemies like a lion, will speak eloquently and nobly in an assembly, have Rājasik (energetic and active) nature, live long, build up bright fame, be possessed of exceptional intellectual acumen and will become victorious by dint of his valour. *Śakaṭayoga* : This is different from the one we saw among the Ākṛtiyogas. This is brought about when the Moon is posited in the 6th, 8th or 12th place from Jupiter. However, there is an exception : If the Moon is posited in a Kendra house from the Lagna, Śakaṭayoga is nullified. *Effects of Śakaṭa* : His fortune will be fluctuating — sometimes he will lose every thing and after sometime make good the loss. He will not be a man of consequence in the world and will be miserable on account of some secret trouble which he cannot get rid of. There is another *Mālāyoga* different from the one mentioned in the context of Dalayogas. Here it is called *Śubhamālā*, because all the benefics are to be posited in regular order in the 5th, 6th and 7th houses from the Lagna. It is important in this yoga that all the three houses should be occupied by benefics. You can now compare this with the Lagnādhiyoga, where it is not absolutely necessary for the benefics to occupy all the three houses, 6, 7 and 8, at the same time, while in this yoga it is not so. *Effects of Śubhamālā*: The person will be a governor or a similar high officer of the State, praised by kings, will enjoy pleasures, give charity freely, help others in need, be fond of kinsmen, blessed with worthy sons and wife, and be brave. Opposed to this yoga there is one called *Aśubha Mālā* which is formed when these benefics are posited in regular order in the three bad houses viz. 6th, 8th and 12th. *Effects* : He will be addicted to bad ways, miserable, ungrateful, a murderer, timid, without respect for Brahmins, quarrelsome and one cursed by the people. Another important Yoga is *Lakṣmī* yoga. When the lord of the 9th house and Venus are posited in Kendras or Koṇas identical with their own houses or exaltations, it is called *Lakṣmī* Yoga. In addition to this if the Moon is also aspected by Jupiter, the resulting Yoga is called *Gauri*. *Effects of Lakṣmīyoga* : The person will always enjoy the blessed company of his good and auspicious wife, be free from illness, be very rich, brilliant, protector of his kith and kin, an abode of the Grace of the Goddess Mahālakṣmī, will ride horses and elephants, will be carried in palanquins, best of kings, pleasing all his subjects and munificent in gifts. *Effects of Gauriyoga* : He will have a charming personality, will belong to an illustrious family, be a friend of kings, possessed of obedient and virtuous children; his face will resemble the lotus and his victories will be eulogized by one and all. *Sarasvatīyoga* is caused when the three benefics, Mercury, Jupiter and Venus, are posited in Kendras, Koṇas or the 2nd house which should happen to be their own houses or exaltations or the houses of friends. In addition to this Jupiter should be possessed of strength. *Effects* of this Yoga : He will be very intelligent, clever in dramaturgy, prose compositions, poetry, mathematics and rhetorics, a poet, a great scholar in the Śāstras, very famous throughout the world, very rich, blessed with wife and children, fortunate and honoured by great sovereigns. There is another yoga called Śaradā which is quite different from Sarasvati. This *Sāradāyoga* is formed under the following conditions : The lord of the 10th house must be in the 5th house, Mercury in a Kendra, the Sun being strong in his own house, Jupiter in a Koṇa from the Moon or the 11th house from Mercury, and Mars in a Koṇa from Mercury. The effects of this Yoga are practically the same as those of Sarasvatī. After you have understood the Yoga bearing the names of the three Goddesses it will be easy for you to know those bearing the names of their consorts. Accordingly you have yogas such as the Śrīnātha, Śrikaṇṭha and Viriñci or Brahmā. *Śrīnāthayoga* is formed when the lord of the 9th house, Venus and Mercury are in Kendras or Koṇas identical with their own, exaltation or friendly houses. From this definition you can easily understand that the yoga of the husband-God is obtained by a slight extension of that of the wife-Goddess. *Effects of Śrīnāthayoga* : The person becomes wealthy, clever in pleasantries and sweet speech, is possessed of marks on his body resembling conch, discus etc. recites always verses in praise of the Lord in the company of His devotees, worships His devotees with zeal, is blessed with worthy wife and sons, pleasing in appearance and very amiable. *Śrīkaṇṭhayoga* — this word means Lord Śiva — is formed if the lord of the Lagna, the Sun and Moon are all in Kendras or Koṇas identical with their own, friendly or exaltation houses. *Effects* : The person concerned will be adorned with Rudrākṣa rosaries and the holy ashes, magnanimous, meditating on the Lord Śiva always, will observe vows to please the Lord, help virtuous men, be tolerant of other religions, brilliant in appearance and taking delight in worshipping the Lord Śiva. *Viriñciyoga* is formed when Jupiter, Saturn and the lord of the 5th house are posited in Kendras or Koṇas identical with their own, exaltation or friendly houses. *Effects* : The person will be intent on getting the knowledge of the Supreme Brahman, very intelligent, virtuous, content, following the scriptural path, will have many disciples, will speak gently, be very rich, have wife and children, be long-lived, will have spiritual lustre, with senses under control and receiving respect and homage from kings. *Parivartanayogas* : When lords of two Bhāvas exchange their positions, the resulting yoga is termed Parivartanayoga in general. Altogether there are 66 such exchanges, some of which are formed by the lords of bad houses viz. 6, 8, 12. If the lord of the 12th exchanges position with that of any one of the remaining

11 houses, 11 kinds of *Dainyayoga* (yoga of misery) are formed. If the lord of the 6th does it with the lord of any one of 1, 2, 3, 4, 5, 7, 8, 9, 10 and 11 houses, *ten* kinds of Dainyayoga are formed. If the lord of the 8th house does the same with the lord of 1, 2, 3, 4, 5, 7, 9, 10 and 11 houses, *nine* kinds of Dainyayoga are formed. These three kinds of yoga come to 30 in all. If the lord of the 3rd exchanges position with that of any of 1, 2, 4, 5, 7, 9, 10 and 11 houses, *eight* kinds of *Khalayoga* are formed. So these 38 yogas are unfavourable. The *Effects of Dainyayoga* are : The person will be a fool, reviler, committing sinful acts, oppressed by enemies, speaking harshly, of wavering mind and having his undertakings always interrupted. *Effects of Khalayoga* are : The person will go astray; sometimes he will lose all his fortune and sometimes he will get much wealth; sometimes he will speak nicely and at other times harshly; at times he will be happy and at others miserable. The remaining 28 yogas are called *Mahāyogas.* They are caused thus : The lord of the Lagna exchanging position with the lord of any one of the following : 2, 4, 5, 7, 9, 10 and 11 = 7. The lord of the 2nd house doing it with the lord of any one of the 6 viz. 4, 5, 7, 9, 10 and 11 = 6. The lord of the 4th house doing it with that of any one of the 5 houses viz. 5, 7, 9, 10 and 11 = 5. The lord of the 5th doing it with that of any one of the four viz. 7, 9, 10 and 11 = 4. The lord of the 7th house doing it with that any one of the three houses, 9, 10 and 11 = 3. The lord of the 9th doing it with that of 10th or 11th house = 2. The lord of 10th exchanging position with that of the 11th = 1. *Effects of Mahāyoga* are : The person will be blessed by the Goddess of Fortune, be very rich, lordly, bedecked with excellent clothes and ornaments, will receive honours and authoritative position from the king and be blessed with good children and vehicles. In the example chart there is one instance of Parivartana between the lords of 7th and 10th. This is a Mahāyoga conferring many a benefit on the native, *Parvatayoga* : This yoga is formed thus : See where the lord of the Lagna is posited. If the lord of the latter house is in a Kendra or Koṇa identical with his own house or his exaltation, this yoga is caused. *Kāhala* yoga is an extension of the preceding yoga. Find where the last planet forming the Parvatayoga is posited. If the lord of that house is in a Kendra or Koṇa identical with his own or exaltation house,

Kāhala is brought into existence. *Effects of Parvata* : The subject will be a king having unimpaired wealth and happiness and will do things whose benefits will be eternally felt. *Effects of Kāhala* : The subject will be ever prospering, noble, cheerful, benevolent, wise and respectable.

Rājayoga : Though there are many Rājayogas (Vide Chapter XIII) an ordinary Rājayoga is now defined. It is formed by the conjunction of the lords of 9th and 10th houses in an auspicious house. You know that this yoga is a particular variety of those that are constituted by the combination of the lords of a Kendra and a Koṇa. If such a combination takes place in a good house, it is called *Śaṅkha* yoga. *Effects of Rājayoga* : The subject will be a king enjoying great pomp and power, being praised by the virtuous. *Effects of Śaṅkha* : He will be a king, enjoyer of pleasures and liberal in gifts.

There are 12 yogas caused by the lords of the 12 Bhāvas when they are bright and well placed and are in their own houses or exaltations, and when the concerned Bhāvas themselves are aspected or occupied by benefics. In other words, a Bhāva must have a benefic in it or it must be aspected by a benefic. Besides that its lord must be strong and in a good Bhāva which is either its own house or its exaltation. These 12 yogas are in order (1) Cāmara, (2) Dhenu, (3) Śaurya, (4) Jaladhi, (5) Chatra, (6) Astra, (7) Kāma, (8) Asura, (9) Bhāgya, (10) Khyāti, (11) Supārijāta, and (12) Musala. These names are practically self-explanatory and stand for the 12 Bhāvas. Now their effects are given in order : (1) The subject will steadily progress day by day, will be very attractive in appearance, famous, a leader of men, longlived and very prosperous. (2) He will enjoy good food and wealth, be very learned in all branches of knowledge, will have a large family, will be blessed with gold, jewels, money and corn like the God of wealth. (3) He will be honoured by his worthy and famous younger brothers, possessed of exceptional valour, wedded to his duty to the State and very famous like Śrī Rāma. (4) He will be rich in cattle, wealth and corn, will have a grand mansion full of relatives, a noble wife, jewels, beautiful garments, ornaments, a very respectable position, will be always happy, have many vehicles, be honoured by kings, devoted to Gods and Brahmins and will cause wells to be sunk and water-sheds to be put up by the road-side.

(5) He will have ideal family happiness, good personality, children and wealth, will be famous, scholarly, sweet-tongued, a minister of some king, respectable, and of a brilliant and sharp intelltect. (6) He will curb his powerful foes by his superior prowess, will be arrogant and cruel in his ways, having many scars on his limbs, with a strong body, and be quarrelsome. (7) He will be blessed with a good wife, children and relatives, not interested in others' wives, will be greater than his father on account of his superior virtues and very prosperous. (8) He will spoil others' work, become tale-bearer, selfish, poor, having forbidden cravings, will commit mean acts and be troubled by the effects of his own bad deeds. (9) He will be of ideal character, will obtain everlasting wealth, have royal paraphernalia like the chowries, will be bowed to by the public, will worship the *manes*, Gods and Brahmins, be of ideal conduct, raise the status of his family and be of a noble heart. (10) He will be a king protecting the virtuous and performing good deeds approved by the world, will be fortunate in respect of children, friends, wife and wealth and be very famous. (11) He will become a king, perform auspicious rituals constantly, hoard lots of wealth, have a good family, be learned and will listen to holy stories. (12) He will get money with much difficulty, will be humiliated, his wealth will be fluctuating, he will spend money only for legitimate purposes, will be unsteady and foolish and will go to heaven after death.

There is another set of 12 Yogas based upon the presence of the lords of the several Bhāvas in the bad houses viz. 6, 8, and 12. These are also caused by the aspect and association of malefics in the case of these 12 Bhāvas. I shall make this statement clear with an example : Let us suppose that in a horoscope the lord of the Lagna is posited in the 6th, 8th or the 12th Bhāva; or let the Lagna be aspected by or conjoined with a malefic. Then a bad Yoga, called *Avayoga* is brought into existence. You have to view the remaining Bhāvas and their lords in the same manner. The names of the twelve Yogas are, therefore : (1) *Avayoga*, (2) *Nisvayoga*, (3) *Mṛtiyoga*, (4) *Kuhūyoga*, (5) *Pāmarayoga*, (6) *Harṣayoga*, (7) *Duṣkṛtiyoga*, (8) *Saralayoga*, (9) *Nirbhāgyayoga*, (10) *Duryoga*, (11) *Daridrayoga*, and (12) *Vimalayoga*. Now I shall give the effects of these yogas in order. (1) The person born under the Avayoga will be quite insignificant, short-lived, utterly miserable, humiliated, associated with the wicked, of bad conduct, of an ugly body and of unstable position. (2) The Nisvayoga makes one a stranger to good words, have a barren wife, undesirable company, ugly eyes and teeth, bereft of intelligence, learning and wealth, his wealth being taken away by enemies. (3) Mṛtiyoga causes defeat at the hands of enemies, loss of brothers, shamelessness, loss of stamina and money, unnecessary trouble and worry arising from improper activities, and unnatural behaviour. (4) One born under Kuhūyoga will lose his mother, vehicles, friends, happiness, ornaments, relatives and position. His place will be destroyed and he will be attached to a woman of ill fame. (5) The Pāmarayoga makes one live a miserable life, indiscriminate, a liar, a cheat, lose his children or have no issue at all, an atheist, a glutton and resort to mean and wicked fellows. (6) Under the Harṣayoga one becomes blessed with happiness, enjoyments, good fortune, a strong physique, wealth, lustre, good friends, renown and sons. He will destroy his enemies, will be afraid of sins, and a favourite of prominent and illustrious personages. (7) The person born under the Duṣkṛtiyoga will lose his wife, will crave for the company of others' wives, will be ugly in appearance, will wander away, be afflicted with venereal diseases like gonorrhoea, will be troubled by the king, grief-stricken and despised by his relatives. (8) Saralayoga makes the native long-lived, resolute, fearless, prosperous, blessed with learning, wealth and sons, successfull over foes, very famous and successfull in his undertakings. (9) The person born under the Nirbhāgya-yoga will lose his paternal house, lands etc., will despise elders and the wise, will be a heretic, clad in tattered clothes, wretched, poor and miserable. (10) Under Duryoga one will have to labour hard for fruitless tasks, will be slighted by the people, will be a traitor to the people around, highly selfish and be a regular wanderer from home. (11) Under the Daridrayoga one becomes highly indebted, fierce, exceedingly penurious, will be suffering from ear-diseases, without love for his brothers, will be engaged in forbidden activities, will speak indecently and be a slave of others. (12) Lastly, the Vimalayoga makes one spend very little and save a lot of money, helpful to all, happy, independent, noted for his virtues and of a respectable profession. From the results enumerated above you must have observed that there are good effects mentioned in respect of only three Bhāvas viz. 6, 8 and 12. This shows that if the lord of one Dusthāna is posited in another Dusthāna, the effect becomes beneficial. This is on a par with the statement that two negatives make an affirmative.

There is another *Duryoga* which is formed thus : The lords of 6, 8 and 12 are very strong, and are posited in Kendras or Koṇas. In addition to this the lords of the Lagna, 4th, 9th and 10th houses must be weak, pale and posited in the Dusthānas. If this position is reversed i.e. the lords of the Dusthānas are weak and posited in those houses only, and the lords of 1, 4, 9 and 10 houses strong and posited in Kendras or Koṇas, the subject will be very fortunate, wealthy, happy, virtuous and a king.

Bhāskarayoga : If Mercury is in the 2nd house from the Sun, if the Moon is in the 11th house from Mercury and if Jupiter is in a Koṇa with reference to the Moon, the resulting Yoga is called *Bhāskara.* For example let us suppose that the Moon is in Pisces. Then the Sun should be in Aries, Mercury in Taurus and Jupiter either in Cancer or in Scorpio. *Effects* : The person concerned will be a hero, equal to a king, handsome, well-versed in Śāstras, wealthy, expert in music, brave, competent and proficient in mathematics.

Indrayoga : If Mars is posited in the 3rd house from the Moon, Saturn in the 7th from Mars, Venus in the 7th from Saturn and Jupiter in the 7th from Venus, the resulting yoga is called *Indra.* In this Yoga Mars and Venus would be together with Jupiter and Saturn in opposition. Of course the Moon would be in the 11th house from Mars and Venus and in the 5th from Jupiter and Saturn. *Effects* : The subject will be famous, virtuous, of good character, a king or his equal, eloquent in speech, and possessed of wealth, diverse ornaments, attractive features and prowess.

Marudyoga or *Vāyuyoga* : In this yoga Jupiter should be in a Koṇa from Venus, the Moon in the 5th from Jupiter and the Sun in a Kendra from the Moon. Let us start with Venus, say in Libra. Then Jupiter will be in Aquarius, the Moon in Gemini and the Sun in Virgo or Sagittarius. Cannot the Sun be in Pisces, as that too is a Kendra from the Moon ? No, because Venus and the Sun cannot be separated so much.

Effects : One born under this Yoga will be an orator, of a generous heart, with a protruding belly, well-versed in the Śāstras, prosperous, clever in transacting business and a king or his equal.

Budhayoga : This is formed when Jupiter occupies the Lagna, the Moon a Kendra from Jupiter, Rāhu the 2nd house from the Moon, the Sun and Mars the 3rd house from the Moon. Let us take Sagittarius to be the Ascendant. Put Jupiter in the Lagna, Moon in Gemini, Rāhu in Cancer and the Sun and Mars in Leo. *Effects* : The subject will have royal splendour, unrivalled strength, exceptional fame, scholarship of the Śāstras, cleverness in trade, intelligence and absence of enemies.

Mahāpuruṣayogas

These are five in number, being based on the positions of the five planets beginning with Mars. If the Yoga-producing planet is posited in a Kendra which is its own house or exaltation, a Mahāpuruṣayoga — a yoga wherein a great and distinguished person is born — is brought about. The Yoga is called *Rucaka* if the planet producing the yoga happens to be Mars; it is called *Bhadra*, if the planet is Mercury; it is *Haṁsa* if caused by Jupiter; it is *Mālavya* or Mālava if caused by Venus; and it is *Śaśa* if caused by Saturn. *Effects of Rucaka* : The subject having this Yoga will have a long face, will acquire much wealth through his prowess, be heroic, strong, destroyer of enemies, arrogant, famous for his virtues, victorious and a commander of armies. *Effects of Bhadrayoga* : The subject will be long-lived, sharp-witted, pure, praised by the learned, a king, very wealthy, and eloquent in an assembly. *Effects of Haṁsayoga* : One will be extolled by the virtuous, a king, with his soles and palms marked with the conch, lotus, and fish, possessed of a beautiful body, virtuous, and will eat sumptuous food. *Effects of Mālavyayoga* : The person will have a sturdy body, be courageous, rich, blessed with children, wife and fortune, ever growing, happy, famous, having good vehicles, learned and with cheerful senses. *Effects of Śaśayoga* : He will be popular, possessed of good strength and servants, a king or head of a village, of bad character, addicted to other women, enjoying others' wealth and happy. *Note* : I have told you that these five Yogas arise from the positions of planets in Kendras. These Kendras may be counted from the Ascendant or from the Moon. If a person has one of these five yogas, or two, three, four or all the five, he will be in order (1) fortunate, (2) equal to a king, (3) a king, (4) an emperor, and (5) one greater than even an emperor.

I am giving below some more Yogas for the benefit of students :—

Matsya-yoga : If there is a malefic in the 9th house from the Lagna, if the 5th house is occupied by both benefics and malefics, and if the 4th or the 8th house is occupied by a malefic, this yoga is ushered in. *Effects* : The person born under this Yoga will be an astrologer, very compassionate, and possessed of virtues, intelligence, strength, physical beauty, fame, learning and penance.

Kūrma-yoga : In this Yoga the benefics should occupy the 5th, 6th and 7th Bhāvas and be at the same time in the Aṁśas or Rāśis belonging to themselves, or their friends or their exaltations, and the malefics should be in the Lagna, 3rd and the 11th houses identical with their exaltation or friendly houses. *Effects* : One will be very famous, will enjoy royal luxuries, be religious-minded, full of the quality of Satva or goodness, brave, happy, a leader of men, and helping others through his kind words.

Khadga-yoga : When the lords of the 2nd and the 9th bhāvas exchange their positions, and when the lord of the Lagna is in a Kendra or Koṇa, it is called Khadga — Sword — Yoga. *Effects* : In this yoga one will be devoted to the study of the scriptures and philosophy, intelligent, full of prowess, strong, valiant, happy, free from jealousy, rising to pre-eminence through his own power, grateful and clever.

Kusuma-yoga (Flower): — In this Yoga Venus should be in the Lagna-Kendra which is a fixed Rāśi, the Moon in a Koṇa and the malefic Saturn in the 10th house. *Effects* : The native will be very generous in charity, enjoyer of pleasures, foremost among kings, born of illustrious families, respected by kings, very famous, and full of valour.

Kalānidhi-yoga : If Jupiter is posited in the 2nd or 5th Bhāva in conjunction with or being aspected by Mercury and Venus, or in the house of either of them, the Yoga is called Kalānidhi. The idea is that if Jupiter in 2nd or 5th house is neither aspected by Mercury and Venus nor conjoined with them, then he should be at least in the house of one of the two, i.e. Gemini, Virgo,

Taurus or Libra. *Effects* : The person will be passionate, amiable for his many virtues, worshipped or honoured by great kings, attended upon by armies and royal paraphernalia, and free from diseases, dangers and enemies.

Aṁśāvatāra-yoga : (Partial Incarnation) : In this Yoga both Jupiter and Venus should be in Kendras, and Saturn in Kendra identical with his exaltation. In addition to this the Ascendant must be a movable Sign. *Effects* : The person born under this Yoga will be one whose holy fame would be sung by all; he will go on pilgrimages, will be well versed in fine arts, will be intent on enjoying pleasures of life, will establish an era, will be of restrained senses, knower of Vedānta philosophy and possessed of royal splendour and dignity.

Hari-Hara-Brahma-yoga : There are three kinds of this Yoga. (1) If the benefics are posited in the 2nd, 12th and the 8th Bhāvas counted from the lord of the 2nd Bhāva, one kind of Yoga is produced. (2) A second is produced when the Moon, Mercury and Jupiter are posited in the 4th, 8th and 9th houses from the lord of the 7th house. (3) A third Yoga is generated when the Sun, Venus and Mars occupy the 4th, 10th and 11th houses from the lord of the Lagna. *Effects* : One born under this Yoga will be a thorough master of the sacred lore, truthful, endowed with perfect happiness, of pleasing address, gallant, victorious over all his foes, a benefactor of all living beings, and be engaged in the performance of holy deeds.

CHAPTER XIII

RĀJAYOGAS

In astrological parlance the word Rājayoga means a peculiar combination of planets at birth which confers special benefits such as honour, prosperity, power and success throughout life in general and during the periods of the Yoga-producing planets in particular. Hence people generally associate the word Yoga with the significance of good fortune. There are many Rājayogas mentioned by ancient sages, but all of them are not of equal power and substance, because the grade of the Yoga depends on the state, position and strength of the planets concerned. Hence great care should be exercised when you pronounce judgments on these yogas. The following are some of the Rājayogas leading to great opulence, authority and kingship :—

(i) The planets occupying Taurus, Gemini, Leo, Virgo, Sagittarius, Aquarius and Pisces.

(ii) They occupying Aries, Taurus, Libra and Pisces.

(iii) They be in Taurus, Sagittarius, Pisces and the four angles.

(iv) They be in Aries, Leo, Virgo, Libra and Aquarius.

(v) If they be in the 3rd, 4th and 5th Bhāvas.

(vi) If the 7 planets be in the 7 Bhāvas viz. I, II, III, IV, V, VII and IX.

(vii) If all the planets be posited in the Moon's Horā.

(viii) Benefics be in IX and XI Bhāvas and malefics in VI and X houses.

(ix) Benefics endowed with strength be in I, IV, VII and X houses, and Mars and Saturn in IX and XI Bhāvas.

(x) Four or more planets (other than the Moon) aspect the Lagna or the Moon in Vargottamāṁśa. (According to some the aspecting planets should be in IV, VII and X houses).

(xi) Venus occupying the asterism Aśvinī be in the Lagna and be aspected by all the planets (i.e. other than the Sun and Mercury).

(xii) Three or more planets be in their own Aṁśas (and not

in the Aṁśas of their depression) and one of them be in the ascendant.

(xiii) All the seven planets be in their own houses.

(xiv) The lord of the ascendant being strong and Venus be in II house which is neither his (Venus') inimical house nor his depression.

(xv) The Moon occupying at night her own Navāṁśa or one owned by a very friendly planet and be aspected by Venus alone.

(xvi) Venus be in Vargottamāṁśa in Pisces which is the ascendant.

(xvii) The lord of the Lagna in strength be in his exaltation and be aspected by the Moon.

(xviii) The Lagna-lord *alone* be in a Kendra identical with his exaltation, provided his Navāṁśa is owned neither by his enemy nor by his debilitation sign.

(xix) The full Moon be in IX house identical with her own, exaltation or friendly Sign, and Saturn and Mars be in X and II houses.

(xx) The strong and full Moon occupying an angle other than the ascendant, be aspected by Jupiter and Venus.

(xxi) Two or three planets be in their exaltation signs, the Moon in Cancer and the ascendant possessed of full strength.

Note :— A person born in a royal family can easily attain to a great position or kingship, but for an ordinary man to rise to that position the planetary positions must be extra-ordinary : If five or six planets are strong and exalted without forbidden Aṁśas, and Jupiter is in the Lagna, even an ordinary person will become a great monarch. We are told that five planets were exalted when Śrī Rāmacandra was born.

(xxii) All the benefics in strength be in exaltation identical with I, II, IV or V house, and malefics in III, VI or XI house.

(xxiii) If Mars occupies the Lagna that is Aries, Leo or Sagittarius, and is aspected by a friend.

(xxiv) If the Sun, Moon and Jupiter possessed of strength occupy III, IX and V houses respectively. (According to some the above three houses are to be counted not from the Lagna, but from Mars).

(xxv) If the lord of the 10th Bhāva is posited in the 8th, in a Navāṁśa belonging to his exaltation, own or friendly Sign, or has attained Pārāvatāṁśa.

(xxvi) If the lord of the Navāṁśa occupied by the lord of IX house be in IV or V; or if Mercury be in conjunction with or aspected by Jupiter; or if Mercury occupying a Kendra be aspected by the lord of IX house, provided Jupiter is in the ascendant.

(xxvii) If Saturn occupy in strength his Mūlatrikoṇa or exaltation identical with a Kendra or Koṇa and be aspected by the lord of XI house.

(xxviii) If the Moon be in I, Jupiter in IV, Venus in X, and Saturn in his own Sign or exaltation; or if benefics be posited in X, XI, XII, I, II, and III houses.

(xxix) If Saturn in strength be in Uttamāṁśa, Jupiter in a Navaṁśa other than his debilitation, and the Sun in a benefic Aṁśa be aspected by benefics.

(xxx) If Rāhu be in X, and Saturn occupying XI be aspected by the lord of IX, and if the lord of the ascendant be unassociated with a planet in debilitation.

(xxxi) Lords of IX and X counted from the Lagna —

Do Do ,, ,, IX house

Do Do ,, ,, X ,,

be in conjunction, in mutual reception (i.e. each occupying the other's sign), aspect each other or be in mutual Kendras and at the same time be connected with the lord of II house (counted from the Lagna).

(xxxii) If Saturn be posited in Aquarius-Ascendant, and if four others be in their exaltation; if Mercury be in Aries-Ascendant, and if Jupiter be exalted.

(xxxiii) If the Moon be in Taurus-Ascendant aspected by the remaining six planets; if one planet be in exaltation and the rest in their own or friendly signs.

(xxxiv) If Jupiter conjoined with Mars and the Moon occupies Vargottamāṁśa or Puṣkarāṁśa;[1] or if the full Moon occupies the 10th house and receives the aspect of benefics.

(xxxv) If the Moon along with Jupiter and Venus be in Sagittarius, Mercury in the Lagna, Mars in Virgo, and Saturn in Capricorn identical with the 4th. house; or if Mercury, the Moon, Mars, Jupiter and Saturn occupy Virgo, Pisces, Gemini,

1. 21st, 14th, 24th and 7th degrees in Aries, Taurus, Gemini and Cancer and their trines are the Puṣkarāṁśas in order.

Sagittarius and Capricorn respectively; or if the full and strong Moon be in Pisces-Ascendant, Mars in exaltation and Saturn in Aquarius.

(xxxvi) If Mars be in Capricorn-Ascendant and the Moon in Cancer; or if Mars, the Sun and Jupiter occupy in order Capricorn, Aries and Aquarius.

(xxxvii) If the full Moon conjoined with any planet other than the lord of the Lagna be aspected by Venus, Mercury and Jupiter; or if Jupiter, Venus and Mars are in Vargottamāṁśas and malefics be not in Kendras.

(xxxviii) If all the planets are in Śirṣodaya Signs (that rise with their head foremost) and the Moon aspected by benefics in Cancer; or if the lord of the ascendant is in IX or X house and the Moon in the Lagna.

(xxxix) If both the Sun and Moon be in the middle of Sagittarius, Saturn being very strong in the Lagna, and Mrs in exaltation; or if the lord of the ascendant be posited in an upacaya house counted from the Moon and benefics in Kendras identical with benefic Signs and Navāṁśas, and if malefics be devoid of strength.

(xl) If the Sun about to go to his exaltation be in trine and the Moon and Jupiter in Cancer; or if the Sun be in trine identical with his Mulatrikoṇa or exaltation, and if the Sun, Venus and Mercury be in the 3rd, 6th and 8th places from the Moon and at the same time occupy their respective Aṁśas.

(xli) If the Sun, Moon, Mercury and Venus be in X house which does not belong to their enemy, where they are neither depressed nor invisible, and in friendly Aṁśas; or if Mars possessed of strength occupies his exaltation and is aspected by the Sun, Moon and Jupiter.

(xlii) If the exalted Mercury be in the ascendant, Venus in X house, Jupiter with the Moon in VII and Mars and Saturn in V.

(xliii) If Jupiter conjoined with Venus be in II house; if the lord of I house be in an angle, that of X house in IV, and that of IX in XI; or if the Sun and Mercury be in IV house, Saturn and the Moon in X and Mars in the ascendant.

(xliv) If the Sun be rising in Leo in an Aṁśa not of Venus, and Mercury be in Virgo; or if Saturn and Mars be in X, V or I house, and the full Moon in a sign owned by Jupiter; or if the lord of the ascendant occupies in strength a Kendra or is aspected by friendly planets.

(xlv) If the Lagna-lord being exalted aspect the Moon.

(xlvi) If Saturn be in the ascendant identical with Libra, Sagittarius and Pisces (as well as Capricorn, Aquarius and Aries, according to some).

(xlvii) If any one of the lords of IX, XI and II houses be in a Kendra with respect to the Moon, and if Jupiter be the lord of XI.

(xlviii) If the Moon and Mars be in I, IX or X house and Jupiter and the Sun be strong.

(xlix) If Mars occupy Aśvīnī, Anurādhā or Dhaniṣṭhā in X house, and the Sun be in the ascendant which is not his debilitation.

(l) If the full and bright Moon be posited in the Sun's Navāṁśa and benefics unassociated with malefics be in Kendras.

(li) If Jupiter, Venus and Saturn be in Pisces, the full Moon in exaltation, and the Sun in Aries-ascendant aspected by Mars (or the full Moon in exaltation be aspected by Mars and the Sun be in Aries-ascendant).

(lii) If for a night birth the benefics be in depression or in inimical houses identical with III, VI or XI house, or be in their highest exaltation and bright, or be all in Kendras, and if the Moon also be in Cancer identical with X house.

(liii) If Jupiter and the Moon occupy Kendras receiving the aspect of Venus, provided there be no planet in depression.

(liv) If the Moon be in the ascendant which is an aquatic sign or whose Aṁśa belongs to an aquatic sign, and be in her own or a benefic Varga, and at the same time there be no malefics in angles (Kendras).

Nīcabhaṅga — Cancellation of Depression

There is another type of Rājayoga which is of a negative nature. It is got by the cancellation of a planet's debilitation under certain conditions : (1) If a planet is debilitated and if the lord of the depression or the lord of the exaltation Sign of the depressed planet is in Kendra from the ascendant or the Moon, the person concerned will become an emperor devoted to Dharma. (2) The same result is achieved, if the lord of the depression sign or the planet that is exalted in that Sign is in a

Kendra from the Lagna or the Moon; (3) if the two planets mentioned in (1) are mutually in Kendra positions; (4) if the planet in depression is aspected by the lord of that sign; (5) if the planet in depression is in a Kendra with respect to the Lagna or the Moon; (6) if the lord of the Navāṁśa of the depressed planet be in a Kendra or Koṇa, and if the ascendant be a movable Sign or if the lord of the ascendant be in a movable Sign or Aṁśa. (7) If Jupiter be depressed in the Lagna, and the 8th house be occupied by a malefic, and if the Navāṁśa of the 8th house be one owned by that malefic; and (8) if two, three or four planets in depression occupy benefic 1/60 portions or their exaltation Navāṁśas, the person will become a great sovereign.

CHAPTER XIV

ISSUE

Birth of worthy children is the legitimate object of marriage which alone makes an individual's personality complete. Our Dharma Śāstras lay down that to propagate the line is one of the duties of man, as otherwise he would become a debtor to his ancestors. Hence the consummation of wedlock is realized in the birth of a son, whom poets designate as the knot binding together the hearts of man and wife. One must, therefore, be very fortunate to have good and long-lived children. All the details of children are read, as you have learnt, from the 5th Bhāva mainly and the 9th as well as from their lords and the planets connected with them. Jupiter who is the Kāraka or significator of issue also must needs be well placed and strong. In this connection you will do well to remember the signs of the zodiac that are termed '*Alpasuta*' or '*of few children*'. They are *Taurus*, *Leo*, *Virgo* and *Scorpio*.

A person can expect good children under the following conditions :—

(1) Jupiter and the lords of V house counted from the ascendant and the Moon should be well placed.

(2) The 5th Bhāva itself be conjoined with or aspected by benefics or lords of auspicious houses (i.e. other than the 6th, 8th and 12th).

(3) The lords of the ascendant and V house should be conjoined, in mutual reception (i.e. exchange houses) or aspect each other.

(4) Both Jupiter and the lord of V house are in Vaiśeṣikāṁśa and are aspected by the lord of IX house. One is blessed with a son early in life, if the lord of V be in a Kendra or Koṇa and be conjoined with benefics.

Similarly examine the 5th Bhāva counted from Jupiter as well. If there are malefics in this house as well as in the two mentioned above (i.e. 5th house from the ascendant and the Moon), or if malefics aspect or surround them and if the lords of these V houses are posited in inauspicious houses, without benefic aspect or association, one cannot hope to be blessed with issue. Now let us suppose that the lord of the 5th house who is a natural malefic occupies it. Would it destroy the house ? No, because the owner of a house cannot and will not destroy it. So birth of children is assured in that case. On the other hand the presence of a malefic in V house owned by a benefic will harm progeny.

(i) If one of the Signs designated as *Alpasuta* happens to be the 5th house, one will have no issue or have it very late in life. (ii) If the Sun be in such a Sign happening to be the 5th house, Saturn in the 8th and Mars in the Lagna, one might expect to have a child with difficulty late in life. (iii) The same effect will follow if Saturn, Jupiter and Mars occupy in order I, VIII and XII houses, and the 5th house be an *Alpasuta* sign. (iv) Similar is the effect, if the Moon be in XI house, and the 5th house reckoned from Jupiter be occupied by a malefic and there be many planets in the ascendant. (v) Jupiter in Pisces and Sagittarius as the 5th house causes very few children and issue after much difficulty respectively, whereas in Cancer and Aquarius, no issue at all. (vi) Not many children can be expected if the Moon or Mercury occupies singly the 5th house identical with Cancer. If the Sun, Mars or Venus be in that position, one would get children by a second wife. On the other hand Saturn in such a position will cause many children. Jupiter in the same place, however, will lead to the birth of many daughters. Now you must be anxious to know the rules for predicting birth of sons and daughters. The following conditions govern male births :— (i) The 5th Bhāva and/or its lord (who being a male planet himself) should be situated in a male Sign or Aṁśa and/or be in conjunction with or aspected by male planets. (ii) The lord of this Bhāva, Jupiter, Mars and the Sun in the chart should all be posited in male Aṁśas anywhere. The goodness or otherwise of the children is to be measured from the strength of the lord of the 5th house. To get the rule for female births substitute the word "*female*" for '*male*' in rule (i) above. Similarly birth of girls is to be predicted, when the lord of V or IX house occupies VII or an even Sign and is conjoined with or aspected by the Moon or Venus. One would have many children, if V house be a Varga (Sign, Horā etc.) of Venus or the Moon and be aspected by or conjoined with either of them, and if at the same time no malefics occupy this Bhāva. In spite of afflictions one could have one son at least, if the lord of the Aṁśa occupied by the owner of the 5th house be in his own Sign or Aṁśa.

The following planetary configurations indicate loss of children and issuelessness :—

(i) The lord of the 5th house should be in depression, in inimical house or be eclipsed, or be in conjunction with the lord of the 6th, 8th or 12th house without any benefic aspect or conjunction.

(ii) Mars and Saturn should aspect the 5th house (No issue).

(iii) The lord of the 7th house should be in V house (No wife or issue).

(iv) Rāhu occupying V Bhāva and its lord a Dusthāna (inauspicious house) — (Loss of children).

(v) Lord of V house being conjoined with Mars or Rāhu (Do.).

(vi) Lord of V house and Jupiter being conjoined with Mars. (No issue).

(vii) Lord of V being conjoined with the Sun and Venus. (Do.).

(viii) Jupiter and lords of I, V and VII houses being weak (Do.).

(ix) A malefic being in I house, its lord in V, lord of V in III and the Moon in IV. (Do.).

(x) The Moon being in V which is an odd sign or Aṁśa and being aspected by the Sun. (Do.):

Note :— The last two conditions may lead to great sufferings to the person in respect of children.

The following planetary combinations lead to family extinction :—

(i) Malefics occupying the 6th, 8th and 12th houses counted from the house of issue.

(ii) The IV, VII and X houses being occupied respectively by a malefic, Venus and the Moon.

(iii) The Lagna, 5th, 8th and 12th houses being tenanted by malefics.

(iv) Venus and Mercury being in VII, Jupiter in V and malefics in IV house.

(v) The Moon being in V and malefics in I, VIII and XII houses.

(vi) Malefics being in I, VII, IX and XII occupying inimical Vargas.

(vii) The Moon and Jupiter together being in I, Mars or Saturn in VII and all malefics in IV house.

(viii) A malefic being in I, the Moon in IV and the lord of the ascendant devoid of strength being in V house.

Adoption

The following planetary configurations indicate a son by adoption :—

(i) The 5th Bhāva owned by Saturn or Mercury being aspected by or conjoined with Māndi or Saturn.

(ii) The lord of V house being weak and having no connection whatsoever with the lords of the 1st and 7th houses.

(iii) There should be a planet possessed of full strength occupying the 5th house, and the lord of the 5th be in the invisible half.

(iv) The Moon being in a malefic Sign and the lord of the 5th house in IX house and the lord of the ascendant in a trine.

(v) The lord of the 5th being in the ascendant which is an even sign, or in the 4th house in an Aṁśa belonging to Saturn.

(vi) The lord of the 5th being conjoined with the Sun and Mercury should be in an Aṁśa owned by an even Sign or by Saturn.

(vii) The above lord in a Navāṁśa of Saturn, and Jupiter and Venus in their own houses. In this case the person is likely to beget a son after adopting a child.

(viii) The planets must be strong in the bright half of the month and be situated in the Aṁśa of Saturn, and Jupiter be in the 5th house.

(ix) If the lords of the 1st and 5th houses occupy an inauspicious house (Dusthāna) and are aspected by benefics, one will have both a son born to him and an adopted one. Now to understand wherefrom the adoption is made proceed thus :— Find out the Vargas of the cusp of the 5th house, the planet posited therein and Jupiter. These Vargas point to certain Signs. Now find out which of such signs are *unoccupied.*

That house will show the relationship of the person from whose family the adoption will be made.

You should also know the method of finding out the number of children one would have and when the event may be expected. The number of children should be gauged from the planets posited in the 5th house and those conjoined with its lord, this process being repeated in respect of the 5th houses counted from the house occupied by Jupiter and the Sign representing the Sun's Navāṁśa, taking care to eliminate those that are posited in the Aṁśas of their enemies and depression. The number of children may be equal to the Navāṁśas that have been covered by the 5th Bhāva. The number will correspond to the Aṁśas owned only by benefics. If there is the aspect of benefics, this number will have to be doubled. In the case of malefics similar deductions have to be made. This can also be calculated thus :— Convert the Navāṁśas that have elapsed in V house into minutes and multiply it by the benefic aspect on it (in Rūpas). Divide the product by 200. The quotient will represent the number of children one will have. Another method :— Leaving out the Signs convert the degrees etc. of the 5th Bhāva into minutes. Then multiply it by the figure (in Virūpas) representing the benefic aspect and divide the product first by 60 and again by 200. The final quotient will represent the number of children. The result obtained from malefic aspect on the Bhāva will indicate the loss of issue one will have. Yet other methods : (i) Take the sum of the longitudes of Jupiter, the Moon and the Sun. This will show a particular Sign and Navāṁśa. The number of the Navāṁśas will represent the number of children. (ii) Add the longitudes of the lords of IV, V and IX Bhāvas and ascertain as before the number of past Navāṁśas in the result obtained. This will give you the required figure. (iii) Similarly add the longitudes of the planets, if any, occupying the 4th, 5th and 9th Bhāvas. Take the past Navāṁśas in the result for the required number.

You can find out the time of fruition of this Bhāva thus :— (i) Add the longitudes of the lords of the 5th and the 1st. Bhāvas. The result will indicate a certain Sign and Aṁśa. When Jupiter in transit passes through this and its triangular position, one may beget a son or daughter. (ii) Add the longitudes of the 1st, 5th and 7th houses. The sum will represent a particular Sign and asterism. Now find out the Mahā Daśā for that asterism. Children may be born during this major period and in the sub-period of (1) the planet occupying the 5th house, (2) the one aspecting it, and (3) the one owning the 5th house. (iii) The event may be expected to take place when Jupiter in transit arrives at the Rāśi and Navāṁśa indicated by the sum of the longitudes of the lord of V house, Jupiter, the planet occupying V and the one aspecting it. On the other hand, Saturn's arrival at the same place will indicate possible harm to children. (iv) It may be expected during the Daśā or Apahāra of any one of the following :—(1) The lord of the Lagna, (2) the lord of the 7th. (3) the lord of the 5th, (4) the lord of the 9th, (5) Jupiter, (6) one aspecting the 5th and (7) the one occupying the 5th house. (v) It may take place when Jupiter in transit arrives at the Sign or Navāṁśa occupied by the lord of the 5th house or Yamakaṇṭaka (upagraha of Jupiter). (vi) It may take place when the lord of the ascendant conjoins during his transit with the lord of the 5th house in a Sign which is the former's exaltation or own house, or when he (lord of ascendant) comes to the 5th house or the house occupied by its lord at birth. (vii) Birth of a son may be expected during the major or minor period of the strongest of the following :—(1) The lord of 5th house, (2) Jupiter, and (3-6) the lords of the Signs and Navāṁśas occupied by (1) and (2). (viii) It may take place when Jupiter passes during his transit through a Sign (or its trine) representing the Rāśi or Aṁśa occupied by the lord of the 5th house counted from Jupiter. (ix) Add the longitudes of the two planets owning respectively the natal star and the 5th from it (Pratyaktārā). When Jupiter passes in transit through the Sign represented by the sum or through a trine, the event may occur.

If the lord of the 5th house be conjoined with Rāhu. a child born in the sub-period of the former will be short-lived, whereas one born in the Bhukti of Rāhu will live long. What is the rationale behind this ? It is very simple : The lord of the Bhāva is spoilt by Rāhu, while Rāhu takes upon himself the nature of the other and so cannot do any harm to the house.

Now it may interest you to know the appropriate time for conception as well as the relationship between conception and birth. Conception is likely to take place when the Sun and Venus for men, and Mars and the Moon for women, are possessed of strength and pass through Apacaya houses (i.e. other than the 3rd, 6th, 10th and 11th houses) identical with their own Signs or Aṁśas. The birth of a child is expected to take place when the Sun in transit comes to the 3rd Sign or its trine reckoned from the Lagna at impregnation. If the Lagna at birth happens to be V or IX from that at impregnation, it should be declared as very fortunate. To find out the relationship between the Moon at impregnation and at the birth of a child proceed thus : Note the Dvādaśāṁśa ($2\frac{1}{2}$ degree portion) of the Moon at the time of impregnation. It belongs to one of the 12 Signs. Now count its number from Aries. The Moon at birth will be so far removed from Aries or from the Sign of the Dvādaśāmśa as the above number. Similarly we can find out whether it will take place at night or daytime. Find out the diurnal or nocturnal nature of the rising Sign at *Niṣeka* or impregnation. See also what fraction of it had elapsed. The birth will take place when so much of the day or night will have elapsed. The portion of the day or night passed will correspond to the degrees that have risen in the Rāśi. This may also be calculated from the degree passed by the Moon. The Ghatī of birth will correspond to the 1/60 portion that is rising. The Sārāvalī states that some sages are of opinion that the natal star will be the 10th from the one at conception, while Bādarāyaṇa puts it in the 7th house from the ascendant or the Moon at impregnation.

The following principles taken from Sepharial's "Manual of Astrology" can be tried with advantage :—

(1) When the Moon at birth is waxing and visible, or waning and invisible, the period intervening between Ādhāna (impregnation) and birth will be less than the time taken for 10 lunar revolutions or 9 solar months.

(2) If the Moon at birth is waxing and invisible or waning and visible, the interval will be of more than 10 lunar revolutions.

(3) The number of days in excess or short (of ten lunar revolutions) can be calculated by finding the distance of the Moon from the horizon, the distance being counted from the ascendant when the Moon is invisible, and from the 7th house when the Moon is visible. Convert this distance into degrees and divide it by 12. The quotient gives the number of days required to be added or subtracted. (The number of days required for 10 lunar revolutions $= 27.32305 \times 10$).

(4) If the birth is in the bright half, the Lagna will represent the Moon's position at conception.

(5) If the birth is in the dark half, the 7th house from Lagna will give the Moon's position at conception.

(6) The Rāśi occupied by the Moon at birth will be rising or setting at conception according to as the Moon is waxing or waning.

Now let us work out an example according to these principles :—There was a birth at 5.58 A.M., I.S.T. on 1952-7-6, Lat. 12.5 N. The positions of the Moon, Sun and Ascendant are given below :—Moon = 7s-29°-40′-21″. Sun = 2s-20°-40′-43″. Asc. = 2s-17°-1′-32″. See the chart on page 178. Here the Moon is waxing and invisible. Hence the interval between conception and birth is greater than 10 lunar revolutions. As the Moon is invisible we have to deduct the ascendant from the Moon's position :—7s-29°-40′-2″ minus 2s-17°-1′-32″ = 5s-12°-38′-49″ = 162.647 degrees. On dividing this by 12, we get 13.554. This is the number of days we have to add to 273.2305. By addition we get 286.7845. This is the period preceding birth or the interval between conception and birth. As it is bright fortnight, the ascendant viz, Gemini, should represent the Moon's position at conception. We cannot blindly follow here the Rule No. 6. For in that case the conception or Niṣeka would take place in broad daylight. Of course scientifically this is not untenable, as they say that sometimes actual fertilization of the ovum takes place some time after copulation i.e. 3 to 13 days. We can say in this particular case that the union took place when the Rāśi containing the Moon at birth viz. Scorpio, was setting and not rising. So it must have taken place when the 30th degree of Taurus was rising i.e. at about 11-30 P.M. on Sunday the 23rd of September 1951. The two charts are given below for convenient reference : As the conception-Lagna is the very end of Taurus, a nocturnal sign, the birth took place practically at the fag end of the night. However, there is a strong doubt about the correctness of this conclusion. For according to the report the date arrived at happens to be in the safety-period and conception should have taken place on the 2nd of October 1951 or thereafter. On this date though the ascendant does not change, the Moon's position is in Libra. It is also observed that sometimes birth takes place in the same constellation as that of conception. If we adopt this principle, the conception should have taken place at about the time noted above on the 5th of October 1951. Note also the following rules : (1) The Moon at birth is equidistant from the Lagnas at birth and coitus. (2) The Lagna at conception may be as

—	Jup.	—	Sun Ven. Lag.
—	Birth 1952-7-6		Merc. Ketu
Rāhu			—
—	Moon	Mars	Sat.

R. Jup.	—	Lag.	Moon
Rāhu	Conception 1951-9-23		Mars
—			Merc. R. Ven. Ketu
—	—	—	Sat. Sun

far away from the Moon at birth as she is from the Lagna at birth. (3) The Lagna at conception may be the central point between the Lagna and the Moon at birth.

I have come across another method for arriving at the Niṣeka-time from the birth-data : Note the exact positions of the Sun, Moon and ascendant at birth. Now subtract the ascendant from the Moon and convert the result into degrees. Keep this in two places. Divide one of these figures by 16 and add the quotient to the figure kept apart. Divide this result by 14. To the quotient thus got add the constant Ahargaṇa of 246. This will give the number of days preceding the birth i.e. the day of conception. Now let us apply this rule to the same example : By deducting the Lagna from the Moon we get 162°-38′-49″. Keep this in two places and divide one by 16. We get then 10°-9′-55″. Adding this to the figure, 162°-38′-49″, we get 172°-48′-44″. Dividing this by 14 we get 12°-20′-90″. Adding the constant Ahargaṇa of 246 to this we get 256°-20′-39″. This means that the conception took place on the 256th day preceding the day of birth. Now to find out the weekday, divide this number by 7. The remainder is 4. The day of birth was a Saturday. So subtract 4 from 7, number of Saturday which is the 7th day in the week. We get 3 which indicates a Tuesday. This is the weekday of Niṣeka. Still something more remains to be done : Divide the number 256°-20′-39″ by 63 and add the quotient to it. The quotient 4 being added to 256-20-39 gives 260-20-39. Now divide this by 30. Then you get 8 months and 20 days. This brings us to Tuesday the 16th of October 1951.

According to the same authority the exact time of copulation is found out thus :—Take the Sun's position in the morning on the day of Niṣeka found out just now. Add to it the precession of the equinox. Find out the Bhogya—portion to be covered—in that Sign and also the time required for that portion of the Sign to rise, taking into consideration the measures of the several Rāśis for the particular latitude. Now take the Moon's longitude at *birth-time* and add the precession of the equinox to it. Here too find out the time required for the portion of the sign that has already risen (Bhukta). Now add these two results i.e. the Bhogya of the Sun and the Bhukta of the Moon. Add to this sum the total time required for the rising of the signs that intervene between the Moon and the Sun mentioned above. Divide this result in Palas by 60 to get the Ghaṭīs. This will give the exact time of Niṣeka after sunrise. Let us apply these principles to the present example :

The Sun's longitude on the morning of Niṣeka = 5s-28°-39′
Precession of the equinox = 0-23-11

Adding these two we get	=6-21-50	
∴ the portion of Libra yet to rise	=0-8-10	
Time required for Libra to rise at	Palas	Tatparas
this lat.	304	50
∴ time required for 8°-10′ to rise	=82-59 (A)	
Moon's longitude at birth	=7-29-40-21	
Adding the precession to this we get	=8-22-52-13	
∴ the Bhukta portion of Sagittarius	=0-22-52-13	
Time required for this to rise	P.	T.
(Total time for Dhanus is 330-20)	=251	47(B)
Adding up (A) and (B) we get	=334-46(C)	

Now find out time of rising of all the Rāśis from the position of the Moon at birth to that of the Sun on the day of the Niṣeka.

In Sagitt. time required for the remaining	P.	T.
portion to rise	78	33(1)
For Capricorn etc. upto Virgo	2644-40 (2)	

(313-20+278-10+253-10+253-10+278-10+313-20+330-20+320-10+304-50)

Time required for 21-50 of Libra to rise	=221-51 (3)
Totalling up (1), (2) and (3) what we get	=2945-4 (D)
Adding up (C) and (D) what we get	=3279-50
Dividing this by 60 we get Ghaṭīs	=54-40

This figure viz. 54 G.-40 P. is the exact time of Niṣeka on Tuesday/Wednesday night. The exact longitude of the Sun for this time is 5^{s}-29°-33′-48″ and that of the Moon 0^{s}-22°-17′-12″.

Let me give another example of birth and copulation :

Female born at 6-30 A.M. on 1952-3-6. Ascendant= 10^{s}-23°-51′-26.″ Moon=2^{s}-19°-20′-30″, Sun=10^{s}-22°-13′-6″. The reported time of copulation is about midnight on 1951-6-2. Lagna=10^{s}-7°-40′-0″. Moon=0^{s}-27°-1′-51″.

If we apply the principles of Sepharial to the data of birth in order to get the time of conception, the latter would take place five days earlier than the one given above and the Moon would be in Aquarius. On the other hand, if we apply the second method, the conception should have taken place on Tuesday the 12th June 1951. On that day Moon is in Leo. But I do not think that it is necessary to alter the time of copulation for this purpose. For by applying the principle based on the Navāmśa of the Moon at conception we can tide over the difficulty. The Moon's Navāṁśa Rāśi is Sagittarius in the second chart. At birth, therefore, the Moon is actually passing through the 7th house from it i.e. through Gemini. In this case the ascendants at both coitus and birth are the same

Jup. Merc.	—	—	Moon
Lagna Sun Rāhu	Birth		—
Venus			Ketu
—	—	Mars	R. Sat.

Jup.	Merc. Moon	Sun Mars	—
Rāhu Lagna	Copulation		Venus
—			Ketu
—	—	—	Saturn

viz. Aquarius, which is a diurnal sign. The birth was also in the morning after sunrise. We must now be able to formulate some theories about the relationship between the ascendant and the Moon at copulation and birth :—(1) The birth may take place in the same ascendant as the one at conception or the 7th from it or its Navāṁśa. (2) The Moon too may occupy the same position at both the events. (3) The Moon may occupy the Navāṁśa Rāśi or the Rāśi 7th from it. (4) The ascendant at birth may be the same as or opposite to the Moon or her Navāṁśa at conception. In the following example the Moon is in the same Sign, but the Lagna is different. Still the Lagna at birth is 7th from the Moon at copulation.

Rāhu 5	—	Lagna 4	—
R. Jup. 8	Copulation 1950-10-12 about 9-30 P.M.		—
—			—
—	Mars 9	Moon 10	Sun 5 Merc. 1 Ven. 3 Sat. 10 Ketu 11

Jup. 10	Lagna 8	Māndi 2	Mars 10 Sun 2
Rāhu 12	Birth 1951-7-12 at 1-42 A.M.		Merc. 8
—			Ven. 4 Ketu 6
—	—	Moon 8	Sat. 11

We may also consider the following example :—

R. Jup. Lagna	—	—	—
Rāhu	Copulation 1951-8-16 at about 9-30 P.M.		Sun Mars
Moon			Merc. R. Ven. Ketu
—	—	—	Saturn

Asc. = 11^s-21. Sun = 3^s-29-47.
Moon = 9^s-23°-30′

—	Jup. Merc. Venus	Sun	—
Moon Rāhu	Male born at 4-7 P.M. on 1952-5-17		—
—			Ketu
—	—	R. Mars	R. Sat. Lagna

Asc. at birth = 5^s-28°-21′-52″
Sun ,, = 1-3-15-24
Moon ,, = 10-14-4-22

Here too the Navāṁśa Rāśi of the Moon at copulation is Leo and the Moon at birth is in the 7th house from that i.e. Aquarius. The ascendant at birth is the 7th from that at copulation.

Sometimes the father dies before the birth of a child. The following conditions indicate the same :—(i) The Sun should be in a Dusthāna (inauspicious house) and the Dvādaśāṁśa of the ascendant be either Leo or Pisces. (ii) The Moon being weak should occupy the ascendant, Jupiter being combust a Sign belonging to Saturn and all the malefics triangular houses.

People sometimes wish to know if their sons would be able to perform their last rites or be by their side in their last moments. The following planetary configurations suggest these things : (i) If the Sun or the Moon occupies a Kendra (angle) which is a movable sign, the native will not be able to do the cremation of his parents. (ii) On the other hand if they occupy dual signs identical with angles, the death and cremation of parents will not take place in the same period. (iii) If the lords of IV and IX houses be in the invisible part of the zodiac (between the 1st and the 7th houses), the person would be unable to see his parents in their last moments. (iv) If the lord of the 5th house be in the invisible half, one would not be able to see the son's face at the time of one's death.

There is a method for finding out if a couple hankering after progeny stands any chance of success : Add up the longitudes of Jupiter, the Moon and Mars in the horoscope of the woman. If the result shows an even sign and an even Navāṁśa, the woman's fertility is assured. If it is mixed (i.e. Sign even and Aṁśa odd, or *vice versa*), success may be obtained after much hardship. Similarly add up the longitudes of the Sun, Venus and Jupiter in the man's horoscope. If the result gives an odd sign and an odd Aṁśa, the man's virility becomes evident. If these are mixed, success also will be doubtful. Let us apply this rule to the charts of a couple. The two charts are given hereunder :—

Lag. 11 Ketu 11 Sun 8 Moon 8 Merc. 4	Venus 4	—	—
Jup. 11	Male 1903-3-29 at 7-15 A.M.		—
Saturn 2			—
—	—	—	R. Mars 2 Rāhu 5

(1) Sun = 11^{s}-14°-42′-0″ (3) Jup. = 10-16-2-0
(2) Moon = 11-14-54-19 (4) Venus = 0-13-5-22
Adding up (1), (3) & (4) we get
10^{s}-13°-49′-22″

This gives us sign Aquarius and the same in Navāṁśa also. So the fecundity of the male must be adjudged to be very high.

—	R. Jup. 1 Lagna 9	—	Ketu 3 Moon 3
—	Female 1916-12-12 at 4-10 P.M.		R. Sat. 6
—			—
Rāhu 9 Mars 5 Merc. 3	Sun 12	Venus 2	—

(1) Sun = 7s-27°-25′-37″ (3) Mars = 8-15-30-0
(2) Moon = 2-29-36-37 (4) Jup. = 0-2-58-48
Adding up (2), (3) and (4) we get
11^{s}-18°-5′-25″

This is Pisces in Rāśi and Sagittarius in Navāṁśa. The former is even and the latter odd. The result, therefore, must be mixed.

I shall give yet another method of working this out : Take the husband's horoscope first and subtract the Sun's longitude from the Moon's. Multiply the balance by 5. Repeat this process in the case of the wife's chart also. The product in each case will be in signs, degrees etc. Now reduce it into degrees. From this find out what Tithi (lunar day) is indicated.[1]

If it is a non-Chidra Tithi in the bright half of the month, success is assured. If it is in the dark fortnight, success is doubtful. In both the fortnights success depends on the moon's strength. Success is impossible, if the result is Amāvāsyā, or one of the *Chidra* Tithis, or *Viṣṭi* Karaṇa[2] or one of the *Sthira*

1. You know that it is Amāvāsyā — New Moon — when both the luminaries are together. As the Moon goes away from the Sun, the lunar days or Tithis (i.e. phases) increase at the rate of 12 degrees until the Moon's distance is 180° when it is called Full Moon. Then the dark fortnight begins and the Tithis are calculated in the same manner until the distance between the two luminaries becomes nil again. Hence to get the Tithi what you have to do is to subtract the Sun's longitude from that of the Moon. Let us take an example : Let the Sun's position be 8s-3°-29′-37″ and the Moon's 3s-20°-26′-20″. By subtracting the former from the latter we get 7s-16°-56′-43″ By reducing it to degrees we get 227 roughly. As this is more than 180°, it is the dark fortnight. Now divide this by 12° and find out the lunar day : It is 18 and plus something. That means that it is the 19th Tithi or the 4th (caturthī) in the dark fortnight. For our purpose in this particular case, however, you have to calculate the Tithi from the product mentioned above. In this case what you have to remember is that there are certain lunar days that are called "Chidra" or unholy. They are the 4th, 6th, 8th, 9th, 12th and 14th lunar days in both the halves.

2. Karaṇa means a half-lunar day. There are altogether 11 Karaṇas distributed among the 30 Tithis in a lunar month at the rate of 2 Karaṇas for each Tithi. Out of the 11 Karaṇas four viz. (1) Catuṣpād, (2) Nāga, (3) Kiṁstughna, and (4) Śakuna, are termed Sthira or Stable, which means that their sway is constant : They rule over the 4 half Tithis in order viz., (1) The latter half of the 14th lunar day in the dark half, (2) first half of Amāvāsyā, (3) second half of the same, and (4) first half of Pratipad (1st lunar day) in the bright half. The remaining 7 are called Cara or movable. They are (1) Bava, (2) Bālava, (3) Kaulava, (4) Taitila, (5) Garaja, (6) Vaṇij and (7) Viṣṭi or Bhadra. These are repeated 8 times in a lunar month beginning from the latter half of the first Tithi in the bright fortnight. Remember that the places assigned to the Stable Karaṇas should not be tampered with. If these principles are known for arriving at the lunar day and Karaṇa, you can easily locate the forbidden Karaṇas.

or *Stable* Karaṇas. If we apply this rule to the male, we get 0^s-1°-1′-35″, which means the very beginning of the first day of the lunar month, which is practically the same as the Amāvāsyā as far as the Moon's strength is concerned. It is also a Sthira Karaṇa. In the case of the female it is 11^s-10°-55′-0″, which yields the 14th Tithi of the dark fortnight, which is a Chidra Tithi, and the Karaṇa Viṣṭi. According to the first formula, the couple could have issue after initial difficulties, but according to the second they cannot have it at all. And they are actually issueless. If we look at the two horoscopes in the ordinary manner, then too it will be quite clear to us that they have absolutely no chance of having issue. In the male chart the Lagna is hopelessly afflicted by malefics, both by presence and aspect. The same is the case with the 7th house. What about the 5th house ? It is aspected by Saturn, its lord is cent per cent combust and afflicted. The Putra-kāraka is surrounded by malefics. We may examine the 5th house and its lord from this Kāraka too.

Cause of Childlessness :— When the concerned Bhāvas and planets are ill-placed, eclipsed or otherwise afflicted, you can conclude that the trouble is due to some sin committed by the person in the previous incarnation. After finding out the details of the sins an astrologer should suggest proper remedial and propitiatory measures. Astrology should not make you a confirmed fatalist. In that case all our Śāstras which enjoin self-exertion and self-help would be meaningless. For, fate is nothing but the effect of our own deeds. Hence it is upto us to redeem our past deeds and build up a brighter future. If the afflicted planet responsible for the trouble be the Sun, you have to conclude that it is due to the displeasure of the Lord Śiva or Garuḍa or the *manes*; if it be the Moon, to that of the mother, an auspicious lady or the Goddess Durgā; if Mars, to that of the village deity, Lord Kārtikeya, enemies or cousins; if Mercury, to that of Lord Viṣṇu or a Brahmacārin (young religious student); if Jupiter, to that of the family deity, a friend or a preceptor or to the sin caused by destroying a fruit-laden tree; if Venus, to that of a chaste woman, cattle or a Yakṣī or to the sin caused by the destruction of flower-laden trees; if Saturn, to that of the God of Death, ghosts or goblins or as a result of cutting down the sacred Aśvattha (peepul) tree; if Rāhu be in the 5th house or conjoined with its lord, it is due to the curse of serpents; if Ketu, it is due to the curse of a Brahmin; and in the case of Gulika (or Māndi), it is due to the curse of discarnate spirits. If Venus and the Moon in conjunction with Māndi be in the 5th house, the cause is the murder of a cow or woman; and if Jupiter or Ketu be there along with Māndi, it is due to the murder of a Brahmin. These troubles can be warded off or minimized by performing appropriate propitiatory ceremonies. There is nothing unscientific in this. For, if you offend a person, you try to assuage his wounded feelings by sincere apologies and such other acts.

CHAPTER XV

MATRIMONY

Male and female are but the two aspects, or two sides, of Nature. Hence it is natural for them to be united. For, otherwise there would be incompleteness, nay it would be '*paradise lost*'. Even in the ultimate stage of the soul, we are told, it gets merged in the Super-Soul and becomes one with it. Human marriage is but a gross reflection of this grand spiritual union. The ancients have, therefore, called the wife a house-wife, a minister, a friend, a slave etc. She is also the Goddess of the house, encouraging her husband to earn wealth, name and fame. She stands by him in times of crisis. Though marriages are made in heaven, human beings are not aware of their would-be partners in life. Hence they search for a suitable person to fill the vacancy. Their anxiety is all the greater as the selection is made but once in a lifetime.

The wife will be long-lived and good if the lord of VII house counted from the ascendant or the Moon be well placed, well associated and well aspected. So is the case when this Bhāva itself is occupied or aspected by the lord of the 9th house, benefics or its own lord. The Significator of this Bhāva viz. Venus, too should be strong, in a good house receiving benefic aspects. On the other hand, if the Bhāva and its lord are afflicted i.e. by occupation and aspect, the result would not be happy. There will be misery in conjugal life or loss of wife in case there are malefics in the 12th, 4th and 8th from Venus, or if Venus is conjoined with, aspected or surrounded by malefics. The following planetary configurations (Yogas) lead to undesirable effects with regard to conjugal life :—

(i) The lord of VII Bhāva be in V house — loss of wife or progeny.

(ii) Lord of V or VIII house in VII — Do.

(iii) Weak Moon in V and malefics in I, VII and XII houses — Wifeless and childless.

(iv) The Sun and Rāhu in VII — Loss of wealth as a result of association with women.

(v) Venus in Scorpio which is VII house — loss of wife.

(vi) Mercury in Taurus identical with VII—Do.

(vii) Jupiter in VII in depression—Do.

(viii) Saturn or Mars in Pisces identical with VII—Do.

(ix) Saturn and Moon in VII house—wifeless or issueless.

(x) Venus and Mars in VII—Loss of wife.

(xi) The Sun and Venus in I or VII—Wife is barren.

(xii) The 7th house or its Aṁśa be owned by Mars, and the lord of the Aṁśa be either weak or eclipsed — the wife will be wicked, a slave and abandoned by him.

(xiii) VII house falling in Rāśi occupied by the Upagraha Dhūma— No marriage.

(xiv) The 7th house coinciding with Kodaṇḍa—She dies.

(xv) The 7th house coinciding with Pariveṣa—Of bad character.

(xvi) The 7th house coinciding with Ketu—Barren.

(xvii) Venus and lord of VII be in Dusthānas, aspected and surrounded by malefics—Two wives.

(xviii) Lords of II, VI and VII as well as Venus occupying the ascendant being conjoined with or aspected by malefics— The man becomes libidinous.

(xix) Malefics along with lords of I, II and VI occupy VII— He will be addicted to other women.

(xx) Venus and the Moon occupying the 7th house from Mars and Saturn—Wifeless or childless.

(xxi) An impotent planet in VII house and two planets in the 11th house—Two wives.

(xxii) Lord of VII and Venus being posited in dual Signs or Aṁśas—Do.

(xxiii) Malefics occupying or aspecting the 2nd and 7th houses—Loss of wife.

(xxiv) Malefics in their depression or inimical sign occupying the 2nd, 7th or 8th house—Death of wife.

(xxv) The Moon in the Aṁśa of the Sun and in I or VII Bhāva—Wife becomes unchaste.

(xxvi) The Moon in I or VII identical with her depression, or inimical house or in a state of eclipse, or in a decanate termed Serpent, Bird, Noose or Fetters, or in a Ṛkṣa-sandhi (concluding portion of Cancer, Scorpio or Pisces) — the wife falls from her vow or becomes a widow.

(xxvii) Venus in a Varga of Mars or Saturn or aspected by either—addicted to other women.

(xxviii) Malefics in VII or VIII house and Mars in XII and the lord of VII be in the invisible half—he takes another wife.

(xxix) Lord of the ascendant conjoined with the lord of the 7th house, but eclipsed — Wife becomes ugly.

(xxx) Many malefics in II house and in VII (or with their lords), and their lords being aspected by malefics—three wives.

(xxxi) The lord of the 7th house be in a Kendra or Koṇa identical with his exaltation, friendly or own Sign or Varga and be aspected by the lord of the 10th house — many wives.

(xxxii) If the lord of the 7th house be Mercury who is in depression or inimical Varga, or occupy the 6th or 8th house in conjunction with, surrounded or aspected by malefics — he will be killed by his wife who will spell ruin to the family.

The following Yogas lead to good results :—

(i) The lord of VII house be in a Kendra, owned by a benefic, aspected by a benefic or occupying a benefic Aṁśa — the wife would be chaste and dutiful and coming from a noble family.

(ii) Cancer be the 7th house occupied by Mars and Saturn—the wife would be beautiful and chaste.

(iii) The lord of this Bhāva be conjoined with the lord of the ascendant—the wife would be excellent.

(iv) The lord of the ascendant be in the 7th house along with a benefic—wife belongs to a good family.

(v) The Moon occupying the 1st or 7th house in her own or exaltation Sign and aspected by a benefic—she is virtuous.

(vi) The 7th house falling in a benefic Sign or Aṁśa, (still better if aspected by benefics)—wife is virtuous.

(vii) The 7th house, its lord and Venus be all in even signs and be bright, and strong—the wife will be very good.

(viii) The lords of II, VII and XII houses occupying Kendras or Koṇas and being aspected by Jupiter, or benefics occupying the 2nd, 7th and 11th houses counted from the lord of the 7th house—the subject will give all happiness to the wife.

The number of wives one is likely to have can be ascertained from the number of planets occupying the 7th house as well as from that of the planets conjoined with Venus and the lord of the 7th house. According to some it is given by the number of planets conjoined with Venus when the 7th house is occupied.

However there is an exception to this rule : If any of the planets conjoined with Venus be in his own Sign or exaltation, then he should not be taken into account. Similarly if the lord of the 7th house be in the 2nd house owned by Venus, then too the number of wives will correspond to the planets conjoined with Venus. Likewise note how many of the planets conjoined with the lord of the 2nd or 7th house are weak and at the same time owners of Dusthānas (6th, 8th and 12th). They will kill so many wives of the subject. If there is only one strong planet (excepting the lord of a Dusthāna) in the above house, the person will have only one wife, So too when the lord of the 2nd or 7th is in his own house. Even a malefic will do good to the Bhāva, if he owns it. On the other hand even a benefic who owns a Dusthāna will not do much good.

Now you may be interested to know the procedure to find out the time of a person's marriage as well as the natal sign and constellation of the would-be bride. Note the Sign and Aṁśa occupied by the lords of the ascendant and the 7th house in a man's nativity. His bride's natal Sign would be the same or one triangular to the above Sign or Aṁśa; or it may be the exaltation or depression Sign of the lord of I or VII house; or it will be the sign 7th from the Lagna, the Moon or Venus; or it may be the sign that contains the highest number of benefic dots in the Moon's Aṣṭakavarga chart of the man (cf. Chapter XXII). The wife would be ideal in every respect, if she be born in the Sign indicated by the sum total of the longitudes of the lords of the 1st and 7th houses in the man's horoscope. Similarly if a girl is born in the Sign owned by the planet occupying or aspecting the 7th house from the Moon in the boy's chart, she will make an attractive wife, loved by the subject.

You can similarly find out the direction or the place of birth of the would-be bride. You know the planets that preside over the different quarters. Now find out which of the three planets viz. the one occupying the 7th house, its owner and Venus, is the strongest. The quarter presided over by that planet will be the direction of the bride's place. It may also be got from the planet that rules the 7th house counted from Venus.

(i) The subject's marriage may take place when Venus or the lord of VII house passes during his transit through the sign or Aṁśa occupied by the lord of the ascendant, or through one trine to it. (ii) Or it may come off when the lord of the ascendant in transit goes to the Sign which houses the 7th Bhāva. (iii) It is likely to happen during the major period of the planet (1) posited in the 7th house, (2) aspecting the 7th, or (3) owning the 7th. (iv) Find out the strongest of the following four planets viz. the Moon, Venus, and the lords of the sign and Aṁśa occupied by the lord of VII house. Marriage will take place in the major period of that planet and during the passage of Jupiter through a sign which represents the Rāśi or Aṁśa occupied by the lord of the 7th house, or its trine. (v) Find the sum of the longitudes of the lords of the 1st and 7th houses. It will represent a certain Sign. When Jupiter in transit passes through that sign, marriage will take place. (vi) The same may take place when Jupiter passes through the sign indicated by the sum of the longitudes of the planets prseiding over the stars occupied by the Moon and the lord of the 7th house. (vii) It may also take place in the Daśā and Bhukti of the lord of the 7th house counted from Venus, or of the lord of the sign occupied by the lord of the 2nd house counted from the Lagna. (viii) It may occur when the Moon and Jupiter in their transit arrive at the sign owned by the lord of the Aṁśa occupied by the lord of the ascendant at birth, or when Jupiter passes through the sign occupied by Venus or the lord of the 7th house, or when Jupiter and the Moon arrive at a Kendra (together or separately). (ix) In the case of the twice-born the event may take place in so many years after their Upanayana (investiture with the sacred thread) as the 7th house is removed from Aries.

You have already learnt which planets yield results in the beginning of their period, which in the middle and which at the end. In respect of marriage too you can ascertain these details. : First of all you have to find out whether a planet gets the portfolio of marriage in any manner. When that is established, you will see if it is a benefic planet and if it is posited in a benefic Sign. If this be the case, it will help marriage at the commencement of its major period. If it is a benefic planet, but posited in a malefic sign, marriage will take place in the middle of the Daśā. If both the planet and the Sign it occupies are malefic, it will take place at the end of the Daśā. A malefic in a benefic house, however, will confer good results throughout the period, especially when it is conjoined with a benefic.

Compatibility of horoscopes :— People generally say that a person who is Maṅgali or has Kuja Doṣa cannot be matched with a girl who does not possess this Doṣa. The person who has this trouble will adversely affect the life of the partner. Hence they look for girls with Kuja Doṣa for counteracting the same in the boy's chart. It is to be remembered that the girl should not have this trouble more than the boy. The reason is quite obvious. While matching horoscopes care should be taken to ascertain the longevity, Daśās, relationship of the Daśā lords, ending periods of Daśās etc. in the two charts. Before proceeding further let us know what Kuja Doṣa is. If Mars is posited in the 12th, 2nd, 4th, 7th or 8th house from the Lagna, Kuja Doṣa is brought into existence. The above places are also to be counted from the Moon as well as from Venus. If the boy alone has this Kuja Doṣa, he will lose the wife soon. Likewise see if there are malefics in the 2nd and 7th houses. For, they too are harmful to the wife. It is also bad for the wife if Mars occupies the 7th house and the Aṁśa belonging to Venus. The native will be passionately attached to his wife, if the lord of the 7th house is aspected by or conjoined with Venus, or occupies a house owned by Venus. The same effect has to be predicted, if the lord of the 2nd house too is under similar circumstances; or if the lord of the 10th house occupies the 7th along with Venus.

Marriage takes place successfully when Jupiter comes to the Sign belonging to the planet that owns the Aṁśa occupied by the lord of the ascendant. On the other hand, if the Navāṁśa belongs to the depression or inimical sign of the lord of the 1st house, the wife may not live long. The time of the wife's death can be found out thus :— Subtract the ascendant from the longitude of the lord of the 7th house. This will give a Sign. When Jupiter arrives at this Sign or its trine, the death of the subject's wife may take place. The same event is likely to take place during the major and minor periods of *Chidra planets*[1] with respect to the 7th Bhāva, when Saturn passes through the sign which is fatal to the wife according to the Aṣṭaka Varga chart of Venus (vide Chapter XXII) and when Jupiter goes to the Navāṁśa owned by that fatal sign.

1. This term applies to seven planets viz. the lord of the 8th, one occupying it, one aspecting it, one conjoined with its lord, lord of the 22nd decanate, lord of the 64th Navāṁśa and the bitter enemy of the lord of the 8th house.

CHAPTER XVI

FEMALE HOROSCOPY

Though the general rules regarding the 7th house are the same for men as well as for women, still there are some special points to be observed in the female charts. This may be due to the special psychological make-up of the woman. Her auspiciousness or *Māṅgalya* is read from the 8th house, issue from the 9th, beauty from the ascendant, husband and attractiveness from the 7th and association as well as chastity from the 4th house. Benefics and their lords in these houses confer good results, whereas malefics cause havoc. Some authorities hold that the Lagna stands for the woman's brilliance, fame and wealth, the 5th house for children and the 9th and the planets posited therein for asceticism and tranquillity. If both the ascendant and the Moon are housed in even signs and aspected by benefics, the woman will be blessed with ideal character, prosperity, ornaments, husband and sons. If the ascendant and the Moon be in odd signs and be aspected by or conjoined with malefics, she would be masculine in disposition, of crooked mind, poor, fierce and not obedient to the husband. The results would be mixed if the nature of the signs and planets be mixed.

If the 7th house or its Navāṁśa be a Sign owned by a benefic, the woman's husbandw ould be possessed of lustre, fame, learning and wealth, provided the planets and the Signs concerned are strong and unafflicted. Otherwise he would be deformed, unintelligent, poor, deceitful or a gambler and will live away from her. If the 7th house and its Aṁśa belong to Mars or if Mars occupies either of them, she will be widowed or will be at loggerheads with the husband. She will be abandoned by her husband if there be a weak malefic in the 7th aspected by a benefic. If, on the other hand, the planets in these places are of a mixed nature, she will be remarried. Presence of malefics in the 8th house without benefic aspect will destroy the husband. However, should there be benefics in the 2nd house, the woman herself would pass away earlier. If the ascendant be an odd sign, the masculine planets as well as the Moon, Mercury and Venus be possessed of much strength and Saturn of moderate strength, she would be a dependant and have many husbands. On the other hand a girl in whose horoscope the ascendant is an even sign and Mars, Mercury, Jupiter and Venus strong, will be famous, chaste, intelligent, learned and wealthy.

The following planetary dispositions lead to bad character on the part of the woman :—

(i) Malefics in the 4th house without the aspect of or conjunction with benefics.

(ii) The ascendant, the Moon and Venus or their Aṁśas being in the signs owned by Mars and Saturn.

(iii) The Moon (or the ascendant, whichever is stronger) in Aries or Scorpio and in a Triṁśāṁśa belonging to Mars, Saturn or Venus.

(iv) The Moon in Taurus or Libra and in a Triṁśaṁśa of Mars or Saturn.

(v) The Moon in Capricorn or Aquarius and in Triṁśāṁśa of Saturn or Mercury.

(vi) The Moon in Cancer and in the Triṁśāṁśa of Mars.

(vii) The Moon in Leo and in a Triṁsāṁśa of Saturn or Venus.

(viii) Venus and Mars occupying each other's Navāṁśa.

(ix) Venus, Mars and the Moon jointly occupying the 7th house — she will go astray with the husband's consent.

(x) A Sign of Saṭurn or Mars being the Lagna, and the Moon and Venus aspected by a malefic occupying it — she leads an immoral life along with her mother.

Note :— The rules mentioned in (iii) to (vi) above may also be applied to the figure obtained by adding the longitude of the Moon and the cusp of the 1st house.

One remains chaste and auspicious till the end of her life under the following conditions :—

(i) The ascendant, the Moon and the 4th house being connected with benefics.

(ii) Benefics occupying Koṇas (trines).

(iii) The Moon or the ascendant in Aries or Scorpio and in the Triṁśāṁśa of Jupiter; or in Taurus or Libra and in that Aṁśa of Jupiter, Mercury or Venus; or in Gemini or Virgo and in that Aṁśa of Jupiter or Mercury; or in Cancer and in the Aṁśa of Jupiter or Venus; or in Sagittarius or Pisces and in the Aṁśa of Mars, Jupiter or Venus.

The effects of the Moon or the ascendant being in the various signs and Triṁśāṁśas are given in the following table :

Lords of Triṁśaṁśas Lords of→ Signs ↓	Mars	Mercury	Jupiter	Venus	Saturn
Mars	Bad character	Becomes deceitful	Good character Aspicious	Bad character	Bad character
Mercury	Fraudulent	Good character	Good character	Pining	Eunuch
Jupiter	Good character	Adept in fine arts	Do	Good character	Indifferent to sexual union
Venus	Bad character	Good character	Do	Do	Bad character
Saturn	A maid-servant	Bad character	Controls her husband	Issueless and poor	Do
Moon	Bad character	Proficient in fine arts	Good character	Good character	She will kill her husband
Sun	A bad wife	of masculine conduct	King's consort	Bad character	Bad character

Note :— The effects in the blank spaces as well as for the signs of Venus have been already given in the previous two lists.

If the 7th Bhāva or its Navāṁśa belongs to a benefic, the woman will have beautiful hips and be auspicious. If the trines are occupied by weak malefics, she may either be barren or will lose her children. If the Moon be posited in the 5th house identical with an *Alpasuta* Sign (Taurus, Leo, Virgo or Scorpio), she will have very few children. If the 7th house or its Navāṁśa belongs to Mars, Saturn or the Sun, her genital organ will be diseased. If the lords of the (1) ascendant, (2) the 7th, (3) 9th house and (4) the sign occupied by the Moon be posited in good houses, conjoined with benefics and be bright, the subject would be clever in doing meritorious deeds, endowed with beauty and good fortune, and respected by her kinsmen. She will be devoted to her husband, of ideal character and be blessed with good sons. The period of her sound health and auspiciousness (Māṅgalya) has to be read from the influence of benefics on the 8th house.

If the Sun occupy the 7th house receiving the aspect of an inimical planet, she would be deserted by her husband. If Saturn be in that position receiving inimical (or malefic) aspect, she would remain a spinster till the end. If the 7th house owned by a malefic be occupied by Saturn, the woman would be widowed.

When the Moon and Venus are posited in the ascendant which is owned by Mars or Saturn, and when the 5th house also is conjoined with or aspected by a malefic, the woman will be barren. Similarly the Moon and Venus occupying the ascendant belonging to Mars would make the subject hate her husband; the Moon and Mercury in that position make her an expert in philosophical disquisitions; Mars and Mercury, voluptuous; the Moon, Mercury and Venus, happy and prosperous; and Jupiter, blessed with good progeny, ornaments and intelligence. If the lord of the Navāṁśa occupied by the owner of the 8th house be malefic, widowhood is certain. If there be benefics in the 9th house, she would live happily with progeny in spite of a malefic's presence in the 7th or 8th. One would be plunged in poverty and sorrow, if there be malefics in the 1st, 7th, 8th and 9th houses. When the lord of the 5th is posited in the 6th house and the lord of the latter in the ascendant, the subject will meet with death through weapons. When planets occupying Signs or Aṁśas of Saturn and Mars are conjoined with Venus and the Moon and are aspected by malefics, the woman would take to immoral ways along with her mother (See P. 196 (x). If there are *two* malefics in the 7th house, she will be lustful and be widowed; if *three*, unchaste and will kill her husband; and if three benefics are there, she will become the spouse of a king endowed with virtues. One would be tormented by excessive lust, if Venus and Saturn occupy each other's Navāṁśa or aspect each other and if the Lagna be Aquarius with Taurus Aṁśa or Taurus with Aquarius Aṁśa.

A malefic in the 7th house from the Moon is likely to cause widowhood, while a benefic will confer royal privileges. If the birth occurs in the ascendant owned by (1) Venus or the Moon and (2) Mercury or Jupiter, she will in order be (1) attractive with virtues and charm, and (2) skilled in fine arts. If Jupiter should occupy at a female birth the 5th, 9th or a Kendra identical with his own, exaltation or very friendly sign, the person would be a paragon of virtues, happy, prosperous and blessed with worthy sons and would bring credit to both the families. If the strong Moon occupies the ascendant which belongs to herself, and if Mercury, Jupiter and Venus are possessed of strength, she will be brilliant, famous and proficient in many Śāstras and in the aesthetic appreciation of fine arts. If there be a malefic in the 7th and another in the 9th, she might take to asceticism applicable to the planet in the 9th house.

When the earlier death of the woman is ascertained, the exact period of the event can be understood through the lord of the 8th house or the planet occupying it. Find out the lord of the Navāṁśa occupied by this lord of the 8th house. In his Daśā too it may occur. The couple may quit the world almost together if the 8th house has mixed strength and is conjoined with or aspected by both benefics and malefics; or if the lords of the ascendant and the 7th house be together or exchange houses and be in conjunction with a benefic.

Nature of Husband

When a girl's horoscope is presented to you for examination, you can have a fair idea as to what kind of a boy she is going to get for a husband. Of course you have already learnt the general rules regarding this in the previous chapter. Here a few more details are given for the benefit of students :—

(i) If the 7th house is devoid of strength and planets and is aspected by malefics and not by benefics, the girl will have a wretched fellow for a husband.

(ii) If the 7th house be occupied by Mercury and Saturn or owned by either of them, the husband would be impotent.

(iii) If the 7th house be a movable Sign and its lord in a movable Sign or Aṁśa, her husband would always be away from home.

(iv) If the Sun be there in his own Aṁśa or Sign, the husband would be gentle in his sexual activities.

(v) If it be the Moon similarly situated (i.e. in her own Rāśi or Aṁśa in the 7th), he would be gentle in his sex life.

(vi) If it be Mars, he would be poor and adulterous.

(vii) If it be Mercury, he would be learned and happy.

(viii) If Jupiter, virtuous and self-controlled.

(ix) If Venus, handsome and ease-loving.

(x) If Saturn, aged and foolish.

(xi) If the lord of the 9th house and Jupiter be in a Dusthāna (6th, 8th or 12th house), the husband would be short-lived; if they be in Kendras or Koṇas, he would be rich and long-lived; if they be conjoined with Mercury or the lord of the 4th house, learned; if conjoined with Mars and Saturn, an agriculturist; if conjoined with Rāhu or Ketu, a villain; and if conjoined with the lord of the 6th house, a leader of gangsters.

CHAPTER XVII

DISEASE

You have understood by now that the planets, zodiacal signs along with their Vargas or parts, houses and constellations possess particular qualities, good or bad, which are revealed in their respective periods and sub-periods. All the effects revealed by a chart are deemed to be the results of one's Prārabdha or past Karma that has begun to yield fruits. Hence these fruits of Karma constitute a person's nature, tendency and mental and physical peculiarities. However much man may try to get over these peculiarities, he finds that his efforts are no match for his '*nature*' or destiny. For, there is a debt that he owes to nature. In other words, man cannot fight shy of reaping the fruits of what he had sown previously, of which, no doubt, he is not aware at present. All relationships, good and bad, all ailments, severe and trivial, are the effects of nature or debts due to nature. Accordingly, we learn from the medical science that when fever is on, it is nothing but the effect of a fight between the system containing disease-resistants and disease germs. If the debt is too heavy, then the battle goes in favour of the germs and the person pays off the final debt of nature. Hence all diseases are of the nature of debts, big or small.

According to Āyurveda illness is caused by vitiation of the various constituents of the body such as the seven Dhātus, the three Doṣas and Malas. In this connection Sage Hārīta states : "The sin committed by a person in his previous life afflicts him in the form of diseases. But one could eradicate them by means of medical treatment, gifts, Japas, sacrifices and worship of Gods."

Each of the planets is capable of causing many a disease when it is afflicted, powerless, ill placed or combust. These depend on various factors like the humours mentioned above.

Blindness

(i) The rising sign Leo being occupied by the two luminaries and aspected by Mars and Saturn, without any benefic aspect.

(ii) The Sun, Moon, Mars and Saturn being posited in the 6th, 8th, 12th and 2nd in any order, the cause of blindness being vitiation of the humour belonging to the strongest of these planets. (iii) malefics occupying the 6th and 8th. (iv) Mars being lord of the 2nd house (i.e. when the ascendant is either Libra or Pisces), the luminaries in the 8th, and Saturn in the 6th or 12th. (v) The Moon in one of the Dusthānas, and Mars and Saturn being together somewhere. (vi) Lord of 2nd in conjunction with a malefic, Mars and Saturn together with Māndi occupying a single house, and the 2nd house itself being afflicted by malefics, and aspected by Saturn. (vii) Lord of the Navāṁśa occupied by the lord of the second house being joined by malefics and occupying the sign belonging to a malefic, and the lord of the 2nd being the Sun or Mars is aspected by Saturn and Māndi. (viii) Lords of 1st and 2nd together occupying a Dusthāna. (ix) Lord of the 2nd occupying a Dusthāna along with the Sun, Venus and lord of the ascendant. (x) 4th and 5th houses being occupied by malefics, and the Moon in a Dusthāna. (xi) Lords of 1st, 2nd, 5th, 7th and 9th occupying Dusthānas, and Venus being associated with the ascendant. (xii) Venus being combined with the Moon and being posited in a Dusthāna. (xiii) Venus occupying the ascendant in conjunction with the luminaries and being aspected by Mars and Saturn. (xiv) The Moon occupying a sign owned by Venus along with three malefics wihtout any benefic aspect. (xv) The lord of the 2nd house being conjoined with Saturn, Mars and the lord of the ascendant, especially in the 6th or 8th house.

Eye-Disease

(i) Many malefics occupying the 2nd house and aspected by Saturn and a weak benefic.

(ii) Mars and Venus together occupying the 2nd house or a sign or Aṁśa which is the debilitation of one and inimical house to the other.

Dumbness

The lord of the 2nd house occupying one of the Dusthānas along with the lord of the 4th house.

Foul smell in the mouth

Venus being in a house owned by Saturn who occupies the ascendant, and the lord of the 6th house being in a sign owned by Mercury or in Capricorn.

Navel Disease

The lords of the Lagna and the lunar sign should be together in the 6th house or joined with its lord.

Tumours

(i) The lord of the ascendant being posited in a Dusthāna along with the Sun causes a burning tumour. (ii) The lords of the ascendant, 6th and 8th being conjoined with the Sun lead to one as a result of fever. (iii) If it be the Moon instead of the Sun, it would be on a gland caused by dropsy or an operation; (iv) if it be Mercury, one caused by vitiation of bile; (v) if Jupiter, by illness; (vi) if Venus, through sex; (vii) if Saturn, through contact with the lowest or thieves; and (viii) if Rāhu or Ketu, through snake-poison.

Smallpox :— Mars occupying the ascendant aspected by Saturn and Sun.

Enlargement of the Spleen :— (i) Sun in Lagna being aspected by Mars. (ii) The Moon along with a malefic should be in the 6th and be aspected by a malefic, and Saturn should be in the 7th. (iii) The Sun, Moon and Mars are to be together in the 6th house. (iv) Mars is in the Lagna and lord of the 6th weak. (v) The waning Moon along with malefics is in the Lagna belonging to Saturn, or in the 6th or 8th house. (vi) Saturn in conjunction with the Moon should be in the 6th or 8th. (vii) If sign Scorpio happens to be the 8th house, or the Navāṁśa occupied by the lord of the 8th. (viii) The Moon is hemmed in betwixt malefics, and Saturn is in the 7th.

Lunacy :— (i) The Sun in the ascendant, and Mars in the 7th. (ii) Saturn in the Lagna, and Mars in the 7th or a trine. (iii) Jupiter in the 1st and Saturn or Mars in the 7th. (iv) The Lagna being occupied by the eclipsed Moon and Mercury. (v) The weak Moon conjoined with Saturn occupying the 12th house. (vi) Weak Moon together with malefics in 1, 2, 8, 9, 12. (vii) The Moon with malefics and with Rāhu in 5th, 8th or 12th.

(viii) If the beginning of Sagittarius be rising, and if the luminaries are in the lagna or trine, and Jupiter in the 3rd or an angle. (According to another view, the day of birth should be Tuesday or Saturday instead of 'beginning of Sagittarius rising).' (ix) Both the Moon and Mercury in angles without benefic Aṁśas. (x) Saturn, the Sun and Moon in angles. There are six varieties of madness. They are (i) born of Bile, (ii) of Wind, (iii) of Phlegm, (iv) of all the three, (v) of mental anguish, and (vi) of poison. Unmāda is one of the spirits attending on the Lord Śiva. Hence a person who defies Him is attacked by the evil spirit. That is why our elders at home advise us not to indulge in sports, drinking, eating, mating etc. at the time of Pradoṣa (dusk). The proper thing to do at that time is to perform the Sandhyāvandana and worship of the Lord. In the physical plane, it is caused by the eating of forbidden, spoilt and impure food, as well as excessive joy, fright, grief and mental agony. Sometimes inordinate sexual craving also produces it.

Epilepsy :— Some of the planetary configurations are not very different from those for lunacy. (i) If the Moon in conjunction with Saturn be aspected by Mars, one gets epileptic fits. (2) The same effect follows if Jupiter and Venus quincunx or 2nd and 12th to each other, be weak, aspected by or conjoined with the lords thereof, and be aspected by malefics at the same time. (3) Another Yoga for this is the presence of the Sun, Mars and Saturn in the 8th house.

Diabetes :— (i) The Moon in Cancer or Scorpio, Rāśi or Aṁśa, being afflicted by a malefic. (ii) If Venus occupies the 8th house and gets the aspect of malefics. (iii) Mercury and the Sun occupying a Sign belonging to Jupiter and receiving the aspect of Saturn. (iv) The 7th house being a watery sign and occupied by Saturn, the Sun, Mars and Rāhu.

Venereal diseases :— (i) If sign Virgo happens to be the 8th house or Navāṁśa occupied by the lord of that house. (ii) Venus and Mars occupying the 7th house receiving the aspect of a malefic. (iii) Lord of the 6th house along with Mercury and Rāhu occupying the ascendant. (iv) Lord of the 6th combined with Mars without any benefic aspect. (v) The Moon in the Aṁśa of Cancer, Scorpio or Aquarius, conjoined with Saturn. (vi) The Moon along with a malefic be in the Rāśi occupied by the lord of the 8th, and the lord of 8th be aspected by Rāhu. (vii) The 8th house being occupied by three or four malefics without any benefic association. (viii) Mars, or the Sun and Saturn being in the 8th house and receiving the aspect of debilitated, inimical or malefic planets.

Stomach-diseases :— (i) Mars be in the ascendant when the lord of the 6th is weak. (ii) Saturn be in the 8th, and Rāhu or a malefic in the Lagna. (iii) The lord of Lagna be in an inimical house or debilitated, and Mars and Saturn occupying the 4th house are aspected by a malefic. (iv) The lord of the 8th house being weak, the ascendant is aspected by malefics, and the 8th house itself is occupied or aspected by Saturn. (v) The Sun, Moon and Mars together occupying the sixth house. (vi) The 8th house be Makara, or the Navāṁśa of the lord of the 8th be the same. (vii) Ketu tenanting the 5th house, and lord of the 5th be weak. We have also seen before that the Moon in Leo tends to upset the stomach. According to one view this ailment is caused by the Moon (weak and afflicted) occupying the sixth house.

Heart-disease :— (i) The Moon (in 1, 4, 6 or 8) hemmed in betwixt Mars and Saturn, and the Sun be in Capricorn. (ii) Such a Moon be also conjoined with the Sun in Capricorn. (iii) The luminaries exchanging Rāśis or Aṁśas. (iv) The Sun and Moon be in conjunction either in Cancer or Leo. (v) Aquarius happening to be the 8th house or the Navāṁśa Rāśi occupied by the lord of the 8th. (vi) The waning Moon be in the 6th or 8th identical with a watery sign in conjunction with a malefic. (vii) Jupiter in the 8th house identical with a watery sign being aspected by a malefic. (viii) Venus in the 8th being aspected by a malefic. (ix) The Sun occupying the Lagna is aspected by Mars. (x) The Moon between two malefics, and Saturn in the 7th. (xi) Saturn conjoined with Māndi be in the 6th aspected by the Sun, Mars and Rāhu, and without any benefic aspect or association. (xii) Mars in the 6th house in a cruel 60th Aṁśa, conjoined with Mercury and aspected by Venus. (xiii) The 4th house being occupied by Jupiter who is aspected or joined by the Sun and Mars. (xiv) The 4th house being occupied by malefics, and its lord conjoined with malefics or hemmed in between them.

Leprosy :— (i) Malefics other than the lord, occupying the ascendant. (ii) The Moon along with Mars or Saturn be in the Aṁśa of Cancer, Pisces or Capricorn (without benefic aspect or association). (iii) The Moon in the ascendant, Sun in the 7th, and Mars and Saturn in the 2nd and 12th. (iv) The Sun and Rāhu occupying the 8th house, more so if Mars too joins them. (v) If the Sun, Venus and Saturn are together in a single house. (vi) The Sun in a house belonging to Mars being aspected by Saturn. (vii) Rāhu in Leo being aspected by Venus. (viii) The lord of the ascendant and Mercury, or Mars and the Moon being conjoined with Rāhu or Ketu anywhere. (ix) The Sun and Mars being conjoined with Saturn. (x) The Moon being conjoined with Mars and Saturn in Aries or Taurus. (xi) Venus, Mars, the Moon and Saturn being together in capricorn, Cancer or Scorpio, provided there is no benefic in the Lagna. (xii) Jupiter or Venus in the 6th and malefics in 1. (xiii) The Moon being surrounded by malefics, and the 7th house occupied by Saturn.

Poison through snake-bite etc. :— (i) Rāhu in the Lagna, and lord of the 3rd house conjoined with the lord of the ascendant. (ii) A planet in depression or inimical house or combustion and aspected by a malefic. (iii) Lords of the ascendant and sixth being conjoined with Rāhu or Ketu. (iv) The 8th house being malefic, owned by a malefic, occupied by malefics and having a malefic asterism. (v) A planet in debility in III and a malefic in VI or inimical house, both aspected by malefics. (vi) The lord of III or the ascendant with its lord in it being combined with Rāhu.

Throat-complaints :— (i) The lord of the third house being conjoined with Mercury. (ii) See (ii) and (v) under Poison. (iii) A malefic in the third house along with Māndi or some other malefic. (iv) The Moon occupying the 4th house in a Navāṁśa belonging to the same Rāśi, and being conjoined with a malefic. (v) Lords of the 2nd and 3rd houses being conjoined along with Rāhu. (vi) Both Mercury and Rāhu being together in the 3rd house.

Ear-ailments :— (i) A malefic in the 3rd house being aspected by another malefic. (ii) Lord of the 3rd occupying a malefic 60th Aṁśa. (iii) Malefics in 3rd, 5th, 9th and 11th without benefic aspect. (iv) Rāhu in the 11th house. (v) The third and eleventh houses and Jupiter being conjoined with or aspected by Saturn and Mars. (vi) Lord of the second house and Mars together occupying the Lagna. (vii) Venus or Mars occupying 2nd or 12th house. (viii) The Moon who is weak, occupying the ascendant other than Aries, Taurus and Cancer.

Fever :— There are many varieties of fever. Many a time fever is only a symptom. (i) Leo or Aquarius is the 8th house or the Navāṁśa of its lord. (ii) Mercury being in Leo is aspected by malefic. (iii) The lord of the ascendant in a Navāṁśa of Aries or Libra. (iv) Lords of the 1st and 6th houses be in conjunction with the Sun. This occurs during the periods and transits of planets. For example, fever is experienced by one in the Sun's own Bhukti of his Daśā, in the sub-period of Rāhu in the Daśā of the Moon, in the Bhukti of Ketu in Rāhu-Daśā, in the Bhuktis of Mars and Rāhu in Saturn-Daśā, and in the Svabhukti of Ketu. So does the Sun cause fever while passing through the 12th house in transit and Mars through the 5th house and the 8th.

Dysentery :— (i) The 8th house or its Navāṁśa being Pisces. (ii) The Moon conjoined and aspected by malefics be in the 6th, and Venus in the 7th house. (iii) The Sun and Mercury being together in a house of Saturn and aspected by a malefic. (iv) The Moon and Venus jointly occupying the 8th, more so if Mars too joins them.

Diarrhoea :— The Moon being posited in the 6th house. (See also under Stomach-complaints). This ailment appears in the Daśā of Venus and Bhukti of the Moon as well as in the Daśā of the weak Moon. Mars in his transit through the 4th house also causes this trouble.

Piles :— (i) The weak Moon occupying the 8th house being aspected by Saturn in strength. (ii) Weak Moon being aspected by strong Mars, and Saturn occupying the 8th house. (iii) Saturn occupying the 8th house. (iv) The lord of the Lagna, Mars and Mercury being together in a Dusthāna or in the 4th aspect the 6th house. (v) The Moon in the 6th or 8th is aspected by Mars, and Saturn occupies the Lagna. (vi) The Sun in Cancer being aspected by Saturn.

Diseases of Teeth :— (i) The Moon or Rāhu posited in the 12th house, Saturn in a trine, and the Sun in the 7th or 8th house. (ii) The above planets occupying Navāṁśas owned by malefics in depression or in inimical houses. (iii) Lord of the 2nd house together with Rāhu occupying a Dusthāna along with the lord thereof. (iv) The Sun in the 2nd house, or the Moon in Leo, or Saturn in Cancer. (v) Rāhu or Ketu in the 6th house. (vi) Jupiter and Rāhu in the Lagna.

Urinary Ailments :— (i) The Moon should be in a watery sign, its lord in the 6th house being aspected by planets occupying watery signs. (ii) All the malefics together occupy 6th or 7th house. (iii) Saturn in the 7th house being aspected by Rāhu. (iv) The 7th house being occupied by a watery planet and its lord in a watery sign or combined with a watery planet, there being no benefic aspect. (v) The 5th house being tenanted by malefics. (vi) The 7th house being a watery sign, and the ascendant being occupied by a watery planet and aspected or joined by a malefic. (vii) The lords of the 6th, 7th and 12th houses being together and aspected by Saturn. (viii) Many malefics being in the 7th house whose lord should be in the 6th or aspected by Rāhu.

Rheumatism :— (i) Jupiter in the ascendant and Saturn in the 7th house. (ii) Saturn in the Lagna, and Mars in the 5th, 7th or 9th house. (iii) The waning Moon and Saturn in the 12th house. (iv) Venus be in the 8th house receiving the aspect of a malefic. (v) The Sun in Cancer being aspected by Saturn. (vi) Saturn being aspected by Mars.

Dropsy :— (i) Saturn should be in Cancer and the Moon in Capricorn. (ii) The 8th house or its Aṁśa be Pisces. This is experienced during the Daśā of debilitated Jupiter.

Diseases of the Testicles :— (i) Rāhu and Mars, or Rāhu and Saturn to be in conjunction especially in the Lagna. (ii) Mars occupying the ascendant. (iii) The lord of the ascendant be in the 8th house which is occupied by Rāhu and Māndi. (iv) Rāhu in the Lagna, Māndi in a trine, and Mars along with Saturn in the 8th. (v) Lord of the Navāṁśa of the Lagna-lord be in conjunction with Rāhu, Māndi, Mars and Saturn, severally or collectively. (vi) Venus and Mars occupying together the 8th house. (vii) Venus and Mars together occupy a sign belonging to Mars. (viii) The Moon and Venus together occupying a sign of Mars and receiving the aspect of both Jupiter and Saturn. (ix) The Navāṁśa of the Ātma-kāraka being occupied by Gulika and aspected by Mercury alone. (x) Mars, Saturn and Rāhu to be in the 6th, and a malefic in the ascendant.

Wounds

(i) The lord of the 6th being posited in the ascendant along with Rāhu or Ketu.

(ii) The lord of the ascendant being in a Dusthāna along with Rāhu or Ketu.

(iii) Saturn and Mars being conjoined in the 6th or 12th house.

(iv) The ascendant or its lord being conjoined with a malefic and aspected by Mars.

Illness at different ages

(i) If Rāhu be in the 6th and Saturn in the 6th therefrom, one would fall ill in the *first* year, and have eye-trouble in the *third* year.

(ii) If the Sun be in the 8th from the 6th house, and the Moon in the 12th therefrom, one would have danger from water in the 5th and 9th years.

(iii) If the lord of the 8th be conjoined with Rāhu in the 8th house itself or in a Koṇa, one would suffer from glandular afflictions in the 12th and 16th years.

(iv) If the lord of the 12th be in the 6th along with its lord, one would suffer from enlargement of spleen in the *third* and *nineteenth* year.

(v) If Saturn be in the 8th and Mars in the 8th or 12th house, one gets nasal catarrh in the eleventh and thirtieth years.

Feminine Diseases :— (i) If the Navāṁśa of the 7th house belongs to Mars, and is aspected by Saturn or by the Sun and Mercury, the woman suffers from a disease in the womb. (ii) The Lagna is owned by Mercury and its Triṁśāṁśa by Saturn. (iii) The ascendant is owned by the Sun and Triṁśāṁśa by Venus. (iv) Jupiter or Venus in the 8th causes abortion. (v) Saturn and the Sun in the 8th house lead to barrenness. (vi) Mercury and Saturn in the 7th (as well as in the 5th) lead to the same effect. In a work entitled the *Mahādeva-Bhāṣya* it has been stated that if Mars occupies the 8th house from the ascendant or the Moon of the girl at the time of marriage, she will have excessive and continuous menstrual flow. Similar diseases crop up when Venus occupies in a woman's horoscope Scorpio (and also is aspected by malefics only). Sometimes the foetus does not develop even after a year or two. Such a case is termed Mūḍha-Garbha in Āyurveda. If the Navāṁśa of the ascendant at Niṣeka (impregnation) belongs to Saturn and if Saturn occupies the 7th house, then the delivery may take place after three or even 12 years

CHAPTER XVIII

DESCRIPTION OF DECANATES

You have seen already that a Rāśi is subdivided into various parts or Vargas, each of which has its own importance in horoscopy.

Parāśara mentions 16 Vargas. But generally six or seven Vargas only are made use of in astrology. The Horāpradīpa has given a clear analysis of the functions of the seven Vargas mentioned above. Everything concerning the body is to be judged from the Lagna as a whole; things pertaining to wealth and property from Horā, the result of Karma from the Decanate, brothers and sisters from Saptāṁśa, issue from Navāṁśa, marriage from Dvādaśāṁśa and lastly death from Triṁśāṁśa. At present we are not concerned with the Vargas other than the Drekkāṇa. The word Drekkāṇa like Tāvuru is not a Sanskrit one. It must be a loan word from Greek where it must have meant an arc subtending an angle of 10 degrees at the centre of a circle. Hence the word Drekkāṇa or decanate corresponds to Daśa in Sanskrit and to decem in Latin. Greek astrologers attached great importance to this decanate possibly on account of the special significance of the number ten. In India too we associate this number with some mystic significance. Look at the ten Avatāras, ten quarters, ten heads of Rāvaṇa etc. The Bible too speaks of the ten Commandments. This ten degree portion of a Sign represents in fact a part of man's existence on this earth. This might also account for the acceptance by ancient scholars of man's span of life to be 120 years in all. The importance of the decanate may be gathered from the fact that great scholars like Varāhamihira have bestowed unusual thought on this subject.

There is difference of opinion among the authorities regarding the ownership of the decanates in the different Signs. Varāhamihira is of opinion that in all Signs the lords of decanates are (i) the lord of the Sign itself, (ii) that of the fifth house therefrom, and (iii) that of the 9th house from the Sign. The Yavanas, however, assign the lordship of the three to the lords of the particular Sign, its 12th and 11th Signs respectively. Yet some others distinguish the lordship on the basis of the nature of the Signs. In a movable house the lordship belongs to the lords of the 1st, 5th and 9th from the particular house; in a fixed house it belongs to those of the 5th, 9th and 1st house; and in a common house it belongs to those of the 9th, 1st and 5th house respectively. But Satyācārya seems to have made a distinction in respect of horoscopy and horary astrology. He states that for horoscopy there should not be any difference in the lordship of the decanates and that should belong to the lords of the 1st., 5th and 9th houses, while for the purpose of queries the lords are to be taken as those of the 1st, 12th and 11th houses. I am inclined to believe that this distinction is very helpful in the case of horary astrology. It is to be borne in mind that every planet is considered to be strong while posited in his own decanate.

These decanates have their own names, forms, characteristic qualities and utilities. The names of the decanates are the following :— (*i*) Sarpa or serpent, (*ii*) Nigala or fetters, (*iii*) Āyudha or weapon, (*iv*) Pakṣin or bird, (*v*) Dahana or fiery, (*vi*) Jala or watery, (*vii*) Saumya or benefic, and (*viii*) Vimiśra or mixed. There is also sex-difference among them. Some of them are also called Catuṣpād or quadruped. The following are termed Serpent decanates which are of course malefic :— The second and third decanates of Cancer, the first and second of Scorpio, and the third of Pisces. According to Balabhadra they are the first and second of Cancer, the same of Scorpio and the last of Pisces. The first one of Capricorn is called Nigala Drekkāṇa. According to the Jātakapārijāta the second decanate of Vṛścika is the Nigala one. Similarly the Sarpa-Drekkāṇas are the first, second and third respectively of Vṛścika, Karka and Mīna. The Āyudha-Drekkāṇas are the last of Gemini, the first and third of Sagittarius, and the third of Capricorn. The Pakṣi Drekkāṇas are the second ones of Gemini and Libra and the first ones of Leo and Aquarius. Another authority gives them as the first decanates of Leo and Capricorn. The Fiery ones are :— The first decanates of Aries, Leo, Scorpio, Capricorn and Aquarius; the second ones of Cancer and Scorpio; and the last ones of Leo, Libra, Scorpio and Pisces. These are eleven in all. There are six Watery decanates; The first ones of Cancer and Pisces; the second ones of Virgo and Pisces; and the last ones of Taurus and Gemini. There are eleven Saumya or benefic ones : The first ones of Gemini, Virgo and Libra; the second ones of Aries, Taurus, Sagittarius, Capricorn and Aquarius; and the last ones of Virgo, Sagittarius and Aquarius. There are eight Mixed decanates. The first ones of Taurus and Sagittarius, the second ones of Gemini, Leo and Libra, and the last ones of Aries, Cancer and Capricorn. The 22nd decanate from the rising one is termed Khara — cruel. All these names are expressive of their characteristic qualities. The following are also designated as Quadruped :— The second of Aries, the second and third of Taurus, the first of Cancer, first and last of Leo, last of Libra and of Scorpio and the first of Sagittarius. The following twelve are feminine :— The first of Taurus, Gemini, Virgo and Scorpio; the second of Aries, Cancer, Scorpio, Sagittarius, Capricorn, Aquarius and Pisces; and the last of Virgo. The remaining except the last of Scorpio are masculine.

Next we shall consider the forms of the decanates as described by Varāhamihira. This description is of paramount importance in that it helps the astrologer in delineating the characteristics, physical and mental of the person concerned. The first decanate of Aries is a man, dark in complexion, fierce in appearance and of red eyes, wearing a white cloth around his hips, holding a raised axe and appearing to be able to protect others. From this description we can easily guess that a person born in this decanate will be a leader of men who would subjugate them by his cruelty, might and promise of protection. The Sārāvali, however, says that the man is charitable, fond of fighting and inflicting heavy punishment on his kinsmen. The second, according to Yavana, is a woman with an equestrian face and pot-like body, clad in red garments and fond of ornaments and eatables. She is also always thirsty. According to the Sārāvali we have to declare a man born in this decanate to be concupiscent, given to pleasures, fond of music, high-minded, handsome and coveting women's and friends' wealth. The third is represented by a man who is cruel, tawny in colour, skilled in arts, active, of broken vows and clad in red clothes and holding a raised club in his hand. According to the Sārāvali he is good but harmful to others, a king's servant, liberal and fond of his own people. This shows a whimsical officer. The first decanate of Taurus symbolizes a woman with her hair curled and cut, her body like a pot, her clothes burnt, being very thirsty and hungry and greedy for ornaments. The second decanate denotes a man with a goat's face, proficient in agriculture and animal husbandry, with raised shoulders and dirty clothes. He is always hungry. This suggests a good but poor farmer. The last one is a man with a huge body like that of an elephant, prominent white teeth, brown complexion, feet like those of the tiger. He is a hunter coveting the meat of sheep and deer. The first decanate of Gemini is a woman without children, beautiful, fond of secret amour, well dressed and ornamented and having raised shoulders. This suggests a clever courtesan. The Sārāvali, however, makes it a man who is rich, tall with a large head, eloquent, receiving honour from kings, pleasure-loving and given to gambling. The second one represents a man standing in a garden, wearing armour and armed with a bow; he is heroic and a professional warrior and has an aquiline face; he thinks of sports, wealth, children and ornaments. If at a query this decanate is rising, one may predict the query to pertain to any of the things mentioned here. The last one is a man bedecked with ornaments, rich in jewels, fastened with a coat of mail and a quiver, and holding a bow. He is a poet and skilled in dance and instrumental music. The first decanate of Cancer is a man holding leaves, roots and fruits, having an elephantine body and feet similar to those of a tiger, face like that of a hog and neck like that of a horse. He is stationed in the forest of the Malaya mountain. The Sārāvali gives a different description altogether. He is an amiable, handsome man, intelligent, helper of others, fair in complexion, unsteady and devoted to Gods and Brahmins. The former is useful in Viyonijanma, birth of birds and beasts, while the latter in human births and queries relating to human beings. The second one is a woman coarse in behaviour, having a snake, with her head decorated with lotuses; she cries aloud holding the branch of a Palāśa tree in a forest. The other authority gives it as a miser fond of sleep, under the thumb of women, sickly and pleasure-loving. The last one is a man with a serpent coiled round, seated in a boat and going out on the sea in search of ornaments for his wife. He wears gold ornaments and has a flat face. This indicates a hen-pecked husband who would do any dangerous deed just to please his beloved. The first decanate of Leo is a combination of a man, quadruped and bird. According to the other, it is a man who is liberal, intent on conquering his enemies, courageous, endowed with many wives and friends, wealthy and a servant of kings. The second is a man with an equestrian shape, wearing white garlands on his head, clad in deer-skin and blanket, with a slender waist and raised nose-tip, holding a bow, and difficult to be approached. The last is a man with his face resembling that of a bear, and movements those of monkeys; he holds a stick, fruit and meat; he has a beard and curled hair. The first decanate of Virgo is a virgin holding a pot full of flowers, clad in soiled garments, and wishing for wealth and clothes and desiring to go to her father's residence. The Sārāvali makes it a tall, darkman who is delicate, modest, eloquent, with an elongated head and eyes like honey. He claims a share in the property of a woman. The second is a man holding a pen in his hand; he is dark in complexion and has a turban on his head; he earns and spends money; he carries a big bow; his body is fully covered with hair. This suggests a poet or an artist. According to the Sārāvali this is good for foreign travel. The last is a woman, yellowish in complexion, wearing a fine white silk Sārī, she is tall and is holding a pot and a ladle. She is pure and is going to temple. The first decanate of Libra is a clever merchant holding a balance in his hand seated in a shop in the bazar. The second is a man with an aquiline face, hungry and thirsty, and wishing to fly away with a pot in order to meet his wife and children. This decanate naturally belongs to Kumbha which is empty. Hence the man is hungry and thirsty. The last is a man with a monkey-like appearance, bedecked with jewels, and having a golden armour and quiver; he frightens animals in the forests and holds fruits and meat in his hand. The Sārāvali gives it as a rogue who is ungrateful, unsteady, ugly, crooked, huge in appearance, unintelligent and one who has lost his credit, friends and wealth. The first decanate of Scorpio is a charming woman bereft of garments and ornaments and coming to the shore from the ocean; she has fallen from her position and her feet are bound with a snake. The second is a woman with her body tied up with a snake; she desires a good position and happiness for the sake of her husband; her body is like a pot or tortoise. The other authority gives it as a man with a golden complexion, who is a good eater, handsome and is possessed of tremulous eyes, and others' wealth. He is good-natured and proficient in arts. The last is of Leonine form with a broad and flat face like that of a turtle. He rules over the Malaya region, scaring away dogs, deer, hogs and jackals. Kalyānavarman gives it as a man without beard and moustaches, cruel, pot-bellied, brown-eyed and courageous. He has massive arms and is devoid of brothers. The first decanate of Sagittarius has a human face and an equestrian body. He holds a long bow and staying in a hermitage guards the ascetics and their sacrificial articles. As this decanate belongs to the same Sign it is significant that the description accords well with that of Sagittarius itself. Jupiter being a spiritual planet is in charge of penance and sacrifice. This is good also for warriors and race-fans. The second is a charming lady with a golden complexion and moderate height. She is seated on a throne and is separating the gems of the sea. According to the other it is a man learned in the Sāstras, a clever expounder of the scriptures and performer of many sacrifices. He goes constantly to sacred places. The last is a man with a beard and golden complexion, seated on a worthy chair holding a rod. He is clad in silks and skins. The first decanate of Capricorn is a man full of hairs with the body like that of hog and a fierce look. He holds in his hands a rope, a net and a trap. The other gives it as a man with long arms, dark complexion, fame, personality, lustre and rougery. He speaks with a smile, is rich and easily won over by women. The second is a woman skilled in arts with long eyes resembling the petals of lotus, and dark complexion. She searches for various types of apparel, and has iron ears adorned with ornament. According to the other book it is a man with a small face and slender waist, given to taking away others' wealth and women, clever, liberal and knower of the ways of the virtuous. The last is a man having a Kinnara-like body and wearing a blanket. He has an armour, bow and quiver. He carries on his shoulder a pitcher inlaid with jewels. This decanate makes one talkative and suffer hardships in a foreign country. The first decanate of Aquarius is a man with an aquiline face, clad in blanket, silk and skin and worried about the acquisition of oil, wine, water and food. He is tall, interested in work, rich and a king's servant. He commands many women and much power and is infamous. The second is a woman seated in a half-burnt carriage containing

Śālmali wood. She carries on her head many pots and is engaged in bringing metals. Her clothes are dirty. If it is a man, he becomes greedy, full of fun and frolic and endowed with many friends. The last is a man, dark in hue, with hair in the ears and a crown on the head. He carries pots filled with barks, leaves, juice and fruits, mixed with metal. The first decanate of Pisces is a man handling sacrificial materials, pearls, conch shells, and wearing ornaments. He undertakes a sea-voyage for the sake of ornaments for his wife. The second is a damsel seated in a boat with flag flying aloft, along with her retinue in order to cross the sea. Her face has a golden colour If man, he eats sumptuously, speaks nicely, and is good at pleasing women and virtuous people. The last one of the last Sign is a man standing naked in a forest near a hole with a serpent coiled round his body. He cries aloud being troubled by thieves and fire. According to the Sārāvali it is a dark man proficient in arts, having large feet. He gives freely to his friends and commands excellent food and drink. He is also very mirthful. When the Rāśi indicated by the decanate is strong and is aspected by its lord, the result will be as stated above.

The development or otherwise of the different limbs of a child is deduced from the nature of the decanates of the 12 bhāvas beginning with the Lagna. The first decanates of the twelve houses represent the head, eye, ear, nostril, cheek, jaw, and mouth on the right side and the same on the left too. Note that the second and twelfth houses stand for the right and left eye respectively. Similarly the second decanates of the houses represent the neck, shoulder, arm, side, heart, chest and navel on the two sides. The last ones represent likewise pelvis, genital organ, testicle, thigh, knee, calf and legs, the 12th being anus. According to some scholars this order should be adhered to only when the first decanate of a Rāśi is rising. Otherwise the order will have to be modified accordingly i.e. if the second decanate of a Rāśi is rising, then we shall have to start with the neck. In my humble opinion it is better to start with the head whichever decanate of the Rāśi rises. If the Rāśi denoted by a particular decanate is well aspected or occupied, if its lord is well situated or aspected, the limb denoted by it will be well developed and good-looking. If the decanate is occupied by malefics, the corresponding limb will have an ulcer. If it is also occupied or aspected by benefics, there will be some mole or mark. If the malefic planet concerned should be in his own Rāśi or Navāṁśa identical with a fixed Sign, then the ulcer would be a congenital one. If the planet causing the ulcer be Saturn, it would be caused by stones or some wind disease; if Mars, by fire, weapon or poison; if Mercury, by mud; if Sun, by a wooden piece or a quadruped; and if Moon, by some liquid or horned creature. Mark, the Moon becomes a malefic when she is weak, and Mercury in association with malefics. A knowledge of the decanates helps the astrologer in predicting the birth of birds and beasts. For example, if a Pakṣi drekkāṇa be rising and be aspected or occupied by Saturn or the Moon, then birds would be born or indicated. In this case Saturn stands for those living on the land and the Moon for those in water. If the last Navāṁśa of Capricorn is rising and if there be three malefics in the 2nd, 3rd and 1st decanates of the Ascendant, the child will be without arms, feet or head as the case may be. If the Moon occupies a decanate owned by Mars, or if the Ascendant belongs to a malefic, and if benefics occupy the 2nd and 11th houses, the native is a snake or human being with a cord coiled round his body. The person born in a malefic decanate will be evil-minded, of wandering habits, addicted to sinful deeds and scandal-mongering. One born in a Watery decanate becomes liberal, enjoyer of pleasures, kind-hearted, intent on agriculture and irrigation, and void of morality. One born in a benefic decanate is compassionate, handsome, and blessed with happiness, wealth and children. And one born in a Mixed decanate is ill-behaved, loose in sexual matters, fickle-minded and of fierce looks. If at a birth the Moon be in her own or a friendly decanate, the subject would have a prepossessing appearance and all virtues; but if she be in a decanate owned by a non-friendly planet, he would have the appearance and qualities pertaining to that planet. If the Moon occupies a Serpent decanate, the subject will be wrathful; if an Armed decanate, he will commit murderous deeds; and if a Quadruped decanate, he will have liaison with worshippable women; if a Bird decanate, he will be a wanderer. If Saturn occupying a Kendra should aspect the Sign represented by the decanate occupied by Mercury, the subject would be an artist or artisan. If the rising decanate at a birth be a Serpent, Fetters or Weapon drekkāṇa, and if the sign represented by the decanate be also aspected by malefics, the person would undergo imprisonment wherein there would be appropriate punishment corresponding to the nature of the decanate. In this Yoga if the 5th and 9th houses are occupied by strong malefics and not aspected by benefics, the native dies in captivity.

We have already seen that the 22nd decanate is termed Khara drekkāṇa which is very important in deciding the nature of the subject's death. If this decanate happens to be Serpent, Weapon or Fetters, the person dies in prison or on account of torture. The lords of the Khara drekkāṇa and of the 8th house play an important role in the despatch of the native. Now let us see the effects of the 36 decanates becoming the Khara drekkāṇa severally :—(1) If it is the first of Aries and is aspected or occupied by malefics, death is due to water, snake poison and vitiation of bile. (2) In the second it is due to water, worms, frost or forest. (3) In the third it is caused by tank, well or precipice. (4) In the first of Taurus it is due to camels, horse, donkey or elephant, (5) In the second it is by vitiation of bile, wind, fire or thief. (6) In the third it is caused by a fall from a vehicle, seat or horse. It may also be caused by weapons in a fight. (7) In the first decanate of Gemini it is due to asthma. (8) In the second it is due to an attack of buffalo, poison or typhoid. (9) In the last it is due to wild animals, wild elephants, (Snake), or a jungle horde. (10) In the first of Cancer it is due to crocodile, liquor, thorn, or somnambulism. (11) In the 2nd it is due to a blow, poisoning etc. (12) In the last it is due to birds, venereal diseases, tumour, blood pressure or poisoning or general lassitude. (13) In the first of Leo it is by water, poison or foot-disease. (14) In the second by dropsy or diarrhoea or in a forest. (15) In the last by poison, weapon, curse or a fall. (16) In the first of Virgo it is by cerebral disease or vitiation of wind. (17) In the 2nd by a wild elephant or snake, in a fortress, forest or from a prince. (18) In the last by camel, donkey, weapon, water, deep chasm or by food served by a woman; (19) in the 1st of Libra by a young woman, quadruped or fall from a height; (20) in the 2nd by stomach ulcer; (21) in the last by snake or aquatic thing; (22) in the 1st of Scorpio by poison, weapon, or food and drink served by a woman; (23) in the 2nd by a bundle of clothes, fall or illness; (24) in the last by pain caused by stones or brickbats, or fracture of the bones of shanks; (25) in the first of Sagittarius by various diseases of the anus; (26) in the second by poison or wind disease; (27) in the last it is in water or by a water-disease, or by gastric trouble; (28) in the first of Capricorn it is by king, violence, tiger or by the amputation of the thigh; (29) in the second by an aquatic creature, poison, snake, a quadruped of uncloven hoofs, fire, weapon, thieves, fever or superhuman agency; (30) in the last by women; (31) in the first of Aquarius by women, water, stomach disease, mountain forest or bipeds; (32) in the second by worries caused by women, or venereal disease; (33) in the last by a couple, quadruped or a disease of the face or mouth; (34) in the first of Pisces by a tumour, rickets, gonorrhoea, woman, abscess on the shanks, or elephant or planetary trouble; (35) in the second by shipwreck, or in water; and (36) in the last by some fell diseases (vide tabulated results on p. 226).

The disposal of the dead body is also known from the nature of this Khara drekkāṇa. If it is Fiery, Watery or Mixed, the body is burnt to ashes; consigned to waters, or exposed to the sun and wind as the case may be. If it is Serpent, it is eaten away by beasts and birds of prey. If there are malefics in the 8th house, the dead body will be cremated. Similarly the previous existence of a soul can be predicted from the lord of the decanate occupied by the stronger of the two luminaries. If it be Jupiter, the soul must have come from the world of immortals; if it is the Moon or Venus, from that of the Manes; if it is the Sun or Mars from that of mortals; if Saturn or Mercury from the infernal regions. The rank of the soul in its previous birth was high, moderate or low according as the owner of the decanate mentioned here is in his exaltation, below that or in his depression. The refuge of the departed is indicated by the lord of the decanate of the 6th house (16th decanate from the rising one) or of the 22nd or by the planet occupying the 7th house. Whichever planet is strongest among these to the world thereof does the departed soul repair. Of course Moksha or final liberation is governed by Jupiter occupying certain positions. Some scholars are of opinion that the refuge of the soul is determined through the ruler of the decanate of the 12th or 2nd house.

The decanate is made use of in preparing Naṣṭaiataka. The

position of Jupiter in the Zodiac at the time of birth of the querent is determined from the decanate that is rising at the time of query. If it is the first decanate of the Sign, Jupiter should be located in the Sign itself which happens to be the Ascendant at the query; if second or third decanate, his position will be in the 5th or 9th as the case may be. The Ṛtu or season at the time of birth should be found out from the ruler of the decanate rising or from the planet occupying the Lagna whichever is stronger. The six seasons Vasanta, Grīṣma, Varṣā, Śarad, Hemanta and Śiśira belong respectively to Venus, Mars and the Sun, the Moon, Mercury, Jupiter, and Saturn. Then the rising decanate determines the month of the Ṛtu according as the first or second half of the decanate is rising. To find the lunar day or Tithi proceed thus — Convert the degrees etc. of the decanate into minutes. Subtract 300 if the minutes are more than 300. From the remainder find out the Tithi at the rate of 10 minutes per Tithi. The Ascendant at birth will be so far removed from the Sign occupied by the Sun at querry as the Sign representing the decanate occupied by the Sun at query is from the rising decanate. Let us take an example. Let the Ascendant and the position of the Sun at query be — 7-22-16 and 4-24-17 respectively. The rising decanate is the third of Scorpio and that of the Sun third of Leo. So the Sun is in the 28th decanate from the rising one. Take off multiples of 12 from 28. The remainder is 4. Hence count four Signs from Leo, the position of the Sun. It is Scorpio which should be the Ascendant at birth. There is another way of looking at this problem. The Rāśi representing the Lagna decanate is Cancer and that of the Sun Aries. So it is the 10th Rāśi. Now counting 10 signs from Leo we come to Taurus.

For travel too this decanate is very helpful. The decanate rising at the start of a journey must be owned, occupied and aspected by benefics. Its form and characteristics must be auspicious. If these conditions are satisfied the travel will be fruitful. The Serpent and other malefic decanates should be scrupulously avoided.

The decanate helps the astrologer in locating lost or stolen articles. Pṛthuyaśas states in his Ṣaṭpañcāśikā, "If the first decanate of a Rāśi is rising, the missing article is at the gate of the house; if it is the second, it is inside the house; and if it is the last one, the article is behind the house." The same author adds that the thief is to be determined from the decanate that is rising. The forms of the various decanates have been already noticed by us. This knowledge would help one to a large extent. Similarly the nature, caste etc. of the thief can be deduced from the qualities given to the ruler of the decanate. The planets aspecting and associating with the ruler also will have to be taken into consideration.

CHAPTER XIX

DEATH

Nobody knows about the soul before its incarnation as well as after its discarnation or physical death. During this interval it plays a wonderful role on the stage of life. Hence both the initial and final points of its life assume unusual importance. As we have already seen the planetary conditions necessary for incarnation, we shall now take up those for its exit from the body.

You are aware that the house concerned with death is the 8th. So are the planets that are connected with this house. If the 8th house is neither occupied nor aspected by planets, then death could be expected as a result of the special nature or humour of the sign representing the 8th house, or of the Navāṁśa Sign occupied by the lord of the 8th. The following are the effects of the 12 houses beginning with Aries, happening to be the 8th house or the Aṁśa of its lord :

Aries :— Death will be due to fever, poison, stomach disease and biliousness.

Taurus :— It is due to the vitiation of all the humours, weapons or fire.

Gemini :— It is caused by cough, asthma, excessive heat, colic etc.

Cancer :— It is through rheumatism, insanity or diarrhoea.

Leo :— It is due to boils (tumour), poison, weapons, fever etc.

Virgo :— It is through stomach-complaints, diseases of the private parts, quarrel, fall from a precipice etc.

Libra :— It is caused by aberration of the mind, fever or typhoid.

Scorpio :— Through jaundice, diarrhoea, enlargement of the spleen and the like.

Sagittarius :— Through a tree, water, weapon or wooden piece. (The effect is sure if the concerned Sign or Aṁśa is occupied by a malefic).

Capricorn :— It is by impalement, ploughing or mental derangement. If there is a malefic in the Sign or Aṁśa, death is likely through wild animals like tigers, cough, fever, consumption or some unnatural cause.

Aquarius :— If it is occupied by malefics, death is likely through tigers, weapons, serpents, cough, fever or consumption.

Pisces :— It may be due to snake-poison, exhaustion of a journey, storm, machine, ship-wreck or fall of lightning.

In case the 8th house is occupied by any one of the seven planets beginning with the Sun the end may be brought about by (i) fire, (ii) water, (iii) weapon, (iv) fall, (v) fever, (vi) thirst or diabetes, and (vii) starvation, in order. On the other hand if this house is aspected by strong planets, the cause of death may be the particular humours belonging to them. Now we can also see if the subject is going to die in his own house or place or abroad. If the 8th house is a movable sign, death will take place in a foreign country; if it is a fixed one, at home; and if a dual one, on the way or near home.

Now I shall give some yogas (planetary configurations) for the exit of the soul under different circumstances :—

(i) If the Sun and Mars occupy at birth the 10th and the 4th house respectively, one's death may be caused by a fall from the top of a mountain.

(ii) If Saturn, the Moon and Mars be in the 4th, 7th and 10th houses respectively, one would die by falling into a well.

(iii) If the Sun and the Moon occupying Virgo are aspected by malefics, death results from one's own kinsmen.

(iv) If the luminaries occupy the ascendant which is a dual sign, the person will find a watery grave.

(v) If Saturn be in Cancer and the Moon in Capricorn, dropsy would be the cause of death.

(vi) If the Moon be in a sign owned by Mars and be hemmed in betwixt malefics, death would be due to weapons or fire.

(vii) If the Moon is in Virgo under the above condition, it is due to vitiation of blood or consumption.

(viii) If the same Moon be in a sign of Saturn, it would be by hanging, fire or a fall.

(ix) If there are two malefics in the 5th and 9th houses without benefic aspect, death will be in captivity.

(x) If the decanate of the 8th house is Sarpa (Serpent), Pāśa (Noose) or Nigaḍa (Fetters), the result is the same as (ix).

(xi) If Virgo happens to be the 7th house occupied by the

Moon along with a malefic, Venus be in Aries and the Sun in the ascendant, one will die at home on account of a woman.

(xii) If the Sun or Mars be in the 4th, Saturn in the 10th and the weak Moon conjoined with malefics in the first, 5th or 9th house, death will be by impalement.

(xiii) If the Sun be in the 4th and Mars conjoined with the weak Moon in the 10th house being aspected by Saturn, one will be beaten to death with wooden clubs.

(xiv) The same fate awaits one, if the four planets mentioned in (xiii) are posited in the 8th, 10th, 1st and 4th houses.

(xv) If the above four planets be in the 10th, 9th, 1st and 5th houses, death would be due to suffocation by smoke, to fire, imprisonment or beating.

(xvi) If Mars, the Sun and Saturn occupy in order the 4th, 7th and 10th houses, death would be brought about by a weapon, fire, or king's displeasure.

(xvii) If Saturn, the Moon and Mars be in II, IV and X houses respectively, it would be caused by wounds or worms.

(xviii) If the Sun be in X house and Mars in IV, it would be by a fall from a vehicle.

(xix) Mars in VII and the Sun, Moon and Saturn in Ist house bring about death by a machine.

(xx) Mars in Libra, Saturn in Aries and the Moon in a sign owned by Saturn cause death in the midst of filth and night-soil. The effect will be the same if the weak Moon be in the X, Sun in VII and Mars in IV house.

(xxi) If the weak Moon be aspected by Mars possessed of strength and Saturn be in VIII house, death would be caused by worms (or tumour), instruments or fire in the wake of some disease of private parts.

(xxii) If the Sun, Mars, Saturn and the Moon should occupy in order I, VIII, V and IX houses, it would be by a fall from a precipice, by the fall of thunderbolt or of a wall.

You are aware that the 22nd decanate which falls in the 8th house from the Ascendant is called Khara.. This has great influence on a person's death. The characteristics of this decanate or of its lord would point to the way the soul exits from the body. This method should be applied in the absence of the aforesaid conditions. There are altogether 36 decanates in the zodiacal chart of 12 signs, each sign having three decanates. The following Table gives the effects of all these :—

Signs	First Decanate	Second Decanate	Third Decanate
Aries	Water, Snake-poison, Bile.	Water, Worms, Snow, Forest.	Falling into a tank or well.
Taurus	Elephant, Horse, Ass, Camel.	Bile. Fire, Wind, Thieves.	Fall from a vehicle, seat or horse or through weapons in battle.
Gemini	Cough, Asthma.	Buffalo, Poison, Typhoid Fever.	Wild animals, Mountain, Snakes or Elephants, Foresters or Forests.
Cancer	Crocodile, Liquor, Thorns, Sleep.	Blows, Drinking poison.	Birds, Diabetes, Tumour, Blood-vitiation, Sleepiness.
Leo	Water, Poison, Disease of the feet.	Dropsy, Diarrhoea, Forest.	Poison, Instruments, (Operation), Curse, Fall
Virgo	Head or Brain Disease, Wind.	Wild Elephant, Snake, Forest, Mountain, Prince's Displeasure.	Chasm, Food & Drink, Woman, Weapon, Water, Donkey, Elephant.
Libra	Young Woman, Animal, Fall.	Stomach Diseases.	Snake, Water.

Signs	First Decanate	Second Decanate	Third Decanate
Scorpio	Poison, Weapon, Woman, Food.	Clothes, Load, Fall, Disease.	Pain caused by clods and stones, Fracture of the Shank.
Sagittarius	Diseases of Anus, Wind-complaints.	Poison, Wind-Diseases.	In water or water-complaints, Stomach diseases.
Capricorn	Torture at the hands of the King, Tiger, Breaking of thighs, Aquatic animals, Poison, Snake, Animal of uncloven hoofs.	Fire, Weapons, Thieves, Fever, Piercing by a non-human agency.	Women.
Aquarius	Women, Water, Stomach complaints, Savages.	Women, Venereal Diseases.	Sexual Excess, Quadrupeds, Facial Diseases.
Pisces	Tumour, Diarrhoea, Diabetes, Young Women, Disease of the Shanks and Water, Elephants, Evil Spirits.	Ship-Wreck.	Fell Diseases.

Note :— The above effects will come to pass especially when the concerned decanate sign is conjoined with or aspected by malefics.

When the cause of death is known through the rules mentioned above, you can find out the kind of place where death takes place. It is indicated by the planet occupying the ascendant or by the one owning the rising Navāṁśa. In case there is no planet in the Lagna, it will be indicated by the ruler of the sign occupied by the lord of the Lagna or of the rising Navāṁśa. If the lord of the Lagna or of its Navāṁśa is conjoined with or aspected by any planet, that planet too will have its say in modifying the place of death. [For the places assigned to the planets vide Chapter II page-19].

According to another authority the place of death should be read from the sign or Aṁśa occupied by the lord of the 8th house. You are aware of the directions and characteristics such as watery, dry etc, represented by the 12 signs of the zodiac.

If the ascendant is a Nocturnal sign, death will occur at night, and if Diurnal at daytime. It is understood that if there are planets in the Lagna, they would influence the effects.

One dies with many others, if there are many planets in the 4th, and the lord of the ascendant is conjoined with that of the 8th house.

One would die along with one's wife or son, if the lords of the ascendant and the 8th house, are conjoined with that of the 7th or 5th house, as the case may be.

If the lord of the Lagna be in a watery sign or Aṁśa being aspected by the Moon and Venus, and if the 8th and 12th houses are occupied by malefics, death will be in water.

If the birth takes place during the period of Viṣa Ghaṭis and if the 8th house be occupied by a malefic, death would be through poison, fire or weapons.

If the Moon be in the *Fatal* degree in the ascendant, 8th or 12th house, it would be through water or machinery.

If the lord of the 8th house be posited in a Navāṁśa which is termed Viṣa, and be conjoined with a malefic, death would be by snake-poison, by vultures or by wild boars according to the name of the particular Navāṁśa.[1]

1. The *first* Navāṁśa of Aries, Taurus, Virgo and Sagittarius the *middle* of Gemini, Leo, Libra and Aquarius, and the *last* of Cancer, Scorpio, Capricorn and Pisces are respectively called *Snake-Poison*, *Vulture-Poison* and *Boar-Poison*.

I am giving below some more combinations for the exit, both natural and unnatural :

(i) Note the Navāṁśa occupied by Māndi at birth. If there are malefics in the 8th from that sign one meets with unnatural death, otherwise peaceful.

(ii) If the Sun and Mars are in each other's sign and also in angular positions (Kendras) from the lord of the 8th house, he will die by impalement and the like on account of the king's wrath. [If Mars and Saturn are in each other's sign or Aṁśa, in the sign or Aṁśa of the 8th house (or in the Fatal degree) and at the same time in Kendras...].

(iii) If the Moon be in I, the Sun devoid of strength in VIII, Jupiter in XII and a malefic in IV house, death will be caused by a fall from the couch or being attacked by hunters at night.

(iv) If the lord of the ascendant is posited in the Navāṁśa of the 8th house, is eclipsed or in the 6th house, he will die of hunger in a place far away from his kith and kin.

(v) If the lords of the 1st and 8th houses be weak, and Mars in conjunction with the lord of the 6th house, he will die in battle or through a weapon.

(vi) If the lord of the Lagna or of the 7th house be in conjunction with the lords of the 2nd and 4th houses, death will be due to indigestion.

(vii) If the lord of the Navāṁśa of the 4th house be conjoined with Saturn or be in a Dusthāna, death will be due to drinking poison.

(viii) If the above lord be together with Rāhu or Ketu, it will be by hanging.

(ix) If the weak Moon conjoined with Mars, Saturn or Rāhu be in the 8th house, death will be due to the trouble of ghosts, to fire or water; if it is in any other Dusthāna, by epilepsy.

(x) If the Sun or Mars devoid of strength occupy the 8th house, and malefics the 2nd house, death would result from a bilious disease.

(xi) If the Moon or Jupiter be in the 8th house which is a watery sign and aspected by a malefic, it would be from consumption.

(xii) If Venus aspected by a malefic be posited in the 8th Bhāva, it would be due to rheumatism, consumption or diabetes.

(xiii) If Rāhu be in the 8th being aspected by malefics, heat-blisters, snake-bite, small-pox or mental disease would be its cause.

(xiv) If the lord of the 8th house be aspected by Venus, and if the Sun or Saturn conjoined with Rāhu be posited in a malefic 60th part of a sign, the subject's head would be chopped off.

(xv) If the Moon occupying a Dusthāna be aspected by the lord of the Lagna and conjoined with Saturn, Māndi and Rāhu, violent death will follow.

(xvi) If benefics occupy the 4th and 10th houses or the 1st and 8th, and be aspected by malefics, one would die by the fall of a spear.

(xvii) If malefics occupy triangular houses (Koṇas) from the Lagna or the Moon, and Mars the 8th house, if would be in captivity or by hanging.

(xviii) If the Sun and Mars be in the 12th house, Rāhu and the Moon in the 7th, Jupiter in any Kendra, one would die far away from home in a temple garden.

Time of Death

The time of demise can be broadly ascertained from the Daśā one is running. Transits of planets too help us in pin-pointing the time. You know that Saturn who moves exceedingly slowly takes about 30 months to cover a sign. So first of all you can see which sign of the zodiac is harmful for the subject as far as Saturn's transit is concerned. For this you will consider the following four planets viz. :— The lord of the 8th house, Māndi, Saturn and lord of the 22nd decanate. Note the signs as well as Aṁśas occupied by these planets. When Saturn in transit passes through any one of these Signs or Aṁśas or their triangular positions, death may occur. It may also happen when Jupiter passes through the sign or Aṁśa (or its trine) occupied by any one of the three planets viz. (1) the lord of the rising decanate, (2) lord of the 8th house and (3) that of the 22nd decanate. Thus Jupiter's transit will provide you with a period of about 12 months. Thereafter the month is got by means of the Sun's transit. For this, note the Sun's Dvādaśāṁśa and the Navāṁśas of the lords of the 8th house and the ascendant. When the Sun passes in transit through any one of these signs or their trines, the event may take place.

After this you may find out the lunar sign of death. It is well known to you that the Moon takes roughly 2¼ days for covering a sign. Now note the sign and Navāṁśa occupied by the Sun as well as the lord of the 8th house. When the Moon passes through any one of these signs or their trines, death may take place. Remember that counting may be done either from the ascendant or from the natal Moon.

The following are some other methods to arrive at the same result :—

(i) Subtract the longitude of Yamakaṇṭaka from that of the lord of the Lagna. Note the resultant Sign and Aṁśa.

(ii) Substract that of the Moon from that of Saturn. Note also the resultant sign and Aṁśa.

(iii) Add the longitudes of the ascendant, Sun and Māndi. Find the sign occupied by the lord of the sign represented by this sum.

When Jupiter in transit passes through any one of these places mentioned above or their trines, death may take place.

The following are some other methods for arriving at the same result :—

(i) Subtract the longitude of Saturn from that of Māndi, and find out the resulting Sign and Navāṁśa. The event may occur when Saturn passes through any one of these or their trines.

(ii) Add the longitudes of the five Upagrahas (subsidiary planets) headed by Dhūma, and note the decanate of the resulting sign. When Saturn arrives at this decanate of the sign, the exit may be expected.

(iii) Add the longitudes of Māndi and Saturn. Multiply the sum by 9. Note the resulting sign and Navāṁśa. When Saturn arrives at this Sign and Aṁśa, the event may take place.

(iv) Add the longtitudes of the lords of the 6th, 8th and 12th houses. The call may come when Saturn comes to this resulting Sign or its trine

(v) Find out the weakest of the three sets of planets, viz. (1) lords of the 8th houses counted from the ascendant and the Moon, (2) lords of the 22nd decanates, and (3) the Moon and Māndi. Note the Navāṁśa occupied by that planet. When Saturn arrives at this Aṁśa or its trine, the call is likely to come.

Note the Sign which happens to be the Navāṁśa occupied by the lord of the ascendant. See how far it is removed from Aries. Count so many signs from the one occupied by the lord of the 8th house. When Saturn comes to this sign during transit, death may overtake the subject. [Suppose Cancer to be the Lagna whose lord, the Moon, is in Leo Aṁśa. This is the 5th Sign from Aries. If the lord of the 8th house i.e. Saturn, is in Aquarius itself, count five signs from it. You get Gemini as the required sign].

(vii) The month of demise is got from the Sign which is the sum of the longitudes of Māndi and the ascendant. The idea is that when the Sun comes in transit to this sign and Aṁśa, it will occur. The Aṁśa will indicate what part of the solar month it is.

(viii) The Moon will occupy at death that sign which is represented by the sum of the longitudes of Māndi and the Moon.

(ix) The time of death or the ascendant of demise will be the sign represented by the sum of the longitudes of the ascendant, Nāndi and the Moon.

(x) Find out the Navāṁśa, Dvādaśāṁśa and decanate occupied by Māndi. When Jupiter arrives at the Navāṁśa, Saturn at the Dvādasāṁsa and the Sun at a trine to the decanate, it will take place. The ascendant at death may also be the sign occupied by the lord of the sign represented by the sum of the longitudes of the three viz. the ascendant, the Moon and Māndi.

(xi) Death may overtake a person when the Moon in transit passes through the following signs :—

(1) The sign occupied by the lord of the 22nd decanate counted from that of the natal Moon, or its trine; (2) the sign representing the natal ascendant; (3) the 8th house from that; (4) the 12th house from the ascendant; (5) the sign occupied by the sun at birth; (6) the asterism occupied by the lord of the 8th house.

(xii) The solar month of death would be identical with the sign occupied by the lord of the 8th house.

(xiii) For a night birth death is likely during the transit of Saturn through a trine of the Sign occupied by Māndi at birth; and for a day birth it is the 7th house from the above.

(xiv) Again for a night birth the event may occur when Saturn passes through the sign and Aṁśa occupied by the Moon or Māndi; and for a day birth, when he passes through the sign and Aṁśa occupied by the Sun or the 5th, 7th or 9th from that.

(xv) Count the distance of Māndi in Signs from the position taken by the lord of the 8th house. Count so many signs from the place of Māndi. When Saturn arrives at that sign, death may happen.

(xvi) When Jupiter passes through the sign indicated by the sum of the longitudes of Rāhu and Jupiter, or through its trine it may be expected.

(xvii) Note the sign occupied by Venus at birth. When the Sun arrives in transit at the 6th, 7th or 12th place therefrom, it may occur.

In conclusion we may say that the transit of Saturn, Jupiter, the Sun and the Moon through the houses occupied by (1) the lords of the Dusthānas, (2) the lord of the 22nd decanate, and (3) Māndi, or their Aṁśas or their trines, may help us in fixing the time of death.

Some persons die without much suffering, while others otherwise. We have seen now the various conditions leading to all kinds of miserable death. To find out if a person's end will be happy proceed thus : Note the Navāṁsa sign of Māndi. If there be a strong benefic unafflicted in the 7th house from that sign, death would be happy. Similarly if the 8th house is occupied by a strong benefic, the same effect will follow.

It is usual with many persons to lose consciousness sometime before they breathe their last. We can find out this period of unconsciousness from the Navāṁśas of the Lagna that are yet to rise. This can be calculated with the aid of the rules already explained in Chapter III. If the rising sign be aspected by its lord, the period is to be doubled. If it is aspected by a single benefic, it is to be trebled, and if by two benefics, it would be six times the original period and so on.

The method of disposal of the dead body is inferred from the nature of the 22nd decanate. If it is Krūra (malefic), the body will be cremated; if Jalacara (Aquatic), it will be consigned to the waters; if Saumya (Benefic), it will be buried; and if Miśra (Mixed), it will be dried up being exposed to the Sun and wind.[1] (For reference see p. 234) However, the above results may be read also from the nature of the planet occupying or owning the 22nd decanate. If the same decanate be Serpent (Sarpa), the dead body would be eaten by vultures, dogs etc.

Next World

If Jupiter occupies (or owns) the ascendant at death, the departed soul goes to Heaven; if the Sun or Mars, to the world of mortals; if the Moon or Venus, to that of the *Manes*; and if Mercury or Saturn, to the infernal regions.

The 12 Signs of the zodiac are allotted for this purpose to the three worlds viz. Bhūloka, Bhuvarloka and Svarloka, at the rate of 4 signs for each.

One goes to hell, if the lord of the 12th house is aspected by malefics and is posited in a malefic Ṣaṣṭyaṁśa (60th part of sign); or if Rāhu occupies the 12th along with Māndi and the lord of the 8th house and is aspected by the lord of the 6th house.

If an exalted benefic planet occupies benefic Vargas in the 12th house and is aspected by both benefics and malefics, the departed soul will enjoy celestial happiness. If Jupiter owning the 10th house occupies the 12th and is aspected by benefics, he will attain immortality.

If Jupiter possessed of strength be in the Sagittarius Navāṁśa of Cancer ascendant, and if three or four planets be in Kendras, the soul will attain Brahman (Absolute). The result will be the same if Jupiter occupies Aries Navāṁśa in Sagittarius ascendant, Venus the 7th house, and the strong Moon Virgo.

Similarly you can deduce the world from which a person has come from the owner of the decanate occupied by the stronger of the two viz. the Sun and the Moon, in the natal chart. The status too in the previous life can be determined through the strength of the planet concerned.

1. For decanates see Chapter IV, page 40 and Chapter XVIII. There they are subdivided into four groups. The following Table gives the groups :—

Krūra — Malefic		Jalacara — Aquatic	Saumya — Benefic	Miśra — Mixed
Leo — I	Decanate	Cancer — I	Aries — II	Capricorn — III
Aries — I	,,	Pisces — I	Sagittarius — II	Aries — III
Aquarius — I	,,	Do — II	Taurus — II	Cancer — III
Scorpio — I	,,	Virgo — II	Aquarius — II	Taurus — I
Capricorn — I	,,	Taurus — III	Capricorn — II	Sagittarius — I
Pisces — III	,,	Gemini — III	Libra — I	Gemini — II
Scorpio — III	,,		Virgo — I	Libra — II
Leo — III	,,		Gemini — I	Leo — II
Libra — III	,,		Sagittarius —III	
Cancer — II	,,		Virgo — III	
Scorpio — II	,,		Aquarius — III	

Chapter XX

PROFESSION

I shall show in this chapter how astrology can help people in finding out which profession would suit them best. Likewise we can read from a person's horoscope what profession his would be father-in-law is following. As you are aware the 10th house is called the house of profession or Karma, which forms the very foundation, as it were, of the edifice of human life. It should be borne in mind that man is nothing without action. Action is the be-all and end-all of human existence. Man takes birth only to work out his past Karma and to do better Karma in this life in preparation for a better life hereafter. Accordingly, the Īśāvāsyopaniṣad declares, "One should wish to live for a hundred years here only performing actions." It is through action, therefore, that we judge a man. Hence, Karma, action or profession, forms one of the most fundamental factors of man's mundane life. Accordingly the 10th house is called the Meridian, highest point. It is also designated as Māna, self-respect, honour or pride. Among the Kendras too the 10th house is important from another point : The Lagna-Kendra is known as Brahma-Kendra, place of creation; it is the East; it is the Head of Kālapuruṣa. Now the 10th signifies Pauruṣa or manliness or martial power. It is, therefore, Kṣatriya-Kendra. It is based on Rajoguṇa which goads man into action. When man renounces all activities, he attains purity of Satva which makes him eligible for entering the portals of self-realization or the Summum Bonum of existence.

Students of astrology are aware that the general method of reading a person's profession is through the lord of the Navāṁśa occupied by the lord of the 10th house. But this is not a sure and infallible method. There are many other factors which go into the making of profession. Man follows some avocation because he likes it and through that he wishes to earn his livelihood. If one gets a good deal of honour and wealth from his profession, he is said to have a good and comfortable profession.

So generally professional success is measured in terms of lucre. In other words, it revolves round Artha and Kāma, wealth and enjoyment of pleasures. There are also several grades of professional status. One may be a menial, another a clerk, yet another a minister, and so on. How are we to judge whether a person's profession is high, moderate or low ? First of all we have to consider the Ascendant, its lord, aspects and planets posited in it. For, the first Bhāva represents the Body with which we have to perform all our actions. Accordingly says Kālidāsa, "Śarīramādyaṁ khalu dharmasādhanam" — The body is the first and foremost means of achieving Dharma. Then the position and strength of the Moon also have to be taken into consideration, as the Moon represents the Cosmic Mind — Candramā manaso jātaḥ — the Moon was born of the Mind of the Creator, and consequently is the significator for the human mind. Then we have to note the strength and position of the Sun who is the Soul of the universe — 'Sūrya ātmā jagatas tasthuṣaśca.' The strength and good positions of the benefics also are essential for ensuring a good and happy life. Benefics should generally occupy in strength Kendras and malefics the 3rd, 6th and 11th receiving benefic aspects. It is also important that benefics should generally be more powerful than malefics. But the lord of Bhāgya — fortune — whoever he might be, must be strong, well-aspected and well-situated. The lord of Karma too must be similarly placed in a Koṇa, which is at least a friendly house. It is better if there is connection between the lords of the Lagna, Bhāgya and Karma. Similarly the lords of wealth and gain (2nd and 11th) among others must be strong and well placed. The same remark applies to the lords of happiness and intelligence (4th and 5th). If all these conditions are satisfied, the subject is sure to occupy a high position of honour, getting plenty of money and homage. He will also discharge his duties efficiently and honourably.

In fact, when you consider a particular Bhāva, all the other Bhāvas also come into the picture in some relationship or other, as they are all intrinsically connected with it. For example, the 6th house becomes the 10th from the house of Fortune. Hence no Bhāva examined in isolation could give an accurate account of itself. It is not these Bhāvas and their lords alone that give us a clue to a man's position, mode of life and activities.

There are certain positions of planets in the Signs of the zodiac and Yogas which at once tell you whether the subject is a prince or peasant, wealthy or bankrupt, physician or patient, and so on. For example, it is said that one would be seated on a throne, if it be the 6th of the Candra-Kriyās. Similarly, when the full Moon occupying Pisces is aspected by a friendly planet, a pre-eminent monarch delighting the world is born. When all the planets occupying the Navāṁśa of Jupiter are situated in Kendras 9th or 2nd house, the subject becomes an ascetic from his boyhood. If Jupiter be posited in the 8th house, the native would be poor and earn his living as a menial. On the other hand, should he be in the 9th, he could aspire to become a minister. So too Venus occupying the 2nd house makes one a poet and wealthy. The same planet in the 10th enables one to have a comfortable profession. Saturn in the Lagna identical with his own or exaltation house produces one equal to a king, or a mayor. Birth in the several Lagnas indicates some sort of professional leanings. For example, one born in the Vṛṣabha Lagna would be engaged in agriculture. One born in Mithuna could read other's thoughts or become a psychologist, and take interest in dancing and music. Birth in Virgo gives the power of interpreting Śāstras or scriptures. Libra makes one clever in trade; Scorpio a government servant or an employee in a palace; Capricorn a religious hypocrite. Similarly different constellations produce different leanings.

The existence of excellent Yogas like Mahāyogas, Rājayogas, Mahāpuruṣa Yogas, Mahābhāgya, Kesari, Adhiyoga, Vasumat, Puṣkala, Lakṣmī, Sarasvatī etc. contributes to great fortune, eminence and certain professional bias. All these things drive us to the conclusion that the whole horoscope should be judged as a single unit and its status ascertained before venturing on a prediction. Even in the horoscope of a beggar there might be some kind of Rājayoga. In that case how could he be in that position ? The idea is that he may become the leader of beggars.

I am giving hereunder some Yogas which indicate professional aptitudes :—

When all the planets occupy Kendras and Paṇapharas only, the person will become a king or landlord. It is to be noted here that the benefics and the Moon should be strong and free from the aspect of or conjunction with malefics.

(a) If the full and strong Moon is situated in her exaltation, own house or friend's house identical with the 9th, 4th, 7th or 10th and is aspected by or conjoined with Jupiter or Venus;

(b) if Mars and Saturn are similarly endowed with strength and benefic aspect etc., and occupy the 2nd and 10th houses, the person will become illustrious, almost omniscient, a paragon of virtues, munificent and beloved of the people.

If the lord of the Ascendant should occupy the 1st, 2nd or 3rd decanate of the Lagna, the native would be a judge, governor or village-headman, as the case may be. If on the other hand, the planet concerned should be aspected by or conjoined with Venus, Jupiter or Mercury, and be situated in a benefic Varga or in his exaltation, he would become an emperor.

The Moon occupying different signs and aspected by the several planets also shows some kind of professional inclination :

(i) In Gemini she being aspected by Mars and Saturn makes one a blacksmith and a weaver respectively. In modern world the appellation blacksmith would include mechanical engineer, worker in a type foundry, iron works etc.

(ii) In Leo she being aspected by Mercury makes one an astrologer, and by Saturn a barber.

(iii) In Scorpio aspected by Venus, she makes one a soldier.

The Navāṁśa occupied by the Moon gives some guidance in this direction :—

(i) The Moon in a Navāṁśa of Mars being aspected by the Sun produces a policeman.

(ii) In the Aṁśa of Venus the Moon being aspected by Mercury makes one a good poet; by Jupiter, an author of excellent literary works.

Conjunctions of planets also give some clues to professional tendencies :—

(i) The Sun & Moon in conjunction make one skilled in machinery and stone-work.

(ii) Venus and the Moon conjoined produce an adept in weaving, tailoring or dyeing of clothes.

(iii) Mars & Mercury conjoined make one a druggist or physician.

(iv) Mars & Venus joined together make one a wrestler or gambler.

(v) Gulika posited singly or in conjunction with others in different Bhāvas also indicates some avocations.

Many a time the planets occupying or aspecting the Ascendant contribute their qualities for the formation of avocation. Still the most common and popular method is to read the profession from the lord of the Navāṁśa occupied by the lord of the 10th house counted from the strongest of the three viz. Ascendant, Moon, and Sun. The professions and avocations belonging to the several planets have been already enumerated in Chapter II. Regarding the 10th house too there are several factors to be taken into consideration : (i) lord of that Bhāva (ii) lord of the Sign occupied by the lord of the 10th, (iii) planets in the 10th house, (iv) planets aspecting the 10th, (v) lord of the Navāṁśa forming the cusp of the 10th, and (vi) lord of the Navāṁśa occupied by the lord of the 10th. All these planets or the strongest of them will contribute his share to formulate the native's profession. According to some authorities, if the 10th house is not tenanted by any planet, then the owner of that house should determine the profession. In all cases, if the planet concerned be very strong, the subject would be able to earn wealth without much effort and be quite happy. Otherwise the result will vary according to the planet's strength. If the sign mentioned above is occupied or aspected by its own lord, the person will earn his living in his own country. On the other hand, if the planet owning the Rāsi or Aṁśa is in a movable sign, he will earn money in a foreign country. If the said lord is retrograde, he will earn money from various sources. But one's measure of wealth entirely depends on one's fortune—9th house, its lord etc. A single benefic in the 10th from the Moon or Lagna without contact with or aspect of inimical planets will usher into the world a person enjoying the company of a large family and ever-lasting fame.

Engineer :—If a benefic is in the sign and decanate belonging to Mercury and if the lord of the 10th is aspected by Saturn (or if Mercury is in the 2nd and in his own decanate), the subject will be an engineer.

Landlordship :—(i) One will own plenty of lands if the lords of the 4th and 10th houses are in mutual reception, and if Mars is possessed of strength; (ii) if the owner of the sign occupied by Mars be conjoined with the lord of the 4th or is in the 4th house; (iii) if Mars is aspected by the lord of the 4th; or by those of the 9th and 10th houses; (iv) if the lord of the 4th house occupies in strength the 10th house which is a friendly sign; (v) if the lord of the 10th house is aspected by or conjoined with the Moon and Venus.

Earning by Self-Effort :—The following planetary combinations lead to this effect :—(i) When the Lagna lord is in the 11th aspected by benefics and the lords of the 2nd and 11th houses; (ii) when the lord of the ascendant is in the 2nd, 9th or 10th identical with his exaltation or friendly house, aspected by the lord of the 11th; (iii) when the lagna-lord is in the 10th, or in a Kendra from the lord of the 9th or 10th, or in his exaltation, and conjoined with the lord of the 11th house.

Cruel Command :— One gives cruel orders (i) if the Sun or Mars be in the 10th and its lord in a Kendra; (ii) if the 10th house is occupied by Rāhu and Saturn; (iii) if Rāhu or Ketu be in the 8th and the 10th-lord in debilitation; (iv) if the lord of the 10th be conjoined with Saturn and aspected by the lord of the 8th and be posited in a malefic Navāṁśa.

One performs meritorious deeds if benefics occupy the 10th house counted from the Lagna or the Moon, or its Navāṁśa. Malefics in the above positions make one commit evil deeds. So does one, if the lord of the sign occupied by owner of the 10th house or its Aṁśa be malefic and conjoined with an Upagraha like Dhūma.

I am giving below the effects of the presence of the several planets in the 10th house counted from the Moon :— (i) If it be the Sun, the subject becomes a great administrator who succeeds in all his big undertakings; (ii) if it be Mars, he will be adventurous and of a sinful disposition; (iii) if it be Mercury, learned; (iv) if Jupiter, equal to a king; (v) if Venus, enjoy comforts; and (vi) if Saturn, sorrow-stricken.

If in the above house the Sun be conjoined with (i) Mars, the person will be addicted to wine and other women; (ii) with Mercury, he will be well-versed in astrology and be fond of his wife, wealth, ornaments and trading with foreign countries; (iii) with Jupiter, he will be blessed and honoured by Kings; (iv) with Venus, possessed of royal favour, women and wealth; and (v) with Saturn, wretched and indigent.

If in the above house Mars be conjoined with (i) Mercury,

the subject will live by means of his knowledge of Sāstras i.e. he will be a teacher; (ii) with Jupiter, he will be the leader of low-class people; (iii) with Venus, he will be doing business in foreign countries; and (iv) with Saturn, he will do daring deeds and be childless.

If in the above house Mercury be conjoined with (i) Jupiter, he will be impotent, of servile speech, famous and in royal favour; (ii) with Venus, he will be blessed with learning, wealth and wife; and (iii) with Saturn, he will be a writer (copyist or clerk) of books, and be engaged in perverse activities.

If in the above position Jupiter be conjoined (i) with Venus, he will be the protector of Brahmins, favourite of kings and very learned; and (ii) with Saturn, he will succeed in giving trouble to one and all, and tenaciously cling to his undertakings.

If Venus and Saturn are together in that house, he will become a pharmacist manufacturing scents etc., and be a physician and merchant.

Let me give below some charts by way of illustration :—

I. *A Very Successful Doctor* :— (The figures represent Navāṁśa Rāśis) Ascendant Cancer 5 with Mars 8; Venus 5 Leo; Sun 10 and Mercury 6 Virgo; Rāhu 8 Libra; R. Sat. 9 Sagittarius; R. Jup. 2 Capricorn; Moon 8 Pisces. The lord of Lagna is in Bhāgya whose lord is in the 7th (Koṇa-lord in Kendra) and being retrograde becomes strong. Lord of the 8th is in the 6th in strength and Vargottamāṁśa thereby producing Viparīta Rājayoga. The Sun with Mercury (lord of the sign tenanted by him) is in the house of power and influence which is aspected in its turn by Fortune-lord, who aspects the Lagna, and lord of Karma as well as the house of acquisition. Mars, Yogakāraka, with his own Aṁśa, though debilitated has attained Nīcabhaṅga Rājayoga. Note also that he as the lord of 10th is in the Ascendant, which is very significant from the point of profession. The Lagna-lord is full in the 9th. Even the cusp of the 10th house is the 1st Navāṁśa of Aries. Mars, you know, has the portfolio of a surgeon. Note also that both the 10th house and its lord are in movable houses. Hence the subject is living in a foreign country. Note also the lords of 9th and 10th are in watery signs.

II. *An Officer of Air Force* :— Lagna Taurus 1 with Jup. 1; Moon 11 Ketu 9 Gemini; R. Saturn 10 Cancer; Mars 10 Virgo;

Sun 5, R. Mercury 8, Sagit.; Venus 5 Capricorn. Benefic lord of gain is in the Lagna; Yogakāraka Saturn is in the 3rd, a watery sign, (in own Aṁśa) whose lord is full. Lord of Lagna is in Fortune with the Aṁśa of Happiness. The Yogakāraka and Lagna-lord are in mutual Kendra and aspect. No doubt this chart is not free from blemishes i.e. weaknesses. The profession of this chart should be one relating to Saturn and Mars, the former presiding over wind and the latter over weapons and machines.

III. *A Major in the Army* :— Lagna Cancer 11; Sun 8 Leo; R. Venus 11, Rāhu 2, Merc. 4 Virgo; Mars 4 Scorpio; R. Saturn 1 Capri.; R. Jup. 2 Aquarius; Moon 11 Taurus. Look at the fine dispositions of planets in this chart. The Lagna-lord is exalted in the 11th. There is Kesari Yoga. Mars, Mercury and Saturn are in their own houses. The Moon is at the apex of an equilateral triangle. There are many kinds of Rājayoga and two Mahāpuruṣa Yogas, Rucaka and Śaśa. The 10th-lord is Mars and he is the lord of the Navāṁśa occupied by the 10th-lord from the Moon. The Bhāgya-lord, though posited in the 8th, aspects the lord of wealth. The lords of 10, 2, 9 and 1 are in mutual Kendras.

IV. *An Astrologer of Note* :— Lagna Gemini 10 with Saturn 2; Rāhu 1 Leo; Jupiter 9 Libra; Mercury 9 Pisces; Sun 4, Mars 4 Aries; Moon 11, Venus 2 Taurus. Mercury has Nīca-bhaṅga. Lord of 10th aspects 11th with two planets, one of whom is exalted and the other though in his own house is combust, Lagna and Bhāgya. Venus in Vargottamāṁśa in own house is conjoined with the exalted Moon, lord of wealth, though in 12th. The Ascendant and the lord thereof in Pisces indicate this profession. So too does Jupiter, lord of the Navāṁśa occupied by him. For both Mercury and Jupiter have the portfolio of Astrology.

V. *Metallurgist* :— Aries 7 Lagna; Mars 11 Taurus; Rāhu 10 Gemini; Moon 9 Cancer; Saturn 8 Scorpio; Jup. 11, Merc. 11, Sun 7, Venus 1 Aquarius. Mars comes to Lagna Bhāva. Lords of Lagna and 10th aspect each other. The latter has Vargottamāṁśa. Lords of 2, 3 and 9 are in Lābha and those of 1, 2, 9 & 10 are in mutual Kendras. Mars presides over metallurgy, of course.

VI. *Scholar Administrator* :— Cancer 6 Ascendant with

Ketu 10; R. Jup. 4 Leo; Saturn 6 Scorpio; Mercury 6 Capri.; Sun 1 Moon 1 Aquar.; Venus 2 Aries; Mars 6 Taurus. Mars and Venus are in mutual reception. The presence of Ketu in Lagna tends to give the gentleman a philosophical outlook on life. Venus in his own Aṁśa in the 10th conduces to an aesthetic disposition. Lord of Bhāgya in the 2nd aspects the lords of both Lagna and 2nd house. 10th-lord is in the 11th. There is Kesari Yoga. Jupiter, Mars, Sun and Moon and Saturn are in mutual Kendras. Presence of Venus in the 10th suggests authorship of works of cultural interest. The house of speech is well entrenched by the presence of the strong Jupiter. Hence his reasoned and seasoned speeches. Though lords of 1st and 2nd are in the 8th, yet they receive the aspect of Jupiter, lord of 9th. The luminaries are in the house of gain from the house of Command. The complete surrender of the Moon to the Sun suggests the sublimation and subjugation of the mind by the Ātman. It also shows that he is a true servant of the State. As Mars is in the 11th, we can say that his gain is through a position of command. Both Lagna-lord and 2nd-lord are in the Aṁśa of Mars. The lord of 10th, Mars, aspects the house of wealth. Mercury, lord of the concerned Navāṁśa, is not generally associated with administrative powers. Still in the Uttara-kālāmṛta the word Mahātantra occurs in the list of Mercury's portfolios. That word means among other things "great administrative status".

VII. *A Great Sage* :— Libra 9 Lagna; Mars 5 Scorpio; Moon 2 Capri.; Sun 3 Merc. 11, Rāhu 2 Aquar.; Venus 4 Pisces; Jup. 7 Aries; Saturn 3 Gemini. Look at this marvellous horoscope of a Great Seer. Jupiter is in 7th Kendra aspecting its lord Mars. The Yogakāraka is in Bhāgya; lord of the Lagna is exalted; there is exchange of positions between the lords of 5th and 9th; Mars is in his own house. The great spiritual planet has considerable influence on this chart. The Moon has exaltation Aṁśa. Saturn, the planet of renunciation is in the house of Pūrvapuṇya. That shows that he was born for Sannyāsa and spiritual ministration of the people. In Bhāva Saturn comes to the 10th. There are many good Yogas such as Kesari. Out of 7 planets 5 are in Kendras and Koṇas. Lord of Bhāgya, Mercury, has Vargottamāṁśa. The Moon is in the house of Saturn, which is significant. The house of intellect is occupied by Āditya, the ideal of Brahmacārins and Brahmavādins, along with Mercury, the scholar. The lord of Penance is in the house of Happiness, thereby indicating that he took to penance as duck to water. Saturn's aspect over Lābha shows the maxim, "Ādānaṁ hi visargāya" — Acquisition is only for bounteous gifts.

Chapter XXI

TRANSITS

You have come across the terms such as Aṣṭakavarga, Gocāra (or transit) etc. I should like to tell you something about this Gocāra before proceeding further. The word Gocāra simply means movement of planets along the circle of the zodiac. Though the word *Go* means cow, ray etc. here it stands for planets that are possessed of rays or lustre. You have already seen how a planet produces effects, good or bad, during its Daśā. This Daśā-methodology is based upon the natal chart as a whole. The Gocāra-system, however, is based upon the transit or movement of planets from time to time through the various Signs of the zodiac starting, of course, from a fixed point viz. the position of the natal Moon. No doubt there are important factors in a horoscope viz. the Ascendant, the Moon's Sign and the one occupied by the Sun. So the effects of transit must be considered with reference to all these three factors. Still the ancients have given greater weight and consideration to the Moon's position at birth. The reason for this is not far to seek. For, the Moon is the Cosmic Mind or the one born of the mind of the Supreme. Historically too her importance cannot be minimized, as her phases were observed by men in the dim past and were connected by them with their vicissitudes and changes in weather etc. Again, it is the mind that is responsible for the happiness and misery of man. When the mind is content, even a beggar does not fear a king. When such is the case, it is but right that the Moon should be considered as the pivot for the changing fortunes of all beings. Moreover, in the case of this Gocāra system generally the planets as such are considered and not as owners of Bhāvas. So if you want to apply this system with the Sun or Lagna as the starting point, you should not say that this or that planet is good or bad in such and such houses counted from the Sun or Lagna. But you have to consider the planets as lords of houses (counted of course from either the Sun or Lagna) transiting the various Bhāvas from either. Now I shall give the details of the usual Gocāra system. Taking the natal Moon as the starting point you have to proceed to consider which planets are good or bad and in which houses. In this case too you must be exact and scientific in your method. For this purpose you must make a new Bhāva chart with the longitude of the Moon at birth as the Lagna. If this is done properly, you can say whether a planet in transit is in one or an other house from the Moon. For example, let us suppose that the Moon is in the 29th degree of Meṣa. If the Sun in transit comes to the 4th degree of Vṛṣabha, you should not think that the Sun is in the 2nd house from the Moon. He should be considered to be in the first house itself. The Sun produces good effects when he passes in transit through the 3rd, 6th, 10th and 11th houses from the Moon. So the effects of his transit through the other house are to be understood to be bad. Similarly Mars, Saturn, Rāhu and Ketu produce good effects only in the 3rd, 6th and 11th houses from the Moon. The Moon is beneficial in 1, 3, 6, 7, 10 and 11 places from herself. Mercury is auspicious in 2, 4, 6, 8, 10 and 11 places from the Moon. Jupiter is good in 2, 5, 7, 9 and 11 places. Venus is favourable in 1, 2, 3, 4, 5, 8, 9, 11 and 12 places. Generally the nine planets beginning with the Sun take respectively the following periods to pass through a Rāśi : (1) 1 month; (2) $2\frac{1}{4}$ days; (3) 2 months; (4) 1 month; (5) 1 year; (6) 1 month; (7) $2\frac{1}{2}$ years; (8) and (9) $1\frac{1}{2}$ years. Though a planet is expected to produce its effects, good or bad, throughout the period of its passage over a house, still it has a particular part of that period which is considered most potent. They are respectively for the planets beginning with the Sun (1) the first 5 days; (2) the last 3 Ghaṭīs; (3) the first 8 days; (4) throughout the period of 1 month; (5) 2 months in the middle; (6) 7 days in the middle; (7) the last six months; (8) & (9) the last 3 months. The same idea may be put in another form as follows :— The Sun and Mars produce effects when they pass through the initial 10 degrees of a Rāśi, Jupiter and Venus in the middle 10 degrees, the Moon and Saturn in the last 10 degrees, and Mercury and Rāhu throughout their passage.

It is true that there are varieties of good and bad effects which I am going to explain shortly. But before I take up that task I should like to tell you some other detail about this. It is what is called VEDHA, which means *piercing* in literal parlance, but here "undoing" or "cancellation". For every place producing good or bad effects there is a place called Vedha which when occupied by some other planet nullifies the previous effects. For example, the Sun is good in transit when he passes through the 3rd house, but its Vedha is the 9th house. The idea is that although the Sun transiting the 3rd house from the natal Moon should yield very good results, still there would be nothing good coming out of this position if at that time some planet (other than Saturn) transits the 9th house from the Moon. In the same manner bad effects too are nullified by their Vedha positions being tenanted by some other planets at the same time. The following table gives the Vedha positions of all the planets :—

Table of Vedha

Planets.	I	II	III	IV	V	VI	VII	VIII	IX	X	XI	XII
						houses						
Sun	1	2	9	3	6	12	7	8	10	4	5	11
Moon	5	1	9	3	6	12	2	7	10	4	8	11
Mars	1	2	12	3	4	9	6	7	8	10	5	11
Mercury	2	5	4	3	7	9	6	1	8	10	12	11
Jupiter	1	12	2	5	4	6	3	7	10	9	8	11
Venus	8	7	1	10	9	12	2	5	11	4	3	6

Explanation :—Under I against the Sun you see the number 1 for Vedha. What does it mean ? It means that when the Sun passes through the natal Moon at any time if there is some other planet transiting the same Rāśi i.e. there is some other planet with the Sun, at the time, the effects (here, bad) are cancelled. Similarly in the case of the second house.

The Vedha positions of *Saturn* and *Ketu* are the same as those of Mars. An important exception to the Vedha-rule is that it does not operate in the case of planets that are related as father and son. For example, there is no Vedha between the Sun and Saturn as they are respectively father and son. So too there is no Vedha between the Moon and Mercury. The idea is that in the case of the Sun even if a Vedha position be occupied by Saturn, there would not be any cancellation of the previous effects.

Now I intend telling you in detail the effects of Gocāra or transit of the several planets through the twelve houses counted from the Sign occupied by the Moon at birth. When the *Sun* passes through the *First* house (the Sign tenanted by the natal Moon), the following bad effects will be experienced :— Fatigue, loss of money, irritability, illness and wearisome journeys. When he transits the *Second* house, there will be loss of wealth, unhappiness, chance of being deceived and avarice. When he passes through the *Third* house, there will be acquisition of a good position, very handsome income, happiness, good health and destruction of enemies. When he passes through the *Fourth* house, the native will suffer from ailments, will be unhappy and be deprived of the company of his wife and kinsmen. When the same planet transits the *Fifth* house, there will be mental agitation, frequent illness, delusion etc. When he transits the *Sixth* house, there will be an end of ailments, enemies, grief and delusion. When he passes through the *Seventh* house, the subject will undertake wearisome journeys; he will have illness caused by stomach and anus troubles; he will also be subjected to humiliation. When he transits the *Eighth* house, there will be illness, fear, quarrels, troubles from the King or government and excessive heat. When he passes through the *Ninth* house, there will be danger, humiliation, separations from one's relatives and mental agony. His passage through the *Tenth* house will enable the subject to accomplish a mighty undertaking. His passage through the *Eleventh* house will help the native to acquire a good position, honour, wealth and cure of diseases. His transit through the *Twelfth* house will produce great strain, loss of wealth, quarrel with friends and fever. The *Moon* will produce the following effects when she passes through the 12 houses counted from her natal position :—(1) Rise of fortune, (2) loss of money, (3) success, (4) fear, (5) sorrow, (6) sound health, (7) all kinds of happiness, (8) untoward events, (9) sickness, (10) attainment of desired objects, (11) joy, and (12) expenditure. Mars will give the following effects when he passes through the 12 houses :—(1) mental grief, separation from one's kith and kin and diseases caused by the vitiation of blood and bile as well as those caused by excessive heat. (2) When he passes through the *Second* house, there will be fear, indiscreet words or verbal warfare and loss of wealth.

(3) In the *Third* he will give rise to victory, acquisition of gold ornaments and great joy. (4) In the *Fourth* he causes loss of position, illness of the stomach and sorrow on account of kinsmen. (5) In the *Fifth* house he will create fever, improper desire or thoughts, sorrow on account of children and quarrels with one's relatives. (6) When he passes through the *Sixth* house, there will be cessation of enmities and quarrels, recovery from sickness, victory, financial gain and success in all undertakings. (7) In the *Seventh* house he causes misunderstandings with one's wife, eye-disease and stomach-trouble. (8) In the *Eighth* house there will be fever, bleeding and loss of wealth and honour. (9) In the *Ninth* there will be humiliation caused by loss of wealth etc., and retarded gait through physical weakness and loss of vitality. (10) In the *Tenth* house he causes wicked activities, obstacles to one's projects, and physical strain. (11) In the *Eleventh* house he produces wealth, health and addition to landed property. (12) Lastly in the *Twelfth* house he engenders loss of wealth, excessive heat, fever etc.

Mercury brings about the following effects in order when he passes through the 12 houses beginning with the Janma Rāśi :—
(1) Loss of money, (2) wealth, (3) fear of enemies, (4) acquisition of wealth (5) quarrel with one's wife and children, (6) victory, (7) obstruction, (8) begetting children and earning money, (9) impediments, (10) all-round happiness, (11) progress, and (12) fear of defeat.

Jupiter causes the following effects while transiting the 12 houses in order :—(1) Quitting one's birth-place, loss of wealth and hostility. (2) Gain of wealth, family happiness and effectiveness of one's words. (3) Loss of position, separation from the near and dear ones, illness and impediments to one's work. (4) Sorrow on account of relatives, humiliation and danger from quadrupeds. (5) Birth of a son, association with the virtuous and royal favour. (6) Trouble from enemies and one's own relatives and diseases. (7) Good journey for auspicious purposes, conjugal happiness and birth of a son. (8) Fatigue through needless journeys, illuck, loss of money, and miseries. (9) All-round prosperity and joy as well as happiness and good fortune. (10) Trouble to one's property, position, children etc. (11) Acquisition of children, position, honour etc. (12) Grief and danger to wealth.

Venus produces the following effects in the 12 houses :— (1) Enjoyment of all kinds of pleasures. (2) Financial gain. (3) Progress and prosperity. (4) Increase of happiness and friends. (5) Birth of children. (6) Adversity. (7) Trouble to wife. (8) Wealth. (9) Happiness. (10) Quarrel. (11) Safety and security. (12) Good income.

Saturn is supposed to bring about the following effects in the 12 houses :— (1) Illness and performance of funeral rites. (2) Trouble to wealth and children. (3) Acquisition of position, wealth and servants. (4) Loss of wife, relatives and wealth. (5) Decline of prosperity, children and mental powers. (6) All-round happiness. (7) Sickness of one's wife, long journeys and fear. (8) Loss of children, cattle, friends and wealth, and sickness. (9) Poverty, obstacles to the performance of religious rites, death of an elder equal to the father, and continuous misery. (10) Interest in forbidden activities, loss of honour, and sickness. (11) All kinds of happiness, acquisition of many kinds of wealth and unique renown. (12) Fatigue owing to worthless business, loss of wealth through enemies, and illness of wife and children.

Rāhu produces the following effects while passing through the 12 houses :— (1) Death or serious illness. (2) Loss of wealth. (3) Happiness. (4) Sorrow. (5) Loss of money. (6) Happiness. (7) Loss. (8) Danger to life. (9) Loss. (10) Gain. (11) Happiness (12) Loss. The effects of the transits of Ketu are the same as those of Rāhu. There is one common feature that is found among the four planets viz. the Sun, Mars, Jupiter and Saturn. That is, when these transit through the 12th, 8th, and the 1st houses, they tend to produce danger to life, and loss of position and wealth. The following point also should be noted with regard to the transits of the Moon, Mars. Rāhu, Venus, Jupiter, the Sun, Saturn and Mercury :— When the Moon passes through the 8th house, Mars through the 7th, Rahū through the 9th, Venus through the 6th, Jupiter through the 3rd, the Sun through the 5th, Saturn through the 1st house, and Mercury through the 4th, there is every likelihood of loss of wealth and honour, and death.

Nakṣatra-Gocāra :— Connected with the subject of Gocāra or planetary transits there is a method of finding out whether a particular period is favourable or not. This is done by noting the nature of the star occupied by the Sun in transit and its relationship with one's natal asterism and some other stars which bear close kinship with that. For this purpose a diagram is needed, which is called the *Saptaśalākā-Cakra*. In this figure what you have to do is that you should draw seven horizontal lines and seven vertical lines crossing the previous ones. While drawing the lines see that the ends of all the lines jut out so that you may get 28 points. In this scheme there is one more asterism called Abhijit which comes in between Uttarāṣāḍhā and Śravaṇa. The first asterism that should be written at the point in the North-eastern corner is Kṛttikā. So the last will be Bharaṇī. Now look at the figure on page 252 for clarification.

Now you must know how to read from this diagram whether there is any untoward transit of the Sun with regard to the natal star etc. In this figure you note that some stars face one another. For example, Kṛttikā and Śravaṇa, Āśleṣā and Anurādhā, Bharaṇī and Maghā, Dhaniṣṭhā and Viśākhā. This means there is mutual affliction or *Vedha* between these two stars. The idea is that if the natal star is Kṛttikā and if the Sun transits at the time the star Śravaṇa, you have to conclude that there is trouble in store for the native. In this connection you are required to remember some more technical terms : The natal star is called Janma-nakṣatra, the second one form that is Sampat or wealth, the 3rd is Vipat or danger, the 4th is Kṣema or happiness, the 5th one is Pratyak (Pratyra) or obstruction, the 6th one is Sādhana or achievement, the 7th one is Nidhana or death, the 8th is Maitra or friendly, the 9th is Paramamaitra or very friendly, the 10th is Karma or action, the 19th is Ādhāna or depositing and the 23rd is Vaināśika or destructive. So if on a particular day or period the Sun is transiting a star which happens to be the Vedha one for one's natal asterism, then it is to be inferred that there is danger to the native's life. Suppose the star occupied at the time by the Sun happens to be the Vedha not for the natal star but for the Ādhāna star i.e. the 19th one from the natal star, then the effect would be fear and anxiety. Let us suppose your natal star to be Mṛgaśiras. Then its Vedha is Uttarāṣāḍhā. If the Sun is transiting Uttarāṣāḍhā, you have to think that there is danger to life. On the other hand, if the Sun is passing through not Uttarāṣāḍhā but through Viśākhā, which is the Vedha for the star that is 19th from the natal star viz. Dhaniṣṭhā (it becomes the Ādhāna), there will

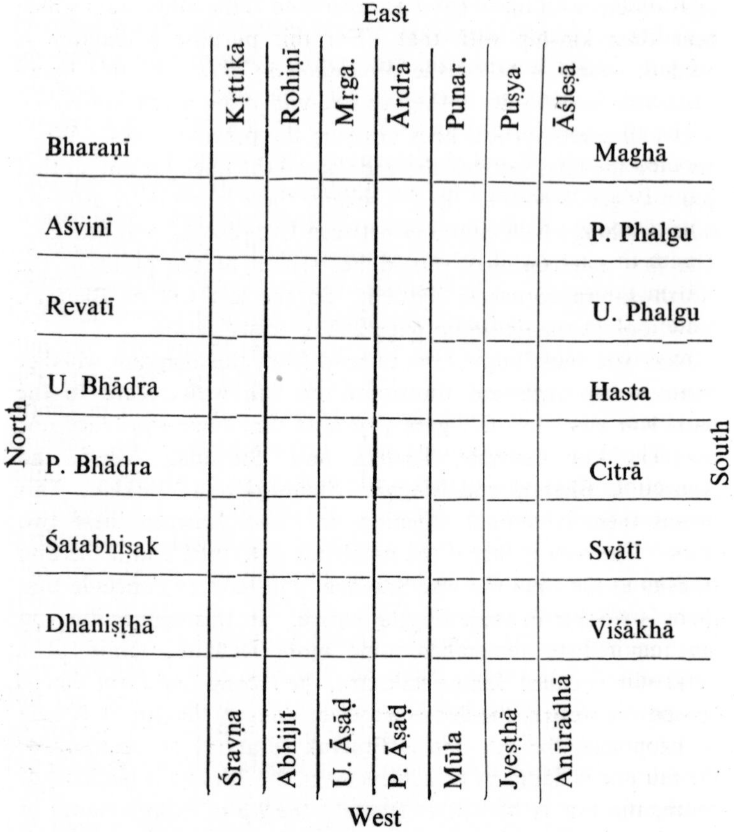

be fear. Similarly if the star tenanted by the Sun happens to be Vedha for Karma-star i.e. 10th from the natal one, there will be loss of money. In addition to the above if the Sun is also conjoined with a malefic, death will be the result. In the same manner see also if other malefics, (i.e. other than the Sun) occupy in transit stars which are Vedha for the three stars viz. the natal one, the 10th and the 19th. In such a case too the result will be death. If both malefics and benefics transit such stars, there will be no danger to life.

There is yet another way of finding out bad effects of transit : If malefics should transit the natal star, the 3rd from it, the 5th, the 7th, 10th, 19th or the 23rd (all counted from the natal star), then too there will be danger to life. If these positions are occupied by benefics in transit, then there will be only failure of undertakings. Now you see that this is another kind of Vedha different from the one indicated by the Saptaśalākā figure. Remember also that this is different from the Rāśi-procedure and its Vedha which have been already explained. The 10th and 19th stars counted from the natal asterism are also called respectively Anujanma and Trijanma. This means that the 10th is the natal star in the second round and the 19th in the third round. See also if the natal star in any round synchronizes with the Sun's entry into another Sign of the zodiac. If it does, then the effect is very bad. It may be death or great danger to life. The same effect will take place, if the same natal star in any round happens to synchronize with the change of sign of any other planet, or with an eclipse, planetary war, falling of meteors or with any other extra-ordinary event.

There are some more points to be remembered in this connection : You have understood now as to which planets give unfavourable results and in which stars and signs. This is not all. Even if a planet is found to be capable of yielding unfavourable results on account of its transit, the bad effects will be nullified by the aspect of a benefic on that planet. The same argument holds good in the case of a planet supposed to produce excellent results but aspected by a malefic. Similar is the effect in the case of one aspected by its enemy. So while pronouncing judgment on Gocāra effects you should be extremely cautious. It is not enough if you simply note the basic rule regarding good and bad houses for the planets in transit. Even if a planet occupies a very bad house according to the rules of transit, it cannot give bad effects in case it occupies at the time its own house or its exaltation. On the other hand, it will yield most excellent results when it transits a good house which is its own house or its exaltation. You have also to note if a planet in transit is in its debilitation, inimical house or combustion. In such a condition even the good effects that are expected would not materialize, and the bad effects would be greatly aggravated.

There is yet another method of finding out the Gocāra effects from the limbs of the native occupied by the planets. Certain stars counted from the natal one are assigned to different limbs of the person. For example, in the case of the Sun's transit the natal star is called the Face. So if the Sun transits the natal star of a person, he is supposed to be seated on the face of the native. The effect of this is not at all happy. I am tabulating below for your convenience the stars constituting the limbs and their effects in the case of the *Sun* and other planets separately.

Sun

Stars	*Limbs*	*Effects*
(a) First star or the natal star	Face	Destruction
(b) 2nd, 3rd, 4th and 5th	Head	Great prosperity
(c) 6th, 7th, 8th and 9th	Chest	Victory
(d) 10th, 11th, 12th and 13th	Right hand	Wealth
(e) 14th, to 19th (six stars)	The feet	Poverty
(f) 20th to 23rd (four stars)	Left hand	Physical ailments
(g) 24th and 25th	The eyes	Gain
(h) 26th and 27th	Genital organ	Danger to life

Note that here the counting is done always from one's natal star, and not from Aśvinī.

Moon

Stars	*Limbs*	*Effects*
(a) 1st and 2nd	Face	Great fear
(b) 3rd to 6th (four)	Head	Happiness
(c) 7th and 8th	Back	Victory over foes
(d) 9th and 10th	Eyes	Financial gain
(e) 11th to 15th (five)	Heart	Happiness
(f) 16th, 17th and 18th	Left hand	Hatred
(g) 19th to 24th (six)	Feet	Going abroad
(h) 25th, 26th and 27th	Right hand	Financial gain

Mars

Stars	*Limbs*	*Effects*
(a) 1st and 2nd	Face	Death
(b) 3rd to 8th (six)	Feet	Fighting
(c) 9th, 10th, 11th	Chest	Success
(d) 12th to 15th (four)	Left hand	Indigence
(e) 16th and 17th	Head	Gain
(f) 18th to 21st (four)	Face	Excessive fear
(g) 22nd to 25th (four)	Right hand	Happiness
(h) 26th and 27th	Eyes	Going away from home

Mercury, Jupiter and Venus

Stars	*Limbs*	*Effects*
(a) 1st, 2nd, 3rd	Head	Sorrow
(b) 4th, 5th, 6th	Face	Gain
(c) 7th to 12th (six)	Hands	Disaster
(d) 13th to 17th (five)	Belly	Plenty of wealth
(e) 18th and 19th	Genital organ	Loss or destruction
(f) 20th to 27th (eight)	Feet	Fame and position

Saturn, Rāhu and Ketu

Stars	*Limbs*	*Effects*
(a) 1st star	Face	Grief
(b) 2nd to 5th (four)	Right hand	Happiness
(c) 6th, 7th and 8th	Right foot	Travel
(d) 9th, 10th & 11th	Left foot	Loss or destruction
(e) 12th to 15th (four)	Left hand	Gain
(f) 16th to 20th (five)	Belly	Enjoyments
(g) 21st, 22nd, 23rd	Head	Happiness
(h) 24th and 25th	Eyes	Happiness
(i) 26th and 27th	Back	Death

Lattā :— This word Lattā means Vedha or affliction. It appears to be of foreign origin like Kriya for Aries, Tāvuru for Taurus etc. This means, as far as transit is concerned, that a planet transiting a particular asterism afflicts another asterism occurring at a particular distance. This distance is measured in the forward direction in some cases and in the opposite direction in the case of others. The former is called Purolattā and the latter Pṛṣṭhalattā. To the former group belong the Sun, Mars, Jupiter and Saturn, and to the latter the Moon, Mercury, Venus and Rāhu. In the case of the Sun the Lattā on the 12th asterism counted in the regular order from the one occupied by him at the time. The idea is that if the Sun is now passing through the star Uttara Phālgunī, the Lattā will fall on Dhaniṣṭhā. So if Dhaniṣṭhā happens to be the natal star of a person, he will have illness and sorrow as the effect of this affliction. In the case of Mars the Lattā — forward — falls on the 3rd star. Now he is in the asterism Mṛgaśīrṣa. So the

Lattā falls on Punarvasu. Hence it should be inferred that a person whose natal star is Punarvasu is likely to fare ill at this time. In the case of Jupiter the Lattā — forward — falls on the 6th star. As Jupiter is now in Mūla, his Lattā falls on Śatabhiṣak. In the case of Saturn it falls on the 8th star. As he is now in Pūrvāṣāḍhā, his Lattā will fall on Revatī. In the case of the Moon the *backward* Lattā would fall on the 22nd star. So if the Moon be in Rohiṇī today, her Lattā would be on Maghā, because here the counting is done backwards. In the case of Mercury it will fall on the 7th star counted backwards. So if Mercury be now in the star Hasta, then his Lattā would be on Punarvasu. So the transit of Mercury becomes unfavourable to a person whose natal star is Punarvasu. In the case of Venus it falls on the fifth star counted backwards. If Venus is in Citrā now, his Lattā will be on Maghā. Lastly the Lattā of Rāhu falls on the 9th asterism counted backwards. So if Rāhu is transiting the star P. Phalgunī, its Lattā will be on Kṛttikā. If the natal star comes under the Lattā of two or more planets, the bad effects will be greatly enhanced. Though the general effect of Lattā has been given as trouble, yet different effects are given for the different planets producing the Lattā. The effect of the Sun's Lattā is loss of one's entire effects, the Moon's great loss, Mars' utter ruination, Mercury's fall and disaster, Jupiter's death, ruin of relatives and insecurity, Venu's quarrel, Saturn's the same as that of the Sun, and lastly that of Rāhu and Ketu misery.

CHAPTER XXII

AṢṬAKAVARGA

I had mentioned to you in this connection that *Aṣṭakavarga* — effects of the seven planets and the Ascendant — plays an important role in measuring the effects of transits. Hence that subject must needs be taken up now. This *Aṣṭakavarga* is nothing but the benefic and malefic dots contributed by all the seven planets and the Lagna in the chart of a particular planet at birth. So first of all you must have before you the natal chart of the person concerned. A planet is said to be good in certain positions counted from his own original place in the radical chart and from those of other planets in the same, including the Lagna. So what you have to do is to put a dot in such places and leave the unfavourable positions blank. The aggregate of all these benefic dots is called the Aṣṭakavarga of that one planet. In this manner you will have to prepare the Aṣṭakavarga charts for the remaining planets. In the case of Aṣṭakavarga charts the counting of houses is done Rāśi-wise and not Bhāva-wise. The Bhāva ideology does not work here. Let us take an example chart.

Moon Lagna	Mars	—	—
—	Natal Chart —		—
Sun Venus			—
Merc.	Sat.	—	R. Jup.

In this chart only the 8 elements that are necessary for the purpose of the Aṣṭakavarga are given. We have to start now with the Sun, as we are going to find out the benefic dots in the Aṣṭakavarga of that planet. For this purpose you must have a blank chart by the side of the above chart in order to mark the benefic dots contributed by the Sun and other significators in the Aṣṭakavarga of the Sun. Now let us see in which houses the Sun is favourable from himself and so contributes benefic dots. He produces beneficent influences on the houses, 1, 2, 4, 7, 8, 9, 10 and 11 counted from his position at birth. Now put a vertical line, instead of a dot, for the sake of clearness, in the first house i.e. Capricorn and 2nd i.e. Aquarius, 4th i.e. Aries, 7th i.e. Cancer, 8th i.e. Leo, 9th i.e. Virgo, 10th i.e. Libra and 11th i.e. Scorpio. What does this mean ? It means that as far as his transit is concerned the above houses where he has contributed benefic dots are good. In the same manner you will have to find out the contributions of the other significators. Count separately the same places from the natal positions of Mars and Saturn. The idea is that the Sun is good in transit in these houses counted from Mars and Saturn. You see that Mars is in Aries at birth. So count 1, 2, 4, 7, 8, 9, 10 and 11 from Aries and put another vertical line in each of these places. Repeat this process from the position of Saturn viz. Scorpio. Thus we have disposed of three significators. Now take up Jupiter's contribution. The Sun is good in the 5th, 6th, 9th and 11th places from Jupiter. Where is Jupiter ? He is in Virgo. So put a mark in these places counted from Virgo i.e. in Capricorn, Aquarius, Taurus and Cancer. The Sun is good in the 6th, 7th, and 12th places from Venus, So mark Gemini, Cancer and Sagittarius. He is good in places, 3, 5, 6, 9, 10, 11 and 12 counted from Mercury. So put the lines in Aquarius, Aries, Taurus, Leo, Virgo, Libra and Scorpio. He is good in 3, 6, 10 and 11 from the Moon. Hence mark the signs Taurus, Leo, Sagittarius and Capricorn. Lastly the Sun is good in places 3, 4, 6, 10, 11 and 12 from the Ascendant. So mark the signs Taurus, Gemini, Leo, Sagittarius, Capricorn and Aquarius. Now look at the chart on p. 258 containing the Sun's Aṣṭakavarga. In this chart you see one house without a single benefic dot.

—	11 1	1111 11	11 1
111 111	Sun's Aṣṭakavarga Total 48		111 11
111 11			111 11
111 11	1111	111	111

Only those houses which contain more than 4 benefic dots are considered to be auspicious. In this chart of the Sun's Āṣṭakavarga Taurus and Aquarius contain 6 benefic dots each. Cancer, Leo, Sagittarius and Capricorn contain 5 each. Though Aquarius is the 12th house from the Moon, yet the Sun's transit through that house will not prove harmful inasmuch as he has acquired 6 benefic dots in that house. Similarly Leo which is the 6th from the Moon should give good results, as it contains 5 benefic dots and belongs to himself. Similar considerations of one's exaltation, friendly house etc., inimical, depression etc. should also be made before assessing the value of Gocāra-effects. Aries is no doubt the exaltation of the Sun. But it contains only 3 dots. This means that it has 5 malefic dots and only 3 benefic ones. So the effect of his transit through this house will not be that good. Look at the 8th house from the Moon. It has only 3 benefic dots. So the transit effects must be extremely bad. So remember this general principle : A bad house in transit will not be so bad if it contains more than four benefic dots. Similarly a good house in transit will not be so good if it contains 4 or less than 4 benefic dots. Even though a Rāśi may contain many benefic dots, still the effects will not be good if the particular house happens to be the concerned planet's depression, inimical or Apacaya house. If a house has no benefic dot in a planet's Aṣṭakavarga, the effect is that the native is likely to lose his life when the planet transits that house. The effects of benefic dots commencing with one and ending with eight are in order (1) destruction, (2) loss, (3) & (4) fear, (5) gain of wealth, (6) acquisition of a damsel, (7) prosperity and (8) kingship or high government position.

Now you may be interested to know as to when exactly the effects of Gocāra are experienced. Some theories have already been given. Another principle is that a planet produces good or bad effects when it has advanced exactly the same degrees in transit as it had advanced at birth. Next we should work out the Aṣṭakavarga chart of the Moon. She is good in the 3rd, 6th, 7th, 8th, 10th and 11th places from the Sun. So put a mark in Pisces, Gemini, Cancer, Leo, Libra and Scorpio. She is good in places, 1, 3, 6, 7, 10 and 11 from herself. So enter the mark in Pisces, Taurus, Leo, Virgo, Sagittarius and Capricorn. She is good in places, 2, 3, 5, 6, 9, 10 and 11 from Mars. Now Mars is in Aries at birth. So put benefic marks in the above places viz. Taurus, Gemini, Leo, Virgo, Sagittarius, Capricorn, and Aquarius. She is good in 1, 3, 4, 5, 7, 8, 10 and 11 from Mercury. So make marks in Sagittarius, Aquarius, Pisces, Aries, Gemini, Cancer, Virgo and Libra. She is good in 1, 2, 4, 7, 8, 10 and 11 places from Jupiter. So put the mark in Virgo, Libra, Sagittarius, Pisces, Aries, Gemini, and Cancer. She is good in 3, 4, 5, 7, 9, 10 and 11 places from Venus. So mark the signs, Pisces, Aries, Taurus, Cancer, Virgo, Libra and Scorpio. She is good in 3, 5, 6, and 11 places from Saturn. So mark the signs, Capricorn, pisces, Aries, and Virgo. Lastly she is good in 3, 6, 10 and 11 places from the Ascendant. So mark Rāśis, Taurus, Leo, Sagittarius and Capricorn. The result is shown in the chart on p. 261. You will see therein that the total number of benefic dots in the Moon's Aṣṭakavarga is 49.

You see in this chart of the Moon only three Rāśis contain more than four benefic dots. They are Pisces with 6 dots, Virgo with 6 dots and Sagittarius with 5 dots. You know that a planet yields beneficial results when it transits certain houses counted from the Moon's position at birth, which in addition happen to be its own, friendly and exaltation houses. Now the moon's transit is good in 1, 3, 6, 7, 10 and 11 houses from her natal position. In the chart, of course, the first house contains 6 dots. So the transit through that house must be excellent. The third house which ought to give very good results as it is her exaltation, cannot be good here, because it contains only 4 benefic dots. The same remark applies to the 6th. The 7th and 10th houses are good.

111 111	111 1	11 11	11 11
11	Moon's Aṣṭakavarga Total 49		11 11
111 1			11 11
111 11	11	11 11	1111 11

Next we have to erect the Aṣṭakavarga chart of Mars. He is good in 3, 5, 6, 10 and 11 places from the Sun. So put the marks in Pisces, Taurus, Gemini, Libra and Scorpio. He is good in 3, 6 and 11 places from the Moon. So mark Taurus, Leo and Capricorn. He is good in 1, 2, 4, 7, 8, 10 and 11 places from himself. So mark the signs Aries, Taurus, Cancer, Libra, Scorpio, Capricorn and Aquarius. He is good in 3, 5, 6 and 11 places from Mercury. Hence mark Aquarius, Aries, Taurus, and Libra. He is good in 6, 10, 11 and 12 places from Jupiter. So inscribe Rāśis, Aquarius, Gemini, Cancer and Leo. He is good in 6, 8, 11 and 12 places from Venus. So mark these houses from Capricorn. He is good in 1, 4, 7, 8, 9, 10 and 11 places from Saturn. So mark the Rāśis beginning with Scorpio. Lastly he is good in 1, 3, 6, 10 and 11 places from the Lagna. So mark the Rāśis commencing with Pisces. Show the results as given in the adjoining chart. The total number of benefic dots of Mars is 39.

You will notice in this chart only two Rāśis viz. Taurus and Leo, containing more than 4 benefic dots. His own signs and his exaltation do not possess many benefic dots.

11	11	111 111	11 11
11 11	Mars' Aṣṭakavarga Total 39		11 1
11 1			111 11
11	11 11	11 1	1

Next we have to work out the chart of Mercury. He is good in 1, 3, 5, 6, 9, 10, 11 and 12 places from himself. He is in Dhanus. So enter the marks in the appropriate Rāśis. He is good in 5, 6, 9, 11 and 12 places from the Sun. So put the marks in Vṛṣabha, Mithuna, Kanyā, Vṛṣcika and Dhanus. He is good in 2, 4, 6, 8, 10 and 11 places from the Moon. You know the Moon is in Pisces. So count these houses from Pisces and enter the marks therein. He is good in 1, 2, 4, 7, 8, 9, 10 and 11 places from Mars and Saturn. Remember that Mars and

11	111 111	111 11	11 11
111 11	Mercury's Aṣṭakavarga Total 54		11 1
11 11			1111 11
111 111	111 11	11 11	11 11

Saturn are not in the same Rāśi. So counting will have to be done separately. He is good in 6, 8, 11 and 12 places from Jupiter. He is good in 1, 2, 3, 4, 5, 8, 9, and 11 places from Venus. He is good in 1, 2, 4, 6, 8, 10 and 11 places from the Lagna. The total benefic dots of Mercury is 54. Now draw the figure and enter the results as shown in the following tables.

In this chart you will observe that Pisces has only 2 benefic dots. Cancer has three. His own houses too contain only 4 dots each.

Next Jupiter is good in 1, 2, 3, 4, 7, 8, 9, 10 and 11 places from the Sun; in 2, 5, 7, 9, and 11 places from the Moon; in 1, 2, 4, 7, 8, 10 and 11 places from Mars; in 1, 2, 4, 5, 6, 9, 10 and 11 places from Mercury; in 1, 2, 3, 4, 7, 8, 10 and 11 places from himself; in 3, 5, 6 and 12 places from Saturn; in 2, 5, 6, 9, 10 and 11 places from Venus; and finally in 1, 2, 4, 5, 6, 7, 9, 10 and 11 places from the Lagna. Now carefully enter the benefic marks in the respective places counted from the different significators. Then show the results as given below :—

111 11	1111 111	111	111
111	Jupiter's Aṣṭakavarga Total 56		111 11
111 111			111
111	111 111	111 111	111 111

Here the total number of benefic dots is 56. You see in this chart seven houses with more than four benefic dots each. Though Janmarāśi is not good for Jupiter's transit, yet in this chart it happens to be his own house and in addition to that it contains 5 benefic dots. His exaltation too must produce excellent results for the same reason. Even the 8th house which is bad for transit cannot be so bad as it contains six benefic dots. In this manner you assess the value of the effects of Gocāra.

Next we must take up the Aṣṭakavarga of Venus. He is auspicious in 8, 11 and 12 places from the Sun; in 1, 2, 3, 4, 5, 8, 9, 11 and 12 places from the Moon; in 1, 2, 3, 4, 5, 8, 9, and 11 places from the Lagna; in 1, 2, 3, 4, 5, 8, 9, 10 and 11 places from himself; in 3, 5, 6, 9, 11 and 12 places from Mars; in 3, 4, 5, 8, 9, 10, and 11 places from Saturn; in 3, 5, 6, 9 and 11 places from Mercury; and finally in 5, 8, 9, 10 and 11 places from Jupiter. Now carefully enter the mark in the proper places counted from the different significators and show the results as given below :—

111 11	111 11	111 11	111 11
111 11	Venus's Aṣṭakavarga Total 52		111 1
111 11			111 11
11	111 1	111 1	111

In this chart you see many Rāśis with five benefic dots. You know that Venus is not good in 6, 7, and 10 places in transit. Here the 6th house contains 5 benefic dots. Hence it cannot give very bad effects. The 7th and 10th places contain only 3 and 2 dots respectively. So their effects must be extremely bad. The 7th being his depression must produce very bad results too.

Saturn is good in 1, 2, 4, 7, 8, 10 and 11 places from the Sun; in 3, 6 and 11 places from the Moon; in 3, 5, 6 and 11 places from himself; in 3, 5, 6, 10, 11 and 12 places from Mars; in 5, 6, 11 and 12 places from Jupiter; in 6, 8, 9, 10, 11 and 12 places from Mercury; in 1, 3, 4, 6, 10 and 11 places from Lagna; and finally in 6, 11 and 12 places from Venus. Now enter the mark in the several places noted above from the different significators and show the results in a chart as shown in the adjoining figure :—

111	11	111	111
111	Saturn's Aṣṭakavarga Total 39		111
111 111			111 111
11	111	11	111

The total benefic dots in Saturn's Aṣṭakavarga is 39. In this chart there are only two Rāśis which possess six dots each. They are Leo and Capricorn. And these happen to be the 6th and 11th places from the natal Moon. Though the 3rd place also is said to be good, still here as it contains only 3 benefic dots it cannot produce any good effect. The 6th viz. Leo, though belonging to his enemy, yet must produce good effects as it contains 6 dots. The 11th house, in addition to being his own, contains also 6 dots. So it must produce excellent results. In this manner you have now learnt the method of the Aṣṭakvarga system. If you add up all the benefic dots of all the seven planets, you will see that they come to a grand total of 337 which is called the Samudāya-Aṣṭakavarga. The total of the benefic dots of individual planets is called Bhinnāṣṭakavarga.

I have told you that if a Rāśi contains benefic dots fewer than four, then the effects of transit will not be good. Still a distinction is to be made here. For, even a bad effect cannot be continuously operating. There must be a silver lining in the cloud of unhappiness. Now how can we find out as to which period will have this silver lining ? Let us suppose that in a planet's Aṣṭakavarga chart certain Rāśi contains only one benefic dot. This benefic dot must have been contributed by one of the 8 significators. Now these significators have been given certain order of precedence. So if you divide a Rāśi into 8 equal parts, this benefic dot will take its due position somewhere. When this planet, whose Aṣṭakavarga is under consideration, transits the particular part of the Rāśi to which the benefic dot belongs the native will have some relief. Now let us see the order of precedence of the 8 significators. When you divide a Rāśi into 8 equal divisions the first division would belong to Saturn, the second to Jupiter, the third to Mars, 4th to the Sun, 5th to Venus, 6th to Mercury, 7th to the Moon and the 8th to the Ascendant. The order of these depends on the distance of the orbits of the heavenly bodies. You know that the orbit of Saturn is the remotest of all. Thus for ascertaining the interval of relief in an otherwise bad period we have to understand which planets have contributed the benefic dots. For example, in our example chart in the Sun's Aṣṭakavarga we have seen three benefic dots in Aries. Which are the planets that have contributed these three dots ? They are contributed by Mars, Sun and Mercury. These three planets preside over the third, fourth and sixth parts of Aries in order. This means that when the Sun passes through these three benefic areas there will be some relief to the native. They are from 7°-30′ to 11°-15′; from 11°-15′ to 15°; and from 18°-45′ to 22°-30′. While marking the benefic dots contributed by the 8 significators in the several Rāśis what you could do with advantage is that you should write the numbers 1 to 8 in the Rāśis of all the Aṣṭakavargas. The figure I would indicate the Sun who contributes the benefic dot. Similarly 2 would show the Moon to be the contributor and so on. If you find the number 8, it means the contributor is the Lagna. Now I give on the next page the planets' Aṣṭakavarga charts in this form :—

—	134	2345 78	678
1345 78	Sun's		13567
12358			12478
23678	1347	134	147

18	34	1234 78	1567
34 57	Mars'		357
238			25678
68	1367	134	7

14578	1234 578	346	568
136	Jupiter's		123 58
1234 78			148
458	1235 68	1345 67	124 568

1245 67	4567	2368	1345
34	Moon's		1456
2378			1238
23458	16	1456	2345 67

68	2345 68	13467	1278
345 67	Mercury's		357
2368			24678 5
1234 78	13167	2348	1467

23678	24568	24568	23578
23467	Venu's		2578
25678			13467
31	1268	2468	367

378	17	248	368
135	Saturn's		145
123 578			123 458
68	146	14	347

This kind of separating the benefic dots contributed by the planets is called Prastāra-Aṣṭakavarga. In other words, in the Bhinnāṣṭakavarga of the planets you try to find out which planet has contributed benefic dots and in which Rāśi. For each planet's Aṣṭakavarga this Prastāra or spreading is done as follows:

Draw 9 parallel lines and cross them by 13 parallel ones. Write the Rāśis in the 12 columns and the 8 significators beginning with Saturn and ending with the Lagna as shown on page 271.

This chart refers to the *Sun's* Aṣṭakavarga. In this manner you can diversify the dots in the Aṣṭakavarga charts of other planets as well.

Now I shall tell you another feature of the Sarvāṣṭakavarga i.e. consolidated results of the Aṣṭakarvagas of all the seven planets. What you have to do in this connection is that you should add up the benefic dots in Aries and other signs severally of the seven Aṣṭakavarga charts. For example, in our given chart take the sign Aries of all the seven Aṣṭakavarga charts. You find 3 dots in the Sun's, 4 in the Moon's, 2 in that of Mars, 6 in Mercury's, 7 in Jupiter's, 5 in that of Venus, and 2 in Saturn's Aṣṭakavarga. If you add up all these you get 29. In this manner you add up the benefic dots after entering them in a Table as shown on page 272, for all the seven planets.

What is the use of this chart ? It is to find out which of the Signs have sufficient number of benefic dots and are therefore

Prastāra-Aṣṭakavarga of the Sun	Meṣa	Vṛṣa.	Mithu	Karka	Siṁ.	Kanyā	Tulā	Vṛsci.	Dhanu	Makar.	Kumbha	Mīna
Saturn		1	1	1	1	1		1	1		1	
Jupiter		1		1						1	1	
Mars	1	1		1			1	1	1	1	1	
Sun	1			1	1	1	1	1		1	1	
Venus			1	1					1			
Mercury	1	1			1	1	1	1			1	
Moon		1			1				1	1		
Lagna		1	1		1				1	1	1	
Total	3	6	3	5	5	3	3	4	5	5	6	—

Sarvāṣṭakavarga Chart

	Sun	Moon	Mars	Mercury	Jupiter	Venus	Saturn	Sarvāṣṭ,
Meṣa	3	4	2	6	7	5	2	29
Vṛṣa	6	4	6	5	3	5	3	32
Mithu.	3	4	4	4	3	5	3	26
Karka	5	4	3	3	5	4	3	27
Siṁha	5	4	5	6	3	5	6	34
Kanyā	3	6	1	4	6	3	3	26
Tulā	3	4	3	4	6	4	2	26
Vṛści.	4	2	4	5	6	4	3	28
Dhan.	5	5	2	6	3	2	2	25
Makar	5	4	3	4	6	5	6	33
Kumbh	6	2	4	5	3	5	3	28
Mīna	—	6	2	2	5	5	3	23
Total	48	49	39	54	56	52	39	337

auspicious, and which not. If you find any Rāśi containing more than 28 dots, you should consider that to be productive of good results during the transit of planets through it. If the number be less than that, the effect would be bad in the form of sufferings etc., their intensity being enhanced with diminishing number. According to another view the effects will be bad up to 25 dots; they will be moderate between 26 and 30; and excellent if above 30.

From the above chart it is clear to you that only six Rāśis have Sarvāṣṭaka figures which are either equal to or more than 28. The rest have lower figures. Still they are not very low, the lowest being 23. Great prominence is given to the Sarvāṣṭaka figures, as it is held that no good work should be commenced when planets pass through Rāśis which have insufficient Sarvāṣṭaka figures. Another point to be remembered in this connection is that even though planets in transit may be passing through Rāśis that may be their exaltation, own, friendly, a Trikoṇa (trinal), a Kendra (quadrant) or Upacaya houses or they may be possessed of strength born of benefic Vargas (Rāśi, Horā etc.), yet they are likely to do harm while passing through Rāśis that are possessed of insufficient Sarvāṣṭaka figures i.e. less than 28 dots. On the other hand even bad houses will prove beneficial provided they contain 28 or more dots in the Sarvāṣṭaka chart. Now you total up the benefic dots found in the houses that are auspicious for the Moon's transit i.e. 1, 3, 6, 7, 10 and 11 places. This is to be done not in the Sarvāṣṭaka chart, but in the Moon's Aṣṭakavarga chart. Similarly find out the total of benefic dots in the auspicious houses for the Sun in his Aṣṭakavarga. You know the 3rd, 6th, 10th and 11th places from the Moon are good for the Sun's transit. If in each case the total is 28 or more, the results must be adjudged as very good. This rule you can apply to each and every planet and find out if the total in each case is above 28. But see that you take only the benefic houses of each planet in respect of transit. Now what is the total of the benefic dots in the case of the Moon ? It is 29. In the case of the Sun it is only 21. What does it indicate ? It proves that even in the favourable houses the Sun's transit will not prove quite beneficial.

After this you must learn how to use the several Aṣṭakavargas for measuring the several Bhāvas counted from the several

Kārakas. For example, you know that the Sun is the Kāraka for father. So use the Sun's place as the Lagna in his Aṣṭakavarga, if you want to read the effects of the different Bhāvas. In his Aṣṭakavarga you see 5 benefic dots in Capricorn which is occupied by the Sun. This is good as far as the father's physical and general well-being is concerned. The second Bhāva too has 5 dots. So his financial position and family affairs must be good. Similarly you will read the other Bhāvas from this new Lagna. For the mother and things relating to her you will take the Moon's position as the starting point and proceed to consider the future. This must be done in the Aṣṭakavarga of the Moon. Hence you will remember the general principle that the transit of any planet over a Bhāva counted from the Lagna of the Kāraka planet will produce good effects provided the concerned Bhāva contains a good many benefic dots. If it is otherwise the effect will not be beneficial. Now look at Jupiter's Aṣṭakavarga. He is the Kāraka, as you know, for issue. Taking his place viz. Virgo, as the new Lagna you proceed to read the strength or weakness of the Bhāvas. What do you see in the 4th Bhāvas which stands for mother, happiness, house, lands etc. ? There are only three benefic dots. So the effects of planetary transit are not expected to be very good.

As this Aṣṭakavarga is to be made use of for various purposes such as computing longevity, health, happiness, Yogas etc. certain rectifications are necessary before the benefic dots are taken into consideration. Such rectifications are two in number viz. (1) Trikoṇaśodhana i.e. correction for the trines, and (2) Ekādhipatya Śodhana, i.e. correction for common ownership. Let us take the first one now. You know that among the 12 Rāśis there are four sets of trines, Aries, Leo and Sagittarius forming one group; Taurus, Virgo and Capricorn the second; Gemini, Libra and Aquarius the third; and lastly Cancer, Scorpio and Pisces the fourth. At a time you can consider only those Rāśis that constitute one group of trines. Now remember the following four rules for the correction of the number of benefic dots appearing in a group of trines :—(1) When all the three signs of a group have benefic dots, if one contains the least number, that should be adopted in the other two too. (2) If one of the houses is devoid of dots, no correction is necessary. (3) If two houses are vacant, make the third also vacant. (4) If all the three houses contain an equal number of benefic dots, put zero in all the three places. Now let us apply these rules to the Sun's A.V. (Aṣṭakavarga) chart. Take the first group of trines. In one there are 3 dots and in the other two 5 each. So use the Rule I and put 3 dots in all the three Rāśis. The same rule applies to the second group too. There too the least number is 3. So put this 3 in all the three Rāśis. In the third group too the same rule has application. Here too you have to write 3 in all the three Rāśis. In the case of the fourth group Rule 2 is applicable as one of the houses viz. Pisces, is vacant. So here no correction is necessary. What is the nett result ? Pisces has zero, Cancer 5, Scorpio 4 and the rest 3 each. In the case of the Moon's A.V. only Rule I is applicable. The result is as follows in the 12 houses : 4, 4, 2, 2, 4, 4, 2, 2, 4, 4, 2, 2. Though I have given the result like this, you will do well to write the numbers in a chart. In the chart of Mars the corrected figures are : 2, 1, 3, 2, 2, 1, 3, 2, 2, 1, 3, 2. In Mercury's A.V. you find Rule IV applicable in the first group. So you have to put zero in all the three places. The result, therefore, is :— 0, 4, 4, 2, 0, 4, 4, 2, 0, 4, 4, 2. In Jupiter's case the result is 3 in all cases except Cancer group which has 5 each. The result in the case of Venus is 2, 3, 4, 4, 2, 3, 4, 4, 2, 3, 4, 4. The result in the case of Saturn's A.V. is 2, 3, 2, 0, 2, 3, 2, 0, 2, 3, 2, 0. After this these figures are to be subjected to another rectification called Ekādhipatyaśodhana i.e. correction for common ownership. You know that all planets except the luminaries own two houses each. Hence the correction relates to the figures appearing in a set of such two houses. This means that there is no correction for the figures found in the houses belonging to the Sun and Moon. Now study the following rules relating to this correction called Ekādhipatyaśodhana : (1) If the two Signs belonging to a single planet are both occupied by planets, there is no crrection. (2) If one of the two signs, whether occupied by planets or not, is vacant i.e. without benefic dots (after the previous correction), then too there is no correction. (3) If one of the houses is occupied by planets and has more benefic dots than the other which is not occupied, put zero in the unoccupied Rāśi. (4) If both the Rāśis are unoccupied and have equal number of dots remove the dots from both. (5) If there is equality of dots in the two Rāśis, of which one is occupied and the other not, remove the dots from the unoccupied Rāśi. (6) If both the Rāśis are unoccupied and have unequal number of dots, put the smaller number in both. (7) If one Rāśi alone is occupied and has a smaller number of dots, put the smaller number in both. Let us now apply these rules to the Sun's A.V. chart which has already been subjected to the correction called Trikoṇaśodhana. You find in that chart 3 dots in Aries and 4 in Scorpio (both belonging to Mars). You know also that both have planets in them, Mars in the former and Saturn in the latter. Now look at Rule I. According to that we should not have any correction for these figures as both are occupied by planets. Next take Taurus and Libra (belonging to Venus) which have 3 dots in each and both are unoccupied. So which rule is to be applied ? Rule IV should be applied here. So put zero in both the Rāśis. Next take the Rāśis of Mercury, which also have an equal number of dots viz. 3, but Gemini is unoccupied, while Virgo is occupied. In this case Rule V has precedence. Hence put zero in Gemini and keep the figure 3 intact in the other. Next take the signs of Jupiter, both of which are occupied but Pisces is devoid of dots. So apply Rule II. And so there is no correction. Lastly take up the Rāśis of Saturn which have 3 dots each, but one of them is without planets. Hence use Rule V and remove the figure from the unoccupied Rāśi. Now you show the chart after this correction as given on page 277.

Note :— I have already made it clear to you that there is no correction to the figures appearing in Cancer and Leo. That is the reason why you see the figures 5 and 3 in these Rāśis even after correction. Now apply the above rules to the charts of other planets which have been already subjected to the previous correction due to the trines. The Moon's chart after this correction will have the following figures in the 12 Rāśis beginning with Aries :— 4, 2, 0, 2, 4, 4, 2, 2, 4, 4, 0, 2.

In the chart of Mars you will get the following figures in the 12 signs after correction :— 2, 1, 1, 2, 2, 1, 1, 2, 2, 1, 1, 2. In Mercury's chart you will find the following figures :— 0, 0, 0, 2, 0, 4, 0, 2, 0, 4, 0, 2. In Jupiter's chart you will see the following :— 3, 0, 0, 5, 3, 3, 0, 5, 3, 3, 0, 5. In that of Venus the following figures will be seen : 2, 3, 3, 4, 2, 3, 3, 4, 2, 3, 3, 4. The following are the figures in Saturn's chart :

2, 2, 0, 0, 2, 3, 2, 0, 2, 3, 0, 0. As these rectified figures are required for various purposes you should keep them carefully and correctly.

—	3	—	—
—	Sun's A.V. after Ekādhipatya		5
3			3
3	4	—	3

After the two kinds of rectification the nett dots in each Rāśi of the several A.V. charts must be multiplied separately by two things called Rāśi-guṇakāra (multpilier for Rāśi) and Grahaguṇakāra (multiplier for the planet occupying a house). The multipliers for the 12 Rāśis beginning with Meṣa are : 7, 10, 8, 4, 10, 5, 7, 8, 9, 5, 11 and 12. The multipliers for the seven planets beginning with the Sun are 5, 5, 8, 5, 10, 7, and 5. Let us now put these figures to use in the A.V. chart of the Sun which has undergone the two kinds of correction. In Meṣa there are 3 dots and its multiplier 7. So the product is 21. Put this result in Meṣa. As Vṛṣabha and Mithuna are devoid of dots, the products are zero in each case. In Cancer you get 20, Leo 30, Virgo 15, Libra 0, Scorpio 32, Sagittarius 27, Capricorn 15, Aquarius and Pisces zero. If you add up these products you will get 160. After this subject the A.V. figures after the two corrections again to the Graha-guṇakāra i.e. multipliers for planets. This will happen only in those Signs which are tenanted by planets. In Aries there is Mars whose multiplier is 8. So multiply 3 by 8 and have the product 24 there. Next Rāśi that has a planet is Virgo where is situated Jupiter whose multiplier is 10. So put $3 \times 10 = 30$. Next Saturn is posited in Scorpio. Saturn's multiplier is 5. So $4 \times 5 = 20$.

Sagittarius is occupied by Mercury whose Guṇakāra is 5. Hence $3 \times 5 = 15$. In Capricorn there are two planets viz. the Sun and Venus. In such cases you have to multiply separately the dots by the Guṇakāra of each planet and then add the two products. The Guṇakāras of the Sun and Venus are in order 5 and 7. So the two products are 15 and 21 and their total is 36. What about the Moon who is in Pisces ? As there are no benefic dots left after the corrections, there cannot be any figure there except zero. Now total up these figures which you have obtained in Aries, Virgo, Scorpio, Sagittarius and Capricorn. The total is 125. Now add up this figure to the total obtained by Rāśi-guṇakāra. So $160+125=285$. Next you will multiply this figure, 285, by 7 and divide the product by 27. The quotient thus obtained represents the A.V. Āyus (longevity) contributed by the particular planet, in this case, the Sun. When this process of multiplication and division is carried out you will get a quotient of 73.9. From this you will remove as many 27s as possible. Only the remainder will represent the Āyus contributed by the Sun. The nett result is 19.9 years. Before you arrive at the decimal figures if you multiply the remainder, 24 by 12 and divide the result by 27, you will get months. If you multiply the remainder by 30 and divide by 27, you will get days. If you want Ghaṭīs, then you will have to multiply the next balance by 60 and divide by 27. According to this method you get 19 yrs. 10 m. 20 days as the Āyus contributed by the Sun. This is not all. There are certain reductions to be effected in the Āyus contributed by the planets. There are some reductions to be done in connection with the various Āyurdāya systems. They are the following : If two planets are together in the same Rāśi, the contribution of each planet is to be halved. In the present case the Sun and Venus are together. So their contributions must be halved. This is one of the reductions. If a planet be in debilitation, its contribution would be reduced to a half. So is the case with a planet that is combust. In the case of a planet occupying an inimical Rāśi there should be a reduction of its contribution by a third. Similarly those planets that are situated in the visible half of the zodiac lose a third of their contribution. This rule applies also to a planet that is vanquished in planetary war. When there are many reductions to be made it is enough if you effect the maximum one. After performing the reductions enjoined you will get a planet's contribution to the longevity of the subject. This figure should finally be multiplied by 324 and the product divided by 365. The quotient will represent the correct contribution of that planet to the person's longevity. You have just found out that the Sun's contribution is 19y-10m-20d. But there are reductions to be effected on several counts such as conjunction with Venus, situation in an inimical house and being in the visible half of the zodiac. Of these three reductions the one for conjunction is the greatest i.e. $\frac{1}{2}$. So we have to reduce the Sun's contribution by a half only. The other reductions should not be done. When this is done you get 9y-10m-11d. This figure should be multiplied by 324 and divided by 365. When this is done you will get the final result as 8y-9m-27d-52g. Next let us take the Moon's A.V. chart which has already undergone the rectification. When you do the Rāśi-multiplication you will get the following figures in Meṣa and other Rāśis :— 28, 20, 0, 8, 40, 20, 14, 16, 36, 20, 0 and 24. The total of these is 226. Similarly do the multiplication for the planets. You will get 32 for Aries, 40 for Virgo, 10 for Scorpio, 20 for Sagittarius, 48 (20 for Sun and 28 for Venus) for Capricorn, and 10 for Pisces. This gives a total of 160. Now add up this and the previous product viz. 226. You get then a grand total of 386. Now multiply this by 7 and divide the product by 27. If the quotient is greater than 27, remove from it as many multiples of 27 as it is possible. The result is 19, 2/27 yrs. As the Moon has already risen, she is in the visible half. So she will lose a third of her contribution. Hence her contribution would be equal to $515/27 \times \frac{2}{3} = 1030/81$ yrs. Now this should be multiplied by 324 and divided by 365. The result will be 11y-3m-13d-34g. Similarly you treat the A.V. of Mars in respect of the Rāśi-multiplication. You will get a total of 146. Then again treat the dots with the Graha-multiplication. You will then get 68. Then the total you get of these products is 214. If you multiply this by 7 and divide the product by 27 you get the quotient, 55 and 13/27. Now take away 54 which is twice 27, from this. Then what remains is 1 and 13/27. This should be again multiplied by 324 and divided by 365. Then you get the result, 1y-3m-23d-25g. Is there any reduction in this ? No, because Mars does not come under any of the rules mentioned above. In the case of Mercury the total of Rāśi-products is 88 and that of Graha-products 108. The grand total is 196. When you do the multiplication and division and then the reduction you get 1286/81 yrs. This when finally multiplied by 324/365 yields 14y-1m-3d-32g. In the case of Jupiter the total of Rāśi-products is 228 and that of Graha-products 155. The grand total of 383 when subjected to the process of reduction etc. yields the Āyus, 10y-9m-27d-52g. In the case of Venus the reduction is one half. The two first products are 286 and 132. So the grand total, 418, yields only 0y-1m-29d-11g. In the case of Saturn the two products are 116 and 92. The grand total of 208 after reduction etc. yields 15y-11m-6d-20g. If you add up the contributions of all the seven planets so obtained, you will get the total longevity or span of life of the native. In this case the total comes to 62yrs-5m-11d. and 46 ghaṭīs. According to many authorities there is no contribution to the span of life by the Ascendant.

In connection with this Aṣṭakavarga you will often come across the term Śodhyapiṇḍa. It means the aggregate of the benefic dots remaining in an A.V. chart after the two corrections viz. Trikoṇa and Ekādhipatya-Śodhanas. I have told you that you have to use the A.V. chart of that planet which happens to be the Kāraka for the particular relative in order to discover the prospects of that relative. One method is to use the Rāsi itself tenanted by the Kāraka-planet as the Lagna. For example, for father you take the Rāśi occupied by the Sun. Another method is to take the 9th house from the one occupied by the Sun. In the case of the mother it is the4 th house from the one occupied by the Moon. This line of reasoning is to be followed in other cases as well. Here I am giving some rules for finding out the critical periods in the life of the subject's father. What is the Śodhyapiṇḍa in the A.V. of the Sun ? It is 24 in our example chart. Which is the 9th house from the one occupied by the Sun ? Here it is Virgo. How many benefic dots are there ? It has only 3 dots. You may have a doubt here : The benefic dots are to be taken from the original A.V. chart or the one after the two corrections ? It is from the original chart. Now what you have to do is to multiply this number of benefic dots by the Śodhyapiṇḍa. So by multiplying 24 by 3 we get 72. This should be divided by 27. The remainder that you get will represent the Star counted from Aśvinī. In this case it is 18 which is Jyeṣṭhā. When Saturn in his transit passes through this star, it is to be expected that the native's father will have great trouble. Or, such a thing or demise of an elder might take place when Saturn transits a trine of the above star i.e. in this case Revatī or Āśleṣā. Similarly you can find out the critical month in the life of the native's father. Note the number of benefic dots in the 8th house from the house occupied by the Sun. Now multiply this number by the Śodhyapiṇḍa of the Sun and divide the product by 12. The remainder gives the Rāśi counted from Aries. When the Sun transits that Rāśi, or its trine, there is likely to be danger to the father's life. In this case the 8th house viz. Leo, has 5 dots. So 24 $\times$ 5 divided by 12 leaves no remainder, or it is 12. That is Pisces. So the bad month is Mīna or its trine i.e. Karkaṭaka or Vṛścika. In the case of the mother you have to take the Moon's A.V. and the 4th house from the one occupied by her. The Śodhyapiṇḍa of the Moon's A.V. is 30, and the 4th house from her contains 4 dots. So 30 $\times$ 4/27 leaves a balance of 12, which represents Uttaraphalgunī star. So the idea is that when Saturn transits this star or its trine viz. Uttarāṣāḍhā or Kṛttikā, there is risk to the mother's life. How would you make use of the A.V. of Mars ? You can find out from this the number of brothers the native will have. Look at the 3rd house from the one occupied by Mars in his A.V. He will have as many brothers and sisters as there are dots in that house. Now in the 3rd house there are 4 benefic dots. This shows that the native will have 4 younger brothers and sisters in all. The 4th house from Mercury's place is said to represent the family of the maternal uncle. In Jupiter's A.V. see how many dots are there in the 5th house from his place. Note also the planets that have contributed the dots. If this house happens to be the contributor's debilitation or inimical house, then his contribution should be deleted and only the remaining ones considered. Now look at Jupiter's A.V. chart wherein I have given the numbers of the contributing planets and Lagna. You will find in Capricorn, which is the 5th house from Virgo wherein is situated Jupiter, six dots and their contributors are 1, 2, 3, 4, 7 and 8. This means they are the Sun, Moon, Mars, Mercury, Saturn and Lagna. You know that the Sun is the natural enemy (in this

A.V. parlance temporary relations are not considered) of Saturn and vice versa. So the Sun is in inimical house. Hence you should not take into account his contribution. Still there are five dots. What does this indicate ? It indicates that the subject will have five children. Here you may note another point also : This is the exaltation of Mars who is one of the contributors. Hence you may draw the inference that the son corresponding to Mars will be very powerful having military or kindred service. I have already explained to you the owners of the 8 parts of a Rāśi. The first belonging to Saturn is likely to cause the birth of a daughter, as this Rāśi is his own, though technically Saturn is a eunuch. This is the mode or line of reasoning you should adopt. Another way of finding out the number of children is to take the Śodhyapiṇḍa of Jupiter and deduct the dots in the malefic houses. Now what is the meaning of 'malefic houses' ? It means the houses occupied by malefics. Hence you have to deduct the dots in Aries, Scorpio and Capricorn. It may also mean the houses owned by the malefics viz. the Sun, Mars and Saturn. Now add up the benefic dots in the original A.V. chart of Jupiter in the 5 houses viz. Aries, Leo, Scorpio, Capricorn and Aquarius. Then you get 25. His Śodhyapiṇḍa is 30. So the balance is five. Hence the subject is likely to beget five children.

Next you must utilize the A.V. of Venus for getting a good partner in life. In his A.V. find out the Rāśi that has the maximum number of benefic dots. That Rāśi should be her Lagna, natal Sign or she should be born in the direction signified by that sign. If this is guaranteed, the wife would bring fortune and prosperity; otherwise i.e. if it is a Rāśi containing very few dots, there will be misery in respect of fortune and issue. In our example, seven Rāśis have 5 dots each. Of these seven the better ones are his own house and exaltation. Here the exaltation happens to be the Lagna. So if the native's partner be born in the same Lagna or with the Moon in Pisces or Taurus the marriage would prove fortunate. The directions, you know, are read in two ways : One method is to take the Lagna and the next three Rāśis as the four cardinal points; and the other is to take Aries and Taurus as the East, Gemini as south-east and so on.

Saturn's A.V. is made use of for finding out the time of the subject's demise. Note the Śodhyapiṇḍa of Saturn and multiply it by the benefic dots, in his original A.V., found in the 8th house counted from the Lagna. Then divide the product by 27. The remainder denotes the asterism counted from Aśvinī. When Saturn or Jupiter transits that asterism, the subject may quit the world. In our example, the Śodhyapiṇḍa is 16. The 8th house from Lagna i.e. Libra, contains only two dots. So multiplying 16 by 2 and dividing the product by 27 we get a remainder of 5. This gives Mṛgaśirṣa star. A note of caution needs to be sounded here. You know Saturn takes roughly 30 years and Jupiter 12 years to make one complete circuit of the zodiac. If a man lives for 100 years Saturn will make three rounds and Jupiter 8. Under these circumstances how are you to predict the time of death ? You know there are many ways of ascertaining the time of death such as the major Daśā-system. When by various methods, which have been explained already you arrive at the broad outline, this is one of the methods used for narrowing the limits. Similarly critical periods are found out in one's life as follows : In Saturn's original A.V. add up all the benefic dots occurring in the Rāśis beginning with the Lagna and ending with the one occupied by Saturn. Similarly add up the dots in all the houses commencing from the one occupied by Saturn and ending in the Lagna. These two figures indicate the two periods in the life of the native which are extremely dangerous to him. Now let us work this out in our chart. The Logna is Pisces; Saturn is in Scorpio. Now adding all the dots in these 9 houses we get 28. In the other set we get 17. This shows that the native is likely to have troubles in his 17th and 28th years of life. If you add up the dots in the Rāśis from the Lagna to the one occupied by Saturn, then multiply it by 7 and then divide the product by 27, the quotient will give the age at which the native will have illness or other troubles. In the example chart we have seen the total to be 28. By multiplying it by 7 and dividing it by 27 we get 7 and 7/27. This shows the native will have some trouble in his 8th year. Similarly treat the total in the other set of Rāśis, which is 17. The result is 4 and 11/27. This gives the 5th year as the period of suffering. This process should be repeated with the total of the dots occurring between the Lagna and Mars and vice versa and between the Lagna and Rāhu and vice versa. In the first case the total is 39. When this is similarly treated it yields 10 and 3/27 i.e. 11th year. In the other case the total is only 5. This being similarly treated gives the 2nd year as of ill health. In our chart Rāhu is in Scorpio along with Saturn. As we have already worked out the years with reference to Saturn, you know the results for Rāhu too. The above process may be gone through with the figures in the Sarvāṣṭakavarga.

You can find out auspicious and prosperous periods by adding the figures in the houses occupied by benefics, and multiplying the same by 7 and then dividing the product by 27. In this case the quotient will give the age at which the subject will be fortunate and happy. This should be done with the figures in the Sarvāṣṭakavarga chart. In that chart you see Pisces containing 23 dots, Virgo 26, and Sagittarius 25, which makes an aggregate of 74 dots. This multiplied and divided by 7 and 27 respectively gives 20th year. So that is the year of prosperity for the native. If you were to ask me if this was the only period of progress for the native, I would say this is not all. You repeat the above process in the A.V. chart of each of the natural benefics, and add up the results of all.

Another point to be remembered in connection with the Sarvāṣṭakavarga is that a person would be happy and prosperous if the total number of dots in the 11th house exceeds that in the 10th, and the figure in the 12th is less than that in the 11th, and lastly the figure in the Lagna is greater than that in the 12th house. In our example the Lagna has 23 dots, 12th house 28, 11th 33 and 10th 25. Here all the conditions except the last one are fulfilled. So though he may be a spend-thrift yet he will have plenty of money and enjoyments. In the Sarvāṣṭakavarga chart you make three divisions of four Rāśis each commencing from Pisces. These three divisions repesent the three stages of life of the subject. That part of life which has the maximum number of benefic dots will prove to be the happiest one. In our example chart the three groups have respectively 110, 113, and 114. Hence we have to conclude that the last period of life will be the happiest. According to another view the grouping must be done not with Pisces as the starting Rāśi, but with the one that happens to be the 12th from the

Lagna Rāśi. According to that you will have to begin with Kumbha in our example chart. According to that calculation the three groups will have in order 112, 113 and 112 benefic dots. There is yet another view : You should not take into consideration the benefic dots occurring in the Rāśis that represent the 8th and 12th Bhāvas. If this view is accepted, we will have to make a fresh calculation. In our chart Tulā and Kumbha are the Rāśis to be avoided. Then we would get according to the first method, 110, 87 and 86 respectively, and according to the other 84, 113 and 86. In the same manner you will have to find out which group has the greatest number of benefic planets and which malefic ones. According to this the period of life of the native will be happy or otherwise, as the case may be.

If the subject has good Yogas in his chart, you can find out from the Sarvāṣṭakavarga as to when his good Yoga will begin to fructify. Look for the figure in the Rāśi representing the native's Lagna. In the age corresponding to that figure there will be acquisition of good fortune like wealth, vehicles, wisdom etc. In our chart the figure in the Lagna Rāśī i.e. Pisces, is 23. This means that fortune will begin to smile upon the native in his 24th year. If the Ascendant is a Sign owned by Saturn, and if the lord of the 12th house occupies the Lagna, and if the lords of both the Lagna and 8th house are weak, the native will live for as many years as there are benefic dots in the Lagna in the Sarvāṣṭakavarga. There is another way of looking for Rāja-yoga through this Sarvāṣṭakavarga : See if in your chart the lords of the ascendant and the 4th are in mutual reception (i.e. have exchanged positions). If that be the case, see if these two houses have 33 benefic dots each. If this condition also is fulfilled, you will be a king endowed with royal splendour. See also if the 1st, 4th and 11th Bhāvas have more than 30 benefic dots each. In that case the person concerned would come by power, wealth and kingdom after his 40th year. This condition cannot be seen in our example chart. On the other hand, if the dots in the 4th and 9th Bhāvas are between 25 and 30, the subject will be very rich at his 28th year or thereafter. This condition is fulfilled in our example chart. Now look at another Rājayoga : The Lagna must be Aries with the Sun in it and the

4th house must be occupied by Jupiter in exaltation and this latter house must have 40 benefic dots. If these conditions are fulfilled, the subject will be a king commanding a vast army of horses. Another Rājayoga is the following : The Ascendant must have 40 benefic dots, Jupiter must be in Sagittarius, Venus in Pisces, Mars in Capricorn and Saturn in Aquarius.

Om Tat Sat

APPENDIX

WHAT IS PAÑCĀṄGA?

What is its Relevance to Modern Man?

Human activities are carried on within the frame-work of time and space. Even a good work suffers sometimes if it be done at a wrong time. Similar is the case of uncongenial environments. We are reminded in this connection of Kālidāsa's remark to the effect that a submission made at an appropriate time by a servant to the master bears fruit immediately. The importance of time is recognised by all human beings on the basis of their experience in life. Now who is responsible for time? We know that it is the Sun, who, though situated thousands of miles away from our earth, causes days and nights as well as seasons by his apparent motions. For, the denizens of this terrestrial sphere consider the Sun's movements, rising, moving to the zenith of the sky and setting and disappearing and causing nights, as real, though the Vedas declare that the Sun never rises, nor sets. He is visible always to the inner eye of the enlightened Seers: "Sadā paśyanti sūrayaḥ, divīva cakṣur ātatam". "Seers perceive Him always. He is the wide-open or out-stretched Eye in the heavens, as it were." The Sun's Effulgence is immortalized in the illustrious Ṛgvedic Mantra known as *Gāyatrī*, which states that when we meditate on that divine, most beneficent (but destructive to sins) effulgence of that Lord, He guides our intellect along the path of self-realization which is the goal of human life. Everyone knows that but for the Sun's heat and light even inanimate objects could not exist on earth, much less living beings including human beings. Great Yogins know how to tap the Sun's Suṣumnā ray (Nāḍī) for all their material and spiritual requirements. Paramahaṁsa Yogānanda refers to the wonderful life of a lady named *Giribālā*, who lived an active life without taking any food or drink. The reason given by her was that her Guru had taught her the mode of tapping the Sun's rays for her sustenance. Modern science is now trying to utilize solar energy for heating, lighting etc. as fuel scarcity is increasing day by day in the world. That is the reason why the ancient Seers declared in the *Ṛg Veda*: "The Sun is the Soul of all beings, moving and stationary". It does not behove, therefore, the so-called rationalists to denounce Sun-worship practised by ancient civilisations all over the world as a superstition. Indian thinkers have already affirmed that man is not a mere body, but a knowing, feeling, willing soul residing in a material body. Even so the Supreme Effulgence is residing in the orb of the Sun, a huge Ball of Fire. Scientists have now established that Time is the fourth dimension.

When we come to realize the importance of time, it is incumbent on us to know it in its entirety. Unless we know its parts or limbs we cannot have a complete understanding of its whole body. The ancients have divided Time into five subdivisions or limbs as human body is divided into eight limbs (which is the subject of the science of Āyurveda). It is appropriate to call the five limbs as *foundation* of Time. For, in South India the foundation of a building is called Pañcāṅga, as it has five parts. Hence it is essential for us to study well the five limbs of Kāla, Time, whose personification or Soul is the Sun called Kālātmā. To know the Pañcāṅga is to worship Him in order to obtain all that we need for our living here and hereafter. These five elements are known as i) Tithi or Lunar Day, ii) Vāra or weekday, iii) Nakṣatra or Lunar Mansion, iv) Yoga or combination of the longitudes of the Luminaries, and v) Karaṇa or a *Half Tithi.*

In astrology the Moon occupies a pre-eminent position inasmuch as she represents the Cosmic Mind. We read in the Veda: "Candramā manaso jātaḥ": The Moon was born of Puruṣa's Mind. It is also well known that it is the mind that controls man's health, behaviour and social and personal activities. The lunar day corresponds to the phases of the Moon, which in their turn are called the Moon's progress along the Zodiacal belt after she leaves the cosy embrace of the Sun at the New Moon. When the longitudes of the two luminaries are identical it is called Amāvāsyā and when the Moon moves 12 degrees away from the Sun, the first lunar day of the light half ends and the second Tithi begins. At the rate of 12 degrees per Tithi the full Moon or Pūrṇimā ends, when the Moon's distance is 180 degrees from the Sun's longitude. As the Tithis advance, so do the Moon's phases increase and when the Moon's orb is full and complete, round, she is supposed to have developed all her 15 digits. Incidentally it may be interesting to know that the lunar months are named after the constellations in which the Full Moon is stationed. I shall not in this connection go into the discussion regarding the beginning and ending of the lunar month. In the dark fortnight the phases of the Moon decrease as she progresses towards the Sun. On the new Moon day there is no lunar digit at all, as she has sacrificed all her digits, containing ambrosia, at the altar of the Gods and *Manes* or Pitaraḥ. There are altogether 30 lunar days in a lunar month, divided into two fortnights of 15 days each. The bright half is especially favourable for the performance of all auspicious ceremonies, while in the dark fortnight the first five days are good and the next five moderate and the rest are generally to be avoided.

The Tithis too have their own presiding deities which are explained by Varāhamihira in his *Bṛhat Saṁhitā* XCIX. They are in order: 1) Brahmā, 2) Vidhātā (according to Parāśara, Bṛhaspati), 3) Viṣṇu, 4) Yama, 5) Moon, 6) Kārtikeya, 7) Indra (Muni says Parā.), 8) Vasus, 9) Serpent (Piśāci), 10) Dharma, 11) Rudra, 12) Sun, 13) Manmatha, 14) Kali (Rudra), 15) Viśvedevas, and 30) Pitaraḥ (Parāśara makes no difference between the Full and New Moon regarding their deities). The Tithis are further divided into five classes as 1) Nandā—the First, Sixth and Eleventh Tithis, 2) Bhadrā—2nd, 7th, and 12th, 3) Jayā—3rd, 8th and 13th, 4) Riktā—4th, 9th and 14th, and 5) Pūrṇā—5th, 10th and 15th. Sage Parāśara, however, gives separate names to the ten Tithis beginning with the 6th as Māsā, Mitrā, Mahābalā, Ugrasenā, Sudhanvā, Sunandā, Yamā, Jayā, Ugrā and Siddhi. It is to be understood that though all the Tithis are based on the phases of the Moon, yet they are not alike in effect. Some are beneficial, some moderate and others harmful in the case of auspicious functions. Each Tithi has been allotted certain functions according to its innate qualities. For example, one should not elect the Fourth lunar day, presided over by Yama, for any work except murderous and cruel deeds. Varāhamihira prescribes Nandā Tithis for permanent works, Bhadrā for treatment, tours, house-construction, marriage and progressive undertakings. The Third lunar day is good for controlling cattle, servants etc. as well as sowing, brewing etc. The 4th as said above is fit for dreadful deeds. The 5th is to be utilized for lasting works such as house-construction, eating new rice, taking tonics etc. The 6th is good for permanent works like building temples. The 7th day is for doing friendly acts, preparing ornaments etc. The 8th day is good for manufacturing arms, digging moats, tunnels etc. The 9th Tithi is for killing enemies, capturing, removal of poisons etc. The 10th is for stable works leading to fame, for sinking wells, laying gardens, holy places etc. The 11th is stable and good for kitchen construction, performing sacrifices and convening an assembly of Vedic scholars. The 12th Tithi is good for keeping treasures, and store-houses. The 13th is for ornamental works, clothes, making women attractive, shaving etc. The 14th is for cruel deeds. The Full Moon day is for worshipping of gods, and Brahminical works. On the New Moon day sacrifices for the ancestors, construction of mangers etc. may be done. For oil-bath the 6th, 8th and 14th Tithis are forbidden.

Some lunar days are termed CHINNA (Cut) Tithis which are to be avoided for auspicious deeds. They are the 6th, 8th and 12th along with the Riktās viz. 4th, 9th and 14th. Some include New Moon too in this list. They are further grouped as i) Sthirā or Stable, ii) Kṣiprā or Quick, iii) Mṛdu or Tender, iv) Mṛdu-dāruṇā or Tender-Dreadful, v) Krūra-dāruṇā or Cruel-Dreadful. Under i) come the First, Tenth and Eleventh Tithis; under ii) the Second, Seventh and Twelfth, under iii) the Third, Thirteenth and Fifth, under iv) Sixth and Eighth, and under v) Fourth, Ninth and Fourteenth Tithis. Another authority brings the Tithis under six heads as Kṣiprā, Carā, Mṛdu, Ugrā, Sthirā and Tīkṣṇā. They are also divided into three categories as Ūrdhvāsyā or Facing Upward, Tiryaṅmukhā or Facing Sideways, and Adhomukhā or Facing Downward.

The second element of the Almanac is Vāra or Weekday. Those that are presided over by the benefics are auspicious days: Monday, Wednesday, Thursday and Friday. As the weak Moon becomes a malefic, even Monday will be inauspicious during that period. The days owned by malefics are meant for particular functions. For example, Sage Vasiṣṭha opines that Tuesday is the best for agricultural operations, Wednesday and Thursday moderate and the rest bad. However, when the Moon is strong Monday is good for agriculture. Some authorities accept even Saturday for entering an agricultural field. According to them Friday should be discarded, but it is good for forest-cropping. The above rule applies to the entrance of goats and buffaloes and to mountaineering. Some condemn Tuesday and Saturday for all good works. Vasiṣṭha says that for the growth of crops the weekdays, Vargas, and rising of Venus, the Sun, Moon and Jupiter are good, whereas Tuesday and Saturday cause disease to crops. As far as marriage is concerned Sunday is said to lead to separation of the couple, Tuesday widowhood and bad character, and Saturday to penury and rheumatic trouble, while Monday confers happiness, Wednesday good progeny, Thursday piety, wealth and children and Friday personal attractiveness and love of kinsmen. According to Sage Gārgya marriage on a Saturday will culminate in the death of the bridegroom, on Tuesday in that of the bride, and on Sunday in poverty. It is to be remembered in this connection that the lord of the weekday should be strong, so too that of the Kālahorā, and still more the planet that owns the Aṁśa rising at the time. When the Sun is posited in an Upacaya house from the natal Moon or in the ascendant at the elected time, Sunday can very well be used for works connected with gold, copper, horses, wood, woollen garments, perfumes, coronation of rulers, medicine etc. Similarly on Monday or when the Moon is in the Lagna or an angle, or when Cancer is rising, works connected with ornaments, pearls, silver, sacrifice, women, milk, agriculture, flowers and clothes can be done with advantage. Tuesday causes success in respect of the following: Mines, ores, gold, fire, corals, weapons, cruel deeds, physicians, nocturnal activities etc. On Wednesday or when Mercury is in the Lagna (not in association with malefics) green substances, gems, dramatic work, scientific pursuit, fine arts, Mantras, alchemy etc. will flourish. Similarly it is in the case of other planets and their weekdays. According to Garga house-warming can be done on Saturdays, but travelling is forbidden. For voyages one should elect the weekdays and Aṁśas of the Moon, Mercury, Jupiter and Venus. For boating Thursday is said to be ideal, while Monday and Friday cause floods, and Wednesday break of the pole. The *Vidyāmādhavīya* states that sometimes the weekdays of Mercury and Venus are not beneficial to women and cows for journey. Certain foods are prescribed for the different weekdays before starting on a journey: They are in order 1) Ghee, 2) Milk, 3) Jaggery, 4) Sesamum, 5) Curds, 6) Barley and 7) Blackgram. According to Śrīpati, however, they are Mārjika (a kind of buttermilk?), Ghee and Milk porridge, Kāñjikā, Sugar and Milk, Curds, Fresh Milk and Tilodana or Rice and Sesamum. Monday, Wednesday and Saturday alone are recommended to oil-bath. The lords of the weekdays are in order Śiva, Gaurī, Guha, Viṣṇu, Brahmā, Indra and Kāla. Their secondary lords are Agni, Water, Earth, Hari, Śakra, Śacī and Viriñci. The Yonis or animals of the weekdays are said to be Lion for Friday, Tiger for Monday, Elephant, Donkey, Boar, Cow, and Dog for the rest. In addition to this there is Vāraśūla—weekday Spike— which should be avoided for journeys in the particular direction: There is Śūla on Monday and Saturday towards the East; on Thursday towards the South; on Sunday and Friday towards the West, and on Tuesday and Wednesday towards the North. However, there are some exceptions to this rule during emergencies: Monday and Saturday Śūla will not do any harm after Eight Ghaṭīs have elapsed; on Tuesday and Wednesday after Twelve Ghaṭīs; on Sunday and Friday after Fifteen Ghaṭīs; and on Thursday after Twenty-two Ghaṭīs. As far as Śrāddhas are concerned, Monday and Saturday are the best; Tuesday and Friday are the worst; and the rest tolerable.

The third limb of the Almanac is the Nakṣatra or constellation whose importance must needs be specially noted by all in general and by students of astrology in particular. There are 27 asterisms—excluding Abhijit which is placed in Capricorn—which are made use of for all kinds of auspicious rituals, travels, litigation, treatment of ailments, marketing commodities and the like. It is the experience of the faithful that when they are forced by circumstances to commence a good work under a forbidden star, invariably they fail to achieve success. This remark applies to omens as well. Some persons who are called men of progressive views might dub those that believe in omens etc. as superstitious. Whatever they might say, such people as are endowed with a sincere heart and unflinching faith in God and statements of great sages of yore, entertain no doubt whatsoever in their minds about the veracity of the influence of planets on terrestrial beings as well as of auguries, whose correctness they have tested by observation and personal experience. In astrology the Zodiacal belt is considered as the Body of Time or Kāla-Puruṣa, which is divided into twelve Signs or Rāśis, which in turn contain 27 (or 28) constellations that are divided equally among the twelve Signs at the rate of Two and a Quarter stars or nine quarters, per sign of 30 degrees. The Circle of constellations is said to be stationary and to have an independent status. Hence this Circle of stars too is regarded as a separate Deity known as Nakṣatra-Puruṣa or

Stellar Deity, and worshipped. As the description of Gods is done from foot upwards, we have to start with the Feet of the Stellar Deity. The asterism Mūla represents its Feet; Rohiṇī—Shanks; Aśvinī—Knees; the Two Āṣāḍhas—Thighs; Phalgunīs—Privities; Krittikā—Hips; P & U. Bhādrapadās—Two Sides; Revatī—Stomach; Anurādhā—Breast; Dhaniṣṭhā—Back; Viśākhā—Arms; Hasta—Hands; Punarvasu—Fingers; Āśleṣā—Nails; Jyeṣṭhā Neck; Śravaṇa—Ears; Puṣya—Mouth; Svātī—Teeth; Śatabhiṣak—Laughter, Maghā—Nose; Mṛgaśiras—Eyes; Citrā—Forehead; Bharaṇī—Head; and lastly Ārdrā—Hair. Worship of the Stellar Deity with Lord Viṣṇu is done on a day ruled by the star Mūla synchronizing with the eighth lunar day of the dark fortnight of the month of Caitra. This worship ought to be conducted strictly in the order of the limbs i.e. from Mūla onwards, the second day worship is to be done on a day ruled by Rohiṇī.

Sage Garga declares that by worshipping this Deity one could attain sound health, happiness and personal charm. Nakṣatreṣṭi or Sacrifice to the Stars, their Presiding Deities and Subsidiary Deities is done sometimes in South India. Years ago it was performed at New Delhi by some Vaidik Brāhmaṇas from the South.

Among the constellations the following nine are eschewed for auspicious functions: Bharaṇī, Kṛttikā, Ārdrā, Āśleṣā, the three Pūrvas, Viśākhā and Jyeṣṭhā. The Stars are also divided into three categories as Male, Female, and Eunuch; stars 1, 4, 7, 8, 13, 17, 22, 25 and 26 are Male; Mūla, Mṛga, and Śatabhiṣak Eunuch; and the remaining 15 are Female. They are also sub-divided into three groups as Divine, Human and Demoniac. The first group of Divine asterisms consists of the nine stars, nos. 1, 5, 7, 8, 13, 15, 17, 22 and 27. The Human group is made up of 2, 4, 6, 11, 12, 20, 21, 25 and 26. The remaining stars belong to the Demoniac class. They are also classified as Antaraṅga (of the Inner Circle) and Bahiraṅga (of the Outer Circle). The First class consists of 16 stars of four groups of four stars each: Kṛttikā and the next three, Maghā and the three next, Anurādhā and the three next and Dhaniṣṭhā and the succeeding three. The Outer Circle consists of four triads headed by Punarvasu, Citrā, U. Āṣāḍhā (including Abhijit in the middle), and Revatī. The stars are further classified on the basis of their face, sight, and characteristics. They are 1) Facing upward, 2) Facing Downward and 3) Facing Sideways. Their Sight is Manda (Dull), Madhya (Moderate), Sudṛk (Nice Sight) and Andha (Blind). They are Quick, Fierce, Sharp, Tender, Stable and Unstable.

The next limb of the Almanac is Yoga. The meaning of this word is union or sum. In other words it is nothing but the sum-total of the longitudes of the two luminaries. There are 27 Yogas corresponding to the 27 constellations. Just as the longitude of a star is 13°-20′, even so the value of a Yoga is the same number of degrees and minutes. When the sum of the longitudes of the Sun and the Moon is Zero, the first Yoga, Viṣkambha, starts, and it is also the end of the 27th Yoga, Vaidhṛti. Let us see it in practice. On Friday the 13th July 1984 Vaidhṛti expires at 5-35 P.M. (according to Lahiri's Ephemeris). The longitudes of the Sun and the Moon are respectively 2-27-37-22 and 9-2-22-38 at 5-35 P.M. The sum of these two figures is Zero. From this point every Yoga needs 13°-20′. In this manner you can calculate from the sum of longitudes of the luminaries for any time of a particular day the ruling Yoga at the rate of 13°-20′ per Yoga. These Yogas are called Nitya Yogas or Daily Yogas. There are five other Yogas brought about by the combination of (1) weekday and lunar day; (2) weekday and star; (3) weekday, star and lunar day; (4) star and lunar day; and (5) Rāśi and lunar day. Ānandādi Yoga, which is used for journeys is caused by the combination of the star and weekday. We are not concerned with these at the present juncture. Out of the 27 Nitya Yogas the following are generally shunned: Viṣkambha, Parigha, Vyatīpāta, Vajra, Vyāghāta, Vaidhṛti, Śūla, Gaṇḍa and Atigaṇḍa.

Even if these untoward Yogas are to be employed under emergencies, the following rule should be strictly adhered to: 7 Ghaṭīs, 30G., 9G., 3G., 15G., 5G., 7G., 6G. and 6G. respectively at the end should be discarded. According to one commentator the number of Ghaṭīs mentioned here are to be avoided both in the beginning and at the end. According to Śrīpati only the first Quarter of the inauspicious Yogas need be rejected for auspicious ceremonies. However, the entire body of Vyatīpāta and Vaidhṛti is malignant and hence to be discarded. Similarly only the first half of Parigha Yoga is to be discarded.

Karaṇa is so called because it cuts the Tithi into two equal parts. So in a lunar month of 30 days there must be 60 Karaṇas. These Karaṇas are divided into two groups viz. Movable (cara) and Immovable (Sthira). The former group consists of seven Karaṇas viz. Bava, Bālava, Kaulava, Taitila, Gara or Garaja, Vaṇik, and Bhadra or Viṣṭi. The second group of fixed ones has only four Karaṇas Viz. Śakuni, Catuṣpāt, Nāga, and Kiṁstughna. The fixed ones can be easily recognised, because they are permanently allotted to four half Tithis: Śakuni is assigned to the latter half of the 14th Tithi of the dark fortnight; Catuṣpāt and Nāga to the two halves of the New Moon; and lastly Kiṁstughna to the first half of the first lunar day (Pratipat) of the light half. What remains of the 60 halves of the lunar month is 56. These are to be shared among the movable Karaṇas that are 7 in number. So they will be repeated eight times. In this scheme Bava will be assigned to the later half of the first lunar day of the bright fortnight. Bālava and Kaulava will go to the first and second halves of the second Tithi (Śukla); Taitila and Garaja to the two halves of the third Tithi; and Vaṇik and Viṣṭi (Bhadra) to the two halves of the fourth lunar day. This process will be repeated until you reach the first half of the 14th Tithi of the dark half. Let me illustrate this with an example: on Sunday the 29th July 1984 bright fortnight is mentioned. That day the first lunar day ends at 14-15 hrs. It started the previous day at 17-21 hrs. So the total duration of this Śukla Pratipat (First day of the light half) is 20-54 hrs. Out of this the first half of 10-27 hrs should go to the fixed Karaṇa, Kiṁstughna. So the later half is to be given to Bava, the first of the moving Karaṇas. Thus on the 29th Bava will be ruling from 3-48 hrs. upto 14-15 hrs. The Yonis or animal origins of the Karaṇas viz. Movable ones, are in order Lion, Tiger, Boar, Donkey, Elephant, Cow and Dog. Their Lords, according to Bharadvāja, are Viṣṇu, Prajāpati, Moon, Jupiter, Vasus, Maṇibhadra and Yama respectively. However, Varāhamihira gives their names as Indra, Brahmā, Mitra, Aryamā, Bhū, Śrī and Yama. The Yonis of the four fixed Karaṇas are Dog, Bull, Serpent and Cock respectively. Their lords are in order Kali, Vṛṣa, Phaṇi and Māruta. Among the movable Karaṇas Viṣṭi or Bhadra is of dreadful consequences, and the rest are good. Among the fixed ones Nāga is used for permanent works, cruel deeds, forcible and hateful activities. Others are meant for auspicious and progressive acts. According to Garga, Bava is good for Brahmins; Taitila for political and court work as well as for ornaments: Gara is for house-hold work and agriculture; Vaṇik is good for trade and commerce.

It may be noted that some of the Tithis, stars, Karaṇas and Muhūrtas have common presiding deities. Hence whatever work is recommended under a constellation can be done on a corresponding Tithi etc. For example, Pratipad Tithi and Star Rohiṇī have a common lord. So whatever is allowed under Rohiṇī is good for the Pratipad also. Similarly for Śrāddhas Star Maghā and New Moon are ideal, as they have the same lord viz. Manes. So too lunar mansions and Karaṇas having the same lord may be employed for appropriate functions. For example, star Jyeṣṭhā and Bava Karaṇa, Rohiṇī and Bālava, Anurādhā and Kaulava, U. Phālgunī and Taitila, Jyeṣṭhā and Garaja, Śravaṇa and Vaṇik, Bharaṇī and Viṣṭi, Āsleṣā and Śakuni, Rohiṇī and Catuṣpāt, Āśleṣā and Nāga and Svātī and Kiṁstughna are treated as equals in electional astrology.

Sage Bharadvāja gives a rough method for finding out the movable Karaṇa on a particular day thus: Note the number of the Tithi and double the number and add 1 to it. Divide the sum by 7. The remainder gives the number of the Karaṇa ruling at the end of the Tithi. For example, take 18th August 1984. It is the 6th Tithi (Dark) ending at 10-38 A.M. So doubling 6 and adding I to the result we get 13. Being divided by 7, it leaves a remainder of 6, which is Vaṇik that is co-extensive with the later half of the Tithi. So it too ends at 10-38 A.M. As Bhadra or Viṣṭi Karaṇa is considered as extremely malefic, a simple method has been given by sage Mārkaṇḍeya for locating it for the purpose of avoiding it. He tells us also whether it belongs to the first half or the second half of the particular lunar day. In the bright fortnight Viṣṭi occurs in the first half of the 8th Tithi and Full Moon: and in the second half on the 4th and 11th lunar days, while in the Dark Fortnight it occurs in the First half of the 7th and 14th lunar days; and in the second half of the 3rd and 10th Tithis. The sage adds that this Karaṇa which is of dire consequence travels in the three worlds: when the Moon is tenanting any of the Signs Meṣa, Vṛṣabha, Karka and Makara, Bhadra dwells in Heaven; when she is in Mithuna, Kanyā, Tulā, and Dhanus, it is in the Nether-world; and when she is in Siṁha, Vṛścika, Kumbha and Mīna, it will be on the Earth. When Bhadra is in Heaven, Nether-world and Earth, works done will contribute in order i) to auspicious results; ii) acquisition of wealth, and iii) Utter ruination. The reason given is that in Heaven Bhadra looks upwards; in the Nether-world downwards, and on Earth it confronts all beings. This dreaded Karaṇa will prove harmless at night provided it starts prior to sunset. Similarly it would be beneficial for a diurnal function, provided it commences before sunrise. These exceptions prove very handy for astrologers in electing good Muhūrtas for marriage etc.

It may be argued by some that a knowledge of the Pañcāṅga is unnecessary for a modern man. If we consider calmly the disturbing and enervating conditions under which modern man lives and ekes out his livelihood, it would be clear to a dispassionate thinker that more than his forbears the modern educated man is in dire need of a firm, reliable support for maintaining his mental peace and sanity in order to be able to save himself from dangerous situations. Such a support is an unshakable faith in the protective power and wisdom of God. A man of faith is guided in his life by the precepts of Śāstras as well as by the practices of great men of yore who have bequeathed to us Vedas and Vedāṅgas, which include the science of Jyautiṣa, Astronomy and Astrology. Let me digress here a little: The other day a certain gentleman railing against astrology remarked that while Astronomy was a science Astrology was not. Such people forget that the basis of astrology is nothing but the astronomical science. If the cause is scientific, the effect also should be scientific. Now coming to the subject of Pañcāṅga, we can safely declare that no man can live and act in society effectively unless he is conversant with the parts of Calendar. In Indian parlance especially in religious matters this calendar takes the form of the Almanac which shows many other things apart from the above-named five elements. One ought to know them too in order to be able to steer clear of inauspicious moments while setting out on a journey or commencing some good work such as constructing a house and sending children to school. After all every moment conceals in its womb vast potentiality for the future. No two moments are alike in their potentialities. Hence even scientists ought to choose a good moment for their research work. Great scientists and poets get inspiration for scientific inventions or for writing inspiring poetry at certain specific moments and under congenial environments. When your mind is dejected or when you are not physically hale and hearty, you cannot undertake any major project. Hence it is necessary to see which lunar day, which weekday, which lunar mansion, which Yoga and Karaṇa are in harmony with your birth star, weekday etc. The very fact that the ancient seers have advised us to elect good elements of the calendar for starting any good work, is proof positive for the statement that man is not an automaton blindly following an inexorable Fate. No doubt, Fate is powerful because Fate is nothing but the resultant of our own past Karma (Prārabdha). What we had sown in our previous existence, we have to reap its fruit in this life. Spiritualists have demonstrated through seances the continuity of the Soul or personality after its physical death. Edgar Cayce has stated in trance: "The Twelve signs of the Zodiac represent soul-patterns.... The soul of the entity is part of the universal consciousness and has dwelt in these environs....The planets are the Looms, the will is the weaver." He has given verifiable details of his clients' previous lives. The intensity and poignancy of the result of past Karma, according to the Śāstras, can be mitigated by our repentent actions such as Japa, Homa and Worship of the Lord Supreme. If personal effort had no value at all, all the injunctions of our Śāstras would be null and void.

Now what are the other items you have to consider while reading the Pañcāṅga daily in the morning? They are Viṣa and Amṛta Ghaṭīs. Each star has a particular period Viṣa Ghatīs as well as Amṛta Ghatīs. Generally their duration is of four Ghaṭīs or I hr. 36 mt., provided the constellation is of 60 Ghaṭī-duration. If it exceeds or is short of that, proper change will have to be made. In the almanac a certain number of Ghaṭīs is given against Amṛta and Viṣa. It means that the Viṣa or Amṛta period starts from that Ghaṭī. For the commencement of these two periods of each asterism please refer to page 50 *supra*. In the opinion of authors of works on Muhūrta the Amṛta Ghaṭī period is highly prized in spite of some blemishes. Hence in urgent circumstances Amṛta Ghaṭī is to be sought for. Similarly no Muhūrta is prescribed during the Viṣa period by any astrologer.

In modern society man has to face many a challenge: In the matter of admission to school and college, in submitting applications for jobs, for starting to take competitive examination, or appearing before a committee of interviewers, or going on a journey, one is naturally very apprehensive about the result. When he finds himself helpless, he is forced to follow the elders in the house regarding the choice of the time and day for the chosen project. One may ask: Even if one selects a good time for writing one's application for a post, if one does not get even an Interview Call, what value can be attached to the good Muhūrta one has chosen? There is a saying in Sanskrit which means that if you fail in spite of your efforts, you are not to blame. As we are born to a hoary cultural tradition, we are bound to observe its principles. Otherwise we would be going against our own nature. The argument why you should respect the sayings of the great Seers of yore who had no axe to grind, is that it is better to fail by following the advice of noble persons rather than succeed by the advice of corrupt and ignoble people. Because people die even after taking medicine, don't patients consult a qualified physician or surgeon? By consulting almanacs and astrologers one gets at least psychological satisfaction and mental peace which are a great asset for man in our troubled world.

The Sages have assured the faithful that by reading daily in the morning the five limbs of the almanac one could secure prosperity through the lunar day (Tithi), longevity through weekday, health and freedom from sins through the constellation, relief from illness through Yoga, and success in one's efforts through the Karaṇa. Elsewhere it is stated that the lunar mansion confers good health, Muhūrta wealth, Tithi success, ascendant comfortable journey, and generally a strong Moon, all good things.*

---

*By Courtesy of the *Vidyā*, Calcutta-48

INDEX

A

E

G

M

U

Y

4901